The American Record

Fifth Edition

The American Record

IMAGES OF THE NATION'S PAST

Volume II: Since 1865

Edited by

William Graebner
State University of New York
College at Fredonia

Leonard Richards
University of Massachusetts, Amherst

Boston   Burr Ridge, IL   Dubuque, IA   Madison, WI   New York   San Francisco   St. Louis
Bangkok   Bogotá   Caracas   Kuala Lumpur   Lisbon   London   Madrid   Mexico City
Milan   Montreal   New Delhi   Santiago   Seoul   Singapore   Sydney   Taipei   Toronto

Higher Education

THE AMERICAN RECORD: IMAGES OF THE NATION'S PAST, VOLUME II: SINCE 1865

Published by McGraw-Hill, a business unit of The McGraw-Hill Companies, Inc., 1221 Avenue of the Americas, New York, NY 10020. Copyright © 2006, 2001, 1995, 1988, 1982 by The McGraw-Hill Companies, Inc. All rights reserved. No part of this publication may be reproduced or distributed in any form or by any means, or stored in a database or retrieval system, without the prior written consent of The McGraw-Hill Companies, Inc., including, but not limited to, in any network or other electronic storage or transmission, or broadcast for distance learning.

This book is printed on acid-free paper.

1 2 3 4 5 6 7 8 9 0 DOC/DOC 0 9 8 7 6 5

ISBN 0-07-294959-7

Editor in Chief: *Emily Barrosse*
Publisher: *Lyn Uhl*
Senior Sponsoring Editor: *Steven Drummond*
Marketing Manager: *Katherine Bates*
Developmental Editor: *Larry Goldberg*
Editorial Assistant: *Jessica Badiner*
Managing Editor: *Jean Dal Porto*
Project Manager: *Meghan Durko*
Manuscript Editor: *Gretlyn Cline*
Art Director: *Jeanne Schreiber*
Associate Designer: *Srdjan Savanovic*
Text Designer: *Ellen Pettengell*
Cover Designer: *Ellen Pettengell*
Associate Art Editor: *Ayelet Arbel*
Senior Photo Research Coordinator: *Nora Agbayani*
Photo Researcher: *Robin Sand*
Cover Credit: *CNAC/MNAM/Dist. Réunion des Musées Nationaux/Art Resource, NY. Cover art (c) James Rosenquist/Licensed by VAGA, New York, NY.*
Production Supervisor: *Janean A. Utley*
Composition: *10.5/12 Jansen by ElectraGraphics, Inc.*
Printing: *45 # New Era Matte, R. R. Donnelly and Sons, Inc./Crawfordsville, IN.*

Library of Congress Cataloging-in-Publication Data

The American record : images of the nation's past / edited by William
Graebner, Leonard Richards.-- 5th ed.
     p. cm.
   Includes bibliographical references.
   ISBN 0-07-294958-9 (pbk. : acid-free paper) 1. United
States--History. 2. United States--History--Sources. I. Graebner,
William. II. Richards, Leonard L.
   E178.6 .A4145+
   973--dc22

2004063180

The Internet addresses listed in the text were accurate at the time of publication. The inclusion of a website does not indicate an endorsement by the authors of McGraw-Hill, and McGraw-Hill does not guarantee the accuracy of the information presented at these sites.
www.mhhe.com

About the Editors

William Graebner is Professor of History Emeritus at the State University of New York at Fredonia. He received the Frederick Jackson Turner Award from the Organization of American Historians for *Coal-Mining Safety in the Progressive Period: The Political Economy of Reform*. Another book, *A History of Retirement: The Meaning and Function of an American Institution, 1885–1978*, was published in 1980. He is also the author of *The Engineering of Consent: Democracy and Authority in Twentieth-Century America* (1987); *Coming of Age in Buffalo: Youth and Authority in the Postwar Era* (1990); *The Age of Doubt: American Thought and Culture in the 1940s* (1991), and the editor of *True Stories from the American Past* (1993, 1997). In 1993, he was Fulbright Professor of American Studies at the University of Rome. He currently serves as Associate Editor of *American Studies*.

Leonard Richards is Professor of History at the University of Massachusetts at Amherst. He was awarded the 1970 Beveridge Prize by the American Historical Association for his book *"Gentlemen of Property and Standing": Anti-Abolition Mobs in Jacksonian America*. Professor Richards is also the author of *The Advent of American Democracy, The Life and Times of Congressman John Quincy Adams*, which was a finalist for the Pulitzer Prize; *The Slave Power: The Free North and Southern Domination, 1780–1860*, which was the second-place winner of the 2000 Lincoln Prize; and *Shays's Rebellion: The American Revolution's Final Battle*. He is currently writing a book on the California Gold Rush and the coming of the Civil War.

Contents

Preface

During the past three or four decades, the study of history in the United States has become in many ways more sophisticated and more interesting. Until the mid-1960s the dominant tradition among American historians was to regard the historian's domain as one centered on politics, economics, diplomacy, and war. Now, at the start of the twenty-first century, historians are eager to address new kinds of subjects and to include whole sections of the population that were neglected in the traditional preoccupation with presidential administrations, legislation, and treaties. Women and children, the poor and economically marginal, African Americans and native Americans, have moved nearer the center of the historians' stage. We have become almost as eager to know how our ancestors dressed, ate, reared their children, made love, and buried their dead as we are to know how they voted in a particular presidential election. In addition, ordinary Americans now appear on the stage of history as active players who possess the power to shape their lives, rather than as passive victims of forces beyond their control. The result is a collective version of our national past that is more inclusive, more complex, and less settled.

About the New Edition

The fifth edition of *The American Record* continues the effort begun in previous editions. We have attempted to bridge the gap between the old history and the new, to graft the excitement and variety of modern approaches to the past on an existing chronological and topical framework with which most of us feel comfortable. Most of the familiar topics are here; we have included essays on the early colonial settlements, the Revolutionary War, the Constitution, progressivism, the Great Depression, and the consensual society of the 1950s. But by joining these essays to primary sources, we have tried to make it possible for teachers and students to explore the links between the Puritan social order and the lessons children learned from their primers; between the Revolutionary War and the colonial class structure; between the Constitution and the physical layout of the nation's capital; between progressivism and the photographs of Lewis Hine; between the Great Depression and the murals that were painted on post-office walls across the nation in the mid-1930s; and between the so-called "consensus" of the 1950s and the integration of Little Rock, Arkansas's public schools. The fifth edition also takes up themes and materials that are not so universally familiar, but that are beginning to reshape our understanding of the American past—among them religion, the rise of a consumer society, the history of popular music, the impact of television, draft resistance, and, most recently, the war in Iraq. Reflecting the book's subtitle, both volumes make liberal use of draw-ings, cartoons, photographs, advertisements, and other visual materials. *The American Record* teaches the skill of making sense of one's whole world.

Throughout, we have attempted to incorporate materials with *texture:* documents that are not only striking but can be given more than one inter-pretation; photographs that invite real examination and discussion; tables and maps that have something new and interesting to contribute; and essays, such as James H. Merrell's account of the "New World" as it appeared to the Catawba Indians, Ronald Takaki's treatment of the wartime relocation of Japanese-Americans, or Beth Bailey's analysis of post-World War II dating customs, that are at once superb examples of recent historical scholarship and accessible to undergraduates. As a foreground to the agency of ordinary people, we have included sections called **Voices,** which feature firsthand commentaries such as Sarah Winnemucca's account of the California migra-tions and the testimony of John Morrison, a New York machinist, before the U.S. Senate in 1883. Another section, labeled **Debates,** juxtaposes differing perspectives on selected issues, including the adoption of the Constitution, the expansion of slavery into the territories, imperialism, Vietnam (featuring a young John Kerry), and 21st century nation-building. The fifth edition introduces a new **On the Web** feature, designed to encourage students to pursue topics of interest using some of the splendid materials available on the Internet.

Learning Aids for Students

From the beginning, we realized that our approach to American history would require some adjustment for many students and teachers. It was one thing to call on students to place an address by Albert J. Beveridge in the context of turn-of-the-century imperialism, yet quite another to ask them to do the same with a young woman's account of the African exhibit at the 1901 Pan-American Exposition in Buffalo, New York. For this reason, we have of-fered a good deal of guidance. **Introductions** to primary and secondary materials are designed not just to provide basic background information, but to suggest productive avenues of interpretation. Interpretive essays and questions are intended to create a kind of mental chemistry that provides students with enough information to experience the excitement of putting things together, and yet not so much guidance that conclusions become obvious. Each chapter concludes with a brief section called **The Big Picture,** where some of the larger questions are posed. In the second vol-ume, we have often taken the The Big Picture a step further, presenting miniessays that we hope will offer students a sense of how the materials in a chapter can yield a broad understanding or interpretation.

Acknowledgments

We remain indebted to R. Jackson Wilson, who inspired the first edition of this book. We also wish to thank our past editors at Alfred A. Knopf and McGraw-Hill—first David Follmer and Chris Rogers, later Niels Aaboe and Peter Labella, and Kristen Mellitt and Lyn Uhl—for their patient supervision of previous editions. For the fifth edition, we have been fortunate to work with Steve Drummond and Larry Goldberg; we thank them for their concern and assistance at every stage of the project. And we are grateful to the teachers and students who used the first, second, third, and fourth editions of *The American Record* and showed us how to make the book better. In particular, we would like to thank the following reviewers of the fourth edition for their many helpful suggestions: Lane Fenrich, Northwestern University; Harvey H. Jackson, Jacksonville State University; Rusty Monhollon, Hood College; Christopher Olsen, Indiana State University; William A. Pencak, The Pennsylvania State University; Peter Richards, St. John's Preparatory School; and Rebecca S. Shoemaker, Indiana State University.

William Graebner
State University of New York
at Fredonia

Leonard Richards
University of Massachusetts
at Amherst

Chapter 1

Reconstruction

When it was first coined in the crisis months between the election of Lincoln and the beginnings of the Civil War, the term "Reconstruction" meant simply the reunification of the nation. By the time the war ended in 1865, the idea of Reconstruction was more complicated: it now meant more than simple political reestablishment of the Union; it meant reconstructing the South, refashioning its social and economic life to some degree or other. For the freedmen—many only days removed from slavery—Reconstruction would soon come to represent freedom itself. Even in 1865, most southern blacks realized that without thoroughgoing Reconstruction, in which freedmen obtained land as well as the right to vote, freedom would mean only a new kind of economic oppression.

 Twelve years later, in 1877, many people, north and south, realized that Reconstruction had ended. But by then the term had taken on intense moral meanings. To most white southerners, it was a term of resentment, the name of a bleak period during which vindictive Yankee politicians had tried to force "black rule" on a "prostrate South." The North tried and finally failed, for the South had, in the end, been "redeemed" by its own leaders. Slavery had ended, but white supremacy had been firmly reestablished. To perhaps a majority of whites in the North, Reconstruction had over the years become a nuisance, and they were glad to let go of it, to reaffirm the value of the Union, and to let the bitter past die. There were other northerners, however, who looked back from 1877 to twelve years of moral failure, of lost opportunities to force freedom and equality on an unrepentant South.

There were hundreds of thousands of freedmen who experienced this "moral failure" in very real ways. Instead of farming their own land, they farmed the lands of whites as tenants and sharecroppers. Far from benefiting from meaningful voting rights, most blacks were denied the franchise, and those who continued to exercise it did so in a climate of hostility hardly conducive to political freedom. Nonetheless, it was possible for blacks to look back positively at the Reconstruction experience. The 1866 Civil Rights Act granted blacks both citizenship and all the civil rights possessed by whites. When the constitutionality of that statute seemed in doubt, Congress made ratification of the Fourteenth Amendment (accomplished in 1868) a precondition for southern restoration to the Union. In theory, that amendment made the federal government the protector of rights that might be invaded by the states. Under "Radical" Reconstruction, carried out by Congress after 1867, hundreds of thousands of southern blacks voted, and many held high elective office. And in 1875, when whites had reestablished their authority throughout most of the region, a new civil rights act "guaranteed" blacks equal rights in theaters, inns, and other public places. If in the end it proved impossible to maintain these gains, Reconstruction still remained the bright spot in the lives of many former slaves.

Promised Land

Elizabeth Rauh Bethel

Most accounts of the Reconstruction period have been written largely from the perspective of powerful white men such as presidents, northern congressmen, or southern "Redeemers." As a result, students often get the impression that all decisions were made by whites, and blacks were idly sitting on their hands, just the beneficiaries or victims of white actions. That was not the case. Throughout the South black men and women, just months after the end of slavery, actively shaped their own futures and challenged the power and prejudices of their white neighbors. Most wanted to own land and become family farmers. The odds against them were immense, and many struggled valiantly only to see their hopes dashed by their lack of money, or by political decisions made in distant Washington, or by white terrorists such as the Ku Klux Klan. But some, as Elizabeth Rauh Bethel documents in the following selection, overcame great obstacles and established tightly knit communities. What do you think accounts for the courage and determination of the families Bethel describes? Do you think the course of American history would have been changed if most black families during Reconstruction had obtained a forty-acre farm? In what respect?

The opportunity to acquire land was a potent attraction for a people just emerging from bondage, and one commonly pursued by freedmen throughout the south. Cooperative agrarian communities, instigated in some cases by the invading Union Army and in other cases by the freedmen themselves, were scattered across the plantation lands of the south as early as 1863. Collective land purchases and cooperative farming ventures developed in the Tidewater area of Virginia, the Sea Islands of South Carolina and Georgia, and along the Mississippi River as refugees at the earliest contraband camps struggled to establish economic and social stability.

These initial land tenure arrangements, always temporary, stimulated high levels of industrious labor among both those fortunate enough to obtain land and those whose expectations were raised by their neighbors' good fortunes. Although for most freedmen the initial promise of landownership was never realized, heightened expectations resulted in "entire families laboring together, improving their material conditions, laying aside money that might hopefully be used to purchase a farm or a few acres for a homestead of their own" during the final years of the war.

From Elizabeth Rauh Bethel, *Promiseland: A Century of Life in a Negro Community*, Temple University Press, Philadelphia, 1981, pp. 5–8, 17–21, 23, 25–33, 39–40. © 1981 by Temple University. Reprinted by permission of Temple University Press.

The desire for a plot of land dominated public expressions among the freedmen as well as their day-to-day activities and behaviors. In 1864 Secretary of War Stanton met with Negro leaders in Savannah to discuss the problems of resettlement. During that meeting sixty-seven-year-old freedman Garrison Frazier responded to an inquiry regarding living arrangements by telling Stanton that "we would prefer to 'live by ourselves' rather than 'scattered among the whites.'" These arrangements, he added, should include self-sufficiency established on Negro-owned lands. The sentiments Frazier expressed were not unusual. They were repeated by other freedmen across the south. Tunis Campbell, also recently emancipated, testified before the congressional committee investigating the Ku Klux Klan that "the great cry of our people is to have land." A delegate to the Tennessee Colored Citizens' Convention of 1866 stated that "what is needed for the colored people is land which they own." A recently emancipated Negro representative to the 1868 South Carolina Constitutional Convention, speaking in support of that state's land redistribution program, which eventually gave birth to the Promised Land community, said of the relationship between land-ownership and the state's Negro population: "Night and day they dream" of owning their own land. "It is their all in all."

At Davis Bend, Mississippi, and Port Royal, South Carolina, as well as similar settlements in Louisiana, North Carolina, and Virginia, this dream was in fact realized for a time. Freedmen worked "with commendable zeal . . . out in the morning before it is light and at work 'til darkness drives them to their homes" whenever they farmed land that was their own. John Eaton, who supervised the Davis Bend project, observed that the most successful land experiments among the freedmen were those in which plantations were subdivided into individually owned and farmed tracts. These small farms, rather than the larger cooperative ventures, "appeared to hold the greatest chance for success." The contraband camps and federally directed farm projects afforded newly emancipated freedmen an opportunity to "rediscover and redefine themselves, and to establish communities." Within the various settlements a stability and social order developed that combined economic self-sufficiency with locally directed and controlled schools, churches, and mutual aid societies. In the years before the Freedmen's Bureau or the northern missionary societies penetrated the interior of the south, the freedmen, through their own resourcefulness, erected and supported such community institutions at every opportunity. In obscure settlements with names like Slabtown and Acreville, Hampton, Alexandria, Saxtonville, and Mitchelville, "status, experience, history, and ideology were potent forces operating toward cohesiveness and community." . . .

. . . In South Carolina, perhaps more intensely than any of the other southern states, the thirst for land was acute. It was a possibility sparked first by General William T. Sherman's military actions along the Sea Islands, then dashed as quickly as it was born in the distant arena of Washington politics. Still, the desire for land remained a goal not readily abandoned by the state's freedpeople, and they implemented a plan to achieve that goal at the first opportunity. Their chance came at the 1868 South Carolina Constitutional Convention.

South Carolina was among the southern states that refused to ratify the Fourteenth Amendment to the Constitution, the amendment that established the citizenship of the freedmen. Like her recalcitrant neighbors, the state was then placed under military government, as outlined by the Military Reconstruction Act of 1867. Among the mandates of that federal legislation was a requirement that each of the states in question draft a new state constitution incorporating the principles of the Fourteenth Amendment. Only after such new constitutions were completed and implemented were the separate states of the defeated Confederacy eligible for readmission to the Union.

The representatives to these constitutional conventions were selected by a revolutionary electorate, one that included all adult male Negroes. Registration for the elections was handled by the army with some informal assistance by "that God-forsaken institution, the Freedman's Bureau." Only South Carolina among the ten states of the former Confederacy elected a Negro majority to its convention. The instrument those representatives drafted called for four major social and political reforms in state government: a statewide system of free common schools; universal manhood suffrage; a jury law that included the Negro electorate in county pools of qualified jurors; and a land redistribution system designed to benefit the state's landless population, primarily the freedmen.

White response to the new constitution and the social reforms that it outlined was predictably vitriolic. It was condemned by one white newspaper as "the work of sixty-odd Negroes, many of them ignorant and depraved." The authors were publicly ridiculed as representing "the maddest, most unscrupulous, and infamous revolution in history." Despite this and similar vilification, the constitution was ratified in the 1868 referendum, an election boycotted by many white voters and dominated by South Carolina's 81,000 newly enfranchised Negroes, who cast their votes overwhelmingly with the Republicans and for the new constitution.

That same election selected representatives to the state legislature charged with implementing the constitutional reforms. That body, like the constitutional convention, was constituted with a Negro majority; and it moved immediately to establish a common school system and land redistribution program. The freedmen were already registered, and the new jury pools remained the prerogative of the individual counties. The 1868 election also was notable for the numerous attacks and "outrages" that occurred against the more politically active freedmen. Among those Negroes assaulted, beaten, shot, and lynched during the pre-election campaign months were four men who subsequently bought small farms from the Land Commission and settled at Promised Land. Like other freedmen in South Carolina, their open involvement in the state's Republican political machinery led to personal violence.

Wilson Nash was the first of the future Promised Land residents to encounter white brutality and retaliation for his political activities. Nash was nominated by the Republicans as their candidate for Abbeville County's seat in the state legislature at the August 1868 county convention. In October of that year, less than two weeks before the general election, Nash was attacked and shot in the leg by two unidentified white assailants. The "outrage" took place in the barn on his rented farm, not far from Dr. Marshall's farm on Curltail Creek. Wilson Nash was thirty-three years old in 1868, married, and the father of three small children. He had moved from "up around Cokesbury" within Abbeville County, shortly after emancipation to the rented land further west. Within months after the Nash family was settled on their farm, Wilson Nash joined the many Negroes who affiliated with the Republicans, an alliance probably instigated and encouraged by Republican promises of land to the freedmen. The extent of Nash's involvement with local politics was apparent in his nomination for public office; and this same nomination brought him to the forefront of county Negro leadership and to the attention of local whites.

After the attack Nash sent his wife and young children to a neighbor's home, where he probably believed they would be safe. He then mounted his mule and fled his farm, leaving behind thirty bushels of recently harvested corn. Whether Nash also left behind a cotton crop is unknown. It was the unprotected corn crop that worried him as much as his concern for his own safety. He rode his mule into Abbeville and there sought refuge at the local Freedman's Bureau office where he reported the attack to the local bureau agent and requested military protection for his family and his corn crop. Captain W. F. DeKnight was sympathetic to Nash's plight but was powerless to assist or protect him. DeKnight had no authority in civil matters such as this, and the men who held that power generally ignored such assaults on Negroes. The Nash incident was typical and followed a familiar pattern. The assailants remained unidentified, unapprehended, and unpunished. The attack achieved the desired end, however, for Nash withdrew his name from the slate of legislative candidates. For him there were other considerations that took priority over politics.

Violence against the freedmen of Abbeville County, as elsewhere in the state, continued that fall and escalated as the 1868 election day neared. The victims had in common an involvement with the Republicans, and there was little distinction made between direct and indirect partisan activity. Politically visible Negroes were open targets. Shortly after the Nash shooting young Willis Smith was assaulted, yet another victim of Reconstruction violence. Smith was still a teenager and too young to vote in the elections, but his age afforded him no immunity. He was a known member of the Union League, the most radical and secret of the political organizations that attracted freedmen. While attending a dance one evening, Smith and four other League members were dragged outside the dance hall and brutally beaten by four white men whose identities were hidden by hoods. This attack, too, was an act of political vengeance. Like other crimes committed against politically active Negroes, this one remained unsolved.

On election day freedmen Washington Green and Allen Goode were precinct managers at the White Hall polling place, near the southern edge of the Marshall land. Their position was a political appointment of some prestige, their reward for affiliation with and loyalty to the Republican cause. The appointment brought them, like Wilson Nash and Willis Smith, to the attention of local whites. On election day the voting proceeded without incident until midday, when two white men attempted to block Negroes from entering the polling site. A scuffle ensued as Green and Goode, acting in their capacity as voting officials, tried to bring the matter to a halt and were shot by the white men. One freedman was killed, two others injured, in the incident that also went unsolved. In none of the attacks were the assailants ever apprehended. Within twenty-four months all four men—Wilson Nash, Willis Smith, Washington Green, and Allen Goode—bought farms at Promised Land.

Despite the violence surrounding the 1868 elections, the Republicans carried the whole of the state. White Democrats refused to support an election they deemed illegal, and they intimidated the newly enfranchised Negro electorate at every opportunity. The freedmen, nevertheless, flocked to the polls in an unprecedented exercise of their new franchise and sent a body of legislative representatives to the state capitol of Columbia who were wholly committed to the mandates and reforms of the new constitution. Among the first legislative acts was one that formalized the land redistribution program through the creation of the South Carolina Land Commission.

The Land Commission program, as designed by the legislature, was financed through the public sale of state bonds. The capital generated from the bond sales was used to purchase privately owned plantation tracts that were then subdivided and resold to freedmen through long-term (ten years), low-interest (7 percent per annum) loans. The bulk of the commission's transactions occurred along the coastal areas of the state where land was readily available. The labor and financial problems of the rice planters of the low-country were generally more acute than those of the up-country cotton planters. As a result, they were more eager to dispose of a portion of the landholdings at a reasonable price, and their motives for their dealings with the Land Commission were primarily pecuniary.

Piedmont planters were not so motivated. Many were able to salvage their production by negotiating sharecropping and tenant arrangements. Most operated on a smaller scale than the low-country planters and were less dependent on gang labor arrangements. As a consequence, few were as financially pressed as their low-country counterparts, and land was less available for purchase by the Land Commission in the Piedmont region. With only 9 percent of the commission purchases lying in the up-country, the Marshall lands were the exception rather than the rule.

The Marshall sons first advertised the land for sale in 1865. These lands, like others at the eastern edge of the Cotton Belt, were exhausted from generations of cultivation and attendant soil erosion; and for such worn-out land the price was greatly inflated. Additionally, two successive years of crop failures, low cotton prices, and a general lack of capital discouraged serious planters from purchasing the lands. The sons then advertised the tract for rent, but the land stood idle. The family wanted to dispose of the land in a single transaction rather than subdivide it, and Dr. Marshall's farm was no competition for the less expensive and more fertile land to the west that was opened for settlement after the war. In 1869 the two sons once again advertised the land for sale, but conditions in Abbeville County were not improved for farmers, and no private buyer came forth.

Having exhausted the possibilities for negotiating a private sale, the family considered alternative prospects for the disposition of a farm that was of little use to them. James L. Orr, a moderate Democrat, former governor (1865 to 1868), and family son-in-law, served as negotiator when the tract was offered to the Land Commission at the grossly inflated price of ten dollars an acre. Equivalent land in Abbeville County was selling for as little as two dollars an acre, and the commission rejected the offer. Political promises took precedence over financial considerations when the commission's regional agent wrote the Land Commission's Advisory Board that "if the land is not bought the (Republican) party is lost in this district." Upon receipt of his advice the commission immediately met the Marshall family's ten dollar an acre price. By January 1870 the land had been subdivided into fifty small farms, averaging slightly less than fifty acres each, which were publicly offered for sale to Negro as well as white buyers.

The Marshall Tract was located in the central sector of old Abbeville County and was easily accessible to most of the freedmen who were to make the lands their home. . . .

The farms on the Marshall Tract were no bargain for the Negroes who bought them. The land was only partially cleared and ready for cultivation, and that which was free of pine trees and underbrush was badly eroded. There was little to recommend the land to cotton farming. Crop failures in 1868 and 1869 severely limited the local economy, which further reduced the possibilities for small farmers working on badly depleted soil. There was little credit available to Abbeville farmers, white or black; and farming lacked not only an unqualified promise of financial gain but even the possibility of breaking even at harvest. Still, it was not the fertility of the soil or the possibility of economic profit that attracted the freedmen to those farms. The single opportunity for landownership, a status that for most Negroes in 1870 symbolized the essence of their freedom, was the prime attraction for the freedmen who bought farms from the subdivided Marshall Tract.

Most of the Negroes who settled the farms knew the area and local conditions well. Many were native to Abbeville County. In addition to Wilson Nash, the Moragne family and their in-laws, the Turners, the Pinckneys, the Letmans, and the Williamses were also natives of Abbeville, from "down over by Bordeaux" in the southwestern rim of the county that borders Georgia. Others came to their new farms from "Dark Corner, over by McCormick," and another nearby Negro settlement, Pettigrew Station—both in Abbeville County. The Redd family lived in Newberry, South Carolina before they bought their farm; and James and Hannah Fields came to Promised Land from the state capital, Columbia, eighty miles to the east.

Many of the settlers from Abbeville County shared their names with prominent white families—Moragne, Burt, Marshall, Pressley, Frazier, and

Pinckney. Their claims to heritage were diverse. One recalled "my grandaddy was a white man from England," and others remembered slavery times to their children in terms of white fathers who "didn't allow nobody to mess with the colored boys of his." Others dismissed the past and told their grandchildren that "some things is best forget." A few were so fair skinned that "they could have passed for white if they wanted to," while others who bought farms from the Land Commission "was so black there wasn't no doubt about who their daddy was."

After emancipation many of these former bondsmen stayed in their old neighborhoods, farming in much the same way as they had during slavery times. Some "worked for the marsters at daytime and for theyselves at night" in an early Piedmont version of sharecropping. Old Samuel Marshall was one former slaveowner who retained many of his bondsmen as laborers by assuring them that they would receive some land of their own—promising them that "if you clean two acres you get two acres; if you clean ten acres you get ten acres" of farmland. It was this promise that kept some freedmen on the Marshall land until it was sold to the Land Commission. They cut and cleared part of the tract of the native pines and readied it for planting in anticipation of ownership. But the promise proved empty, and Marshall's death and the subsequent sale of his lands to the state deprived many of those who labored day and night on the land of the free farms they hoped would be theirs. "After they had cleaned it up they still had to pay for it." Other freedmen in the county "moved off after slavery ended but couldn't get no place" of their own to farm. Unable to negotiate labor or lease arrangements, they faced a time of homelessness with few resources and limited options until the farms became available to them. A few entered into labor contracts supervised by the Freedman's Bureau or settled on rented farms in the county for a time.

The details of the various postemancipation economic arrangements made by the freedmen who settled on the small tracts at Dr. Marshall's farm, whatever the form they assumed, were dominated by three conscious choices all had in common. The first was their decision to stay in Abbeville County following emancipation. For most of the people who eventually settled in Promised Land, Abbeville was their home as well as the site of their enslavement. There they were surrounded by friends, family, and a familiar environment. The second choice this group of freedmen shared was occupational. They had been Piedmont farmers throughout their enslavement, and they chose to remain farmers in their freedom.

Local Negroes made a third conscious decision that for many had long-range importance in their lives and those of their descendants. Through the influence of the Union League, the Freedman's Bureau, the African Methodist Church, and each other, many of the Negroes in Abbeville aligned politically with the Republicans between 1865 and 1870. In Abbeville as elsewhere in the state, the alliance was established enthusiastically. The Republicans promised land as well as suffrage to those who supported them. If their political activities became public knowledge, the freedmen "were safe nowhere"; and men like Wilson Nash, Willis Smith, Washington

Green, and Allen Goode who were highly visible Negro politicians took great risks in this exercise of freedom. Those risks were not without justification. It was probably not a coincidence that loyalty to the Republican cause was followed by a chance to own land.

. . . The Land Commission first advertised the farms on the Marshall Tract in January and February 1870. Eleven freedmen and their families established conditional ownership of their farms before spring planting that year. They were among a vanguard of some 14,000 Negro families who acquired small farms in South Carolina through the Land Commission program between 1868 and 1879. With a ten-dollar down payment they acquired the right to settle on and till the thin soil. They were also obliged to place at least half their land under cultivation within three years and to pay all taxes due annually in order to retain their ownership rights.

Among the earliest settlers to the newly created farms was Allen Goode, the precinct manager at White Hall, who bought land in January 1870, almost immediately after it was put on the market. Two brothers-in-law, J. H. Turner and Primus Letman, also bought farms in the early spring that year. Turner was married to LeAnna Moragne and Letman to LeAnna's sister Francis. Elias Harris, a widower with six young children to raise, also came to his lands that spring, as did George Hearst, his son Robert, and their families. Another father-son partnership, Carson and Will Donnelly, settled on adjacent tracts. Willis Smith's father, Daniel, also bought a farm in 1870.

Allen Goode was the wealthiest of these early settlers. He owned a horse, two oxen, four milk cows, and six hogs. For the other families, both material resources and farm production were modest. Few of the homesteaders produced more than a single bale of cotton on their new farms that first year; but all, like Wilson Nash two years earlier, had respectable corn harvests, a crop essential to "both us and the animals." Most households also had sizable pea, bean, and sweet potato crops and produced their own butter. All but the cotton crops were destined for household consumption, as these earliest settlers established a pattern of subsistence farming that would prevail as a community economic strategy in the coming decades.

This decision by the Promised Land farmers to intensify food production and minimize cotton cultivation, whether intentional or the result of other conditions, was an important initial step toward their attainment of economic self-sufficiency. Small-scale cotton farmers in the Black Belt were rarely free agents. Most were quickly trapped in a web of chronic indebtedness and marketing restrictions. Diversification of cash crops was inhibited during the 1870s and 1880s not only by custom and these economic entanglements but also by an absence of local markets, adequate roads, and methods of transportation to move crops other than cotton to larger markets. The Promised Land farmers, generally unwilling to incur debts with the local lien men if they could avoid it, turned to a modified form of subsistence farming as their only realistic land-use option. Through this strategy many of them avoided the "economic nightmare" that fixed the status of other small-scale cotton growers at a level of permanent peonage well into the twentieth century.

The following year, 1871, twenty-five more families scratched up their ten-dollar down payment; and upon presenting it to Hollinshead obtained conditional titles to farms on the Marshall Tract. The Williams family, Amanda and her four adult sons—William, Henry, James, and Moses—purchased farms together that year, probably withdrawing their money from their accounts at the Freedmen's Savings and Trust Company Augusta Branch for their separate down payments. Three of the Moragne brothers—Eli, Calvin, and Moses—joined the Turners and the Letmans, their sisters and brothers-in-law, making five households in that corner of the tract soon designated "Moragne Town." John Valentine, whose family was involved in A.M.E. organizational work in Abbeville County, also obtained a conditional title to a farm, although he did not settle there permanently. Henry Redd, like the Williamses, withdrew his savings from the Freedman's Bank and moved to his farm from Newberry, a small town about thirty miles to the east. Moses Wideman, Wells Gray, Frank Hutchison, Samuel Bulow, and Samuel Burt also settled on their farms before spring planting.

As the cluster of Negro-owned farms grew more densely populated, it gradually assumed a unique identity; and this identity, in turn, gave rise to a name, Promised Land. Some remember their grandparents telling them that "the Governor in Columbia [South Carolina] named this place when he sold it to the Negroes." Others contend that the governor had no part in the naming. They argue that these earliest settlers derived the name Promised Land from the conditions of their purchase. "They only promised to pay for it, but they never did!" Indeed, there is some truth in that statement. For although the initial buyers agreed to pay between nine and ten dollars per acre for their land in the original promissory notes, few fulfilled the conditions of those contracts. Final purchase prices were greatly reduced, from ten dollars to $3.25 per acre, a price more in line with prevailing land prices in the Piedmont.

By the end of 1873 forty-four of the fifty farms on the Marshall Tract had been sold. The remaining land, less than seven hundred acres, was the poorest in the tract, badly eroded and at the perimeter of the community. Some of those farms remained unsold until the early 1880s, but even so the land did not go unused. Families too poor to consider buying the farms lived on the state-owned property throughout the 1870s. They were squatters, living there illegally and rent-free, perhaps working a small cotton patch, always a garden. Their condition contrasted sharply with that of the landowners who, like other Negroes who purchased farmland during the 1870s, were considered the most prosperous of the rural freedmen. The freeholders in the community were among the pioneers in a movement to acquire land, a movement that stretched across geographical and temporal limits. Even in the absence of state or federal assistance in other regions, and despite the difficulties Negroes faced in negotiating land purchases directly from white landowners during Reconstruction, by 1875 Negroes across the south owned five million acres of farmland. The promises of emancipation were fulfilled for a few, among them the families at Promised Land.

Settlement of the community coincided with the establishment of a public school, another of the revolutionary social reforms mandated by the 1868 constitution. It was the first of several public facilities to serve community residents and was built on land still described officially as "Dr. Marshall's farm." J. H. Turner, Larkin Reynolds, Iverson Reynolds, and Hutson Lomax, all Negroes, were the first school trustees. The families established on their new farms sent more than ninety children to the one-room school. Everyone who could be spared from the fields was in the classroom for the short 1870 school term. Although few of the children in the landless families attended school regularly, the landowning families early established a tradition of school attendance for their children consonant with their new status. With limited resources the school began the task of educating local children.

The violence and terror experienced by some of the men of Promised Land during 1868 recurred three years later when Eli and Wade Moragne were attacked and viciously beaten with a wagon whip by a band of Klansmen. Wade was twenty-three that year, Eli two years older. Both were married and had small children. It was rumored that the Moragne brothers were among the most prominent and influential of the Negro Republicans in Abbeville County. Their political activity, compounded by an unusual degree of self-assurance, pride, and dignity, infuriated local whites. Like Wilson Nash, Willis Smith, Washington Green, and Allen Goode, the Moragne brothers were victims of insidious political reprisals. Involvement in Reconstruction politics for Negroes was a dangerous enterprise and one that addressed the past as well as the future. It was an activity suited to young men and those who faced the future bravely. It was not for the timid.

The Republican influence on the freedmen at Promised Land was unmistakable, and there was no evidence that the "outrages" and terrorizations against them slowed their participation in local partisan activities. In addition to the risks, there were benefits to be accrued from their alliance with the Republicans. They enjoyed appointments as precinct managers and school trustees. As candidates for various public offices, they experienced a degree of prestige and public recognition that offset the element of danger they faced. These men, born slaves, rose to positions of prominence as landowners, as political figures, and as makers of a community. Few probably had dared to dream of such possibilities a decade earlier.

During the violent years of Reconstruction there was at least one official attempt to end the anarchy in Abbeville County. The representative to the state legislature, J. Hollinshead—the former regional agent for the Land Commission—stated publicly what many local Negroes already knew privately, that "numerous outrages occur in the county and the laws cannot be enforced by civil authorities." From the floor of the General Assembly of South Carolina Hollinshead called for martial law in Abbeville, a request that did not pass unnoticed locally. The editor of the *Press* commented on Hollinshead's request for martial law by declaring that such outrages against the freedmen "exist only in the imagination of the legislator." His response was probably typical of the cavalier attitude of southern whites toward the problems of their former bondsmen. Indeed, there were no further reports of violence and attacks against freedmen carried by the *Press*, which failed to note the murder of County Commissioner Henry Nash in February 1871. Like other victims of white terrorists, Nash was a Negro.

While settlement of Dr. Marshall's farm by the freedmen proceeded, three community residents were arrested for the theft of "some oxen from Dr. H. Drennan who lives near the 'Promiseland.'" Authorities found the heads, tails, and feet of the slaughtered animals near the homes of Ezekiel and Moses Williams and Colbert Jordan. The circumstantial evidence against them seemed convincing; and the three were arrested and then released without bond, pending trial. Colonel Cothran, a former Confederate officer and respected barrister in Abbeville, represented the trio at their trial. Although freedmen in Abbeville courts were generally convicted of whatever crime they were charged with, the Williamses and Jordan were acquitted. Justice for Negroes was always a tenuous affair; but it was especially so before black, as well as white, qualified electors were included in the jury pool. The trial of the Williams brothers and Jordan signaled a temporary truce in the racial war, a truce that at least applied to those Negroes settling the farms at Promised Land.

In 1872, the third year of settlement, Promised Land gained nine more households as families moved to land that they "bought for a dollar an acre." There they "plow old oxen, build log cabin houses" as they settled the land they bought "from the Governor in Columbia." Colbert Jordan and Ezekiel Williams, cleared of the oxen stealing charges, both purchased farms that year. Family and kinship ties drew some of the new migrants to the community. Joshuway Wilson, married to Moses Wideman's sister Delphia, bought a farm near his brother-in-law. Two more Moragne brothers, William and Wade, settled near the other family members in "Moragne Town." Whitfield Hutchison, a jack-leg preacher, bought the farm adjacent to his brother Frank. "Old Whit Hutchison could sing about let's go down to the water and be baptized. He didn't have no education, and he didn't know exactly how to put his words, but when he got to singing he could make your hair rise up. He was a number one preacher." Hutchison was not the only preacher among those first settlers. Isaac Y. Moragne, who moved to Promised Land the following year, and several men in the Turner family all combined preaching and farming.

Not all the settlers came to their new farms as members of such extensive kinship networks as the Moragnes, who counted nine brothers, four sisters, and an assortment of spouses and children among the first Promised Land residents. Even those who joined the community in relative isolation, however, were seldom long in establishing kinship alliances with their neighbors. One such couple was James and Hannah Fields, who lived in Columbia before emancipation. While still a slave, James Fields owned property in the state capital, which was held in trust for him by his master. After emancipation Fields worked for a time as a porter on the Columbia and Greenville Railroad and heard about the up-country land for sale to Negroes as he carried carpet bags and listened to political gossip on the train. Fields went to

Abbeville County to inspect the land before he purchased a farm there. While he was visiting, he "run up on Mr. Nathan Redd," old Henry Redd's son. The Fields's granddaughter Emily and Nathan were about the same age, and Fields proposed a match to young Redd. "You marry my grand-daughter, and I'll will all this land to you and her." The marriage was arranged before the farm was purchased, and eventually the land was transferred to the young couple.

By the conclusion of 1872 forty-eight families were settled on farms in Promised Land. Most of the land was under cultivation, as required by law; but the farmers were also busy with other activities. In addition to the houses and barns that had to be raised as each new family arrived with their few possessions, the men continued their political activities. Iverson Reynolds, J. H. Turner, John and Elias Tolbert, Judson Reynolds, Oscar Pressley, and Washington Green, all community residents, were delegates to the county Republican convention in August 1872. Three of the group were landowners. Their political activities were still not received with much enthusiasm by local whites, but reaction to Negro involvement in politics was lessening in hostility. The *Press* mildly observed that the fall cotton crop was being gathered with good speed and "the farmers have generally been making good use of their time." Cotton picking and politics were both seasonal, and the newspaper chided local Negroes for their priorities. "The blacks have been indulging a little too much in politics but are getting right again." Iverson Reynolds and Washington Green, always among the community's Republican leadership during the 1870s, served as local election managers again for the 1872 fall elections. The men from Promised Land voted without incident that year.

Civic participation among the Promised Land residents extended beyond partisan politics when the county implemented the new jury law in 1872. There had been no Negro jurors for the trial of the Williams brothers and Colbert Jordan the previous year. Although the inclusion of Negroes in the jury pools was a reform mandated in 1868, four years passed before Abbeville authorities drew up new jury lists from the revised voter registration rolls. The jury law was as repugnant to the whites as Negro suffrage, termed "a wretched attempt at legislation, which surpasses anything which has yet been achieved by the Salons in Columbia." When the new lists were finally completed in 1872 the Press, ever the reflection of local white public opinion, predicted that "many of [the freedmen] probably have moved away; and the chances are that not many of them will be forthcoming" in the call to jury duty. Neither the initial condemnation of the law nor the optimistic undertones of the *Press* prediction stopped Pope Moragne and Iverson Reynolds from responding to their notices from the Abbeville Courthouse. Both landowners rode their mules up Five Notch Road from Promised Land to Abbeville and served on the county's first integrated jury in the fall of 1872. Moragne and Reynolds were soon followed by others from the community—Allen Goode, Robert Wideman, William Moragne, James Richie, and Luther (Shack) Moragne. By 1874, less than five years after settlement of Dr. Marshall's farm by the new Negro landowners began, the residents of

Promised Land remained actively involved in Abbeville County politics. They were undaunted by the *Press* warning that "just so soon as the colored people lose the confidence and support of the North their doom is fixed. The fate of the red man will be theirs." They were voters, jurors, taxpayers, and trustees of the school their children attended. Their collective identity as an exclusively Negro community was well established. . . .

The representatives to the 1868 South Carolina Constitutional Convention who formulated the state's land redistribution hoped to establish an economically independent Negro yeomanry in South Carolina. The Land Commission intended the purchase and resale of Dr. Marshall's farm to solidify the interests of radical Republicanism in Abbeville County, at least for a time. Both of these designs were realized. A third and unintended consequence also resulted. The land fostered a socially autonomous, identifiable community. Drawing on resources and social structures well established within an extant Negro culture, the men and women who settled Promised Land established churches and schools and a viable economic system based on landownership. They maintained that economic autonomy by subsistence farming and supported many of their routine needs by patronizing the locally owned and operated grist mills and general store. The men were actively involved in Reconstruction politics as well as other aspects of civil life, serving regularly on county juries and paying their taxes. Attracted by the security and prestige Promised Land afforded and the possible hope of eventual landownership, fifty additional landless households moved into the community during the 1870s, expanding the 1880 population to almost twice its original size. Together the eighty-nine households laid claim to slightly more than four square miles of land, and within that small territory they "carved out their own little piece of the world."

To further explore the experience of Reconstruction, visit the "Civil War and Reconstruction, 1861–1877" page of the Library of Congress website and access the links entitled "The Freedmen," "Reconstruction and Rights," and "The Travails of Reconstruction" at http://lcweb2.loc.gov/ ammem/ndlpedu/features/timeline/civilwar/civilwar.html.

SOURCES

The Meaning of Freedom

What did it mean to be free? As Bethel's account of the settlers of Promised Land indicates, there were many obstacles in the path of every freedman and only a few succeeded in becoming independent small farmers. Some twentieth-century writers have argued that the gains for most blacks were miniscule, that being a poor tenant farmer or sharecropper was often even worse than being a slave. But these writers, of course, never experienced the change from slavery to freedom. Here is a man who did.

VOICES

Dayton, Ohio, August 7, 1865

To My Old Master, Colonel P. H. Anderson, Big Spring, Tennessee

Sir: I got your letter and was glad to find you had not forgotten Jourdon, and that you wanted me to come back and live with you again, promising to do better for me than anybody else can. I have often felt uneasy about you. I thought the Yankees would have hung you long before this for harboring Rebs they found at your house. I suppose they never heard about your going to Col. Martin's to kill the Union soldier that was left by his company in their stable. Although you shot at me twice before I left you, I did not want to hear of your being hurt, and am glad you are still living. It would do me good to go back to the dear old home and see Miss Mary and Miss Martha and Allen, Esther, Green, and Lee. Give my love to them all, and tell them I hope we will meet in the better world, if not in this. I would have gone back to see you all when I was working in the Nashville hospital, but one of the neighbors told me Henry intended to shoot me if he ever got a chance.

I want to know particularly what the good chance is you propose to give me. I am doing tolerably well here; I get $25 a month, with victuals and clothing; have a comfortable home for Mandy (the folks here call her Mrs. Anderson), and the children, Milly, Jane and Grundy, go to school and are learning well; the teacher says Grundy has a head for a preacher. They go to Sunday-School, and Mandy and me attend church regularly. We are kindly treated; sometimes we overhear others saying, "Them colored people were slaves" down in Tennessee. The children feel hurt when they hear such remarks, but I tell them it was no disgrace in Tennessee to belong to Col.

From Lydia Maria Child, ed., *The Freedmen's Book*, Ticknor and Fields, Boston, 1865, pp. 265–267.

Anderson. Many darkies would have been proud, as I used to was, to call you master. Now, if you will write and say what wages you will give me, I will be better able to decide whether it would be to my advantage to move back again.

As to my freedom, which you say I can have, there is nothing to be gained on that score, as I got my free-papers in 1864 from the Provist-Marshal-General of the Department at Nashville. Mandy says she would be afraid to go back without some proof that you are sincerely disposed to treat us justly and kindly—and we have concluded to test your sincerity by asking you to send us our wages for the time we served you. This will make us forget and forgive old scores, and rely on your justice and friendship in the future. I served you faithfully for thirty-two years and Mandy twenty years. At $25 a month for me, and $2 a week for Mandy, our earnings would amount to $11,680. Add to this the interest for the time our wages has been kept back and deduct what you paid for our clothing and three doctor's visits to me, and pulling a tooth for Mandy, and the balance will show what we are in justice entitled to. Please send the money by Adams Express, in care of V. Winters, esq., Dayton, Ohio. If you fail to pay us for faithful labors in the past we can have little faith in your promises in the future. We trust the good Maker has opened your eyes to the wrongs which you and your fathers have done to me and my fathers, in making us toil for you for generations without recompense. Here I draw my wages every Saturday night, but in Tennessee there was never any pay day for the negroes any more than for the horses and cows. Surely there will be a day of reckoning for those who defraud the laborer of his hire.

In answering this letter please state if there would be any safety for my Milly and Jane, who are now grown up and both good-looking girls. You know how it was with poor Matilda and Catherine. I would rather stay here and starve and die if it comes to that than have my girls brought to shame by the violence and wickedness of their young masters. You will also please state if there has been any schools opened for the colored children in your neighborhood, the great desire of my life now is to give my children an education, and have them form virtuous habits.

P.S.—Say howdy to George Carter, and thank him for taking the pistol from you when you were shooting at me.

From your old servant,
Jourdon Anderson

The Cartoonist's View of Reconstruction

Thomas Nast was America's foremost political cartoonist. He also was a Radical Republican who had no love for the white South or the Democratic Party. The touchstone cause of Radical Republicans was black civil rights—particularly the right to vote—and conflict with the Democrats and the white South often focused on this issue. Nast's drawings in Harper's Weekly, *as you will notice, illustrated vividly this ongoing battle. The high point for Nast came when Hiram Revels, a black, occupied the Senate seat from Mississippi once held by Jefferson Davis. The low point came shortly afterward. What effect do you think each cartoon had on the electorate? Were any more compelling than the others?*

Columbia—"Shall I trust these men, . . .

and not this man?" Thomas Nast, *Harper's Weekly*, August 5, 1865.

"This Is a White Man's Government."
"We regard the Reconstruction Acts (so called) of Congress as usurpations, and unconstitutional, revolutionary, and void."—Democratic platform. Thomas Nast, *Harper's Weekly*, September 5, 1868, Courtesy of The Research Libraries, The New York Public Library, Astor, Lenox and Tilden Foundations.

"Time Works Wonders Government." Thomas Nast, *Harper's Weekly*, April 9, 1870.

The commandments in South Carolina.
"We've pretty well smashed that; but I suppose, Massa Moses, you can get another
one." Thomas Nast, *Harper's Weekly*, September 26, 1874.

"To Thine Own Self Be True." Thomas Nast, *Harper's Weekly*, October 24, 1874.

The target.

". . . They (Messrs. Phleps & Potter) seem to regard the White League as innocent as a Target Company."—Special dispatch to the *N.Y. Times*, from Washington, Jan. 17, 1875. Thomas Nast, *Harper's Weekly*, February 6, 1875.

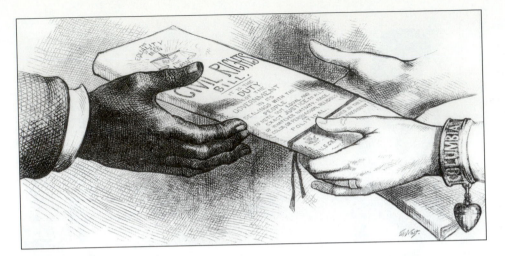

"These Few Precepts in Thy Memory."
Beware of entrance to a quarrel; but, being in,
Bear it that the opposer may beware of thee.
Give every man thine ear, but few thy voice:
Take each man's censure, but reserve thy judgment.
Costly thy habit as thy purse can buy,
But not express'd in fancy; rich, not gaudy:
For the apparel oft proclaims the man.

This above all,—To thine own self be true;
And it must follow, as the night the day,
Thou canst not then be false to any man.
                                              —Shakespeare

Thomas Nast, *Harper's Weekly*, April 24, 1875.

The "Civil Rights" scare is nearly over.
The game of (Colored) fox and (White) goose. Thomas Nast, *Harper's Weekly*, May 22, 1875.

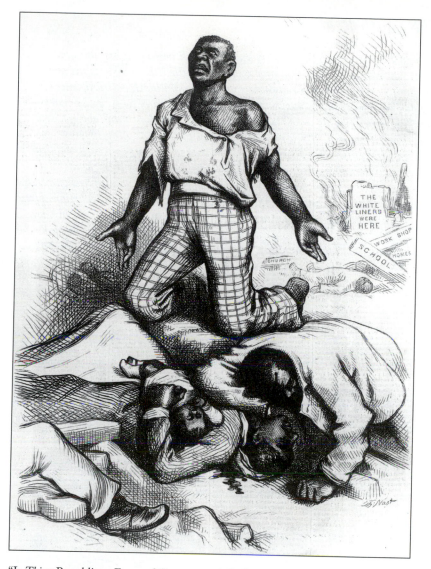

"Is *This* a Republican Form of Government? Is *This* Protecting Life, Liberty, or Property? Is *This* the Equal Protection of the Laws?"
Mr. Lamar (Democrat, Mississippi): "In the words of the inspired poet, 'Thy gentleness has made thee great.'" [Did Mr. Lamar mean the colored race?] Thomas Nast, *Harper's Weekly*, September 2, 1876. The Newberry Library.

To learn more about Thomas Nast and view more of his political cartoons relative to Reconstruction, visit http://cartoons.osu.edu/nast/index.htm.

The South Redeemed

As Nast's cartoons indicate, the crusade for black voting rights and other civil rights ran into stiff opposition and eventually failed. By 1877, white supremacy was firmly reestablished throughout the South, and black political voices were almost completely stilled. The South, according to many white southerners, had been "redeemed" by its white leaders. But the white South did not get back everything it wanted. Black men had refused to work as gang laborers, and black families had refused to let women and children work long hours in the field. Grudgingly, white landowners had let blacks work the land in family plots, usually as either tenant farmers or sharecroppers. Thus, despite "redemption," the southern landscape would look startlingly different from Reconstruction. Here are maps of the same Georgia plantation in 1860 and in 1880. What, in your judgment, were the important features in the new and the old landscape? Do the changes match up with the kinds of attitudes discussed in Bethel's essay? How many of the 1880 families, would you guess, once lived in the old slave quarters?

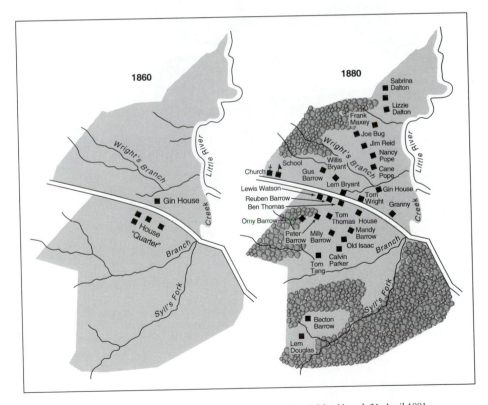

The Barrow plantation, 1860 and 1880. Adapted from *Scribner's Monthly*, vol. 21, April 1881, pp. 832–833.

 ON THE WEB   *To read Frederick Douglass's perception of Reconstruction, visit* http://classiclit.about.com/ library/bl-etexts/fdouglass/bl-fdoug-reconstruction.htm.

THE BIG PICTURE

The problem of Reconstruction was to bring eleven states back into the Union, rebuild the war-torn nation, and achieve racial justice. The latter did not happen. Why didn't it happen? What, in your opinion, would have been an appropriate and effective method for achieving racial justice in 1865?

Chapter 2

The Industrial Age

Nineteenth-century Americans were obsessed with change, progress, development, and growth. And this obsession reached a new peak during the decades after the Civil War. An American who had matured in the 1850s or 1860s could look backward from 1890 or 1900 and remember a lifetime filled with what seemed to be the most astonishing kinds of transformations.

The facts were there to support such memories of change. The population more than doubled between 1870 and 1900. The telegraph, the telephone, the electric light, and the Linotype were only four of the dozens of inventions that made life—and work—remarkably different. In 1850, most workers were artisans, plying their crafts in small shops under employers working beside them on similar tasks. By 1900, larger industrial enterprises were employing thousands of workers; employers seldom had any personal knowledge of their employees; and much of the skill had been removed from the work process. There were new cities, too—six in 1900 with populations of more than 500,000. The United States leapfrogged over England, France, and Germany to become the leading industrial nation of the world. Steel production increased 2,000 percent between the Civil War and the end of the century. Many firms for the first time supplied national and urban markets rather than local and rural ones. This meant new opportunities, more intense competition, and, finally, the emergence of the big corporations that have become the hallmark of the American economy. Change was a whirling, accelerating affair that altered the horizons of experience in every decade.

Above the whirl, a kind of official opinion developed, an orthodox opinion that change was "progress." Presidents and senators, newspaper editors and magazine writers, preachers and book publishers—all the molders of what was coming to be thought of as "public opinion"—voiced a belief that industrialization was creating a better life for the republic. Within this view, industrial growth meant opportunity. Competition meant success. All the inventions created leisure and material comfort. The great new factories meant a sort of democracy of well-being for the workers in them. And, in national terms, industrial growth meant the potential triumph in the world of American principles of freedom and equality.

But the awareness of change also generated problems and anxieties. For the wealthy and the sophisticated, there was the possibility that industrialization might lead to a world of materialism, greed, and speculation, a world with only a thin and false veneer of culture and moral values. This fear was a theme of the book that gave a name to the period, Mark Twain and Charles Dudley Warner's *Gilded Age*, published in 1873.

What became known as the "labor question" or the "labor problem" was really a collection of doubts and anxieties. Could the United States absorb the huge pool of immigrants who were attracted to the industrializing cities and towns? Would the new industrial work force tolerate long hours, factory conditions, and gross disparities of wealth, or would they form labor unions and even take to the streets to protest and redress their grievances? Would ordinary Americans continue to believe in the possibilities of success and self-improvement, and so resign themselves to a place in the new order of things? Or would radical ideologies—socialism, communism, anarchism—thrive in the new industrial environment and bring American capitalism crashing down?

INTERPRETIVE ESSAY

Gunfire and Brickbats: The Great Railway Strikes of 1877

Gerald G. Eggert

In the midst of the great economic changes of the latter half of the nineteenth century, most Americans believed that their country could somehow avoid the deep social conflicts and sharp ideological struggles associated with industrialization in Europe. There were, to be sure, disquieting signs. American workers had come together in unions as early as the 1790s, formed workingmen's political parties in the 1820s and 1830s, and, like Philadelphia textile workers in 1844, gone out on strike against their employers. In the decade after the Civil War, national unions, bringing together workers in similar occupations, had grown dramatically in number and influence, led by the iron molders and the railroad "brotherhoods." Yet even as Americans suffered through the depression of the 1870s, it was easy to believe that race and sectionalism, not class and economics, were the nation's most critical problems.

With the fourth year of the depression came the rude awakening known as the 1877 railroad strike. Although less familiar to most students of American history than the Pullman strike or the Homestead strike of the 1890s, the railroad conflict was probably more significant. It began on a Monday in mid-July, 1877, in Martinsburg, West Virginia, where workers employed by the Baltimore and Ohio Railroad refused to move the trains until the company rescinded a previously announced wage cut of 10 percent. There, and elsewhere, the use of state militia and federal troops to move the trains and bring order angered railroad workers and those in other industries. By the end of the week, the strike had spread to other lines and to other communities in the East, Midwest, and South, including Baltimore, Buffalo, Pittsburgh, Columbus, Chicago, Louisville, and Galveston. In many communities, railroad workers were joined by workers in other industries in citywide "general" strikes, in which most of the city's industries were shut down. The St. Louis general strike was the most important of these confrontations.

Events of this sort would seem highly improbable today, when labor is better organized but also less confident of its ability to confront big business. What conditions—political, economic, social, or technological—made the general strikes of 1877 possible? How did workers understand their situation? What did they want out of the strikes, and were their demands reasonable? What role did ethnicity, class, and race play in the strike? What was the role of government?

The angry band of workmen in the yards of the Baltimore & Ohio Railroad at Martinsburg, West Virginia, who tossed down their tools and refused to allow trains to pass that hot Monday in mid-July 1877, could not have guessed the outcome of their defiance. No doubt they hoped their actions would induce the company to rescind its most recent wage cut. More than likely, however, most of the men were giving vent to pent-up hostilities and frustrations against an employer they could reach in no other way.

Their rebellion quickly caught on. Within days similar work stoppages, some accompanied by riots and looting, swept over the railroad network from one rail center to another in all parts of the country except New England and the Deep South. The disorders of that summer produced the first near-national emergency strike in the country's history, led to massive governmental intervention in a labor dispute, established important precedents for dealing with later strikes, and opened a new epoch in American labor history. The speed with which the movement spread, its ultimate scope, and the abruptness with which it fizzled out must in turn have surprised, cheered, and finally disheartened the Martinsburg strikers.

In 1877 the nation entered the fourth year of the depression touched off by the Panic of 1873. Unemployment was widespread, layoffs and wage cuts were common, commerce was stagnant, business failures were frequent. The prevailing gloom and uncertainty caused tensions and suspicions across class lines, especially when employers tried to economize and protect profits by shifting the burdens of depression onto the workers. Railroad companies were not the only offenders in this regard, nor were their employees the lowest paid of workmen. By reducing the nation to dependence on them for virtually all transportation, however, by the 1870s the railroads had created as many enemies as friends. Their arrogant and autocratic presidents (Tom Scott of the Pennsylvania, William Vanderbilt of the New York Central, Franklin Gowen of the Reading, and John W. Garrett of the Baltimore & Ohio, to name but a few), their arbitrary rates, their rank favoritism to preferred customers, and the influence they wielded over government from county courthouses to Congress contributed to the public outcry against them.

Not all railroad companies were rich and powerful. A number of lines, particularly in the Midwest, had passed into receivership after 1873 and were being managed on behalf of creditors by court-appointed receivers. Those and other lines were forced by shrunken incomes to reduce or even forego dividends. The labor difficulties first arose, however, not on the financially distressed roads, but on the relatively prosperous trunklines of the East. Of those lines only the Erie had passed into receivership. The Pennsylvania in 1876 earned more than enough to pay an 8 percent dividend but distributed only six in order to build up its cash reserves. The New York Central paid its regular 8 percent, the Baltimore & Ohio, ten.

To strengthen their economic position, early in 1877 the trunklines set up a pool to end a rate war that had been eroding profits. They also agreed to a round of wage cuts for their employees. Those lines were not alone; railroad

The Sixth Maryland Regiment, Fighting Its Way Through Baltimore During the Great Strike of 1877. From a photograph by D. Bendann. Library of Congress.

companies in all parts of the country were already slashing wages. The 10 percent cut for Pennsylvania Railroad employees that began June 1 was that company's second reduction since the start of the panic. The B & O, long notorious for paying poorly, announced its second 10 percent cut in eight months—to take effect July 16.

Railroad employees, when compared with most industrial workers, enjoyed steadier work but overall received only average wages. This middling position possibly contributed to the militancy with which they resisted

Robert M. Ammon, the Leader of the Pittsburgh and Fort Wayne Railroad Strike, at His Post, Directing the Movements of the Strikers. From a sketch by John Donaghy. Library of Congress.

attempts to reduce them below that common level of income which hovered ever so slightly above subsistence. For the battle that was shaping up the railroaders lacked organization and leadership. There were unions; the Brotherhood of Locomotive Engineers and the Brotherhood of Locomotive Firemen had come into being during the previous decade. By the time of the 1877 difficulties, however, both had abandoned militancy in hope of winning toleration from the companies. Neither was to play a substantial part in the 1877 strikes. A more radical Trainmen's Union, open to all railroad employees, not just to skilled men in the locomotive cabs, conducted a membership drive on the eve of the strikes but met with little success. As the strikes got under way they were directed, if at all, by impromptu leaders brought to the fore by circumstance. Even at the height of the disorders, no organization or leader could be identified as spokesman for any substantial body of strikers.

Although rumors of strike were rampant on the B & O following announcement of the July 16 wage cut, the workmen made no concerted plans. The day the cut went into effect the men at Martinsburg acted wholly on their own. They simply stopped work and began halting trains that tried to pass through the yards. Supported by sympathetic townspeople, the strikers ignored the pleas of the mayor and orders of railroad officials to return to work. Referring to this situation as "riot," company managers demanded

The Great Strike—Blockade of Engines at Martinsburg, West Virginia, from photograph by D. Bendann.

The Great Strike—Burning of the Lebanon Valley Railroad Bridge by the Rioters. Drawn by Fred B. Schell. *Harper's Weekly* 21 (August 11, 1877). Library of Congress.

that Governor Henry M. Mathews of West Virginia send the militia to re-store order and move the trains. Many of the volunteer militiamen sent to Martinsburg were themselves railroaders who fully understood the workers' grievances. A single feeble attempt was made to run a train with a scab engineer protected by the militia. As the train started up, a workman and a militiaman exchanged gunshots; the striker fell, mortally wounded. The would-be engineer deserted the cab and no one could be found to take his place. During the resulting standoff, President Garrett of the B & O persuaded Mathews to wire the War Department in Washington for Federal troops to help suppress "domestic insurrection" in West Virginia. A small detachment of Regulars arrived July 19 and promptly lifted the blockade. Far from excising the disorder, the action simply spread it westward along the line to Cumberland, Maryland, and other points.

The decision of Governor John L. Carroll of Maryland to dispatch state militiamen to Cumberland at President Garrett's request triggered more serious troubles at Baltimore. The militia were summoned to their armories at about 6:30 P.M. on July 20 by the ringing of all the town's fire bells. But the commotion brought out more than militiamen. Disgruntled railwaymen, assorted troublemakers, the idle and unemployed, excitement-seeking teenagers, and the merely curious all gathered. As one troop of militia marched toward the railroad station, spectators along the way became increasingly hostile. At first they pelted the troopers with insults, then with stones and brickbats. Only strict discipline prevented the men from opening fire on the crowd that injured twenty-five of them as they marched.

A second confrontation between militiamen and a crowd ended less fortunately. Attacked by an angry mob as they were leaving their armory, the troopers opened fire on their tormentors, killing no fewer than ten men and boys. By 9 P.M. a crowd of 15,000 had gathered in the station yard. Despite the presence of militia, troublemakers began tearing up track. Others set fire to railway cars and B & O property in the area, then attempted to block firemen who came to put out the blaze. Hearing rumors that rioters meant to destroy the B & O's property and then burn the whole city, Governor Carroll wired President Rutherford B. Hayes for Federal troops. Although both the fires and the mob were quickly brought under control, Carroll let his request stand. The next day Federal troops moved into an essentially quiet Baltimore.

By the 21st the troubles had begun to spread, westward on the B & O to Newark, Ohio, where state militiamen were called out to end a blockade, and northwestward to Hornellsville, New York, where Erie Railroad employees halted both passenger and freight trains. Because the Erie was in receivership, its officers made what was at that time a novel move: They applied to the court for orders (injunctions) prohibiting interference with property in the possession of the court, and proceeded against the strikers for contempt of court. This device, perfected in the years that followed, became commonplace in later struggles against strikers.

The most serious difficulties of July 21 occurred on the Pennsylvania Railroad at Pittsburgh, where during the next few days the strikes of 1877 would reach their climax. Wage cuts and accumulated grievances of laborers in general, not just of railwaymen, lay behind the riotous disorders in the Iron City. The immediate cause of the outbreak had been the order by Pennsylvania Railroad officers that after July 19 all eastbound trains would be doubleheaders. Ordinarily eastbound trains halted at the mountains until a second locomotive could be attached to assist the crossing. Under the new order, trains would leave Pittsburgh already made up with thirty-six or more cars drawn by two locomotives rather than with seventeen or eighteen cars pulled by a single engine. The company observed that the arrangement would save the time usually spent attaching the second engine. Workmen complained that it also meant men being laid off, more work for those remaining, and increased danger, especially in winter. Doubleheaders, although using two engineers and two firemen, operated with no more conductors, brakemen, or other trainmen than did singleheaders.

On July 19 Pennsylvania employees in Pittsburgh refused to move doubleheaders and prevented strikebreakers from taking their places. As new trains rolled into the yards their crews joined in the stoppage. Within hours the yards filled with trains loaded with freight. Perishables such as meat, fruit, and vegetables soon began to spoil in the summer's heat. Meanwhile, millworkers and other non-railwaymen drifted in, swelling the ranks of the crowd. That night the embryo Trainmen's Union sponsored a meeting of workers to draw up demands on the Pennsylvania Railroad: discontinue doubleheaders, rescind wage cuts, rehire all dismissed strikers. The next day no trains whatever ran in or out of Pittsburgh. Efforts of local government and railroad officials to persuade the strikers to yield met only rebuffs.

An attempt to use militia units from the Pittsburgh area to restore order proved futile. Many men failed to muster and as disorder mounted, militiamen melted into the crowds and disappeared. State officials then bowed to the demand of the Pennsylvania's President Scott that Philadelphia units be dispatched to Pittsburgh. That was a blunder. The two cities had long been antagonistic, their rivalry involving such elements as East versus West, age against youth, inherited mercantile and banking wealth as opposed to new iron and steel fortunes, aristocracy and culture contrasted with a rough proletarian lifestyle. Two trains bearing the Philadelphians ran into hailstorms of stones at Harrisburg, Altoona, and Johnstown before even reaching Pittsburgh.

After a light meal of sandwiches and coffee at the station, the militiamen formed ranks and paraded out to clear the tracks so that doubleheaders could begin operating. Thousands milled around the tracks while others watched from nearby knolls. With bayonets fixed the militia advanced. Now and then steel nicked flesh. Some of the demonstrators tried to wrest rifles from the hands of militiamen. The crowd taunted and jeered. Firecrackers left over from the recent Independence Day celebrations were discharged. Occasionally a pistol shot rang out from the crowd. Suddenly—and without orders—militiamen fired into the crowd. At least ten were killed on the spot, from thirty to seventy others were seriously wounded. The troopers suffered

Great Railroad Strike, Pittsburgh, 1877. Burning of the Offices and Machine Shops of the Pennsylvania Railroad/Burning and Sacking of Freight Trains on the Pennsylvania Railroad and Mob Outside the James Bown & Sons Gunworks. *Harper's Weekly* 21 (August 11, 1877). Library of Congress.

fifteen casualties, though none were killed. The tracks stood clear, but the company found no one willing to run the trains. The militia retired to a roundhouse for the night.

As word of what had happened spread, Pittsburghers, regardless of class, were outraged. Since the state militia had taken over, local constabulary officers refused to take any further responsibility for keeping peace. Workmen, businessmen, and newspaper editors alike denounced the slaughter of fellow townsmen by the alien troopers. Gangs of men and boys looted gunstores for weapons and under cover of night began raining shots down on the roundhouse. Late Saturday night zealots in the crowd started pushing blazing freight cars down the incline leading to the roundhouse.

Forced by resulting fires to abandon their quarters, the militia early Sunday morning hurriedly marched to a nearby Federal arsenal. En route they drew irregular fire from windows of houses as they passed, and from a small band of determined snipers who trailed behind. Denied admission to the arsenal, the dispirited troop continued marching out of the city, eventually finding refuge on the grounds of the Allegheny County Workhouse.

Meanwhile, in Pittsburgh looting and pillaging of freight cars went unchecked for two days, and railroad and other corporate property was put to the torch. By the time the first detachments of Federal troops arrived on Monday morning, the disorders had largely spent themselves. Local officials and Pittsburgh area militiamen quickly reasserted control, cleared the streets, and restored order.

The worst was over, but the strikes continued to spread westward—to Toledo, Fort Wayne, and Indianapolis, to Chicago and St. Louis, and to Kansas City and San Francisco, to name the more prominent trouble spots. In each a familiar pattern developed: Railroad men, following the example set in the East, stopped work and blocked the passage of freight trains. Large crowds of sympathizers, excitement-seeking adolescents, and curious spectators gathered to see what would happen. Pleadings and warnings from business and political leaders were hooted at or ignored. When local police proved unable to maintain order, state militiamen marched in. In the confrontations that followed, depending on circumstances and the discipline of the troopers, order was restored with or without bloodshed.

Each strike also had its distinctive features. At Indianapolis, the resident Federal judge helped form a committee of public safety and raised a force of Civil War veterans to protect lives and property. In San Francisco what started out as a protest against the despised Central Pacific Railway Company turned into a mob action against an even more hated target, Chinese laborers.

Chicago and St. Louis differed from most strike centers in that a Marxist Socialist group, the Workers Party of the United States, attempted to take control of the strikes in those cities. But the hysterical charge that radical communists had stirred up the strikes and planned to repeat the horrors of the Paris Commune of 1871 was completely unfounded. Even in Chicago and St. Louis the strikes began under other auspices. In Chicago striking railway workers and their sympathizers organized roving gangs of men who forced the railroads one by one to suspend operations and then marched from factory to factory to effect a complete closing down of the community. WPUS leaders held rallies, issued pronouncements, and unsuccessfully tried to take command. Their participation ended abruptly with the arrest of their leaders. Meanwhile, the militia, in a series of bloody street encounters, broke the strike at Chicago.

In St. Louis the WPUS was more successful, taking control of the strikes from the beginning. As in Chicago, bands of workers intimidated businesses into shutting down. At St. Louis, however, no blood was shed. When the strikes all around the country began collapsing on July 25, the forces of law and order at St. Louis regained confidence. Organizing and arming reliable forces, they marched on the WPUS headquarters. Radicals who failed to escape were arrested and the affair ended. Although mopping-up actions continued for several weeks, the national trauma was over by the close of the first week in August. The Signal Corps, whose reports from all points during the strikes had kept the administration well posted on developments, ended its report of August 5: *"Pax semper ubique."*

The wave of strikes in July 1877 marked the opening of a quarter-century of dramatic clashes between Capital and Labor in the United States, particularly on the railroads: the Southwest Strikes of 1885 and 1886, the Haymarket Affair in 1886, the Great Burlington Strike of 1888, the Homestead Strike in 1892, the march of Coxey's army of the unemployed and the Pullman Boycott-Strike in 1894, and the Anthracite Coal Strike of 1902. The significance of the 1877 strikes lay not in their being first (there had been, for example, massive but shortlived strikes in the textile mills in Lowell, Massachusetts in the 1830s and among New England shoemakers in 1860), but in that they were so widespread and tied up the country's principal means of transport.

In effect the strikes of 1877 came close to what today would be called a national emergency strike. To be sure, the American economy in 1877 was not yet as integrated and interdependent as it would become in the 20th century, but a score of larger cities and many otherwise isolated communities depended almost wholly on the railroads for meat, grain, milk, and coal. When the strikes paralyzed railroad traffic in 1877, the price of these commodities shot upward. In many communities not directly involved in the strikes, businesses closed down for lack of coal and raw materials. The United States relied so heavily on railroads that canal and river barges and horsedrawn wagons could not and did not provide significant substitute transportation. Apparently no one starved because of the strikes in 1877 and public suffering was limited. Had the strikes been better organized or had they lasted a week or two longer, the consequences for tens of thousands if not millions of people would have been grim.

Reactions of the propertied classes to the strikes ranged from fear and indecision, to bold determination to suppress them. In their zeal some proponents of order became as heedless of obeying the law as those they opposed.

That maintaining the peace was primarily the responsibility of local and state police authorities did not prevent demands for vigorous Federal intervention. James H. Wilson, a distinguished Union cavalry officer in the Civil War and in 1877 receiver of the St. Louis & Southwestern Railroad, urged sending units of the United States Army to St. Louis. "Time has come when President should stamp out mob now rampant," he telegraphed Washington: "The law can be found for it after order is restored." "For God's sake run the freight trains," pleaded an anonymous Democrat in a letter to President Hayes. "If necessary take control of the Roads under the Constitutional right to regulate interstate commerce. . . . Imagine the Commerce between these States stopped for 2 weeks. I'd rather see you fixed in the Presidential chair for 25 years; I would rather see you Emperor than to have Commerce paralyzed."

Hayes and his cabinet met daily during the crisis to consider these and other recommendations. Their course was much more conservative. Existing Federal law offered little guidance in such matters; labor problems per se remained wholly outside the province of government at that time. There were few precedents for Federal intervention in labor disputes—Andrew Jackson had used the Army to break a strike on the Baltimore & Ohio Canal and Federal troops had crushed a number of small local strikes during the Civil War—but these probably were not even known to the administration. The resources at the disposal of the president also limited his response. The Army numbered only 25,000 men. Most were fighting Indians on the frontier—the Custer massacre had taken place just a year before—or were guarding the Mexican border. Because Congress had adjourned without passing an army appropriation bill, the troopers received no pay after June 30.

At no point did Hayes or his advisers consider intervening to mediate the labor troubles even though the president clearly saw the nature of the strikes. They were neither insurrection against the Government nor the start of a communistic-anarchistic revolt, he told newsmen at the height of the rioting in Pittsburgh. They gave "no evidence of a spirit of communism because the attacks of the mob have not been directed against the property of the general public, but against the corporations with which the laboring element is at war."

Precisely because they were economic matters, Hayes regarded offers of Federal mediation as unjustified and undesirable. Under the prevailing doctrines of laissez-faire economics, wages, hours of labor, and general working conditions were matters to be resolved privately by capital and labor within bounds prescribed by the laws of supply and demand. Only if labor differences resulted in outbreaks of lawlessness was the Government justified in intervening—and then only to restore law and order, not to mediate the dispute.

Railroad and other business interests repeatedly urged protection of interstate commerce and the mails as grounds for Federal intervention. Hayes and the Cabinet discussed protecting interstate commerce at only one meeting, then dropped that approach. The issue of protecting the mails arose when strikers, hoping to avoid a clash with Federal authorities, offered to run mail through their blockades provided that it be accompanied by neither passengers nor freight. The Postmaster General passed this offer on to Presidents Vanderbilt of the New York Central and Scott of the Pennsylvania, reminding them of their obligations to move the mail. "R.R.s refuse to carry mails alone," Hayes recorded in his diary. The administration applied no further pressure to the roads, but neither did it use the army against strikers who blocked mail.

Instead, Hayes authorized the United States Army to intervene on three other grounds. Simplest and most obvious was to protect threatened Federal installations such as arsenals and subtreasuries. Most frequently used was the constitutional provision that the president, when called upon by the governor of a state, could send the army to help suppress domestic insurrection that the state could not put down. Hayes routinely refused requests from governors for troops to preserve law and order, to forestall troubles, or even to suppress strikes and riots already underway. Only when a governor would attest that insurrection beyond his capacity to handle was in progress did Hayes send in troops. In the struggle between duty and consistency (Hayes, after all, had said that he saw no evidence that the strikes constituted insurrection against the Government), duty, at least as Hayes saw it, won out.

It should be remembered that the authority of the president to send troops at the request of a state did not require that they be sent automatically. He had both the right and the obligation to determine in each instance whether the alleged insurrection warranted intervention. Hayes appears to have sent troops to both Martinsburg and Baltimore with undue haste and too little information, and perhaps even unnecessarily. On the other hand, in ordering the army to Pittsburgh, though clearly justified, Hayes acted tardily.

The third basis on which Hayes dispatched the army—to enforce Federal court injunctions—proved to be most significant for the future. In many instances in 1877 the courts displayed greater zeal than the executive in meeting the crisis. Because the orders and decisions of judges were carefully recorded and published, they served as ready precedents in later disorders. As already noted, injunctions backed when necessary by force came to be very effective weapons in the labor wars of the late 19th and early 20th centuries.

The use of force in 1877 revealed a number of shortcomings in military establishments both state and Federal. Governors had been prompt—sometimes too prompt—in dispatching militia to strike scenes. Once there, those forces often proved inadequate or inefficient. At the time most state militias consisted of volunteer forces, more social and political than military in nature. Most were small in number, inadequately trained, ill-disciplined, and poorly led. Under pressure they sometimes broke and ran, or what was equally disastrous, they panicked and opened fire. By contrast the United States Army appeared businesslike and disciplined. It commanded respect wherever it went, and as a result neither suffered casualties nor took lives in the course of dozens of encounters with crowds in 1877. Even so, the limited size of the army and the clumsy procedure for calling it into action left much to be desired. As a direct result of the experiences of 1877 several states, led by Pennsylvania, enlarged, reorganized, and reformed their militias. Enlarging and reforming the United States Army had to await the outbreak of war with Spain in 1898.

No over-all consensus arose as to the "lessons" of the strikes. The chief of the Brotherhood of Locomotive Engineers proposed compulsory arbitration of railway labor disputes and many newspaper editors called for strict regulation of railroads by the Government. The editors of *Nation* and *Harper's Weekly* magazines, on the other hand, thought the strikes proved conclusively the need for a larger army. President Scott of the Pennsylvania Railroad, noting that injunctions backed by the army applied only to railroads in receivership, urged that the same protection be extended to all railroads and that army units be stationed in all major commercial centers to enforce court orders.

President Hayes, too, saw the need for far-reaching reform. "The Strikes have been put down by *force*," he wrote in his diary on August 5, "but now for the *real* remedy. Can't something [be] done by education of the strikers, by judicious control of the capitalists, by wise general policy to end or diminish the evil?" Congress, which had not been in session since before the strikes, assembled in special session in October 1877 to consider the long-delayed army appropriations bill. Aside from commending the army for its devotion to duty in the late riots, in his message to Congress Hayes proposed no "wise general policy" to forestall or deal with labor problems. And Congress, unwilling to stir animosities needlessly, avoided any discussion of the riots and passed no laws to guide the Executive in handling future strikes. In the end, except for the courts, Federal officials did nothing to prepare for labor disorders, even though the most optimistic of observers would not have predicted a strike-free future.

Because no preventive measures were adopted between 1877 and the next round of railway strikes, later Federal policy, as in 1877, was fashioned spontaneously in the midst of conflict. And again as in 1877, the role of the Federal Government would be that of breaking strikes rather than attempting to avoid them or mediating them once they got under way. During the next quarter-century, strikers almost always lost in their contests with employers. If not crushed by their employers' superior economic power, the military might of the state or Federal governments ruined them.

The men from Martinsburg who first rebelled at having their wages cut, thereby touching off the strikes of 1877, would have had no difficulty in understanding either the reasons for the later strikes or the near certainty of the strikers' defeat. They also would have sympathized deeply with the losers. What they had no way of knowing was that their defeat in 1877 and all the subsequent defeats of strikers helped to bring about a fundamental change in the public's perception of the labor question. In time, as labor's plight became better understood, public opinion would require that government stand neutral in the clashes between Capital and Labor, that limits be put on the arbitrary issuance of injunctions during labor disputes, that mediation services be provided by government for the peaceful resolution of labor differences, and even that workers be guaranteed the right to organize, to bargain collectively, and to strike. Had the Martinsburg strikers foreseen those developments they might even have taken pride in their apparently futile act of defiance.

For contemporary accounts, documents, and analysis of the 1877 strike in Baltimore, see the Maryland State archives site at www.mdarchives.state.md.us/msa/stagser/121/1797/html. 0000.html. Click on "search" and use the google search engine to locate the material.

The Working Class

In the aftermath of the great labor upheaval of 1877, journalists and social analysts across the country pondered the meaning of the conflict. Among them was E. L. Godkin, the influential editor of The Nation. *In politics, Godkin was a thoughtful, independent liberal; he supported civil service reform and attacked political corruption and the high protective tariffs favored by business. As the following selection reveals, he was also an opponent of organized labor and deeply concerned about the strikes and violence in the summer of 1877. How did Godkin interpret those events? What, according to Godkin, was at stake? What aspects of his analysis do you find most objectionable?*

E. L. Godkin

⮿ *A Widespread Rising . . .*

It is impossible to deny that the events of the last fortnight constitute a great national disgrace, and have created a profound sensation throughout the civilized world. They are likely to impress the foreign imagination far more than the outbreak of the Civil War, because the probability that the slavery controversy would end in civil war or the disruption of the Union had been long present to people's minds both at home and abroad. . . . There has for fifty years been throughout Christendom a growing faith that outside the area of slave-soil the United States had—of course with the help of great natural resources—solved the problem of enabling labor and capital to live together in political harmony, and that this was the one country in which there was no proletariat and no dangerous class, and in which the manners as well as legislation effectually prevented the formation of one. That the occurrences of the last fortnight will do, and have done, much to shake or destroy this faith, and that whatever weakens it weakens also the fondly cherished hopes of many millions about the future of the race, there is unhappily little question. We have had what appears a widespread rising, not against political oppression or unpopular government, but against society itself. What is most curious about it is that it has probably taken people here nearly as much by surprise as people in Europe. The optimism in which most Americans are carefully trained, and which the experience of life justifies to the industrious, energetic, and provident, combined with the long-settled political habit of considering riotous poor as the products of a

"A Widespread Rising . . . against Society Itself," *The Nation*, vol. XXV, August 2, 1877, pp. 68–69.

monarchy and aristocracy, and impossible in the absence of "down-trodden masses," has concealed from most of the well-to-do and intelligent classes of the population the profound changes which have during the last thirty years been wrought in the composition and character of the population, especially in the great cities. Vast additions have been made to it within that period, to whom American political and social ideals appeal but faintly, if at all, and who carry in their very blood traditions which give universal suffrage an air of menace to many of the things which civilized men hold dear. So complete has the illusion been that up to the day of the outbreak at Martinsburg thousands, even of the most reflective class, were gradually ridding themselves of the belief that force would be much longer necessary, or, indeed, was now necessary in the work of government. . . .

The kindest thing which can be done for the great multitudes of untaught men who have been received on these shores, and are daily arriving, and who are torn perhaps even more here than in Europe by wild desires and wilder dreams, is to show them promptly that society as here organized, on individual freedom of thought and action, is impregnable, and can be no more shaken than the order of nature. The most cruel thing is to let them suppose, even for one week, that if they had only chosen their time better, or had been better led or better armed, they would have succeeded in forcing it to capitulate. In what way better provision, in the shape of public force, should be made for its defense we have no space left to discuss, but that it will not do to be caught again as the rising at Martinsburg caught us; that it would be fatal to private and public credit and security to allow a state of things to subsist in which 8,000 or 9,000 day laborers of the lowest class can suspend, even for a whole day, the traffic and industry of a great nation, merely as a means of extorting ten or twenty cents a day more wages from their employers, we presume everybody now sees. Means of prompt and effectual prevention—so plainly effectual that it will never need to be resorted to—must be provided, either by an increase of the standing army or some change in the organization of the militia which will improve its discipline and increase its mobility. There are, of course, other means of protection against labor risings than physical ones, which ought not to be neglected, though we doubt if they can be made to produce much effect on the present generation. The exercise of greater watchfulness over their tongues by philanthropists, in devising schemes of social improvement, and in affecting to treat all things as open to discussion, and every question as having two sides, for purposes of legislation as well as for purposes of speculation, is one of them. Some of the talk about the laborer and his rights that we have listened to on the platform and in literature during the last fifteen years, and of the capacity even of the most grossly ignorant, such as the South Carolina field-hand, to reason upon and even manage the interests of a great community, has been enough, considering the sort of ears on which it now falls, to reduce our great manufacturing districts to the condition of the Pennsylvania mining regions, and put our very civilization in peril. Persons of humane tendencies ought to remember that we live in a world of stern realities, and that the blessings we enjoy have not been showered upon us like the rain from heaven. Our superiority to the Ashantees or the Kurds is not due to right thinking or right feeling only, but to the determined fight which the more enlightened part of the community has waged from generation to generation against the ignorance and brutality, now of one class and now of another. In trying to carry on the race to better things nobody is wholly right or wise. In all controversies there are wrongs on both sides, but most certainly the presumptions in the labor controversy have always been in favor of the sober, orderly, industrious, and prudent, who work and accumulate and bequeath. It is they who brought mankind out of the woods and caves, and keep them out; and all discussion which places them in a position of either moral or mental inferiority to those who contrive not only to own nothing, but to separate themselves from property holders in feeling or interest, is mischievous as well as foolish, for it strikes a blow at the features of human character which raise man above the beasts.

✿ *Almost Part of the Machinery*

The depression of the 1870s finally ended, but conflict between capital and labor did not; every year brought hundreds of strikes, boycotts, and lockouts. In 1883, deeply concerned about the deteriorating climate of labor relations, the U.S. Senate held extensive hearings. One of those who testified was John Morrison, a New York City machinist. With variations, his story is the story of the American industrial working class in the closing decades of the late nineteenth century. In reading Morrison's testimony, imagine that you are E. L. Godkin (see his editorial on page 46), seated in the hearing room, taking notes for an upcoming feature in The Nation. *What is your reaction? Should something be done to help Morrison, or to deal with the problems he reveals? What, if anything, could government do?*

VOICES

By Mr. George:

Q. State your age, residence, and occupation.

A. I am about twenty-three years old; I live in this city; I am a machinist, and have been in that business about nine years.

Q. Do you work in a shop?

A. Yes, sir; I work in different shops.

* * *

Q. Is there any difference between the conditions under which machinery is made now and those which existed ten years ago?

A. A great deal of difference.

Testimony of John Morrison, August 28, 1883, U.S. Congress, Senate, *Report of the Committee of the Senate upon the Relations between Labor and Capital*, Government Printing Office, Washington, D.C., 1885, vol. I, pp. 755–759.

Q. State the differences as well as you can.

A. Well, the trade has been subdivided and those subdivisions have been again subdivided, so that a man never learns the machinist's trade now. Ten years ago he learned, not the whole of the trade, but a fair portion of it. Also, there is more machinery used in the business, which again makes machinery. In the case of making the sewing machine, for instance, you find that the trade is so subdivided that a man is not considered a machinist at all. Hence, it is merely laborers' work and it is laborers that work at that branch of our trade. The different branches of the trade are divided and subdivided so that one man may make just a particular part of a machine and may not know anything whatever about another part of the same machine. In that way machinery is produced a great deal cheaper than it used to be formerly, and in fact, through this system of work, 100 men are able to do now what it took 300 or 400 men to do fifteen years ago. By the use of machinery and the subdivision of the trade they so simplify the work that it is made a great deal easier and put together a great deal faster. There is no system of apprenticeship, I may say, in the business. You simply go in and learn whatever branch you are put at, and you stay at that unless you are changed to another.

Q. Does a man learn his branch very rapidly?

A. Yes, sir; he can learn his portion of the business very rapidly. Of course he becomes very expert at it, doing that all the time and nothing else, and therefore he is able to do a great deal more work in that particular branch than if he were a general hand and expected to do everything in the business as it came along. . . .

Q. Have you noticed the effect upon the intellect of this plan of keeping a man at one particular branch?

A. Yes. It has a very demoralizing effect upon the mind throughout. The man thinks of nothing else but that particular branch; he knows that he cannot leave that particular branch and go to any other; he has got no chance whatever to learn anything else because he is kept steadily and constantly at that particular thing, and of course his intellect must be narrowed by it.

Q. And does he not finally acquire so much skill in the manipulation of his particular part of the business that he does it without any mental effort?

A. Almost. In fact he becomes almost a part of the machinery.

By the chairman:

Q. Then if he gets so skilled that he has not to think about his work, why cannot he compose poetry, or give range to his imagination, or occupy his mind in some other way while he is at work?

A. As a rule a man of that kind has more to think of about his family and his belly than he has about poetry.

THE CHAIRMAN: That is right.

By Mr. George:

Q. Has there been in the last ten or fifteen years any great revolution in the making of machinery so far as regards the capital that is required to start the business?

A. Well, I understand that at this present day you could not start in the machinist's business to compete successfully with any of these large firms with a capital of less than $20,000 or $30,000. That is my own judgment. There have been cases known where men started ten or fifteen years ago on what they had earned themselves, and they have grown up gradually into a good business. One of these firms is Floyd & Sons, on Twentieth Street. That man started out of his own earnings; he saved enough to start a pretty fair-sized shop, and he is occupying it today; but since that time it appears the larger ones are squeezing out the smaller, and forcing more of them into the ranks of labor, thus causing more competition among the workers.

Q. What is the prospect for a man now working in one of these machine shops, a man who is temperate and economical and thrifty to become a boss or a manufacturer of machinery himself from his own savings? Could a man do it without getting aid from some relative who might die and leave him a fortune, or without drawing a lottery prize, or something of that sort?

A. Well, speaking generally, there is no chance. They have lost all desire to become bosses now.

Q. Why have they lost that desire?

A. Why, because the trade has become demoralized. First they earn so small wages; and, next, it takes so much capital to become a boss now that they cannot think of it, because it takes all they can earn to live.

Q. Then it is the hopelessness of the effort that produces the loss of the desire on their part; is that it?

A. That is the idea. . . .

Q. What is the social condition of the machinists in New York and the surrounding towns and cities?

A. It is rather low compared to what their social condition was ten or fifteen years ago.

Q. Do you remember when it was better?

A. When I first went to learn the trade a machinist considered himself more than the average workingman; in fact he did not like to be called a workingman. He liked to be called a mechanic. Today he recognizes the fact that he is simply a laborer the same as the others. Ten years ago even he considered himself a little above the average workingman; he thought himself a mechanic, and felt he belonged in the middle class; but today he recognizes the fact that he is simply the same as any other ordinary laborer, no more and no less.

Q. What sort of houses or lodgings do the machinists occupy as a general rule?

A. As a general rule they live in tenement houses, often on the top floor.

Q. How is it as to the size of the apartments that they occupy, the conveniences and comforts they afford, their healthfulness, the character of the neighborhood and the general surroundings?

A. That depends a great deal upon the size of the families. In most cases they are compelled to send their families to work, and of course they have to have rooms in proportion to the size of their families, and of course it often robs them of their earnings to pay rent; but as a rule the machinists live in the lowest quarters of the city, between Eighth and Eleventh Avenues, on the west side, and on the east side between Third Avenue and the river. You will find the machinists stuck in those quarters on both sides of the city.

• • •

One great trouble with our trade is that there is such a surplus of machinists in the market now that every day sees seven or eight at the door of every shop looking for a job. In fact they are denied the right to labor, and that is what we kick about. About two months ago, I believe there was about one-fifth of our trade in this city entirely out of work.

Q. Do you know from reading the papers or from your general knowledge of the business whether there are places in other cities or other parts of the country that those men could have gone and got work?

A. I know from general reports of the condition of our trade that the same condition existed throughout the country generally.

Q. Then those men could not have bettered themselves by going to any other place, you think?

A. Not in a body.

Q. I am requested to ask you this question: Dividing the public, as is commonly done, into the upper, middle, and lower classes, to which class would you assign the average workingman of your trade at the time when you entered it, and to which class would you assign him now?

A. I now assign them to the lower class. At the time I entered the trade I should assign them as merely hanging on to the middle class, ready to drop out at any time.

Q. What is the character of the social intercourse of those workingmen? Answer first with reference to their intercourse with other people outside of their own trade—merchants, employers, and others.

A. Are you asking what sort of social intercourse exists between the machinists and the merchants? If you are, there is none whatever, or very little if any.

Q. What sort of social intercourse exists among the machinists themselves and their families, as to visiting, entertaining one another, and having little parties and other forms of sociability, those little things that go to make up the social pleasures of life?

A. In fact with the married folks that has died out—such things as birthday parties, picnics, and so on. The machinists today are on such small pay, and the cost of living is so high, that they have very little, if anything, to spend for recreation, and the machinist has to content himself with enjoying himself at home, either fighting with his wife or licking his children.

Q. I hope that is not a common amusement in the trade. Was it so ten years ago?

A. It was not; from the fact that they then sought enjoyment in other places, and had a little more money to spend. But since they have had no organization worth speaking of, of course their pay has gone down. At that time they had a form of organization in some way or other which seemed to keep up the wages, and there was more life left in the machinist then; he had more ambition, he felt more like seeking enjoyment outside, and in reading and such things, but now it is changed to the opposite; the machinist has no such desires.

Q. What is the social air about the ordinary machinist's house? Are there evidences of happiness, and joy, and hilarity, or is the general atmosphere solemn, and somber, and gloomy?

A. To explain that fully, I would state first of all, that machinists have got to work ten hours a day in New York, and that they are compelled to work very hard. In fact the machinists of America are compelled to do about one-third more work than the machinists do in England in a day. Therefore, when they come home they are naturally played out from shoving the file, or using the hammer or the chisel, or whatever it may be, such long hours. They are pretty well played out when they come home, and the first thing they think of is having something to eat and sitting down, and resting, and then of striking a bed. Of course when a man is dragged out in that way he is naturally cranky, and he makes all around him cranky; so, instead of a pleasant house it is every day expecting to lose his job by competition from his fellow workman, there being so many out of employment, and no places for them, and his wages being pulled down through their competition, looking at all times to be thrown out of work in that way, and staring starvation in the face makes him feel sad, and the head of the house being sad, of course the whole family are the same, so the house looks like a dull prison instead of a home.

Q. Do you mean to say that that this is the general condition of the machinists in New York and in this vicinity?

A. That is their general condition, with, of course, a good many exceptions. That is the general condition to the best of my knowledge.

Alice Austen: Images of Work

The photographs in this section are by Alice Austen, a dignified, middle-class woman who lived on Staten Island and took pictures there and in New York City. According to historian Laura Wexler, Austen was the first woman photographer to take pictures on the streets of Manhattan. She took these pictures in the mid-1890s and sold them in portfolios labeled "Street Types of New York." Examine the photographs. What are the elements of Austen's "style"? What message, if any, do the photographs have about the workers in them? Do you think the photos differ from those a man would take? How, and why?

Immigrant and pretzel vendor. Photo by Alice Austen. Library of Congress.

Two bootbacks, City Hall Park. Photo by Alice Austen. Library of Congress.

Sweeper in rubber boots. Photo by Alice Austen. Library of Congress.

Rag pickers with billboard. Photo by Alice Austen. Library of Congress.

THE BIG PICTURE

The materials in this chapter raise two important questions: First, what was the nature of labor's challenge to the new industrial order? Does the violent militancy of the 1877 strikers suggest a desire to change the system in some fundamental way? Or did the workers just want higher wages within the existing order? Similarly, what does John Morrison's 1883 testimony tell us about what he, and workers like him, wanted, or about how he thought of himself and understood his position in society? Second, how did elites—the owners of the railroads, well-placed politicians, newspaper editors (such as William Godkin), and commentators (such as photographer Alice Austen), respond to the threat to the social order posed by workers in an era of rapid industrial change?

Chapter 3

The West

The terms *America* and the *West* had seemed synonymous from the time of the earliest penetration of the Atlantic coastline down into the nineteenth century. But during the years after the Civil War, a new kind of frontier waited to be conquered by white settlers and surrendered in bitter defeat by the Indians. Beyond the Mississippi lay a vast expanse of plains, known officially as "the Great American Desert." Farther west were the seemingly impenetrable mountains and the real deserts of the Southwest. To most Americans, even as late as the 1850s, this half of the continent appeared to be good for little but a permanent reservation for native American tribes.

Amazingly, in little over a generation, the trans-Mississippi West was settled. The first transcontinental railroad was opened shortly after the Civil War. It was followed by others and by a network of rail lines spreading out into Iowa, Missouri, Texas, and the Dakotas. California became a state on the eve of the Civil War, and by the end of the century the process of state making had filled in almost all the continental map. The last effective native American resistance was broken in the 1870s and 1880s, when the old policy of war and extermination was replaced with a new form of aggression, called "assimilation." Mining towns sprang from nothing in Nevada, Colorado, and Montana. Texas and Oklahoma became primary cotton-producing states. Cowboys drove Texas longhorns into the new cow towns of Kansas and Nebraska, where the animals could be loaded onto trains headed for eastern slaughterhouses. New techniques of dry farming created one of the world's most productive wheat belts in the western half of the Great Plains. In 1890, just twenty-five years after Grant had accepted Lee's surrender, the United States Bureau of the Census officially declared that the frontier had ended forever.

The story was not a simple one of geographical expansion. The settlers of the new West were armed with a new technology that helped explain the remarkable rapidity of their success. The repeating rifle and the Gatling gun subdued the native American. The railroad took the wheat and cattle east at incredible speeds. Miners used steam power and dynamite to pry gold and silver from the mountains. Farmers—the big ones, at least—had the new mechanical reaper to bring in wheat at a rate that manual labor could not have approached. Californians were tied to the rest of the Union by the railroad and the new telegraph.

On the surface, then, the experience was one of triumph—at least for the white society. But there was a dark side to things, too. Even dry farming could not overcome periodic droughts, and the droughts came. There was competition from Russian and Australian wheat, so prices were very unstable. Some railroads gouged the farmers. Worst of all, the new technology proved not to be a blessing at all. The new agriculture was just *too* efficient. By 1890, one farmer could produce and get to market what it had taken eight farmers to produce fifty years before. Together, they produced more food than could be sold. So prices fell and stayed down, and farmers often could not recoup the cost of their seed, much less earn the money to pay interest on their mortgages and on the loans they had made to buy their reapers and plows. Agricultural depression was so severe and frequent that the whole second half of the nineteenth century—except for the war years—was really one long and chronic economic crisis for farmers, not only in the new West, but everywhere.

Agriculture in the South labored under a different set of burdens. The Civil War created a long-term capital shortage and, of course, severed the bond that had held slave labor to the plantation. Southerners responded with two systems. The first, designed to establish a link between free black farm workers and the plantation, was sharecropping. Under this system, blacks (and poor whites) agreed to farm the land in return for a share of the crop—usually one-third. Under the second system, the crop-lien, sharecroppers and tenant farmers borrowed money and received credit for supplies and food from merchants and landowners, while pledging in return a percentage of their crop. Together, sharecropping and the crop-lien fostered throughout the South a system of peonage, in which poor whites and blacks were legally bound by debt to work the lands of others.

Farmers sought to redress their grievances through a variety of protest movements, each linked to a particular organization. In the 1860s, midwestern farmers established the Patrons of Husbandry, better known as the Grange. Its purposes were partly social and partly economic—to lower the costs of shipment and storage of grain. Many farmers and ranchers in the South and West strongly opposed national efforts to limit silver coinage and reduce the number of greenbacks in circulation. These "sound money" efforts, which effectively put the nation on the gold standard in 1879, strengthened the American dollar and contributed to economic growth. But they also contributed to a deflationary environment—falling wholesale and consumer prices—that damaged thousands of farmers and ranchers who had borrowed money to buy land, tools, seed, and animals. These debtors lashed out at the nearest target: the banks. By the 1890s, farmers in the South, the Great Plains, and the Far West had turned to state and national politics. Through the People's Party, or Populists, they sought the aid of the national government in inflating a depressed currency and in regulating the railroads and other trusts. Populist influence peaked in 1896, when William Jennings Bryan was the presidential nominee of both the Democrats and the Populists, but declined after Bryan was defeated for the presidency by Republican William McKinley.

There were other, less political, ways of coming to grips with the market revolution, the heritage of slavery, and the dislocation caused by being transplanted, body and soul, onto a remote prairie. Plains farmers brought with them a weapon that helped them overcome the initial reluctance to move onto the hard, unyielding sod of Nebraska and the Dakotas. The weapon was *myth:* the myth that the West was the source of unprecedented opportunity; the myth that climate would respond to the migration of people; the myth that the yeoman farmer—half frontiersman, half man-of-the-soil—could handle anything; the myth that all whites were superior to all native Americans.

Some of these Western myths remain potent, even today, while others have lost some or all of their ability to persuade. The myth of the yeoman farmer remains a part of American culture in the early years of the twenty-first century, even though farmers represent only about 2 percent of the population, and even though most farm products are produced by agribusiness corporations rather than "family" farms. The myth of the West as a place of opportunity is not entirely dead, either, but California—which represented that idea for so long—has recently seen its image tarnished by urban race riots, power shortages, and massive budget deficits.

One of the most durable of all Western myths was the idea of the West as a place of unremitting and brutal violence and lawlessness—of saloon brawls and stagecoach robberies, of farmers and cattlemen at each other's throats over how to use the land, of a sheriff and a gang of outlaws determining a community's future in a dramatic shootout on the edge of town. This is the West that served as the inspiration for the first Western film, Edwin S. Porter's *The Great Train Robbery* (1903), and for countless others, including such classic gunfighter movies as *High Noon* (1952), *Shane* (1953) and, in a more negative and less nostalgic form, *McCabe and Mrs. Miller* (1972). Many scholars have made the point that the West wasn't as violent as the movies would have us believe. To be sure, the cow towns of Kansas and the mining towns of the Black Hills (during the 1874 gold rush) and Coeur d'Alene, Idaho (the 1883 rush), were full of armed, drunk twenty-four-year-old young men, spoiling for a fight. But the cattle and mining "frontiers" did not last long, and it is arguable that the East—the East of labor-management conflict and industrial accidents—was in its way much more violent than the West. What has lasted, a product of our changing desires and needs, is the myth of the violent West, a curious combination of truth and fiction.

INTERPRETIVE ESSAY

America's Robin Hood

Kent L. Steckmesser

Most Americans would not recognize the names of Bob and Bill Dalton, Sam Bass, or Bill Doolin. Thanks to singer/songwriter Bob Dylan, more would have heard of John Wesley Hardin. And, although Western movies are much less popular than they were before 1970, a very large percentage would know Frank and Jesse James and Billy the Kid by name and reputation. All were criminals—they robbed banks and trains, mostly, and killed people while doing so—and they all could be labeled "social bandits," a term used by historian Richard White that describes people who violate the law but who do so—or appear to do so—with a higher cause in mind. They plied their craft in western Missouri, Oklahoma Territory, and central Texas in the three decades following the Civil War.

In the essay that follows, historian Kent L. Steckmesser examines the story of the most famous outlaw of all, Jesse James, whose gang terrorized railroads and small town banks from Missouri to Minnesota. Jesse first participated at the age of 16 in 1866; he was killed in 1882, the year that marvel of engineering and technology, the Brooklyn Bridge, was opened to traffic between Brooklyn and Manhattan.

Steckmesser's thesis is straightforward: that James was a mythic figure, similar in some respects to Robin Hood, and that he didn't do most of the "good" things that people said he did. But that statement of thesis only makes one want to know more. If James wasn't such a good guy, why did people claim he was? And that question suggests others that can help one use the James story to penetrate and understand some of the forces that were shaping the American nation in the late nineteenth century and that may have caused ordinary people to measure James as a "social bandit," even if he was not.

Using Steckmesser's essay, the introduction to this chapter, and what you have already learned about American history in previous chapters, think about how the story of Jesse James intersects with other elements of nineteenth-century American history. In what sense was Jesse's career of crime—or his reputation—a product of the Civil War? What groups of people might have gotten particular pleasure out of reading about his robberies of banks and railroads (consider what banks and railroads meant to some westerners)? Having read about the 1877 railroad strike in the previous chapter, what connections can you draw between that event and the stories that were told about the James gang? Most broadly, how might a person with the qualities of a Jesse James have appealed to a young man working at one of the new department stores, in a government office, or in one of the large industrial enterprises of the day?

Advertising circular for a production based on the life of Jesse James, c. 1888. Library of Congress. Why is there a black woman on the bar?

The Robin Hood outlaw is a familiar world figure. In Germany he appears as Schinderhannes, in Italy as Fra Diavalo, in Australia as Ned Kelley. Usually driven to outlawry by persecution, he takes from the rich to give to the poor, and inevitably dies by a traitor's hand. Many of his exploits belong to folklore rather than history. Indeed, some English scholars now believe that Robin Hood himself never existed, that he was simply created by balladeers who knew what their audiences wanted. But there is no question about the actual existence of America's own Robin Hood, Jesse Woodson James. Newspaper accounts and court records tell the story of a classic criminal career. Like the prototypic English bandit, Jesse is said to have been brave, generous, and good-natured. His victims thought otherwise, but the continuing appeal of this legend tells us much about the human imagination.

Jesse James was born in Clay County, Missouri, on September 5, 1847. He was the son of a Baptist minister, and many tales have been told about Jesse's own devotion to the church. One choice story has him conducting a Sunday School choir at Unity, Missouri. But religion and a revolver do not go well together. After the first of the bank holdups had been definitely traced to Jesse James in 1869, he was excluded from the Mount Olive Baptist Church. As for the choir story, it is shattered by the testimony of Jesse's sister-in-law that he was tone-deaf.

In 1850 the Reverend Robert James left for California goldfields, and died within a month of his arrival there. Thus Jesse and older brother Frank were raised by Mrs. Zerelda James, certainly one of the most formidable mothers in American history. Though she remarried in 1855 to a Dr. Reuben

Samuel, Mrs. James remained the dominant partner. She was an iron-willed woman who transmitted much of her own self-righteousness to "the boys." One of the causes to which she was committed was the Confederacy; Mrs. James was a Southerner and she owned slaves. Since Clay County was in the troubled Kansas–Missouri border region, it was inevitable that the family would become involved in the Civil War.

The regular Confederate army was driven out of Missouri in 1862. The Southern effort was henceforth conducted by guerrilla bands which ranged over the state burning bridges, cutting telegraph lines, and attacking Federal patrols. Frank and Jesse James both served in these irregular outfits. In 1862 Frank joined the band of William Clarke Quantrill, the most dreaded bush-whacker of the border wars. In 1864 Jesse started his horse-and-pistol career by joining Fletcher Taylor, one of Quantrill's lieutenants. Though ostensibly fighting for the Confederacy, these guerrillas were often serving themselves. Taylor's recruiting slogan, for example, was: "Join Quantrill and rob the banks." So Jesse spent his sixteenth year in this back-alley warfare, which bred a wolfish ferocity in the combatants. He was with "Bloody Bill" Anderson at the Centralia massacre, where 24 unarmed Union soldiers were lined up and shot down. While grown men could learn to forget about these acts when peace came, an impressionable youth might believe that they were "normal."

The guerrillas were in a difficult position when the war ended in 1865. Jesse found out just how difficult it was when he tried to surrender that spring. Some Union soldiers fired on him as he rode into Lexington, Missouri, under a white flag. He was seriously wounded in the chest, and the resulting scars were the means of identifying him when he was killed in 1882. After recovering at his mother's home, Jesse faced the problem of all ex-guerrillas, that of adjusting to a quiet "civilian" life. Many Confederates and indeed many of Quantrill's men settled down and became responsible citizens. But the James brothers took the easy way out and chose to make a profession of bank and train robbery.

"Persecution" is a basic folk explanation of outlawry and a standard theme in the Robin Hood tradition. During certain periods the law becomes corrupt, or it tends to represent a social system in which injustice is the rule. In such situations, so the folk interpretation says, an outlaw of the Robin Hood type appears and resists the oppressors. In medieval England a corrupt priesthood and nobility, personified by the Abbot of St. Mary's and the Sheriff of Nottingham, exploited the poor. Robin Hood became the cham-pion of these helpless people when he robbed the Abbot and distributed the take among them. Though hounded by the Sheriff of Nottingham, the out-law always escaped because he had the support of the commoners.

Historians are skeptical of such folk versions. This is especially true in Robin Hood's case because of the inconclusive evidence regarding the outlaw's existence and because such figures as the Abbot of St. Mary's and the Sheriff of Nottingham cannot be found in any historical records. But the persecution theme is recreated in different historical settings. Thus the "Yankees" would not let wartime hatreds subside, and they continued to harass the James boys. John N. Edwards, newspaperman and former Confederate, formulated the explanation in his *Noted Guerrillas* (1877): "They have been followed, trailed, surrounded, shot at, wounded, ambushed, surprised, watched, betrayed, proscribed, outlawed, driven from State to State, made the objective points of infallible detectives, and they have triumphed."

Such an apologia casts the warm glow of Southern patriotism over Jesse's career. It is true that the Radical Republicans who controlled Missouri could and did make life miserable for many ex-Confederates. But the belief that the boys were forced into banditry because of their devotion to the Southern cause does not stand up under close examination. All but two of the banks they robbed were in Southern states, and they lifted wallets from Confederates and Yankees alike.

Jesse's first venture in the banking business took place at Liberty, Missouri, in 1866. Doubts have been expressed about his participation in this holdup, but it has all the features of his *modus operandi*. On February 13 two men walked into the Clay County Savings Bank and asked cashier Greenup Bird to change a bill. As he did so, the men drew revolvers and forced him to fill their burlap sacks with over 60,000 dollars in gold and government bonds from the vault. The bandits then joined several companions outside. As the gang galloped out of town they shot down an innocent bystander, a local college student named George Wymore. This wanton killing was the first of many that would mark the rise and fall of the James gang.

Banker Bird was unable to identify the outlaws, although none of them had worn masks. A local farmer named Minter said he had sold grain sacks used in the robbery to Frank and Jesse James, but he later decided that he had been mistaken. Intimidation of witnesses was a standard tactic in Jesse's operations. But letters and documents have linked the James gang to the robbery. The negotiable bonds were sold by former members of "Bloody Bill" Anderson's band. For example, George Shepherd, a well-known associate of Jesse James, cashed a 1,000 dollar note in Memphis, Tennessee.

The Robin Hood outlaw always has a sense of humor, and Jesse seems to qualify in this respect. As he locked Mr. Bird inside the bank's vault, the leader of the outlaws remarked that "all Birds should be caged." But the local people did not think that the epigram was amusing. In fact the *Liberty Tribune* described the whole episode as "one of the most cold-blooded murders and heavy robberies on record," and went on to pray that "the villains may be overhauled and brought to the end of a rope."

There is little evidence of Jesse's activities until 1869. Then on December 7 the bank at Gallatin, Missouri, was robbed by two men who killed cashier John Sheets. The horse of one of the gunmen bolted, and he had to double up behind his companion to escape. The runaway animal was identified in the *Kansas City Times* as "belonging to a young man named James, whose mother and stepfather live about four miles from Centerville, Clay County." This reference indicates that Jesse was not a well-known bandit at this time. But Gallatin was a turning point, for the brothers were henceforth ostracized by the better element of their home county. Their new notoriety was also indicated by Governor McClurg's offer of 500 dollars for the capture or killing of each.

Jesse proceeded to build an awesome reputation in both history and folklore. On June 3, 1871, four men robbed the bank at Corydon, Iowa. The celebrated politician Henry Clay Dean was addressing a large crowd when the outlaws interrupted him on their way out of town: "The fact is, Mr. Dean, some fellows have been over to the bank and tied up the cashier, and if you-all ain't too busy you might ride over and untie him. We've got to be going." Who else but Jesse could have spoken with such colossal impudence?

Audacity also marked the gang's robbery of the Kansas City fairgrounds the next year. Three gunmen seized the cashbox amidst a crowd estimated at ten thousand people. The only casualty in the wild gunfire that followed was a little girl shot through the leg. Major Edwards, the leading apologist for the James boys, eulogized them in a *Times* editorial entitled "The Chivalry of Crime." This described the robbery as "a feat of stupendous nerve and fearlessness that makes one's hair rise to think of it, and with a condiment of crime to season it, becomes chivalric, poetic, superb." Jesse himself wrote an alibi letter to the paper claiming that "I can prove where I was at the very hour the gate was robbed." Such letters were usually a good indication that the gang had been involved in the crime.

Another folk belief is that the Robin Hood outlaw "takes from the rich and gives to the poor." The outlaws themselves find it useful to nourish such illusions. Schinderhannes, the German bandit of the 1790's, claimed that "we take only from the Jews." Ned Kelley, an Australian "bushranger" of the 1870's, boasted that he robbed only wealthy landowners. After the robbery of the Kansas City fairgrounds, a letter from one of the James gang appeared in the *Times*. Signed JACK SHEPHERD, DICK TURPIN, CLAUDE DUVAL, it proclaimed that "we rob the rich and give to the poor." No evidence shows, however, that any money from the Kansas City robbery, or from any of the gang's other robberies, ever found its way into the pockets of the deserving poor.

Jesse decided to branch out into railroad and stagecoach operations. The move was not only profitable but was also good public relations. Many Midwestern farmers hated the railroad companies, who squeezed their customers for "all the traffic would bear." In fact, the Anti-Monopoly party of the Seventies and the later Populist party were more formal expressions of popular hatred for the railroads. The James brothers became symbols of retributive justice for many Missourians, who liked to see the fat bosses get fleeced for a change. Jesse took advantage of these sentiments by hitting practically every railroad in a three state area. The only Missouri line exempted from his exactions was the Hannibal and St. Joe, which had taken the precaution of giving Mrs. Samuel a lifetime pass.

The gang's first railroad job was a Rock Island train which was deliberately wrecked near Council Bluffs, Iowa, on July 20, 1873. When the train hit a loosened rail the locomotive toppled over, scalding the engineer to death. The bandits lifted some 2,000 dollars from the express-company safe in the baggage car, and then walked through the derailed cars taking money and jewelry from the passengers. As usual, they departed with rebel yells and the firing of guns.

A succession of other train robberies over the next eight years gave the James brothers a reputation as the greatest outlaws in American history. Actually train robbery had been "invented" by the Reno brothers of Indiana, and some member of the James gang probably learned the proper techniques from them in prison. Usually railroad ties would be placed across the tracks, and the halted train would then be looted from cowcatcher to caboose. The boys always took a true craftsman's pride in their accomplishments. At the Gad's Hill, Missouri, holdup in 1874 they gave the conductor a press release containing an exact description of the holdup, with a headline of "THE MOST DARING TRAIN-ROBBERY ON RECORD."

Jesse also profited from stagecoach robberies. In January of 1874 he held up the stage near Hot Springs, Arkansas. Folklore has it that Jesse James never stole from preachers, widows, or ex-Confederates. A newspaper report of this robbery stated that the bandit leader returned a gold watch to one of the victims upon learning that he had been a Confederate soldier. In fact, however, Jesse kept all the jewelry. A watch and stickpin taken from Mr. John Burbank in this robbery were found among Jesse's possessions at the time of his death. The supposed ex-Confederate, a Mr. Crump of Memphis, did not mention the return of the watch in his affidavit. The boys did not take time to inquire about the political beliefs of their victims. They were usually in too great a hurry.

Jesse's success in his chosen profession gave him the means to marry. In June of 1874 he wed his first cousin, Zerelda Mimms. She bore him two children and followed him faithfully during eight anxiety-ridden years.

In 1874 Pinkerton detectives hired by the railroad and express companies began to appear in Missouri. They had little success in following the cold trails which usually ended in Clay or Jackson counties. The sleuths were handicapped by the fact that many residents sympathized with the boys, and others were afraid to talk for fear of reprisals. In addition, few people knew what Jesse or Frank James looked like. There were no photographs of them to tack up on police department walls. Members of the gang traveled openly and appeared in Kansas City, Independence, Nashville, and elsewhere without apparent fear of arrest.

The Pinkerton men seriously mismanaged their campaign against the James boys. On the night of January 26, 1875, they surrounded the Samuel home on a tip that Jesse and Frank were hiding out there. An iron flare lamp filled with kerosene was hurled through a window. When it exploded it killed Jesse's twelve-year-old half brother, Archie Peyton Samuel. The fragments also ripped off Mrs. Samuel's right arm. A wave of indignation swept the state following this outrage. Many citizens were now convinced that the James boys were being hounded by the railroads and the Yankee politicians. In the spring an amnesty bill was even introduced in the state legislature. The bill did not pass, but it indicated a belief among sizeable numbers of Missourians that the boys were victims of persecution rather than out-and-out criminals.

Jesse took advantage of the popular sympathy to continue his train holdups in 1876. Posses were unable to trail the gang to their hideouts. Missouri tradition has it that the boys used to reverse the shoes of their horses so that pursuers would go in the opposite direction. This is a trick which folk belief had attributed to medieval outlaws well before Robin Hood. The effect of such practice, however, would be to make the horse stumble and fall. Jesse escaped because the farmers harbored him, out of either fear or sympathy as the case might be. Many of these humble folk believed Jesse's claim that he was another Robin Hood. Those who doubted the claim found it wise to keep their views to themselves.

The gang's luck held until they left familiar territory. Clell Miller was from Minnesota, and he recommended that the James and Younger gangs join up and rob the First National Bank of Northfield. The eight outlaws who attempted the robbery on September 7, 1876, stirred up a hornet's nest. Alert citizens detected the robbery in progress and opened up on the raiders with rifles and shotguns. The town square became a battlefield on which two of the outlaws died. The others got away, but after several days of trailing the three Younger brothers were all captured and a fourth bandit was killed. Jesse and Frank, however, escaped to the west. They posed as law officers during their flight, telling several citizens that they were confident of catching the James boys.

After the close call at Northfield the brothers decided to take a vacation for reasons of health. Between 1876 and 1879 they lived quietly in Nashville and environs, Jesse under the name of "T. J. Howard" and Frank as "B. J. Woodson." It was at this time that Jesse is said to have had a casual meeting in Louisville with the famous detective D. T. Bligh. The detective told "Mr. Howard" that "I'd like to see Jesse James before I die." A few days later Bligh received a postcard which read: "You have seen Jesse James. Now you can go ahead and die."

Jesse roared out of retirement on October 8, 1879. A train of the Chicago and Alton Road was held up at the Glendale station in Jackson County, and 6,000 dollars went into the outlaws' burlap bags. Then on July 15, 1881, a Rock Island train was stopped and robbed by four men near Winston, Missouri. The conductor and a passenger were shot down by the outlaws in a deliberate, cold-blooded murder. In response to this outrage, Governor Thomas Crittenden offered rewards of 5,000 dollars each for Frank and Jesse James in connection with these two holdups.

Crittenden had been elected Democratic governor in 1880 on a platform which included a "solemn determination to overthrow and to destroy outlawry in this state whose head and front is the James gang." So notorious had Missouri become that newspapers across the country were calling it "The Robber State." But the railroads put up the reward money, and Crittenden started tightening the screws. One result was the surrender of gang member Dick Liddill in January of 1882. His confession left little doubt that Jesse had been the leader of both the Glendale and Winston jobs.

Two new members of Jesse's gang, Bob and Charlie Ford, also became turncoats. They made a secret agreement with the governor to assassinate

THE HOUSE IN WHICH JESSE JAMES → WAS KILLED.

The Home Of Frank & Jesse James

THE BAPTIST CHURCH KEARNEY MO. IN WHICH THE FUNERAL SERVICES WERE HELD.

The mythic home of Jesse James. Library of Congress.
What did the person who drew these pictures want others to think about Jesse James?

their leader, who was living in St. Joseph under his alias of "Thomas Howard." On April 3, 1882, Jesse removed his revolvers and got up on a chair to straighten a picture which was entitled "God Bless Our Home." In this rather incongruous setting of domestic tranquility, Bob Ford fired one bullet into Jesse's head, terminating his earthly career at 34 years and seven months. The legend was to have a much longer life.

The manner of Jesse's death was made to order for a folk hero. The Judas figure is as familiar in outlaw narratives as detectives and Merry Men. If he did not exist, folklore would invent him. Thus tradition tells us that Robin Hood was betrayed by his cousin, the prioress of Kirklees. And after Jesse James was killed, the newspapers talked about "hired criminals" and "blood bargains." Jesse's biographers called Bob Ford "a veritable snake in the grass," while the famous ballad refers to him as "the dirty little coward who shot Mr. Howard." Ford may have been a Judas but he was no coward. That kind of job required icy nerves.

Thousands of curious citizens converged on the house after reading newspaper headlines which announced that "Jesse James Bites the Dust." They saw the body of a man five feet eleven inches in height, with a solid, compact body. He was fair complexioned with black hair and a carefully trimmed sun-browned beard. Many people at the time, and in subsequent years, refused to believe that Jesse James had really been killed. But Mrs. Samuel and Zerelda James both identified the body at the inquest. Dick

Liddill also remarked, in the characteristically unsentimental fashion of out-laws, "That's Jess all right, I'd know his hide in a tanyard."

Jesse had assets of only 250 dollars when he died. The commercializa-tion of his legend, which began immediately, yielded much greater profits. The owner of the house in St. Joseph sold blood-soaked shavings from the floor where Jesse had died. When these ran out he smeared new chips with chicken blood. The *National Police Gazette* ran sensational articles detailing "thrilling episodes of the Bold Bandit." Cheap paperback biographies by J. W. Buel and J. A. Dacus were published within a few months of the slay-ing. Dime novelists also turned out dozens of James boys' stories under var-ious imprints. Frank Tousey's "New York Detective Library" alone had 18 titles on the boys. These were written by "D. W. Stevens" (John R. Musik), who had never seen Jesse James. But he kept his young readers popeyed with tales of Jesse's escapes from the law.

The people, however, did not need commercial writers to help them put a halo on Jesse James. In folk songs and tales they created their own Robin Hood. They gave him all the classical outlaw virtues: generosity, courtesy, and wit. The ballad of Jesse James, possibly composed by a Negro convict, occupies a central place in this lore. It was apparently being sung shortly after Jesse's death, although printed versions did not appear until 1900. The lyrics are quite specific about the outlaw's generosity:

> *Jesse James was a lad, who killed many a man*
> *He robbed the Glendale train.*
> *He took from the rich and he gave to the poor*
> *He'd a hand and a heart and a brain.*

In point of fact, Jesse took from both rich and poor, and kept the loot for himself.

Anecdotes tell of his kindness to the unfortunate. The story of Jesse and the Poor Widow is a well-known bit of Americana. The boys once stopped at a lonely farmhouse for dinner. The tearful widow informs them that she is about to lose her home to the banker because she cannot pay the 1,400 dol-lar mortgage. Kindhearted Jesse immediately gives her the money as a gift. He and Frank then lie in wait and hold up the banker as he returns to town. This episode has been placed in Tennessee, Arkansas, and Missouri, al-though there are no printed references to it before 1897. It is significant that identical stories have been attributed to other American outlaws.

On yet another occasion Jesse appears as the Protector of Womankind. A schoolteacher on her way home with a month's wages had to go through a lonely stretch of woods. She asked a passing horseman to escort her, as she had heard Jesse James was in the neighborhood and was afraid of being robbed. The horseman took her home, and then said: "Now, lady, tell your friends that Jesse James helped you safely through the woods."

While tales of this type have continued to circulate on a local level, the idealized Jesse James has been made known to larger audiences through mo-tion pictures and television. Historians naturally regard these filmed versions

Cover of *An Authentic Life of Billy the Kid*, by Pat F. Garrett (1882).
Why the word authentic?

as being far off the mark. But producers face some difficult problems, since both mediums have their own industry "codes" which prohibit glorification of crime and criminals. Twentieth Century Fox faced this dilemma in 1939 when it filmed the classic *Jesse James*. The audience was treated to scenes of Tyrone Power, one of Hollywood's handsomest actors, eluding dull-witted posses in a series of magnificently photographed Technicolor sequences. Close-ups of the hero revealed him wearing beautiful sports clothes that could only have come from Abercrombie and Fitch. The "code" was observed in the last reel, where the happily domesticated Jesse was finally killed off to prove that crime really doesn't pay after all.

The script writers employed the "persecution" theme by blaming the railroads for Jesse's troubles. He was made to say: "The railroads have the police, the courts, everything. . . . I hate the railroads." Their perfidy is revealed when the detectives throw a bomb and kill Jesse's mother, a heartrending scene but one manifestly untrue. As the granddaughter of Jesse James said after viewing this film: "About the only connection it had with facts was that there was once a man named James and he did ride a horse."

The television series on "The Legend of Jesse James," which ran during the 1965–66 season, followed the same interpretation. Allen Case, who portrayed Frank James, said in an interview that "the railroad approached the James people and they wouldn't take the price offered, so the railroad blew up their house. As a result the James brothers started robbing trains and giving money back to the people." But audiences had become somewhat more critical, and the series foundered on its own improbabilities. Baby-faced Christopher Jones, playing the lead role, acted a pale imitation of his be-whiskered and bloodthirsty prototype. Nor could the producers decide whether the character really was a hero. They slid away from the question by asserting that "the series explores the enigma that was Jesse without condoning or condemning his deeds." The fans couldn't buy it; they knew too much history for their own good.

Despite some current skepticism about Jesse's generosity, his Robin Hood reputation is quite secure. This is so because the outlaw represents certain ideals, particularly social justice, which people hold dear. In 1949 Harry S. Truman spoke for many when he remarked that "Jesse James was a modern-day Robin Hood. He stole from the rich and gave to the poor, which, in general, is not a bad policy." Jesse's crimes are forgotten, while the legend of his idealism lingers on. Furthermore, the parallels between Robin Hood and Jesse James illustrate the persistence of such folk beliefs across several centuries. They also demonstrate the ease with which the popular imagination can overcome even the most stubborn facts.

Growing Up Indian, in a White Man's World

Zitkala-Să

In the following account, Zitkala-Să recalls her Indian childhood. Born Gertrude Simmons in 1876 on a Sioux reservation in South Dakota, she was the daughter of an Indian woman and a white man. Zitkala-Să, as she later christened herself, left the reservation at the age of eight for White's Manual Institute in Wabash, Indiana, a school operated by Quakers that followed the assimilationist policies of the Bureau of Indian Affairs, described by Richard White in the previous essay. Written without the assistance of an interpreter or editor, the stories first appeared in 1900 and 1901 in Harper's *and the* Atlantic Monthly, *where they were meant to inform and entertain the elite, liberal readers of those magazines.*

Why did Zitkala-Să want to leave the reservation, and why did her mother agree to allow her to do so? How did Zitkala-Să experience the Institute? More generally, how should one evaluate her reaction to the white man's school? Is it appropriate to see what happened to Zitkala-Să as a kind of tragedy? Or should one view her experience as an understandable and necessary aspect of her transition from one culture to another?

 # VOICES

The Big Red Apples

The first turning away from the easy, natural flow of my life occurred in an early spring. It was in my eighth year; in the month of March, I afterward learned. At this age I knew but one language, and that was my mother's native tongue.

From some of my playmates I heard that two paleface missionaries were in our village. They were from that class of white men who wore big hats and carried large hearts, they said. Running direct to my mother, I began to question her why these two strangers were among us. She told me, after I had teased much, that they had come to take away Indian boys and girls to the East. My mother did not seem to want me to talk about them. But in a day or two, I gleaned many wonderful stories from my playfellows concerning the strangers.

"Mother, my friend Judéwin is going home with the missionaries. She is going to a more beautiful country than ours; the palefaces told her so!" I said wistfully, wishing in my heart that I too might go.

Mother sat in a chair, and I was hanging on her knee. Within the last two seasons my big brother Dawée had returned from a three years' education in the East, and his coming back influenced my mother to take a farther step from her native way of living. First it was a change from the buffalo skin to the white man's canvas that covered our wigwam. Now she had given up her wigwam of slender poles, to live, a foreigner, in a home of clumsy logs.

"Yes, my child, several others besides Judéwin are going away with the palefaces. Your brother said the missionaries had inquired about his little sister," she said, watching my face very closely.

My heart thumped so hard against my breast, I wondered if she could hear it.

"Did he tell them to take me, mother?" I asked, fearing lest Dawée had forbidden the palefaces to see me, and that my hope of going to the Wonderland would be entirely blighted.

With a sad, slow smile, she answered: "There! I knew you were wishing to go, because Judéwin has filled your ears with the white man's lies. Don't believe a word they say! Their words are sweet, but, my child, their deeds are bitter. You will cry for me, but they will not even soothe you. Stay with me, my little one! Your brother Dawée says that going East, away from your mother, is too hard an experience for his baby sister."

Thus my mother discouraged my curiosity about the lands beyond our eastern horizon; for it was not yet an ambition for Letters that was stirring me. But on the following day the missionaries did come to our very house. I spied them coming up the footpath leading to our cottage. A third man was with them, but he was not my brother Dawée. It was another, a young interpreter, a paleface who had a smattering of the Indian language. I was ready to run out to meet them, but I did not dare to displease my mother. With great glee, I jumped up and down on our ground floor. I begged my mother to open the door, that they would be sure to come to us. Alas! They came, they saw, and they conquered!

Judéwin had told me of the great tree where grew red, red apples; and how we could reach out our hands and pick all the red apples we could eat. I had never seen apple trees. I had never tasted more than a dozen red apples in my life; and when I heard of the orchards of the East, I was eager to roam among them. The missionaries smiled into my eyes and patted my head. I wondered how mother could say such hard words against him.

"Mother, ask them if little girls may have all the red apples they want, when they go East," I whispered aloud, in my excitement.

The interpreter heard me, and answered: "Yes, little girl, the nice red apples are for those who pick them; and you will have a ride on the iron horse if you go with these good people."

I had never seen a train, and he knew it.

"Mother, I am going East! I like big red apples, and I want to ride on the iron horse! Mother, say yes!" I pleaded.

My mother said nothing. The missionaries waited in silence; and my eyes began to blur with tears, though I struggled to choke them back. The corners of my mouth twitched, and my mother saw me.

"I am not ready to give you any word," she said to them. "Tomorrow I shall send you my answer by my son."

With this they left us. Alone with my mother, I yielded to my tears, and cried aloud, shaking my head so as not to hear what she was saying to me. This was the first time I had ever been so unwilling to give up my own desire that I refused to hearken to my mother's voice.

There was a solemn silence in our home that night. Before I went to bed I begged the Great Spirit to make my mother willing I should go with the missionaries.

The next morning came, and my mother called me to her side. "My daughter, do you still persist in wishing to leave your mother?" she asked.

"Oh, mother, it is not that I wish to leave you, but I want to see the wonderful Eastern land," I answered.

My dear old aunt came to our house that morning, and I heard her say, "Let her try it."

I hoped that, as usual, my aunt was pleading on my side. My brother Dawée came for mother's decision. I dropped my play, and crept close to my aunt.

"Yes, Dawée, my daughter, though she does not understand what it all means, is anxious to go. She will need an education when she is grown, for then there will be fewer real Dakotas, and many more palefaces. This tearing her away, so young, from her mother is necessary, if I would have her an educated woman. The palefaces, who owe us a large debt for stolen lands, have begun to pay a tardy justice in offering some education to our children. But I know my daughter must suffer keenly in this experiment. For her sake, I dread to tell you my reply to the missionaries. Go, tell them that they may take my little daughter, and that the Great Spirit shall not fail to reward them according to their hearts."

Wrapped in my heavy blanket, I walked with my mother to the carriage that was soon to take us to the iron horse. I was happy. I met my playmates, who were also wearing their best thick blankets. We showed one another our new beaded moccasins, and the width of the belts that girdled our new dresses. Soon we were being drawn rapidly away by the white man's horses. When I saw the lonely figure of my mother vanish in the distance, a sense of regret settled heavily upon me. I felt suddenly weak, as if I might fall limp to the ground. I was in the hands of strangers whom my mother did not fully trust. I no longer felt free to be myself, or to voice my own feelings. The tears trickled down my cheeks, and I buried my face in the folds of my blanket. Now the first step, parting me from my mother, was taken, and all my belated tears availed nothing.

Having driven thirty miles to the ferryboat, we crossed the Missouri in the evening. Then riding again a few miles eastward, we stopped before a massive brick building. I looked at it in amazement, and with a vague misgiving, for in our village I had never seen so large a house. Trembling with fear and distrust of the palefaces, my teeth chattering from the chilly ride, I crept noiselessly in my soft moccasins along the narrow hall, keeping very close to the bare wall. I was as frightened and bewildered as the captured young of a wild creature. . . .

The Cutting of My Long Hair

The first day in the land of apples was a bitter-cold one; for the snow still covered the ground, and the trees were bare. A large bell rang for breakfast, its loud metallic voice crashing through the belfry overhead and into our sensitive ears. The annoying clatter of shoes on bare floors gave us no peace. The constant clash of harsh noises, with an undercurrent of many voices murmuring an unknown tongue, made a bedlam within which I was securely tied. And though my spirit tore itself in struggling for its lost freedom, all was useless.

A paleface woman, with white hair, came up after us. We were placed in a line of girls who were marching into the dining room. These were Indian girls, in stiff shoes and closely clinging dresses. The small girls wore sleeved aprons and shingled hair. As I walked noiselessly in my soft moccasins, I felt like sinking to the floor, for my blanket had been stripped from my shoulders. I looked hard at the Indian girls, who seemed not to care that they were even more immodestly dressed than I, in their tightly fitting clothes. While we marched in, the boys entered at an opposite door. I watched for the three young braves who came in our party. I spied them in the rear ranks, looking as uncomfortable as I felt.

A small bell was tapped, and each of the pupils drew a chair from under the table. Supposing this act meant they were to be seated, I pulled out mine and at once slipped into it from one side. But when I turned my head, I saw that I was the only one seated, and all the rest at our table remained standing. Just as I began to rise, looking shyly around to see how chairs were to be used, a second bell was sounded. All were seated at last, and I had to crawl back into my chair again. I heard a man's voice at one end of the hall, and I looked around to see him. But all the others hung their heads over their plates. As I glanced at the long chain of tables, I caught the eyes of a paleface woman upon me. Immediately I dropped my eyes, wondering why I was so keenly watched by the strange woman. The man ceased his mutterings, and then a third bell was tapped. Every one picked up his knife and fork and began eating. I began crying instead, for by this time I was afraid to venture anything more.

But this eating by formula was not the hardest trial in that first day. Late in the morning, my friend Judéwin gave me a terrible warning. Judéwin knew a few words of English; and she had overheard the paleface woman talk about cutting our long, heavy hair. Our mothers had taught us that only unskilled warriors who were captured had their hair shingled by the enemy. Among our people, short hair was worn by mourners, and shingled hair by cowards!

We discussed our fate some moments, and when Judéwin said, "We have to submit, because they are strong," I rebelled.

"No, I will not submit! I will struggle first!" I answered.

I watched my chance, and when no one noticed I disappeared. I crept up the stairs as quietly as I could in my squeaking shoes,—my moccasins had been exchanged for shoes. Along the hall I passed, without knowing whither I was going. Turning aside to an open door, I found a large room with three white beds in it. The windows were covered with dark green curtains, which made the room very dim. Thankful that no one was there, I directed my steps toward the corner farthest from the door. On my hands and knees I crawled under the bed, and cuddled myself in the dark corner.

From my hiding place I peered out, shuddering with fear whenever I heard footsteps near by. Though in the hall loud voices were calling my name, and I knew that even Judéwin was searching for me, I did not open my mouth to answer. Then the steps were quickened and the voices became excited. The sounds came nearer and nearer. Women and girls entered the room. I held my breath and watched them open closet doors and peep behind large trunks. Some one threw up the curtains, and the room was filled with sudden light. What caused them to stoop and look under the bed I do not know. I remember being dragged out, though I resisted by kicking and scratching wildly. In spite of myself, I was carried downstairs and tied fast in a chair.

I cried aloud, shaking my head all the while until I felt the cold blades of the scissors against my neck, and heard them gnaw off one of my thick braids. Then I lost my spirit. Since the day I was taken from my mother I had suffered extreme indignities. People had stared at me. I had been tossed about in the air like a wooden puppet. And now my long hair was shingled like a coward's! In my anguish I moaned for my mother, but no one came to comfort me. Not a soul reasoned quietly with me, as my own mother used to do; for now I was only one of many little animals driven by a herder. . . .

The Devil

Among the legends the old warriors used to tell me were many stories of evil spirits. But I was taught to fear them no more than those who stalked about in material guise. I never knew there was an insolent chieftain among the bad spirits, who dared to array his forces against the Great Spirit, until I heard this white man's legend from a paleface woman.

Out of a large book she showed me a picture of the white man's devil. I looked in horror upon the strong claws that grew out of his fur-covered fingers. His feet were like his hands. Trailing at his heels was a scaly tail tipped with a serpent's open jaws. His face was a patchwork: he had bearded cheeks, like some I had seen palefaces wear; his nose was an eagle's bill, and his sharp-pointed ears were pricked up like those of a sly fox. Above them a pair of cow's horns curved upward. I trembled with awe, and my heart throbbed in my throat, as I looked at the king of evil spirits. Then I heard the paleface woman say that this terrible creature roamed loose in the world, and that little girls who disobeyed school regulations were to be tortured by him.

That night I dreamt about this evil divinity. Once again I seemed to be in my mother's cottage. An Indian woman had come to visit my mother. On opposite sides of the kitchen stove, which stood in the center of the small house, my mother and her guest were seated in straight-backed chairs. I played with a train of empty spools hitched together on a string. It was night, and the wick burned feebly. Suddenly I heard some one turn our door-knob from without.

My mother and the woman hushed their talk, and both looked toward the door. It opened gradually. I waited behind the stove. The hinges squeaked as the door was slowly, very slowly pushed inward.

Then in rushed the devil! He was tall! He looked exactly like the picture I had seen of him in the white man's papers. He did not speak to my mother, because he did not know the Indian language, but his glittering yellow eyes were fastened upon me. He took long strides around the stove, passing behind the woman's chair. I threw down my spools, and ran to my mother. He did not fear her, but followed closely after me. Then I ran round and round the stove, crying aloud for help. But my mother and the woman seemed not to know my danger. They sat still, looking quietly upon the devil's chase after me. At last I grew dizzy. My head revolved as on a hidden pivot. My knees became numb, and doubled under my weight like a pair of knife blades without a spring. Beside my mother's chair I fell in a heap. Just as the devil stooped over me with outstretched claws my mother awoke from her quiet indifference, and lifted me on her lap. Whereupon the devil vanished, and I was awake.

On the following morning I took my revenge upon the devil. Stealing into the room where a wall of shelves was filled with books, I drew forth The Stories of the Bible. With a broken slate pencil I carried in my apron pocket, I began by scratching out his wicked eyes. A few moments later, when I was ready to leave the room, there was a ragged hole in the page where the picture of the devil had once been.

Iron Routine

A loud-clamoring bell awakened us at half-past six in the cold winter mornings. From happy dreams of Western rolling lands and unlassoed freedom we tumbled out upon chilly bare floors back again into a paleface day. We had short time to jump into our shoes and clothes, and wet our eyes with icy water, before a small hand bell was vigorously rung for roll call.

There were too many drowsy children and too numerous orders for the day to waste a moment in any apology to nature for giving her children such a shock in the early morning. We rushed downstairs, bounding over two high steps at a time, to land in the assembly room.

A paleface woman, with a yellow-covered roll book open on her arm and a gnawed pencil in her hand, appeared at the door. Her small, tired face was coldly lighted with a pair of large gray eyes.

She stood still in a halo of authority, while over the rim of her spectacles her eyes pried nervously about the room. Having glanced at her long list of names and called out the first one, she tossed up her chin and peered through the crystals of her spectacles to make sure of the answer "Here."

Relentlessly her pencil black-marked our daily records if we were not present to respond to our names, and no chum of ours had done it successfully for us. No matter if a dull headache or the painful cough of slow consumption had delayed the absentee, there was only time enough to mark the tardiness. It was next to impossible to leave the iron routine after the civilizing machine had once begun its day's buzzing; and as it was inbred in me to suffer in silence rather than to appeal to the ears of one whose open eyes could not see my pain. I have many times trudged in the day's harness heavy-footed, like a dumb sick brute.

Once I lost a dear classmate. I remember well how she used to mope along at my side, until one morning she could not raise her head from her pillow. At her deathbed I stood weeping, as the paleface woman sat near her moistening the dry lips. Among the folds of the bedclothes I saw the open pages of the white man's Bible. The dying Indian girl talked disconnectedly of Jesus the Christ and the paleface who was cooling her swollen hands and feet.

I grew bitter, and censured the woman for cruel neglect of our physical ills. I despised the pencils that moved automatically, and the one teaspoon which dealt out, from a large bottle, healing to a row of variously ailing Indian children. I blamed the hard-working, well-meaning, ignorant woman who was inculcating in our hearts her superstitious ideas. Though I was sullen in all my little troubles, as soon as I felt better I was ready again to smile upon the cruel woman. Within a week I was again actively testing the chains which tightly bound my individuality like a mummy for burial.

The melancholy of those black days has left so long a shadow that it darkens the path of years that have since gone by. These sad memories rise above those of smoothly grinding school days. Perhaps my Indian nature is the moaning wind which stirs them now for their present record. But, however tempestuous this is within me, it comes out as the low voice of a curiously colored seashell, which is only for those ears that are bent with compassion to hear it.

Many of the published works of Gertrude Simmons Bonnin (Zitkala-Ša) are available at http://guweb2.gonzaga.edu/faculty/campbell/enl311/zitkala.htm. *That site also has a biography by Roseanne Hoefels and a useful commentary on how to teach the work of Zitkala-Ša by Kristin Herzog.*

Visualizing Assimilation

Zitkala-Sǎ does not appear in either of the "before and after" photographs below, but she would surely have empathized with the children in them. The photos were taken at the Hampton Normal and Agricultural Institute in Hampton, Virginia, probably in the 1880s. A trade school and teacher-training center, the Hampton Institute enrolled African Americans and Native Americans. The photographs retain their original captions.

    What observations can you make from each photograph? Do you think the children share the perspective of the institution and its photographer? Would you conclude from these photographs that Hampton's assimilation effort was a success, or a failure?

On arrival at Hampton, Va: Carrie Anderson—12 yrs., Annie Dawson—10 yrs., and Sarah Walker—13 yrs. Used with the permission of the Peabody Museum of Archaelogy & Ethnology.

Fourteen months after. Used with the permission of the Peabody Museum of Archaeology & Ethnology.

The Worlds of Quanah Parker: A Photo Essay

Comanche chief Quanah Parker (ca. 1852–1911) was the son of a Comanche chief, Peta Nocone, and Cynthia Ann Parker, a white woman taken captive during an 1836 raid on Parker's Fort, Texas. Between 1867 and 1875, Parker led raids on frontier settlements. After his defeat and surrender, he lived another kind of life, one illustrated in the photographs on these pages. What adjectives would you use to describe the Quanah Parker revealed in these photographs?

Quanah Parker, Seated Next to a Portrait of His Mother. Photo by H. P. Robinson, Fort Sill, Oklahoma Territory. Courtesy Oklahoma Historical Society.

Quanah Parker, on the Porch of His Home, c. 1895. Photo by Irwin and Mankins. Courtesy Oklahoma Historical Society.

Comanche Chief Quanah Parker on Horseback Near His Home, Cache,
Oklahoma Territory, c. 1901. Photo by N. Losey. Courtesy Oklahoma Historical Society.

Quanah Parker's Home, 1912. Photo by Bates, Lawton, Oklahoma. Courtesy Oklahoma
Historical Society.

Quanah Parker, with One of His Seven Wives. Courtesy Oklahoma Historical Society.

The Significance of the Frontier in American History

Frederick Jackson Turner

*To the majority of Americans—who lived in cities or small towns "back East"—
the West was a mirror of what Americans were and wanted to be. One of the most
influential expressions of this idea was Frederick Jackson Turner's essay, "The
Significance of the Frontier in American History," which he read to an audience
of fellow historians assembled in Chicago on the occasion of the 1893 world's fair.
Chicago was even then a great manufacturing and distribution center, and the city
had a reputation as a hotbed of conflict between capital and labor. Labor troubles
at the McCormick Harvester works, culminating in an 1886 bombing in
Haymarket Square, had made middle-class Chicagoans tense and anxious, and
perhaps overly fearful that their city was being overrun by radicals and
immigrants. And as Turner spoke, there was trouble brewing just a few miles
beyond the city's southern boundary, where workers at the Pullman Palace Car
Company were soon to go on strike, triggering more upheaval and violence.
Although Turner's subject was the West, it was also very much about what was
happening in Chicago and other points "East."*

*According to Turner, what was it that defined the West, and why was it
important? What did Turner's perspective imply about the future of the nation,
looking forward into the twentieth century?*

In a recent bulletin of the Superintendent of the Census for 1890 appear
these significant words: "Up to and including 1880 the country had a frontier of settlement, but at present the unsettled area has been so broken into
by isolated bodies of settlement that there can hardly be said to be a frontier
line. In the discussion of its extent, its westward movement, etc., it can not,
therefore, any longer have a place in the census reports." This brief official
statement marks the closing of a great historic movement. Up to our own
day American history has been in a large degree the history of the colonization of the Great West. The existence of an area of free land, its continuous
recession, and the advance of American settlement westward, explain
American development.

Behind institutions, behind constitutional forms and modifications, lie
the vital forces that call these organs into life and shape them to meet changing conditions. The peculiarity of American institutions is, the fact that they
have been compelled to adapt themselves to the changes of an expanding
people—to the changes involved in crossing a continent, in winning a
wilderness, and in developing at each area of this progress out of the primitive economic and political conditions of the frontier into the complexity of
city life. Said Calhoun in 1817, "We are great, and rapidly—I was about to

From Frederick Jackson Turner, "The Significance of the Frontier in American History,"
American Historical Association, *Annual Report for 1893*, Government Printing Office,
Washington, D.C., 1894, pp. 199–201, 205, 208, 215–217, 219, 220–223, 226–227.

say fearfully—growing!" So saying, he touched the distinguishing feature of American life. . . . American development has exhibited not merely advance along a single line, but a return to primitive conditions on a continually advancing frontier line, and a new development for that area. American social development has been continually beginning over again on the frontier. This perennial rebirth, this fluidity of American life, this expansion westward with its new opportunities, its continuous touch with the simplicity of primitive society, furnish the forces dominating American character. The true point of view in the history of this nation is not the Atlantic coast, it is the great West. . . .

The frontier is the line of most rapid and effective Americanization. The wilderness masters the colonist. It finds him a European in dress, industries, tools, modes of travel, and thought. It takes him from the railroad car and puts him in the birch canoe. It strips off the garments of civilization and arrays him in the hunting shirt and the moccasin. It puts him in the log cabin of the Cherokee and Iroquois and runs an Indian palisade around him. Before long he has gone to planting Indian corn and plowing with a sharp stick; he shouts the war cry and takes the scalp in orthodox Indian fashion. In short, at the frontier the environment is at first too strong for the man. He must accept the conditions which it furnishes, or perish, and so he fits himself into the Indian clearings and follows the Indian trails. Little by little he transforms the wilderness, but the outcome is not the old Europe, not simply the development of Germanic germs, any more than the first phenomenon was a case of reversion to the Germanic mark. The fact is, that here is a new product that is American. . . .

By 1880 the settled area had been pushed into northern Michigan, Wisconsin, and Minnesota, along Dakota rivers, and in the Black Hills region, and was ascending the rivers of Kansas and Nebraska. The development of mines in Colorado had drawn isolated frontier settlements into that region, and Montana and Idaho were receiving settlers. The frontier was found in these mining camps and the ranches of the Great Plains. The superintendent of the census for 1890 reports, as previously stated, that the settlements of the West lie so scattered over the region that there can no longer be said to be a frontier line. . . .

The Atlantic frontier was compounded of fisherman, fur-trader, miner, cattle-raiser, and farmer. Excepting the fisherman, each type of industry was on the march toward the West, impelled by an irresistible attraction. Each passed in successive waves across the continent. Stand at Cumberland Gap and watch the procession of civilization, marching single file—the buffalo following the trail to the salt springs, the Indian, the fur-trader and hunter, the cattle-raiser, the pioneer farmer—and the frontier has passed by. Stand at South Pass in the Rockies a century later and see the same procession with wider intervals between. The unequal rate of advance compels us to distinguish the frontier into the trader's frontier, the rancher's frontier, or the miner's frontier, and the farmer's frontier. When the mines and the cow pens were still near the fall line the traders' pack trains were tinkling across the Alleghenies, and the French on the Great Lakes were fortifying their posts, alarmed by the British trader's birch canoe. When the trappers scaled the Rockies, the farmer was still near the mouth of the Missouri. . . .

The frontier promoted the formation of a composite nationality for the American people. The coast was preponderantly English, but the later tides of continental immigration flowed across the free lands. This was the case from the early colonial days. The Scotch Irish and the Palatine Germans, or "Pennsylvania Dutch," furnished the dominant element in the stock of the colonial frontier. With these peoples were also the freed indented servants, or redemptioners, who at the expiration of their time of service passed to the frontier. . . . Very generally these redemptioners were of non-English stock. In the crucible of the frontier the immigrants were Americanized, liberated, and fused into a mixed race, English in neither nationality or characteristics. The process has gone on from the early days to our own. . . .

The legislation which most developed the powers of the National Government, and played the largest part in its activity, was conditioned on the frontier. . . . The pioneer needed the goods of the coast, and so the grand series of internal improvement and railroad legislation began, with potent nationalizing effects. Over internal improvements occurred great debates, in which grave constitutional questions were discussed. Sectional groupings appear in the votes, profoundly significant for the historian. Loose construction increased as the nation marched westward. But the West was not content with bringing the farm to the factory. Under the lead of Clay—"Harry of the West"—protective tariffs were passed, with the cry of bringing the factory to the farm. The disposition of the public lands was a third important subject of national legislation influenced by the frontier. . . .

It is safe to say that the legislation with regard to land, tariff, and internal improvements—the American system of the nationalizing Whig party—was conditioned on frontier ideas and needs. But it was not merely in legislative action that the frontier worked against the sectionalism of the coast. The economic and social characteristics of the frontier worked against sectionalism. The men of the frontier had closer resemblances to the Middle region than to either of the other sections. Pennsylvania had been the seed-plot of frontier emigration, and, although she passed on her settlers along the Great Valley into the west of Virginia and the Carolinas, yet the industrial society of these Southern frontiersmen was always more like that of the Middle region than like that of the tide-water portion of the South, which later came to spread its industrial type throughout the South.

The Middle region, entered by New York harbor, was an open door to all Europe. . . . It had a wide mixture of nationalities, a varied society, the mixed town and county system of local government, a varied economic life, many religious sects. In short, it was a region mediating between New England and the South, and the East and the West. It represented that composite nationality which the contemporary United States exhibits, that juxtaposition of non-English groups, occupying a valley or a little settlement, and presenting reflections of the map of Europe in their variety. It was democratic and nonsectional, if not national; "easy, tolerant, and contented;" rooted strongly in material prosperity. It was typical of the modern United States. . . .

But the most important effect of the frontier has been in the promotion of democracy here and in Europe. As has been indicated, the frontier is productive of individualism. Complex society is precipitated by the wilderness into a kind of primitive organization based on the family. The tendency is anti-social. It produces antipathy to control, and particularly to any direct control. The tax-gatherer is viewed as a representative of oppression. . . .

The frontier States that came into the Union in the first quarter of a century of its existence came in with democratic suffrage provisions, and had reactive effects of the highest importance upon the older States whose peoples were being attracted there. An extension of the franchise became essential. It was *western* New York that forced an extension of suffrage in the constitutional convention of that State in 1821. . . .

So long as free land exists, the opportunity for a competency exists, and economic power secures political power. But the democracy born of free land, strong in selfishness and individualism, intolerant of administrative experience and education, and pressing individual liberty beyond its proper bounds, has its dangers as well as its benefits. Individualism in America has allowed a laxity in regard to governmental affairs which has rendered possible the spoils system and all the manifest evils that follow from the lack of a highly developed civic spirit. In this connection may be noted also the influence of frontier conditions in permitting lax business honor, inflated paper currency and wildcat banking. The colonial and revolutionary frontier was the region whence emanated many of the worst forms of an evil currency. The West in the war of 1812 repeated the phenomenon on the frontier of that day, while the speculation and wild-cat banking of the period of the crisis of 1837 occurred on the new frontier belt of the next tier of States. Thus each one of the periods of lax financial integrity coincides with periods when a new set of frontier communities had arisen, and coincides in area with these successive frontiers, for the most part. The recent Populist agitation is a case in point. Many a State that now declines any connection with the tenets of the Populists, itself adhered to such ideas in an earlier stage of the development of the State. A primitive society can hardly be expected to show the intelligent appreciation of the complexity of business interests in a developed society. . . .

From the conditions of frontier life came intellectual traits of profound importance. The works of travelers along each frontier from colonial days onward describe certain common traits, and these traits have, while softening down, still persisted as survivals in the place of their origin, even when a higher social organization succeeded. The result is that to the frontier the American intellect owes its striking characteristics. That coarseness and strength combined with acuteness and inquisitiveness; that practical, inventive turn of mind, quick to find expedients; that masterful grasp of material things, lacking in the artistic but powerful to effect great ends; that restless, nervous energy; that dominant individualism, working for good and for evil, and withal that buoyancy and exuberance which comes with freedom—these are traits of the frontier, or traits called out elsewhere because of the existence of the frontier. Since the days when the fleet of Columbus sailed into the waters of the New World, America has been another name for opportunity, and the people of the United States have taken their tone from the incessant expansion which has not only been open but has even been forced upon them. He would be a rash prophet who should assert that the expansive character of American life has now entirely ceased. Movement has been its dominant fact, and, unless this training has no effect upon a people, the American energy will continually demand a wider field for its exercise. But never again will such gifts of free land offer themselves. For a moment, at the frontier, the bonds of custom are broken and unrestraint is triumphant. There is not *tabula rasa*. The stubborn American environment is there with its imperious summons to accept its conditions; the inherited ways of doing things are also there; and yet, in spite of environment, and in spite of custom, each frontier did indeed furnish a new field of opportunity, a gate of escape from the bondage of the past; and freshness, and confidence, and scorn of older society, impatience of its restraints and its ideas, and indifference to its lessons, have accompanied the frontier. What the Mediterranean Sea was to the Greeks, breaking the bond of custom, offering new experiences, calling out new institutions and activities, that, and more, the ever retreating frontier has been to the United States directly, and to the nations of Europe more remotely. And now, four centuries from the discovery of America, at the end of a hundred years of life under the Constitution, the frontier has gone, and with its going has closed the first period of American history.

THE BIG PICTURE

The West was a mirror of what Americans were and wanted to be, and perhaps above all of what they feared they were becoming. Frederick Jackson Turner's idea of the West was profoundly shaped by his anxiety that the "closing" of the frontier would usher in a new century in which the healthy values of individualism and democracy produced by frontier conflicts and conditions would be gradually overcome by urban decadence. Something similar was responsible for the powerful mythology that has swirled around Frank and Jesse James and other western bandits for well over a hundred years. Whatever the reality, the James gang stands in symbolic opposition to banks, railroads, and other big businesses; to the accumulation of wealth in the Gilded Age and after; and to the growing power of the federal government, which had subdued the rebellious South.

It is common to understand the conflict between Indians and whites in the American West as conflict between a progressive, modernizing, market-based capitalist culture on the one hand, and a deeply resistant, static, primitive, and antimarket Indian culture on the other. That was Turner's view, and there is much truth in it. However, the materials in this chapter suggest a more complex perspective. To be sure, Zitkala-Šǎ's story has its tragic side, and parts of it reinforce the social and cultural differences between the two societies. However, the white culture was also the object of deep desire and even accommodation; Zitkala-Šǎ's mother wanted her daughter to be literate in the ways of the white man. By the same token, Quanah Parker is photographed in Western clothes as well as Indian ones, and next to his wife, who is decked out in a cape and fancy hat. Was Parker hopelessly compromised by Western material values, or was he at ease, and dignified, in white as well as Indian settings?

Cities and Immigrants, Cities and Migrants

In 1860 there were only sixteen cities in the United States with populations over 50,000, and only three cities of more than 250,000. By 1900 the corresponding figures were seventy-eight and fifteen. In the half-century after 1850, the population of Chicago grew from less than 30,000 to more than 1 million. For older, eastern cities, growth meant change in function and structure. Boston—in 1850 a concentrated merchant city of some 200,000 persons, dependent on oceangoing commerce—was by 1900 a sprawling industrial city with a population of more than 1 million.

Entirely new cities arose to meet particular demands of time and place. For George Pullman, of sleeping-car fame, big cities were sordid and disorderly places that spawned crime and violence. He planned and built an entirely new community isolated from disruptive influences where (so he believed) his workers would always be happy (he was mistaken). Western cities also expanded rapidly, usually by virtue of some nearby exploitable resource. Wichita was one of several Kansas towns founded on the cattle trade. Seattle was a timber city. Denver had its origins in the 1857 gold rush, but it remained to service the Great Plains, much as Chicago did the Midwest.

The new urban residents were often either immigrants from abroad or migrants from the nation's small towns and rural areas. In 1910 perhaps one-third of the total urban population were native Americans of rural origin; another one-quarter were foreign-born. Although the nonurban population increased absolutely in each decade before 1950, it diminished relatively. During and after the Civil War, the widespread adoption of a variety of labor-saving devices, including cultivators, reapers, mowers, threshers, and corn planters, allowed fewer and fewer farmers to feed the urban populace. Certain areas, such as rural New England, showed marked reductions in population. "We cannot all live in cities," wrote Horace Greeley in the 1860s, "yet nearly all seem determined to do so."

The emigration to the United States from abroad was, simply put, a major folk migration. There were 4.1 million foreign-born in the United States in 1860, 13.5 million foreign-born in 1910. And to these numbers must be added the children of the foreign-born—15.6 million in 1900, 18.9 million (more than one out of every five Americans) by 1910.

Some cities attracted a disproportionate share of the foreign-born. By 1910, New York City and two older Massachusetts cities, Fall River and Lowell, had more than 40 percent foreign-born residents. Twelve major cities, including Boston, Chicago, Milwaukee, Detroit, and San Francisco, had between 30 and 40 percent foreign-born residents. Seventeen other cities, including Seattle, Portland, Omaha, and Oakland, had over 20 percent foreign-born residents. (Most southern cities had less than 10 percent.)

After 1880, another change of importance occurred. The national origin of the nation's foreign-born population shifted from the northern and western European mix characteristic of previous decades to the southern and eastern European, Jewish and Catholic, mix dominant in 1900. In contrast to the earlier immigrants, a larger proportion of the later immigrants concentrated in the ghettos of northeastern industrial cities. On New York City's Lower East Side, more than 30,000 people were squeezed into half a dozen city blocks.

Ethnic clustering was nothing new, but the unfamiliar languages, customs, and religious practices of the Italians, Russians, Poles, and Slavs seemed to many observers to be associated with slums, unemployment, delinquency, and disease. The later immigrants were also held responsible for the growth of "alien" ideologies—anarchism and socialism—in large American cities in the last quarter of the century. And there was enough truth in this charge to give it some credence. "Red" Emma Goldman, one of the nation's most active anarchists, was Russian-born. Her friend Alexander Berkman, who was born in Poland, made an unsuccessful attempt to kill steel magnate Henry Clay Frick during the 1892 Homestead strike. In Chicago, a center of working-class politics, radical political ideas were especially well represented, and radical leaders were more often than not German-born. Germany, after all, had produced Karl Marx, and Russia, the anarchist Mikhail Bakunin. Europe simply had a more well-developed radical tradition than the United States. Many new immigrants brought with them some portion of this tradition when they set foot on American shores.

After 1880, but especially after 1910, the social character of American cities was altered by another migration, this one inside the country. This internal migration—one of the most important events in all of twentieth-century American history—brought hundreds of thousands, and eventually millions, of African Americans from the rural and urban South to industrial cities of the North and Midwest, and, to a lesser extent, the Far West. Many came with great expectations for a better life, chalking their dreams on the sides of the boxcars that carried them north: "Farewell—We're Good and Gone," "Bound to the Land of Hope," and "Bound for the Promised Land." Aboard a northbound train headed for Chicago from Jackson, Mississippi, in 1925, future novelist Richard Wright wondered what his new circumstances would bring. "If I could meet enough of a different life," he thought, "then, perhaps, gradually and slowly I might learn who I was, what I might be." Another important internal migration brought thousands of young, unmarried women to big cities from farms, towns, and smaller cities.

White or black, from Europe or the American South, many of the migrants found their new communities to be wellsprings of freedom and economic opportunity. But these gifts were not distributed evenly. Most of the immigrants—Italians, Poles, Russian Jews, Irish, Germans, and others—had within a generation or two of their arrival been largely integrated into the American economic and social order. Most of the migrants—African Americans, in particular—found themselves increasingly separated from the rest of society, their political, social, and economic opportunities limited and restricted in ways that could hardly have been foreseen. The complex experience of single women is explored in the essay that follows.

The American city of the late nineteenth and early twentieth centuries was the most complex social space one can imagine: rich and poor, blacks and whites, migrants and immigrants, those who spoke English and those who did not, men and women—all seeking some modicum of success, some version of a good life. This chapter explores just a few of the problems raised by the American urban experience.

Women and Migration
Autonomous Female Migrants to Chicago, 1880–1930

Joanne Meyerowitz

In April 1913, the body of thirteen-year-old Mary Phagan was found in the basement of the National Pencil Factory in Atlanta, Georgia, where Phagan was employed. Leo Frank, the pencil factory's northern, Jewish manager, was wrongly accused of the murder and, in 1915, dragged from prison and lynched by a mob in the town of Marietta, where Phagan had grown up. The case, which was covered by the national press, was about the South and the North, about anti-Semitism, and about race. But it was also about the migration of young women that had brought thousands of Mary Phagans to Atlanta and other cities.

In the selection that follows, historian Joanne Meyerowitz offers us a rich account of the experiences of what she calls "autonomous" women migrants—young women like Mary Phagan who in the half century after 1880 left farms or smaller communities for big cities—in this study, the metropolis of Chicago—and lived "apart from family."

The essay raises a variety of questions. Why did these young women migrate? Did it have something to do with "family breakdown," a term more often used to describe late-twentieth-century families? To what extent was it a "gendered" migration—that is, a migration motivated and determined by the fact of gender? Without romanticizing their lives, Meyerowitz argues that these autonomous female migrants were not "passive victims" but rather women with options and choices. Do you agree?

On a cold Saturday morning in the spring of 1916, an eighteen-year-old white woman arrived in Chicago from Joliet, Illinois. Her aunt had bought her a railroad ticket, given her one dollar, and told her to find a job in the city. Over a year later, in the summer of 1917, a fifteen-year-old black woman wrote to Chicago from New Orleans:

> I wont to come there and work i have ben looking for work here for three month and cand find any . . . the only help i have is my mother . . . and she have four children young then me . . . and she have such a hard time tell she is willing for me to go.

In the late nineteenth and early twentieth centuries, thousands of women migrated to Chicago autonomously. That is, they did not move with families or relatives; instead, they came alone and boarded or lodged in the city.

From the *Journal of Urban History*, vol. 13, no. 2, February 1987, pp. 147–163. Copyright © by Sage Publications, Inc.

The largest group of autonomous female migrants were young, unmarried women who came to Chicago from villages, towns, and cities as well as from rural regions. They included native-born white women who migrated from the Northeast and increasingly from Chicago's midwestern hinterlands, and black women who migrated from Kentucky, Tennessee, Missouri, and, increasingly in the twentieth century, from the Deep South. In addition, some foreign-born women migrated alone to Chicago, especially Scandinavian, Polish, Canadian, and Irish women.

While the exact numbers of autonomous female migrants to Chicago are lost to us, the number of boarders and lodgers in the city offers a rough approximation. In 1900, over 22,000 women, or over one-fifth of the Chicago female labor force, boarded or lodged apart from family and relatives. (These figures exclude domestic servants, many of whom were autonomous migrants living in the homes of their employers.) The Chicago figures reflect national trends. In 1900, nineteen percent of the nonservant urban female labor force boarded or lodged apart from family. The results of a number of surveys conducted in Chicago and other cities between 1880 and 1925 suggest that the number of female boarders and lodgers grew about as rapidly as the number of jobs for women increased, ranging roughly between one-fifth and one-sixth of the nonservant female labor force.

The large-scale migration of women is not a new discovery for historians and demographers. In fact, for at least a century now, social scientists have suggested that, in some historical contexts, more women migrated than men. In 1885, E. G. Ravenstein wrote in his well-known laws of migration: "Females are more migratory than males." In the one hundred years since Ravenstein first set out this dictum, numerous demographers, geographers, sociologists, and anthropologists have reiterated his findings. In early twentieth-century France and recently in Latin America, the Caribbean, the Philippines and other parts of Asia, women predominated in certain streams of internal migration, especially in shorter distance migrations from country to city. In the nineteenth- and early twentieth-century United States as well, historians and sociologists have suggested that more women migrated to cities than did men. We find evidence of female-dominated migrations among young, native-born whites in New England in the 1830s, among free blacks in the antebellum and postwar South, among nineteenth-century Irish immigrants, and among the sons and daughters of farmers in Iowa, Minnesota, Illinois, Michigan, Kentucky, and New York in the late nineteenth and early twentieth centuries. In a national study of the farm population in 1920, the U.S. Bureau of the Census concluded: "The farmer's daughter is more likely to leave the farm and go to the city than is the farmer's son."

Despite this evidence of large-scale female migration to cities, few American historians have investigated autonomous female migration in any detail. Much of the historical literature on American migration and geographic mobility focuses primarily on the migration of men or on the migration of families and kin networks. Many studies assume either that women migrated to cities by association only, joining or following male relatives who searched for urban work, or that the migration of women differed little in motive and outcome from the migration of men.

Granted, the quantitative dimensions of autonomous female migration are particularly elusive. We have few records of internal migration. Furthermore, we cannot accurately determine female persistence rates in the city because women changed their names after marriage. Nevertheless, a wide range of nonquantitative sources makes possible a preliminary investigation of the motives for female migration and the experiences of autonomous female migrants in the city.

Why did women migrate to Chicago? The most obvious reason and the reason most often cited by historians is the need for work. According to many demographers as well, the primary "push" for migration during industrialization was economic hardship at home and the primary "pull" was the availability of work in the city. Especially in working-class, tenant farm, and small farm families, the income of the father often did not suffice to support the entire family. In the eighteenth century, many daughters contributed to the economic well-being of their families by sewing, baking, spinning, and performing other domestic chores. By the end of the nineteenth century, factory production had replaced much of this home manufacture. An unemployed daughter who lived at home drew on the family resources for food, clothing, and shelter, and offered little in return. For example, a black woman, seventeen years old, wrote to the black newspaper *The Chicago Defender* from Alexandria, Louisiana. She hoped to migrate to Chicago:

> I have a mother and father my father do all he can for me but it is so hard. A child with any respect about herself or hisself wouldn't like to see there mother and father work so hard and earn nothing. I feel it my duty to help.

In short, unless she worked for wages, a daughter burdened her family. Accordingly, by 1890, forty percent of all single women in the United States worked for wages. By 1930, over half had joined the paid labor force.

Some women migrated after death, divorce, or desertion disrupted the family economy. In some cases, the death of a primary breadwinner, a relatively common occurrence, threw women wholly on their own resources. Orphans and widows who did not live in large cities often migrated in search of work. In some fatherless families, daughters came to support their mothers or their siblings. Mary Kenney, later a labor leader, supported her invalid, widowed mother. She moved to Chicago in the late nineteenth century when she lost her job in a bindery in Hannibal, Missouri. "I was told there was plenty of business in Chicago," she wrote later. "If I could not get work in a bindery, I'd work at anything, even at washing dishes in a hotel." A smaller group of women migrated when desertion or divorce removed their customary male source of support.

While some women migrated when their families could not support them, other women migrated when their families would not support them. In some cases, daughters left home when parents or guardians chose to terminate their economic obligations. In one such case, a woman from a troubled home in a city in Indiana migrated to Chicago. Her mother was dead;

her father drank and gambled; her stepmother disliked her. When she was seventeen, "her father refused to clothe her and in an awful fit of anger swore that he would do nothing more for her." In times of need, other adult daughters returned to their parents' homes only to find their parents unwilling to care for them. When her husband died in 1916, Philiminia P., a twenty-two-year-old black woman, returned to her parents' home in Colorado. "They treated me so rotten," she said, "I come back [to Chicago]. . . . My family put me and my three brothers out. . . . I couldn't live there." The family economy did not always provide adult daughters with cushions in times of crisis.

Other women had jobs or economic support at home but came to Chicago in search of better-paying or more rewarding work. Black women (and men) from the South expected to find higher-paying jobs and less overt employment discrimination in northern cities. One black woman from New Orleans wrote: "I read and hear daly of the great chance that a colored parson has in Chicago of making a living with all the privileg that the whites have." Other women who desired careers sometimes came to the city with hopes of finding greater opportunities for upward mobility. One white office worker, for example, left a dead-end job in her home town when a friend told her of better opportunities in Chicago. Another woman ran away from her home to pursue a career on the stage. Like men, these women saw the city, especially an expanding city like Chicago, as a place of opportunity.

At first glance, then, it appears that women migrated, as men did, in search of work: they came from families that could not or would not support them, and they came with high ambition to pursue careers. A closer observation, however, reveals that women had, in addition, specifically "female" reasons for migrating.

For one, the distinctive features of the female labor market often governed migrations. That is, the structure of the female labor market compelled many women who needed work to go to a large city like Chicago to find it. Aside from a limited number of positions as servants and a handful of jobs as teachers, job-seeking women found few occupations open to them in rural areas and small towns. As one student of migration wrote in 1924:

> Fewer women than men are needed on the farm. One woman, ordinarily, does the work of the family. . . . Not only are fewer women needed, but the occupations open to them in the country are fewer. Practically the only alternatives to marriage for country girls are teaching school and leaving home to go to the city.

Similarly, some smaller industrial cities had few job openings for women. In cities like Gary, Indiana, and Youngstown, Ohio, where traditionally male heavy industries such as steel predominated, jobs for women were scarce.

In several large northern cities, however, the demand for female workers skyrocketed in the late nineteenth and early twentieth centuries. From 1870 to 1930, the female labor force in Chicago grew from 18,300 to 407,600, or by over 2,000 percent. The rate of increase of the female labor force in Chicago was over four times as great as the rate of increase of the female labor force for the nation as a whole. These figures reflect more general urban trends. In 1900, twenty-three percent of adult women in larger cities worked in the wage labor force; only eighteen percent worked for wages in the rest of the nation. By 1920, the gap had widened. Thirty-three percent of adult women worked for wages in larger cities while only twenty-one percent worked for wages in smaller cities, towns, and rural areas. In both years, this rural-urban gap in jobs per capita was larger for women (more than twice as large) than it was for men. Given the dearth of wage work for women outside of large cities and the plethora of jobs within them, it is not surprising that women sometimes migrated to cities in greater numbers than men. Stated simply, the geography of the female labor market differed from the geography of the male labor market.

Still, the search for employment and the structure of the labor market do not explain fully why many women left their homes. In the personal accounts of migrants and in the case records of social investigators, other explanations appear with frequency. Several of these explanations point to noneconomic female concerns. It is impossible to quantify these motives, and it is equally difficult to assign priorities when women listed several different reasons for leaving home. Nonetheless, the existence of these additional motives points to a private side of the female migration experience often neglected by demographers and historians.

For example, some women left their homes to escape the stigma attached by family and community to an unmarried woman suspected of being sexually active. Raped or pregnant women sought the anonymity of life in a city where no one knew them. One such woman came to Chicago in 1888 after she had been seduced and impregnated by a farmer in a nearby county. Another woman worked as a live-in domestic servant until she met a young man who "ruined and deserted" her. After an attempted suicide, she too fled to Chicago.

In other cases, parents and guardians expelled daughters from their homes for sexual behavior deemed unacceptable. An investigator of prostitution in 1911 found a woman whose parents "made her leave home because she went out at night." She told the investigator that she was "'going to hell proper' now."

Just as blacks and Jews often migrated in family groups to escape racial oppression and religious persecution, so many women who lived in patriarchal families moved out on their own to escape oppressive male relatives. Some women left home because fathers, stepfathers, uncles, or husbands abused them physically. In one such case, a twenty-year-old women "had lived with an uncle in Pennsylvania, who demanded her wages, and upon her refusal beat her." According to the charity worker who interviewed her, "She arrived at our terminal still carrying the bruises." In another case, a Hungarian immigrant came to Chicago from New York to escape her violent and alcoholic husband.

Several cases of incest and attempted incest appeared in the records of social and charity workers. The Travelers' Aid Society of the Young Women's Christian Association reported one such case in 1912:

The girl arrived in the city at midnight without hat or coat, seeking protection. Her stepfather had been making improper advances toward her for some time, but so far she had been able to resist them. Her life was threatened if she told her mother.

But the importunities of the man had become so insistent that the girl was afraid to remain longer and she fled.

Women were not only expelled from their homes by stigmatization or by abuse of patriarchal authority. Increasingly in the early twentieth century, women, especially young women, chose to migrate to escape the restrictions routinely imposed upon daughters in the family economy. Parents, fearful for their daughters' chastity, often restricted their daughters' nightlife, and, in addition, parents often required daughters (and less often required sons) to turn their entire wage into the common family fund. Daughters protested.

Some left home when parents or guardians refused to let them spend their evenings as they chose. One woman ran away from home after her parents threatened to send her away for "go[ing] out with fellows." In the early 1920s, another woman came to Chicago from a town in Michigan after her stepfather attempted to whip her for staying out late on a date. She explained:

We kept having fights back and forth about the boys I went out with and the hours that I kept. He even accused me of wanting to do things which I'd not even thought of doing up to that time. One night the auto I was in broke down—it really did—and I didn't get in until after one o'clock. We had a big fight at home and he even tried to whip me. I told him I wouldn't stand for that and would leave home. . . . I was always willing to stand up for my rights.

Other daughters migrated because they resented their lack of economic independence. One seventeen-year-old woman ran away from home because her father, an alcoholic, demanded her wages. In a letter to the *Farmer's Voice*, Miss Alta Hooper warned farm parents that their daughters would leave home unless accorded greater economic freedom: "She isn't going to 'stay put,' but will get out where she can earn some money of her very own, to buy the little things so dear to the hearts of girls; and she will not be questioned and scolded over every little expenditure."

Some of these women were probably drawn to the city by the new possibilities for urban consumer pleasure. By the early twentieth century, new urban nightlife—movies, dance halls, cabarets—offered women entertainment and the chance to mingle freely with their peers. And advertising broadcast the possibility for consumerism in department and other retail stores. Some women seemed especially eager to have their own money to spend on attractive clothing. An eighteen-year-old Danish woman from Michigan, for example, migrated to Chicago in part "because she could not have the clothes she wanted."

Recent writings in European women's history tend to depict a woman's decision to migrate as part of a "family strategy," an economic calculation based on the needs and decisions of the entire family unit. In this study of migration to Chicago, however, the "family strategy" approach provides only partial explanation and, in some cases, obscures the conflicting interests of individual family members. Within the family, stigmatization and abuse sometimes overshadowed cooperation, and, outside the family, increasing urban opportunities for self-indulgence sometimes appealed to women weary of self-abnegation in the family interest.

This is not to imply (as does Edward Shorter) that migration liberated oppressed women to lives of self-seeking and self-satisfied individualism. Once in the city, a self-supporting female migrant learned that she faced obstacles that a self-supporting man did not. She learned to mistrust strangers who might see her as an especially easy mark for exploitation, and she learned too that strangers often mistrusted her, reading her lone status as a badge of sexual misbehavior. Most important, she discovered that employers paid her the low wages of a dependent daughter or wife.

For some women, the harsh lesson began when they first stepped off the train into the city. Criminals sometimes chose railroad stations as the most likely locations in which to find vulnerable female victims. For example, a newcomer from Cleveland "was taken" from the railroad station to a hotel where "her money $2.00 . . . her satchel and her bag were taken from her." The Travelers' Aid Society of Chicago, the Immigrants' Protective League of Chicago, the National League for the Protection of Colored Women, and other similar organizations were founded specifically to protect the female migrant from those who marked her as their prey.

Criminals may well have cheated and robbed naive male migrants just as often as they cheated and robbed naive female migrants. Criminals, panderers, and mashers, however, chose women newcomers as their primary targets for sexual exploitation. Women newcomers who trusted strangers were vulnerable to sexual crimes such as rape. In one such case, a migrant, in search of a hotel room, accepted the help of a man she met outside the Dearborn Street railway station. He took her to a nearby hotel "where she was outraged and detained for weeks." Other women newcomers encountered procurers who attempted to entice them with offers of high pay for work in brothels. More often perhaps, migrants encountered city slickers who simply hoped to seduce them. The annual reports of the Travelers' Aid Society of Chicago include numerous such cases.

The woman migrant who made her way safely through the depot often faced other obstacles when she searched for housing. In many neighborhoods—immigrant, black, and native-born white—landladies expressed clear preference for male boarders and lodgers whom they considered less demanding. They complained that female lodgers were too fussy, that they used the bathroom too often, and that they broke house rules that prohibited cooking and laundering in the rooms. In addition, landladies and neighbors sometimes suspected lone women of what they considered immoral sexual behavior. Recalling her youth in Chicago, one wage-earning woman who lived in her parents' home said, "If a girl didn't live at home, we thought she was bad." In contrast, men who lived on their own usually found their independent status accepted without suspicion.

Women migrants may also have had greater difficulty finding work than male migrants because employers sometimes discriminated against lone women in hiring. Like landladies and neighbors, some employers suspected the working woman who lived away from family of immoral behavior. Others knew that the wages they paid did not suffice for independent living. In 1894, Edward Hillman of the Boston Store, an employer of about 1,900 women in Chicago, said, "A girl who boards out cannot support herself on a low wage. We have to enforce the rule as to living with the family or with friends to insure the moral character to our employe[e]s." Similarly, in the 1920s, the American Telephone and Telegraph Company had a hiring policy that favored "girls who live at home, who are American, and who are 'respectable.'"

The most important constraint faced by a woman migrant was undoubtedly poverty. In almost all of the jobs an unskilled migrant might obtain, she could expect low, and sometimes below-subsistence, wages. Employers and others assumed that working women lived in families in which working males provided partial support. They conceded readily that they did not expect women workers to live solely on their wages. The wages they paid women workers were intended as supplemental; the wages they paid male workers were intended for self and sometimes family support. A survey of store and factory workers, conducted by the federal government in 1908, found that over half of the self-supporting women in Chicago earned less than eight dollars a week, the widely acknowledged subsistence wage. Nationwide, in 1914, women in twenty-four manufacturing industries earned on average $7.75 per week; in the same industries, men earned on average $13.92.

The poverty, the potential victimization, the stigmatization, and the discrimination in housing and hiring did not produce a class of passive victims. Instead, migrants found and created settings that offered substitutes for family support and companionship. Many women rented rooms in private families where they might be treated as if they were daughters. Some lived in subsidized boarding homes managed by churches or by middle-class women's reform organizations such as the YMCA and the Phyllis Wheatley Home Association. Others shared rooms with roommates and cooperated in other ways with their peers, pooling their resources for rent, food, and entertainment. Still others reentered family life by returning home or marrying as quickly as possible. Living in private families or in organized homes, cooperating with peers, returning home, and marriage were options chosen by male migrants as well as female. Women migrants, however, participated in additional substitutes for family support that were available primarily to women. Two such female options were live-in domestic service and dependence on higher-paid men.

At the turn of the century, probably about half of the lone female migrants to Chicago chose to relinquish their independent status and reenter the family's boundaries as hired household workers. Because the demand often outreached the supply, jobs as live-in servants were readily available to female migrants. The room and board offered to live-in servants appealed to some migrants, especially penniless migrants who needed immediate room and board but could not afford to buy them. In addition, the supposed protection of a family setting attracted women who were afraid of the city. A black woman from New Orleans, for example, tried to arrange a live-in position in Chicago in a "good home with good people" because, she wrote, "its very trying for a good girl to be out in a large city by self among strangers."

Still, as David Katzman has written, the long hours, restricted independence, and personal subservience of domestic work repelled many women. Those women who had other work options avoided domestic service. By 1900, white women, who might find work in offices, stores, and factories, often considered domestic service degrading. And black women, who were excluded from most nonservice occupations, increasingly chose to work as day-working servants rather than live in the homes of their employers. The proportion of wage-earning women in Chicago who worked as live-in servants dropped steadily in the last decades of the nineteenth century and continued to drop in the twentieth.

Another primarily female substitute for family support was dependence on higher-paid men. Although quantitative data are not available, it seems that this option became more widespread or, at least, more visible in the early twentieth-century city. Especially in the furnished-room districts of Chicago, social investigators noted that boarders and lodgers entered unsupervised relationships that offered unmarried women opportunities for male support. At one extreme, women exchanged sexual intercourse for money on a full-time basis. Prostitution, however, was only one of several types of heterosexual relationships that lone female migrants entered with the expectation of financial reward. Other women accepted sexual service jobs that did not require the selling of intercourse. In the new urban commercialized recreation industries, women earned relatively high salaries and tips as chorus girls, masseuses, cabaret dancers, taxi-dancers, and cocktail waitresses.

More women undoubtedly relied less formally on their sexual allure. In the late nineteenth and early twentieth centuries, women depended on men customarily for economic support in marriage. Among autonomous female migrants and other women who lived apart from family, this kind of dependence began to appear outside of marriage in a less permanent, more contractual and partial support. This dependence covered a range of behavior from respectable dating to cynical gold digging to "occasional prostitution." Higher-paid men paid for entertainment, luxuries, gifts, and sometimes necessities. Women, in return, gave limited sexual favors, perhaps charming companionship, a good-night kiss, heavy petting, or maybe sexual intercourse.

At its simplest, a self-supporting woman who could not afford to pay for her own amusements could accept a date with a man who, by convention, paid for the evening's entertainment. A federal report on self-supporting women, published in 1910, stated:

> Even if most of the girls do not spend money for amusements, it is no proof that they go without them. Many of the girls have "gentlemen friends" who

take them out. "Sure I go out all the time, but it doesn't cost me anything; my gentleman friend takes me," was the type of remark heard again and again.

The report went further. It suggested that women who wore attractive clothing could meet men on the streets who would pay for their entertainment:

The majority, even if they have no money to spend or no one to take them out, as long as they have clothes that are presentable, can have some entertainment. They can "take a walk" on the street, go into the free dance halls, where they meet men who will treat them to the entertainment the place affords. . . . Or they will take a car to some amusement park where they often make acquaintances who take them the rounds of the resort.

As this report indicates, commercialized recreation industries promoted this kind of dependence. The new movies, restaurants, cabarets, dance halls, and amusement parks catered to a sexually integrated leisure-time subculture in which men paid for the entertainment, food, and drink of women.

Women were aware of the economics of dating. A waitress said: "If I did not have a man, I could not get along on my wages." A saleswoman in a department store explained why she powdered her face: "I might get invited out to supper and save twenty cents." And a chambermaid in a hotel said: "If the girls are good and refuse invitations to go out, they simply have no pleasure."

This dependence of women on men did not always end with entertainment and meals in restaurants. Some women, like Theodore Dreiser's fictional Sister Carrie, also depended on men for money, clothes, or housing. Some of these women worked in stores, offices, factories, and restaurants during the day and sold their sexual services on occasional nights for extra money. For example, a nineteen-year-old migrant from Indiana worked in a restaurant and lodged in a rooming house on Michigan Avenue. A vice report stated: "Is not a regular prostitute, goes out with men for presents or money. Is poorly paid at restaurant." Other women, "kept" women, moved into homes with the men who supported them, living out of wedlock as if they were married.

These economic relationships sometimes led to devious and dishonest behavior by men and women both. Some men tried to get sexual favors from low-income women by bribing them or hounding them with false promises of material comforts. And some women in turn tried to sucker men into giving them gifts and money. These women were known in stereotype as "gold diggers." One streetwise gold digger described her attitude toward men: "What I earn is mine. And what they have is mine, too, if I am smart enough to get it. . . . I'll show you how to take their socks away."

In the mid-1920s, a sixteen-year-old migrant from Wisconsin, Alma, gave an especially detailed account of one of her gold-digging scams. "The first impression a girl has to make," she said, "is that she is a good girl under hard circumstances." When a man asked her for a date, Alma would first have him pay the wages she would earn if she stayed at the dance hall where she worked: "When he ask[s] how much that is, I make it seven or eight dollars rather than four dollars which it usually is." She would let her date treat her to a meal in a nice cafe or restaurant. Then she might excuse herself for a moment and leave through the back door. Or she might telephone an older woman friend "to come right down to where I am, to walk in and claim me as her niece and to threaten to make a scene." Alma and her friend would leave together; the friend would get half of the "rake-off." Most likely, only a few women engaged in such elaborate and conscious gold digging.

The autonomous female migrant, however, was probably more likely to enter some form of informal dependent relationship than was the woman who lived with family. A lone migrant often lacked the funds for comfortable self-support, and she also often lacked the cushion that family might provide in times of unemployment. Equally important, the woman who lived apart from family escaped the watchful eyes of parental authorities.

Not surprisingly, the possibility of dependence on men outside of marriage disturbed middle-class observers. In the late nineteenth century, the more conservative writers simply vilified women who lived outside of families. In their view, if a female migrant, an orphan, or any woman without kin nearby avoided her proper place as a live-in servant, she was likely a promiscuous gad-about who refused her womanly calling. One particularly vehement observer wrote in response to an expose of Chicago sweatshops in 1888:

> But let me ask who is to blame if they work for two to four dollars per week, which every rational mind knows will not support them? But have we not seen these very girls in their finery and gay toggery on Saturday nights in the streets and on Sundays at the parks better dressed than many virtuous wives and daughters? Your sympathies are misplaced. . . . Today there are thousands of families in this county who would gladly employ these girls as domestics in their homes at two, three, or four dollars per week and board. But these would-be ladies of pants and shirt manufactories prefer this life to home comforts and home influences of good, respectable people. I argue these "poor girls" are themselves to blame if they seek the filth of life instead of the purity of it.

Most writers were more sympathetic. They worried about the chastity of female migrants and sought to protect them in surrogate families. The label "woman adrift" captures this image. A woman without family nearby was thought to be drifting helplessly, buffeted hither and yon by forces beyond her control, specifically buffeted by the ruthless economic competition in the city and by the predatory urban men who skulked in railroad stations, parks, and other public places. One especially effusive writer used the "adrift" metaphor as follows: "There are thousands of homeless women . . . who are like flotsam and jetsam on the ocean of life. They have been cast onto the sea of misfortune and are like shipwrecked beings not knowing how to save themselves." Using a different metaphor, another writer drew a more dismal picture: "Whether foreign born or native the girls all come to the city seeking fame or fortune, burning with high hope and filled with great resolves, but the remorseless city takes them, grinds them, crushes them, and at last deposits them in unknown graves." In the view of these reformers, the family, the haven of love, had failed to protect its daughters, and the cruel city threatened to ruin them. The "woman adrift" symbolized the victimization of the innocent and weak in an urban world without moral standards.

Whether they vilified the migrant or sympathized with her, the concern of these writers demonstrates that contemporaries distinguished the female migrant from her male counterpart. In the late nineteenth and early twentieth centuries, observers rarely focused so keenly on the experience and behavior of male migrants to Chicago.

This preliminary investigation focuses on the more obvious ways in which autonomous female migration to cities in the late nineteenth and early twentieth centuries differed from male migration. A lengthier study would undoubtedly reveal ethnic and racial differences among female migrants. A black laundress, a Polish peasant, and a native-born white typist would all come to the city, of course, with different expectations and would certainly have diverse urban experiences. This study emphasizes those features of female migration that cut across these ethnic and racial barriers.

The women who came alone to Chicago sometimes had distinctly "female" reasons for leaving home. Once in the city, they encountered certain obstacles that male migrants rarely encountered, and some of them found substitutes for family support on avenues open only to women. The female labor market (including the often-neglected sexual service sector), the sexual double standard, women's roles in the traditional family economy, and women's emerging roles in an expanding consumer society influenced women's motives for migration, the constraints they faced as migrants, and the responses they forged in the urban environment. Although they moved beyond the walls of the home, the women migrants to Chicago in the late nineteenth and early twentieth centuries did not escape the institutions and ideologies that shaped American womanhood.

Interior Space: The Dumbbell Tenement

By the 1880s, immigrants to New York and other big cities often found themselves living in "dumbbell" tenements, so called because of their shape. Because it was designed as an improvement on existing structures, the dumbbell was, ironically, labeled a "reform." Perhaps it was, but it also had serious deficiencies. Placed side by side, as was the intention, two dumbbells created an airshaft less than five feet wide between the buildings.

The dumbbell generally housed four families to a floor, with two families living in the four-room apartments (to the left in the diagram) and two in the three-room apartments (to the right). Many families also took in boarders or used the premises to produce goods. The most spacious room, the front parlor, was only 10½ feet × 11 feet; bedrooms were 8½ feet × 7 feet. The cooking apparently was done in what is labeled the "living room." Everyone on the floor shared the bathrooms, marked here with "w.c." (water closet).

From the floor plan reproduced here, imagine what it would have been like to live in a dumbbell tenement. What kinds of experiences would life in such a building promote? And what activities would it inhibit? Speculate on why the building was designed so that the bedrooms in the apartments on the left could be entered from both the living room and the public hallway.

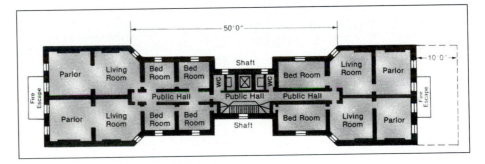

A Typical Dumbbell Tenement.

@ ON THE WEB — *For a virtual tour of the tenements of Manhattan's Lower East Side in the late nineteenth century, see* http://www.tenement.org/index_virtual.html.

The Refined City: A Photo Essay

By virtue of their size and the new relationships they imposed on their inhabitants, American cities of the late nineteenth century required their residents to live and to communicate in ways unknown just a few decades before. Many of the adjustments that people made—and the institutions they created to facilitate those adjustments—involved attempts to reduce racial, ethnic, or class contact where it was felt to be excessive or inappropriate. Which of the following photographs illustrates this kind of effort? This group of illustrations also includes several that might best be understood as mythic images—images that tell us more about what the photographer or illustrator desired or believed than about any existing "reality." Which ones fall in this category, and what does each tell us about how nineteenth-century Americans understood the city?

Central Park, the Drive, Currier & Ives, 1862. Library of Congress.

World's Columbian Exposition, Chicago, 1893. Library of Congress.

Frederick C. Robie House, Chicago, Designed by Frank Lloyd Wright.
Library of Congress.

Delmonico's, New York City, 1903. Library of Congress.

The Threatening City: A Photo Essay

The four images in this grouping are also about big city life—three from New York City, one from Washington, D.C.—but they depict the urban experience very differently. Two of the photographs are almost identical. How do they differ? Why is the first of the two famous, and the second seldom seen?

Turn-of-the-century urban reformers were determined to get rid of the blight and danger that they said characterized the alleys of Washington and other cities. Does the Lewis Hine photograph of "Purdy's Court" support their perspective?

In general, how do you account for the contrasting views of city life presented in the two photo essays?

Bandit's Roost, 39½ Mulberry Street, New York City, c. 1887. Photograph by Richard Hoe Lawrence (previously attributed to Jacob A. Riis). The Jacob A. Riis Collection, Museum of the City of New York.

Bandit's Roost, 39½ Mulberry Street, New York City, c. 1887. Photograph by Richard Hoe Lawrence (previously attributed to Jacob A. Riis). The Jacob A. Riis Collection, Museum of the City of New York.

A Thompson Street Black and Tan Dive on the Lower East Side of New York City, 1887. Photograph by Richard Hoe Lawrence (previously attributed to Jacob A. Riis). Museum of the City of New York.

The photographs of Richard Hoe Lawrence and Jacob Riis are discussed and analyzed at http://historymatters.gmu.edu/mse/Photos/question1.html *and* http://xroads.virginia.edu/~MA01/Davis/photography/riis/riisanalysis.html.

Lewis Hine, "Purdy's Court, near the Capitol," Washington, D.C., 1908. International Museum of Photography at George Eastman House, Rochester, New York.

The Perils of Unrestricted Migration (1894)

Rena M. Atchison

Rena M. Atchison's critique of immigration anticipated by more than a decade the massive influx of "new" immigrants that reshaped the nation early in the next century. In 1894, when her book was published, about 100,000 immigrants from southern and eastern Europe entered the country; in 1907, the number was nearly 1 million.

Even so, the alarm she expressed was widely shared. What was the source of her concern? Which of her arguments now seem dated, and which would have some appeal today, as the nation grapples with the latest influx of immigrants, this one from Latin America and Asia? What key assumption did Atchison use to ground her argument?

VOICES

The Anglo-Saxon believes himself to be the child of destiny. In the American republic he has carried to their logical conclusion the great principles of Magna Carta. The genius of the political and religious reformations which made the land of King John and Cromwell the home of civil liberty and social progress in the Old World has been the molding power in our social and political institutions for two centuries. Within that short period the Anglo-Saxon has set two of the great landmarks of history—the emancipation of the subject—the emancipation of the slave. Word went on the wings of the wind that henceforth there was to be a land where there would be neither bond nor free, where men could worship God in the freedom of their own conscience, where all men should be free, their freedom limited only by that of their fellowmen.

Men who had been scourged with whip and thong from the gates of the Old World's cities and the boundaries of empires by blasphemous superstition; men oppressed by an industrial serfdom more brutalizing than feudal vassalage; adventurers restlessly seeking danger or gold; political iconoclasts seeing only the defects of government and who, like some critics, would tear down a Parthenon because its proportions are not perfect; Jew and gentile, pagan and Christian turned their eyes longingly and covetously to the New El Dorado which seemed to have sprung like some fabled Atlantis from the Western deep.

The great westward tide of immigration brought us for a century, and for the most part as late as 1860, the best muscle and brain of Europe. It came mostly from the great middle class of Europe, representing its best artisanship and its most progressive thought, and it readily assimilated with American

From Rena M. Atchison, *Un-American Immigration: Its Present Effects and Future Perils,* Chicago: C. H. Kerr, 1894, pp. 141–148.

institutions. Since 1860 there has been a constant, and especially during the last twelve years, a rapid deterioration in the character of this immigration, until at the present time the great mass of immigrants are not only totally illiterate but have to be classed as unskilled laborers, or without occupation.

The largest percentage of increase of foreign-born for the present decade (1880–1890) is for persons in Hungary, 441.69 percent; in Russia, 411.29 percent; in Italy, 312.80 percent; in Austria, 218.83; and in Poland, 203 percent.

The increase in number of foreign-born from 1880 to 1890 was 2,569,604, more than twice the number of increase from 1870 to 1880, and very nearly twice the number of increase during the two preceding decades. Of this number, 818,152 came from Germany; from Norway, 140,936; from Sweden, 283,704; from Russia, 146,922; Italy, 138,350; while England sent 244,932, and Canada and Newfoundland 26,378. All other countries sent less than 100,000, Poland leading with 98,833, while Ireland sent 16,777.

The total percent of increase of foreign-born for the decade was 38.47 percent. If we remember that the average percent of increase of native-born for a decade is 20 percent, we shall more fully understand the magnitude of the problem before us. The present immigration law seems to have placed no effectual check upon even some of the worst classes of immigration. The number of Italians landing February 1891 was given as 2,000. During February 1892 over 3,000 Italians landed at the port of New York, showing an increase rather than a restriction. . . .

The European immigrant no sooner sets his foot upon our shores than he becomes at once not only an industrial and moral factor but a political one as well. And herein lies the greater danger. And this danger is greatly heightened by the character of this immigration, insuring a possible transference to American soil of the un-American ecclesiastical domination of priest-ridden Europe. The impertinence of an Italian priest and an Italian subject, unable to speak the English language, dictating to several millions of American citizens the manner and means they shall pursue in the education of future American citizens is a sufficient indication that, while we have struck the fetters from the limbs of 4 million slaves, we have still within our boundaries a far more dangerous form of slavery, the enslavement of at least 10 million of our citizens bound by religious fealty to obey the dictates of an extraneous power on that most vital of all questions in a republic—education. And far more dangerous than the treason of Confederate leaders is the short-sightedness or timidity of American statesmen in dealing with so vital a question.

It is not our purpose to outline an immigration law in this work but to show the perils of the present system. Several remedies, however, must have suggested themselves to the reader as possible and just restrictions upon immigration. Any adequate law should embody the following points:

First, such a law should be general and not special. It should admit the worthy and exclude the unfit of all nations. A law which makes an indiscriminate restriction against any people is inherently unjust, irritates and antagonizes the people discriminated against, and is contrary to the spirit of our institutions.

Second, no immigrant should be permitted to land upon our shores who cannot read and write his native language. This restriction alone would cut off the large mass of illiterate immigrants whose presence in our republic is a menace, socially, industrially, and politically.

Third, every immigrant should be compelled to register and to have sufficient money to insure him from becoming a burden to the state for a period of at least six months. The present condition of the labor market and the vast numbers of immigrants who are stranded in New York every year, some becoming a public burden within twenty-four hours after landing at Castle Garden, are sufficient reasons for such restriction.

Fourth, any immigrant who upon registration or afterward shall be found to have been a criminal in any prison or the inmate of any workhouse or almshouse in his native land within a short time previous to his immigration to America should be deported at the expense of the steamship importing him, and the exportation of criminals and paupers to the United States should be made an international offense.

Fifth, every immigrant should be required to declare at the time of landing and registration his intention or nonintention to become a citizen of the United States.

Sixth, no person should be allowed to vote in any state until he has become a naturalized citizen. Not only should the period for naturalization be extended but no person should be allowed to vote who cannot read the constitution of the commonwealth in which he resides and the Constitution of the United States in the English language. Certainly it is not just that we should be compelled to bear the burden of Europe's illiteracy, pauperism, and crime, and an honest intention of citizenship should be the price paid for the industrial and other advantages offered to the immigrant.

If foreign immigration continues at the present rate and such immigration continues to come from middle, southern, and northeastern Europe, in 1900 the Anglo-Saxon and Anglo-Saxon institutions will no longer be the dominant powers in molding American life and legislation. Will the heir to the heroes of Lexington and Concord, Shiloh and Gettysburg be still the victorious leader on the battlefield of new issues? Will the heir to America's Magna Carta, created by the genius of Hamilton and Washington and sealed by the blood of Lincoln, be still the man of destiny—not only preserving in their integrity our free institutions in the spirit and intent of their founders and defenders but also leading a people, absolutely free, toward the solution of the greater issues on the ever widening horizon of progress?

The closing words of Lincoln's memorable speech on the battlefield of Gettysburg contain all the inspiration and philosophy of the future for our republic:

> It is rather for us here to be dedicated to the great task remaining before us—that from these honored dead we take increased devotion to that cause for which they gave the last full measure of devotion; that we here highly resolve that these dead shall not have died in vain; that this nation, under God, shall have a new birth of freedom; and that government of the people, by the people, for the people shall not perish from the earth.

THE BIG PICTURE

Beginning in about 1890, "reformers" of many stripes—urban planners, ministers, politicians, social workers, photographers, and journalists, among others—would engage the American city as a set of "problems" to be solved. We will read about some of their solutions in Chapter 6, when we examine the reform movement known as progressivism. At this point, however, it should be interesting to try to anticipate progressive ideas by using the materials in this chapter to construct a reform "agenda." To do that, imagine what sorts of reforms photographer Richard Hoe Lawrence might have recommended on the basis of the photographs he took, or how middle-class Americans might have responded after looking at those photographs? How could urban planners and architects, or municipal authorities, have responded to the housing problems represented by the "dumbbell" tenement? What kinds of legislation could have been enacted to help Chicago's "autonomous" young women, or to assist cities in dealing with the consequences of their migration? What political solutions might have been employed to alleviate the social impact of what Rena M. Atchison believed was the "wrong" kind of immigration?

Chapter 5

Empire

In the final years of the nineteenth century, Americans suddenly awoke from their preoccupations with domestic life to find themselves with an empire on their hands. In 1895, while very few Americans paid any attention, inhabitants of Cuba, which was still a Spanish colony, staged an unsuccessful revolution—one more in a series of New World revolutions against European rule that had begun in 1776. But this one failed. The Spanish began a ruthless repression of guerrilla resistance, even herding men, women, and children into concentration camps. The American press took up the Cuban cause in shrill editorials and exaggerated reporting. Before anyone— even those in President McKinley's administration—quite knew what was happening, the American battleship *Maine*, calling at Havana, had been mysteriously sunk, perhaps sabotaged. McKinley asked Congress for a resolution permitting "forcible intervention" in Cuba. An American fleet that Secretary of the Navy Theodore Roosevelt had waiting in the Pacific steamed for Manila Bay in the Philippines to attack Spanish warships there. War was on.

The war lasted for only a few weeks, and when it was over, the United States "possessed" the Philippines, Cuba, and Puerto Rico, and was faced with the task of governing its new colonies for a time under military occupation. The British boasted that the sun never set on their empire. Americans could not yet make the same boast, but they could see from a quick look at the map that the sun never set for *long* on American possessions.

This simple story—of being drawn innocently into "a splendid little war," as John Hay called it, and waking up blinkingly to an unanticipated empire—probably is a fairly accurate summary of the way most Americans experienced the events of 1898 and 1899. But the story misses a lot.

It overlooks, to begin with, the fact that the history of the United States could be written as a history of expansion and conquest. Through exploration, purchase, treaty, and war, the United States had become, in the course of the nineteenth century, a vast nation. And all along there had been plans and dreams to expand even further, down into Mexico and the Caribbean. In this way, the Spanish-American War was a logical outcome to a long history.

The Cuban and Philippine occupations should also be seen as early examples of many similar interventions over the next two decades that together helped define the distinctly American version of empire. Carried out with the support of presidents known as reformers and progressives, these ventures added up to a major extension of American influence around the globe. Roosevelt's aid to Panamanian rebels in 1903 made possible American domination of the Canal Zone. Under William Taft, the United States asserted its right to intervene and to supervise the collection of customs receipts in Nicaragua, another nation with a potential canal route. Woodrow Wilson sent American forces into Haiti and the Dominican Republic, and in 1914, seeking to topple the Mexican government, he landed American troops and occupied the coastal city of Veracruz.

But this new expansion occurred in a new atmosphere. The 1890s was a decade of deep economic and social crisis. The depression of 1893 to 1897 was the worst in the nation's history and gave rise to the specter of collapse, as bands of tramps wandered the countryside in numbers large enough to be called "armies." Two of the most violent strikes in American history—one at Homestead, Pennsylvania, in 1892; the second at Pullman, Illinois, in 1894—intensified the sense that the country was at a desperate crossroads. For many, particularly for people like Theodore Roosevelt, the Spanish-American War and the chance to be an imperial power were a welcome relief from the brooding sense of decline and collapse that the decade had engendered.

In addition, whatever its origins, the new empire appeared to many Americans to be an opportunity, both for commercial and military development and for reform. The connection may seem odd in retrospect, but many Americans looked on the chance to govern Cuba or the Philippines as a chance to recover a sense of mission, to bring to "backward" nations government that was honest, efficient, enlightened, and democratic. In the process, such people hoped, the nation might begin to set its own house in order. Indeed, the experience of empire may have contributed as much as populism did to the emergence of the atmosphere of reform that was to give the first decades of the new century their characteristic flavor.

Black Soldiers and the White Man's Burden

Willard B. Gatewood, Jr.

The quick and decisive defeat of the Spanish in the Philippines did not end conflict on the islands. Led by Emilio Aguinaldo, Filipino nationalists for several years resisted American domination using guerrilla tactics not unlike those employed against another American army by Vietnamese nationalists in the 1960s.

The following selection, by Willard B. Gatewood, Jr., touches on the character of this guerrilla war and the problems it posed for American soldiers. But Gatewood's primary interest is in the Philippines as a site of racial contact and interaction. He chronicles the experiences and feelings of black American combat units, led by white officers, engaging native populations of color and, ironically, taking up the "white man's burden"—and all of this at a time when, back home, whites were legalizing racial segregation and lynching about a hundred blacks each year.

What can be learned about race relations from the experience of these black soldiers in the Philippines? How did the racial contacts brought about by the conflict shape the beliefs of whites, blacks, and Filipinos? What stance did the black troops take toward their role in the imperial process, and how do you explain their outlook?

Black regulars were among the American troops whose service in the Philippines spanned the shift in insurgent strategy from conventional to guerrilla warfare. Arriving in Manila in July and August 1899, Negro soldiers of the Twenty-fourth and Twenty-fifth Infantry immediately took stations around the city from Calacoon to Balic Balic road. By mid-1900 the number of black regulars in the Philippines had increased to 2100 men. In January and February 1900, the Forty-eighth and Forty-ninth Infantry, the two Negro volunteer regiments recruited specifically for service in the islands, disembarked at Manila and remained in the field in Luzon until their enlistment terms expired a year and a half later. Eight troops of the Ninth Cavalry, originally destined for China to help put down the Boxer Rebellion, arrived in mid-September 1900. The Ninth first saw action in southern Luzon in the vicinity of Nueva Caceres and Legaspi, and later participated in operations in Samar and Panay. By December 1900, when the total strength of American forces stood at 70,000 men and officers, there were over 6000 black regulars and volunteers stationed at dozens of small outposts scattered from northern Luzon to Samar.

Willard B. Gatewood, Jr., *Black Americans and the White Man's Burden, 1898–1903*, University of Illinois Press, Urbana, 1975, chapter 10. Used with permission of Willard B. Gatewood, Jr.

During their first weeks in the Philippines the black soldiers became intimately acquainted both with the hazards of a tropical climate and with the deadly tactics of the insurgents. On August 21, 1899, eleven men of the Twenty-fourth Infantry who had started on a reconnaissance mission toward San Mateo drowned when their boat capsized in the Mariquina River, a swift stream swollen by several days of heavy rain. Early in September a party of the Twenty-fourth, on a scouting expedition in the mountains north of Manila, discovered in a valley "a body of Filipinos, drilling on extended order, such as used only in fighting." But upon descending to the site, the soldiers found only "peaceful citizens planting rice"—an occurrence that was to be repeated many times . . . as they pursued their elusive enemy.

Among the numerous engagements in which black regulars participated during the northern offensive, few attracted as much attention as the battle at O'Donnell. The Twenty-fifth, with headquarters at Bamban, learned that a large force of insurgents was encamped fifteen miles away at O'Donnell. Led by a Filipino guide, a detachment of four-hundred black soldiers under the command of Captain H. A. Leonhauser left Bamban on the night of November 17, 1899, headed for O'Donnell on a roundabout route through the foothills of the Zambales Mountains. Arriving at their destination just before sunrise, the troops staged a surprise attack on the insurgent stronghold. Once inside O'Donnell, the colored soldiers "showed a grim and great earnestness in their work of gathering in prisoners, rifles and bolos." One eyewitness reported: "Strong black arms caught fleeing insurgents upon the streets and hauled them from under beds and beneath houses. Native women screamed in alarm and on their knees offered money and food to the American troops." But the soldiers apparently refrained from acts of unnecessary brutality. In fact, a young white officer was deeply impressed by the "humanity and forebearance of the colored men of the 25th Infantry" in their taking of O'Donnell. "There might have been a hundred of these pitiful Filipino warriors killed," he wrote, "but the men apparently couldn't bring themselves to shoot them." Instead, the soldiers were satisfied to capture over one-hundred insurgents and a large supply of weapons, food, and ammunition. . . .

. . . By early 1900 resistance to American rule was almost wholly in the form of guerrilla warfare. Few engagements thereafter deserved to be called battles. But the hit-and-run tactics of Aguinaldo's widely dispersed forces and the marauding bands of robbers (ladrones) proved to be no less deadly to American troops who were constantly on patrol and scouting duty. Black volunteers of the Forty-eighth and Forty-ninth Infantry arrived in the Philippines early in 1900 anxious to confront the insurgents in conventional warfare; they were disappointed to discover that most of their efforts were devoted to "looking for rebel forces which are no where to be found." A Negro lieutenant probably expressed the sentiments of his comrades when on January 31, 1900, he wrote home: "While there is no enemy in sight, yet we are always on the lookout and we have slept in our shoes ever since we landed. The war may be over or it may have just commenced. No one can tell what these devils will do next." . . .

McKinley's victory in November was the signal for General MacArthur* to inaugurate a new policy designed to ensure the establishment of permanent control over the islands. This policy represented a shift from "benevolent pacification" to a more stringent approach, promising punishment for natives who continued to resist American authority and stressing the importance of isolating insurgents from their bases of supply in the villages. It also emphasized the need to protect villagers from intimidation and terror at the hands of insurgents. For the black soldiers, including the Tenth Cavalry, which arrived in May 1901, the new military policy meant not only garrison duty in towns and villages scattered over hundreds of miles across the archipelago, but also an endless succession of expeditions through rice paddies and dense forests and over treacherous mountains and swollen streams. . . .

From early 1901 until their departure from the Philippines more than a year later, the black troops who garrisoned numerous outposts on the islands did more than perform the usual scouting, patrol, and guard duties, and other activities involved in keeping the peace. They also assisted in laying "the foundations of civil government" and generally functioned as agents of the Americanization process. Their civil duties included the supervision of elections, the organization of educational and legal systems, and the maintenance of public health facilities. Lieutenant David J. Gilmer of the Forty-ninth Infantry, a former member of the Third North Carolina Volunteers, not only was popular with enlisted men but also won the affection of the people of Linao as commander of the post there. Gilmer later secured a commission in the Philippine Scouts, an army of natives organized and officered by Americans. Captain Frank R. Steward, also of the Forty-ninth, who was a graduate of the Harvard Law School, served as provost judge in San Pablo; there he organized and presided over the first American-type court. His father, Chaplain Theophilus Steward of the Twenty-fifth Infantry, supervised a series of schools taught by soldiers in the towns and villages north of Manila under the protection of his regiment. According to one observer, the chaplain's command of the Spanish language and capacity for hard work enabled him to achieve excellent results and to instill in Filipinos an appreciation for American values. Black soldiers often displayed considerable pride in their nonmilitary activities, which they described as significant contributions to the improvement of life among the natives. An enlisted man in the Twenty-fifth Infantry boasted in 1902 that "the colored American soldier has taught the Filipino thrift, economy and above all the customs of polite society." . . .

. . . No less than whites, blacks suffered from the boredom endemic to existence in remote outposts. Their diversions sometimes included activities considerably less wholesome than fishing, swimming, playing baseball, or participating in choral groups. Gambling and overindulgence in various alcoholic concoctions constituted the chief diversions of some soldiers, and drinking gamblers had a tendency to spawn fights. Black soldiers on leave in Manila sometimes became involved in disturbances in the tenderloin districts, especially in houses of prostitution that attempted to establish a color line.

*General Arthur MacArthur, military commander in the Philippines.

For many soldiers, black and white, female companionship offered the best respite from a monotonous existence. It was common practice for a Negro soldier to acquire a "squaw." Richard Johnson of the Forty-eighth Infantry claimed that the "first to acquire a querida' or lover (kept woman) was our captain and this set the pattern for all the men." Perhaps, as Archibald Cary Coolidge later wrote, "their pursuits of the native women provoked much anger among the [Filipino] men." But whether such activity gave "rise to fresh insurrection in districts which had been called pacified," as Coolidge claimed, is open to question. Some black soldiers, especially those who planned to remain permanently in the Philippines at the termination of their military service, married Filipino women and settled in various parts of Luzon. For most soldiers, however, these relationships ended when they sailed for the United States in 1902. An enlisted man of the Twenty-fifth observed that in view of the number of deluded women who crowded the pier as soldiers shipped out for home, it was altogether appropriate for the band to play "The Girl I Left Behind."

Whatever the consequences of their relations with native women, black soldiers generally appear to have treated Filipinos with respect and compassion. Throughout the war, and especially after the army adopted a harsher policy toward insurgents, reports of atrocities circulated widely in the United States. Few prompted as much indignation as those regarding the use of the so-called water cure as "a persuader . . . to induce bad hombres to talk." Some Americans maintained that troops in the Philippines engaged in brutalities that surpassed anything committed by "Butcher" Weyler in Cuba. In May 1900, black newspapers in the United States published a letter from a Negro soldier who expressed horror at the looting, stealing, desecration of churches, and daily indignities against Filipinos committed by his white comrades. Even some high-ranking military officers protested against the severity of the war. The charges of unwarranted brutality achieved even greater credence late in 1901 when General Jacob Smith, in retaliation against the insurgents for their massacre of a contingent of American troops in Samar, ordered his army to turn the island into "a howling wilderness" and to kill every human being over the age of ten.

Although one writer asserted in 1904 that "the brutal conduct" of black soldiers "in the interior seriously jeopardized the hope of a peaceful solution" to the Philippine insurrection, the weight of testimony in regard to their treatment of natives contradicts this observation. Oswald Garrison Villard* maintained that "neither the officers nor the men of any colored regiment" figured in "the charges and counter-charges arising out of the use of the water torture, except one man who at the time of his offense was not with his regiment." There were, of course, other exceptions of which Villard was undoubtedly ignorant. For example, Lieutenant Samuel Lyons of the Twenty-fifth confided in a letter to his wife that he and his men had on occasion administered the water cure to recalcitrant insurgents. Nevertheless,

*The liberal, pacifist editor of the New York Evening Post.

it does appear that the black regiments used this particular form of torture far less frequently than some of the white outfits.

The Ninth Cavalry developed its own method for extracting information from captured insurgents. In describing it one authority wrote: "A native . . . was taken into a semi-dark room and securely bound. Then a huge black, dressed only in a loin cloth and carrying a cavalry sabre, entered and danced around the victim making threatening gesticulations with the sabre. To an ignorant Filipino he undoubtedly looked like a devil incarnate." The method proved amazingly successful as a persuader; whatever its psychological consequences, it was obviously preferable to the physical torture inflicted by the water cure.

By the time the black troops departed from the Philippines, it was generally agreed that their relationships with natives were more cordial than those of white soldiers. When the Negro soldiers first arrived in the islands, Filipinos viewed them with awe and fear as an "American species of bête noir." A typical reaction was: "These are not Americans; they are Negritoes." But their fear quickly turned into friendliness and their awe into admiration. Filipinos came to accept black Americans as "very much like ourselves only larger" and gave them the affectionate appellation, "Negritos Americanos." Negro soldiers generally reciprocated the good will of peaceful natives and treated them with consideration and respect. In letters home they often referred to the contempt that white soldiers displayed toward all Filipinos and insisted that such an attitude underlay much of the natives' hostility to American rule. Military authorities, quick to recognize the rapport between black soldiers and natives, generally agreed that in towns and districts "garrisoned by colored troops the natives seem to harbor little or no enmity toward the soldiers and the soldiers themselves seem contented with their lot and are not perpetually pining for home." In 1902 Colonel [Andrew S.] Burt could "not recall of the many places where the 25th Infantry has been stationed on these Islands that the inhabitants were not genuinely sorry when they have been ordered to leave their towns." General Robert P. Hughes fully agreed, noting that black soldiers "mixed with the natives at once" and "whenever they came together, they became great friends." Hughes recalled that when he withdrew "a darkey company" from Santa Rita, the residents wept and begged him to allow the black soldiers to remain.

Not all white Americans in the Philippines were so favorably disposed toward black soldiers and their friendly relations with Filipinos. "While the white soldiers, unfortunately, got on badly with the natives," the correspondent Stephen Bonsal reported, "the black soldiers got on much too well." Some white officers came to suspect that Negro troops had more sympathy for the Filipinos' aspirations for independence than for American policy regarding the islands. Others complained that the racial identity that black soldiers established with the natives had resulted in a color line that discriminated against whites. Governor Taft* apparently shared some of these

*Governor of the Philippines and future president, William Taft.

concerns. He felt that black troops "got along fairly well with the natives . . . too well with the native women"; the result was "a good deal of demoralization in the towns where they have been stationed." Taft was credited with engineering the withdrawal of Negro troops from the islands in 1902 "out of their regular turn."

Whatever the reaction of white soldiers to the rapport between their black comrades and the Filipinos, their overt expressions of racial prejudice toward both only strengthened that relationship. Writing about American forces in the Philippines early in 1900, Frederick Palmer maintained that color was a crucial factor and that if a man was nonwhite, "we include him in a general class called 'nigger,' a class beneath our notice, to which, so far as our white soldier is concerned, all Filipinos belonged." Another correspondent, Albert Gardiner Robinson, reported from Manila that "the spirit of our men is far too much one of contempt for the dark-skinned people of the tropics." White soldiers "almost without exception" referred to the natives as "niggers," and, as Major Cornelius Gardner of the Thirtieth Infantry observed, "the natives are beginning to understand what the word 'nigger' means." In 1899 both the *Manila Times* and the *Army and Navy Journal* became so concerned about the mischief done by the widespread use of the term in referring to black soldiers and Filipinos that they called upon Americans to banish it from their vocabulary. For quite a different reason white southerners in the islands also objected to calling Filipinos "niggers"— a term that they reserved for Negro Americans, soldiers as well as civilians. James H. Blount of Georgia, an officer in the Twenty-ninth Infantry who remained in the Philippines as a civil judge, claimed that southerners "instinctively resented any suggestion comparing Filipinos and negroes," because such comparison implied that their social intercourse with natives was "equivalent to eating, drinking, dancing and chumming with negroes"— things that no self-respecting white man would do.

Black soldiers were keenly aware of the racial attitudes of their white comrades toward all colored people, themselves as well as Filipinos. The men of the Twenty-fifth Infantry had scarcely landed in the islands in 1899 when, as they marched into Manila, a white spectator yelled: "What are you coons doing here?" The sentiment implicit in the question found expression in the establishment of "white only" restaurants, hotels, barber shops, and even brothels, and in tunes such as "I Don't Like a Nigger Nohow" sung by white soldiers. In mid-1900 a Negro regular observed that "already there is nowhere in Manila you can hardly [sic] get accommodated and you are welcomed nowhere." The color line being drawn against the black soldier in the Philippines was, in his opinion, "enough to make a colored man hate the flag of the United States." Patrick Mason of the Twenty-fourth Infantry wrote home not long before he was killed in combat: "The first thing in the morning is the 'Nigger' and the last thing at night is the 'Nigger.'" Such talk, according to Mason, was prompted by the assumption of white soldiers that no one except Caucasians had "any rights or privileges." Late in 1899 a black infantryman on duty near San Isidro wrote: "The whites have begun to establish their diabolical race hatred in all its home rancor . . . even endeavoring to propagate the phobia among the Spaniards and Filipinos so as to be sure of the foundation of their supremacy when the civil rule . . . is established." White officers often expressed admiration for the light-hearted, cheerful mood with which black soldiers undertook even the most difficult assignments, but few indicated an awareness of their deep resentment of the insults and discrimination to which they were regularly subjected.

A major source of black soldiers' grievances was the racial prejudice displayed by some of their white officers. While in the Philippines, the officer personnel of the four Negro regiments of the regular army changed frequently; according to black enlisted men and noncommissioned officers, the replacements too often included whites who, protected by their rank, gave full vent to their animosities against people of color. Though always generous in their praise of white officers whom they considered fair-minded, black soldiers complained bitterly about their treatment at the hands of those with a prejudice against Negroes. Specifically, they charged such officers with cursing and abusing enlisted men and with subjecting them to inhuman treatment for even minor infractions of military regulations. In a few instances the grievances found their way to the War Department; but as a member of the Twenty-fifth who filed a complaint correctly predicted, "an abnegation will confront this statement as has been the case heretofore."

The color prejudice manifested by white Americans in the Philippines substantially affected the black soldiers' view of the Filipino. The soldiers early classified the natives as colored people and looked upon themselves as part of an experiment pitting "Greek against Greek." Although some white Americans claimed that Filipinos deeply resented the presence of black troops because they regarded themselves "as belonging to a race superior to the African," such a view was contradicted by the testimony of black soldiers who almost without exception noted how the affinity of complexion between themselves and the natives provided the basis for mutual respect and good will. After a series of interviews with well-educated Filipinos, a black infantryman reported that although natives had been told of the "brutal natures" of black Americans and had at first feared for the safety of their senoritas, personal experience had demonstrated that Negro soldiers were "much more kindly and manly in dealing with us" than [were] whites.

Black soldiers might refer to Filipino insurgents as "gugus," a term used by white Americans usually to identify hostile natives, but they obviously did not join white soldiers in applying the more general term "nigger" to all Filipinos. Nor did they "kick and cuff" natives at will. According to one Filipino, the black soldier differed from his white comrade in one principal respect: he did not "connect race hatred with duty." Eugene R. Whitted of the Twenty-fifth Infantry agreed that the Negro soldier's lack of racial animosity toward colored people gave him an advantage over whites in dealing with the Filipinos. "Our men met treatment with like treatment," he declared, "and when they were in the field they were soldiers and when in town gentlemen." Despite breaches in the gentleman's code, Negro troops appear, as one Negro regular put it, to have gotten "along well with everybody but American [white] people."

Although color was important in determining the attitude of black soldiers toward Filipinos, it was not the only consideration. Some soldiers early detected a similarity between the predicament of the black man in the United States and the brown man in the Philippines: both were subjects of oppression. For such soldiers the struggle of colored Filipinos against their white oppressors had obvious ideological as well as racial implications. In view of the plight of colored citizens in the United States, it was not surprising that some black soldiers expressed doubts as to whether Filipinos under American rule would "be justly dealt by." Private William R. Fulbright of the Twenty-fifth described the war against the Filipinos as "a gigantic scheme of robbery and oppression." Writing from a military station on Luzon on Christmas Eve, 1900, a Tuskegee alumnus confided to Booker T. Washington that "these people are right and *we* are wrong and terribly wrong." The black soldier assured Washington that he would not re-enlist because no man "who has any humanity about him at all" would desire "to fight against such a cause as this." Another Negro infantryman who believed that the Filipinos had "a just grievance" maintained that the insurrection would never "have occurred if the army of occupation . . . [had] treated them as people." But the occupation forces, he declared, attempted to apply to the Filipinos the "home treatment for colored people," which they would not tolerate.

Few black soldiers were so forthright in expressing doubts about the wisdom and correctness of the American position in the Philippines. More typical was a statement by Sergeant M. W. Saddler: "Whether it is right to reduce these people to submission is not a question for the soldier to decide." Like others, Saddler preferred to emphasize the resolve with which Negro troops in the Philippines performed their duty in order to "add another star to the already brilliant crown of the Afro-American soldier." Captain W. H. Jackson of the Forty-ninth acknowledged that the soldiers of his regiment identified racially with the natives, but he insisted that, as members of the American army, black men took the position that "all enemies of the U.S. government look alike to us, hence we go along with the killing."

Despite such explanations, the correspondence of Negro soldiers revealed that they were continually plagued by misgivings about their role in the Philippines. For black regular William Simms of Muncie, Indiana, such misgivings were forcefully driven home by a Filipino boy who asked him: "Why does the American Negro come from America to fight us when we are much a friend to him and have not done anything to him [?] He is all the same as me and me all the same as you. Why don't you fight those people in America who burn Negroes, that make a beast of you . . . ?" For introspective and thoughtful soldiers like Simms, their racial and ideological sympathy for a colored people struggling to achieve freedom seemed always to be at war with their notions of duty as American citizens and their hope that the fulfillment of that duty would somehow ameliorate the plight of their people at home. As Sergeant John W. Galloway indicated, "the black men here are so much between the 'Devil and the deep sea' on the Philippine Question." But even those without such qualms who believed that the soldier's oath knew "neither race, color, nor nation" were troubled by the increasing hostility of black Americans at home toward the war in the Philippines. Negro soldiers, according to one infantryman, were "rather discouraged over the fact that the sacrifice of life and health has to be made for a cause so unpopular among our people."

Anti-imperialists in the United States were quick to detect the irony involved in the use of black troops to suppress the Filipino insurrection. A succession of poets, novelists, humorists, and journalists attacked the racist notions implicit in the doctrine of the white man's burden and pointed up the disparities between the rhetoric and realities of "benevolent assimilation." George Ade and Finley Peter Dunne called attention to the incongruities in the nation's use of black troops to shoulder the "white man's burden" in the Philippines where they, as representatives of an unassimilated segment of the American population, were supposed to bring about the "benevolent assimilation" of the Filipino. According to Dunne's Mr. Dooley, the government's policy in the Philippines was to "Take up th' white man's burden an' hand it to th' coons." Having succeeded to the presidency in September 1901, upon McKinley's assassination, Theodore Roosevelt admitted that Dunne's "delicious phrase about 'take up the white man's burden and put it on the coons' exactly hit off the weak spot" in his expansionist theory. But Roosevelt assured Dunne that he was not willing "to give up the theory yet."

No less aware of the "weak spot" were the Filipino insurgents, who were also thoroughly familiar with the plight of Negroes in the United States and with the widespread anti-imperialist sentiment within the black community. Cognizant of the ambivalent attitude of the black troops who found themselves combatting an independence movement by another people of color, insurgent propagandists directed special appeals "To the Colored American Soldier." Here is one such proclamation signed by Aguinaldo and addressed to the Twenty-fourth Infantry during its operations in 1899 in the vicinity of Mabalacat:

> It is without honor that you are spilling your costly blood. Your masters have thrown you into the most iniquitous fight with double purpose—to make you the instrument of their ambition and also your hard work will soon make the extinction of your race. Your friends, the Filipinos, give you this good warning. You must consider your situation and your history, and take charge that the blood . . . of Sam Hose proclaims vengeance.

Such appeals were sources of embarrassment for the vast majority of black soldiers, who protested that they were "just as loyal to the old flag as white Americans." Nevertheless, the insurgents' propaganda was not altogether barren of results, and a few black soldiers actually joined the rebel ranks. . . .

Despite the publicity that a dozen or so Negro deserters attracted, the overwhelming majority of black soldiers in the Philippines ignored the blandishments of the insurgents and hoped that their service would result in rewards commensurate with their record. The Negro regular still believed that he was entitled to "a commission from the ranks." During the congressional consideration of the Army Reorganization Bill, which passed in February,

1901, the black press in the United States pleaded not only for an increase in the number of Negro regiments in the regular army, but also for the appointment of black officers. Their efforts were unsuccessful in both respects. . . .

Despite such discrimination, black soldiers throughout their service in the islands reported favorably on opportunities for enterprising black Americans. They described the soil and climate as conducive to productive agriculture and particularly emphasized the openings awaiting the Negro in business. F. H. Crumbley of the Forty-ninth Infantry urged black Americans "of Christian education" who desired to labor "among an appreciative people" to migrate to the Philippines at once. "They should not wait till the field is covered by others," he advised, "but should come in the front ranks and assist in developing these people." Sharing Crumbley's enthusiasm, a black enlisted man of the Twenty-fourth wrote home: "I shall say to all industrious and energetic colored Americans . . . that they cannot do anything more beneficial to themselves than to come over here while the country is still in its infancy and help . . . reap the harvest which we shall soon begin to gather in. In this country will be many fortunes made." The soldiers believed that the friendly relations that they had established with the Filipinos would operate to the advantage of Negro Americans who sought their fortunes in the islands.

On July 2, 1902, President Roosevelt issued a proclamation that, in effect, announced the end of the Filipino Insurrection. Even before his announcement American troops had begun to depart from the Philippines; beginning in May, the first black troops had shipped out of Manila for San Francisco. By mid-autumn all Negro soldiers, except those who chose to be mustered out in the Philippines, had taken stations in the United States. Most of those taking up residence in the islands secured jobs in hotels and restaurants in Manila or appointments as clerks in the civil government. In addition, there were "several school teachers, one lawyer and one doctor of medicine." One black American to remain in Manila when his regiment left in 1902 was T. N. McKinney of Texas, who first served on the city's police force and later as a minor civil servant. Ultimately McKinney acquired considerable wealth as the proprietor of the Manila Commission House Company; he became the recognized leader of the "colored colony in the capital city." Late in 1902 a black veteran of the Philippine campaign stationed at Fort Assiniboine, Montana, made public his views on the emigration of Negro Americans to the islands. Despite the fact that racial prejudice had "kept close in the wake of the flag" and was "keenly felt in that far-off land of eternal sunshine and roses," he was nonetheless convinced that the islands offered "our people the best opportunities of the century."

Combat: An Officer's Account

William Connor

In the spring of 1899, Lt. William Connor wrote the following letter to Lt. Frederick Sladen, describing his experiences in a series of engagements that took place in and around Pasig, Malolos, and other locations within fifty miles of Manila on the island of Luzon. What attitude does Connor take toward the Filipino enemy? Toward combat? What can the account tell us about why Americans went to war in the Philippines and, more broadly, about why the nation became an imperial power?

VOICES

[April 1, 1899]

. . . On Thursday reconnaissances were made in all directions to locate the enemy who had fled precipitately on Wednesday. This developed quite an engagement at Cainta when a Batallion of the 20th routed nearly 1000 natives behind entrenchments with a swamp in front. They then retired to Pasig, the natives burning the town before retiring. Every one who could walk had left Pasig during the bombardment and from the looks of several buildings I fancy they did so wisely. On one bell in the church belfry I counted fourteen bullet marks and four of them had passed through the metal. . . .

On Saturday night some of the Insurgents crept up and attacked a Company of the Washingtons and the outposts of the 22nd Infantry. We lost pretty heavily for a small engagement and the General was mad all through. We chased the Indians that night until 9, bivouacking for the night and all the next day followed them down the shore as far as San Pedro Tuason. (I hope you have a map of the country.) It was a running fight all the way, the Indian loss was heavy and they were going too rapidly to carry off their dead or wounded.

At the end of the week I simply had to come back to Manila and catch up in [sic] the office work (which needed it) so left the brigade and the last part of its operations.

I had burned my face to a blister and that, with a scrubby beard I looked more like a highway ruffian than a U.S. Officer.

Lt. William Connor to Lt. Frederick Sladen, April 1, 1899, Personal Correspondence, Sladen Family Papers (Box 5), Archives, U.S. Military History Institute, Carlisle Barracks, Pennsylvania.

I was in town just a week when I received a telegram from Gen. Wheaton asking if I could accompany him as A.D.C. [aide de camp] on the campaign to be made against Malolos. . . .

Oregon was meantime advancing toward Polo on the left and we could hear the rest of the Division firing on our right. As soon as line[s] could be formed the Indians opened fire and I took orders to General Egbert, 22nd Inft. to advance and take the trenches at the top of the hill. Those were the last orders the little General ever got. I saw him 15 minutes later shot through and through. He died before he got to the dressing station. He recovered from a wound received in the Wilderness in the Civil war, was shot through the lungs in Cuba and recovered and then was caught by a bullet of one of the worthless niggers. The 22nd went right up and over one hill and up the next and the Indian was hunting other quarters at a splendid gait. . . .

The morning of the first advance was beautiful and to see those thousands of men (about 9000) leave the trenches just as day was breaking, to hear how the rifles commenced to crack and a distant boom of Hall's cannon, to see those lines march straight ahead all with their flags flying, to hear the shrill officers whistles and the trumpet calls and the faint [. . .] calls in the insurgent lines, then to see the dust fly up with more and more frequency when bullets struck, to get the Ping: Ping of the Mauser and the Ugh of the Remington and then to see men commence to drop and be carried off to the rear, were all things that now seem more and more like stories told by some one else than actual experience. . . .

There were lots of brave things done that day, many doubtless that will never be known to the world at large, but not done for the world at large, but for duty's sake.

It takes a few weeks of work like this to make one proud that he is an American. The average man here in the Army (Volunteer and Regular) is a type that the country can be proud of, daring fearless and generous. A Mighty poor "peace soldier" but a more than mighty good "war soldier."

William Connor

Picturing Empire: A Photo Essay

As Willard B. Gatewood, Jr.'s essay and Lt. William Connor's letter reveal, the pursuit of empire was a brutal, racist, and masculine undertaking—not for the faint of heart. But that is hardly the impression conveyed by the photographs presented on the following pages. The first two are part of a series taken by Frances Benjamin Johnston aboard Admiral George Dewey's flagship, the Olympia, *in 1899. Someone else took the third photograph, which presents Johnston sharing a meal with the crew. From an elite background, Johnston was an accomplished photojournalist when she took on the assignment. Dewey had become a national hero for his successful attack on the Spanish fleet at Manila Bay the year before.*

Imagine that you are a middle-class American in the fall of 1899, leafing through The Ladies' Home Journal, Cosmopolitan, *and other mass-circulation magazines of the day, and finding Johnston's* Olympia *photographs. What do they tell you about the war in the Philippines, about the men who fought it, about Admiral Dewey? What words would you use to describe Johnston's presentation of American empire? Why do you think Johnston allowed herself to be photographed eating with the ship's crew?*

Admiral Dewey on the deck of the *Olympia* with his dog, Bob. Photo by Frances Benjamin Johnston (1899). Library of Congress.

Dancing sailors. Photo by Frances Benjamin Johnston (1899). Library of Congress.

Johnston in the crew's mess of the *Olympia*. Unknown photographer (1899). Library of Congress.

Debating Empire

DEBATES

Cuba and Puerto Rico, the Philippines and Guam—these were the spoils of the short and bloody war with Spain in the spring of 1898. But what to do with them? Fortunately, the decision on Cuba and Puerto Rico had already been made; the Teller Amendment, passed by Congress before it would agree to a declaration of war, prohibited outright annexation. Besides, most Americans felt reasonably comfortable with a miniempire in the Caribbean, traditionally seen as an American lake.

The Pacific acquisitions were another matter. They were not covered by the Teller Amendment, and their annexation had the look of a European-style empire—of purposeful imperialism. A national discussion began—one of the great debates in all of American history. The debate took place wherever people gathered: in barber shops and women's clubs, in schools and churches, in debating societies and general stores, and on the floor of the United States Senate, where, finally, a tie-breaking vote by the vice president announced that the Philippines would be annexed.

Among the voices that made a difference in that debate were those of Albert J. Beveridge, Republican Senator from Indiana and a spokesman for the pro-empire position; and William Jennings Bryan, the Democratic candidate for president in 1896, and a representative of the anti-imperialist position. The Beveridge and Bryan positions presented here are each taken from two speeches. One of the central issues was whether an overseas empire was consistent with the American historical experience. How did each man deal with that issue?

Albert J. Beveridge

March of the Flag

It is a noble land that God has given us; a land that can feed and clothe the world; a land whose coastlines would inclose half the countries of Europe; a land set like a sentinel between the two imperial oceans of the globe, a greater England with a nobler destiny.

It is a mighty people that He has planted on this soil; a people sprung from the most masterful blood of history; a people perpetually revitalized by the virile, man-producing working-folk of all the earth; a people imperial by virtue of their power, by right of their institutions, by authority of their Heaven-directed purposes—the propagandists and not the misers of liberty.

It is a glorious history our God has bestowed upon His chosen people; a history heroic with faith in our mission and our future; a history of statesmen

Excerpts from "March of the Flag" (1898) and "Our Philippine Policy" (1900), in Albert J. Beveridge, *The Meaning of the Times and Other Speeches*, Bobbs-Merrill, Freeport, N.Y., 1908.

who flung the boundaries of the Republic out into unexplored lands and savage wilderness; a history of soldiers who carried the flag across blazing deserts and through the ranks of hostile mountains, even to the gates of sunset; a history of a multiplying people who overran a continent in half a century; a history of prophets who saw the consequences of evils inherited from the past and of martyrs who died to save us from them; a history divinely logical, in the process of whose tremendous reasoning we find ourselves to-day.

Therefore, in this campaign, the question is larger than a party question. It is an American question. It is a world question. Shall the American people continue their march toward the commercial supremacy of the world? Shall free institutions broaden their blessed reign as the children of liberty wax in strength, until the empire of our principles is established over the hearts of all mankind?

Have we no mission to perform, no duty to discharge to our fellow-man? Has God endowed us with gifts beyond our deserts and marked us as the people of His peculiar favor, merely to rot in our own selfishness, as men and nations must, who take cowardice for their companion and self for their deity—as China has, as India has, as Egypt has?

Shall we be as the man who had one talent and hid it, or as he who had ten talents and used them until they grew to riches? And shall we reap the reward that waits on our discharge of our high duty; shall we occupy new markets for what our farmers raise, our factories make, our merchants sell— aye, and, please God, new markets for what our ships shall carry?

Hawaii is ours; Porto Rico is to be ours; at the prayer of her people Cuba finally will be ours; in the islands of the East, even to the gates of Asia, coaling stations are to be ours at the very least; the flag of a liberal government is to float over the Philippines, and may it be the banner that Taylor unfurled in Texas and Fremont carried to the coast.

The Opposition tells us that we ought not to govern a people without their consent. I answer, The rule of liberty that all just government derives its authority from the consent of the governed, applies only to those who are capable of self-government. We govern the Indians without their consent, we govern our territories without their consent, we govern our children without their consent. How do they know that our government would be without their consent? Would not the people of the Philippines prefer the just, humane, civilizing government of this Republic to the savage, bloody rule of pillage and extortion from which we have rescued them?

And, regardless of this formula of words made only for enlightened, self-governing people, do we owe no duty to the world? Shall we turn these peoples back to the reeking hands from which we have taken them? Shall we abandon them, with Germany, England, Japan, hungering for them? Shall we save them from those nations, to give them a self-rule of tragedy?

They ask us how we shall govern these new possessions. I answer: Out of local conditions and the necessities of the case methods of government will grow. If England can govern foreign lands, so can America. If Germany can govern foreign lands, so can America. If they can supervise protectorates, so can America. Why is it more difficult to administer Hawaii than

New Mexico or California? Both had a savage and an alien population; both were more remote from the seat of government when they came under our dominion than the Philippines are to-day.

Will you say by your vote that American ability to govern has decayed; that a century's experience in self-rule has failed of a result? Will you affirm by your vote that you are an infidel to American power and practical sense? Or will you say that ours is the blood of government; ours the heart of dominion; ours the brain and genius of administration? Will you remember that we do but what our fathers did—we but pitch the tents of liberty farther westward, farther southward—we only continue the march of the flag?

The march of the flag! In 1789 the flag of the Republic waved over 4,000,000 souls in thirteen states, and their savage territory which stretched to the Mississippi, to Canada, to the Floridas. The timid minds of that day said that no new territory was needed, and, for the hour, they were right. But Jefferson, through whose intellect the centuries marched; Jefferson, who dreamed of Cuba as an American state; Jefferson, the first Imperialist of the Republic—Jefferson acquired that imperial territory which swept from the Mississippi to the mountains, from Texas to the British possessions, and the march of the flag began! . . .

And, now, obeying the same voice that Jefferson heard and obeyed, that Jackson heard and obeyed, that Monroe heard and obeyed, that Seward heard and obeyed, that Grant heard and obeyed, that Harrison heard and obeyed, our President to-day plants the flag over the islands of the seas, outposts of commerce, citadels of national security, and the march of the flag goes on! . . .

The ocean does not separate us from lands of our duty and desire—the oceans join us, rivers never to be dredged, canals never to be repaired. Steam joins us; electricity joins us—the very elements are in league with our destiny. Cuba not contiguous! Porto Rico not contiguous! Hawaii and the Philippines not contiguous! The oceans make them contiguous. And our navy will make them contiguous.

Our Philippine Policy

. . . the times call for candor. The Philippines are ours, "territory belonging to the United States," as the Constitution calls them. And just beyond the Philippines are China's illimitable markets. We will not retreat from either. We will not repudiate our duty in the archipelago. We will not abandon our opportunity in the Orient. We will not renounce our part in the mission of our race. And we will move forward to our work, not howling out regrets, like slaves whipped to their burdens, but with gratitude for a task worthy of our strength, and thanksgiving to Almighty God that He has deemed us worthy of His work.

This island empire is the last land left in all the oceans. If it should prove a mistake to abandon it, the blunder, once made, would be irretrievable. If it proves a mistake to hold it, the error can be corrected when we will. Every other progressive nation stands ready to relieve us.

But to hold it will be no mistake. Our increasing trade henceforth must be with Asia. More and more Europe will manufacture what it needs, secure from its colonies what it consumes. Where shall we turn for consumers of our surplus? Geography answers the question. China is our natural customer. She is nearer to us than to England, Germany or Russia, the commercial powers of the present and the future. They have moved nearer to China by securing permanent bases on her borders. The Philippines give us a base at the door of all the East. . . .

And the Pacific is the ocean of the commerce of the future. Most future wars will be conflicts for commerce. The power that rules the Pacific, therefore, is the power that rules the world. And, with the Philippines, that power will be the American Republic. . . .

It will be hard for Americans who have not studied them to understand the people. They are a barbarous race, modified by three centuries of contact with a decadent race. The Filipino is the South Sea Malay, put through a process of three hundred years of dishonesty in dealing, disorder in habits of industry, and cruelty, caprice, and corruption in government. It is barely possible that 1,000 men in all the archipelago are now capable of self-government in the Anglo-Saxon sense. . . .

. . . *it would be better to abandon the Philippines, and count our blood and treasure already spent a profitable loss, than to apply any academic arrangement of self-government to these children.* They are not yet capable of self-government. How could they be? They are not a self-governing race; they are Orientals, Malays, instructed by Spaniards in the latter's worst estate.

They know nothing of practical government, except as they have witnessed the weak, corrupt, cruel, and capricious rule of Spain. What magic will any one employ to dissolve in their minds and characters those impressions of governors and governed which three centuries of misrule have created? What alchemy will change the oriental quality of their blood, in a year, and set the self-governing currents of the American pouring through their Malay veins? How shall they, in a decade, be exalted to the heights of self-governing peoples which required a thousand years for *us* to reach?

William Jennings Bryan

America's Mission

When the advocates of imperialism find it impossible to reconcile a colonial policy with the principles of our government or with the canons of morality; when they are unable to defend it upon the ground of religious duty or pecuniary profit, they fall back in helpless despair upon the assertion that it is destiny. "Suppose it does violate the Constitution," they say; "suppose it does break all the commandments; suppose it does entail upon the nation an incalculable expenditure of blood and money; it is destiny and we must submit."

Excerpts from "America's Mission" (1899) and "Imperialism" (1900), in *Speeches of William Jennings Bryan*, ed. William Jennings Bryan, Funk & Wagnalls, New York, 1909, 2 vols., vol. II.

The people have not voted for imperialism; no national convention has declared for it; no Congress has passed upon it. To whom, then, has the future been revealed? Whence this voice of authority? We can all prophesy, but our prophecies are merely guesses, colored by our hopes and our surroundings. Man's opinion of what is to be is half wish and half environment. Avarice paints destiny with a dollar mark before it; militarism equips it with a sword. . . .

We have reached another crisis. The ancient doctrine of imperialism, banished from our land more than a century ago, has recrossed the Atlantic and challenged democracy to mortal combat upon American soil.

Whether the Spanish war shall be known in history as a war for liberty or as a war of conquest; whether the principles of self-government shall be strengthened or abandoned; whether this nation shall remain a homogeneous republic or become a heterogeneous empire—these questions must be answered by the American people—when they speak, and not until then, will destiny be revealed.

Destiny is not a matter of chance; it is a matter of choice; it is not a thing to be waited for, it is a thing to be achieved.

So with our nation. If we embark upon a career of conquest no one can tell how many islands we may be able to seize or how many races we may be able to subjugate; neither can any one estimate the cost, immediate and remote, to the Nation's purse and to the Nation's character, but whether we shall enter upon such a career is a question which the people have a right to decide for themselves. Unexpected events may retard or advance the Nation's growth, but the Nation's purpose determines its destiny.

What is the Nation's purpose?

The main purpose of the founders of our Government was to secure for themselves and for posterity the blessings of liberty, and that purpose has been faithfully followed up to this time. Our statesmen have opposed each other upon economic questions, but they have agreed in defending self-government as the controlling national idea. They have quarreled among themselves over tariff and finance, but they have been united in their opposition to an entangling alliance with any European power. . . .

This sentiment was well-nigh universal until a year ago. It was to this sentiment that the Cuban insurgents appealed; it was this sentiment that impelled our people to enter into the war with Spain. Have the people so changed within a few short months that they are now willing to apologize for the War of the Revolution and force upon the Filipinos the same system of government against which the colonists protested with fire and sword? . . .

The forcible annexation of the Philippine Islands is not necessary to make the United States a world-power. For over ten decades our Nation has been a world-power. During its brief existence it has exerted upon the human race an influence more potent for good than all the other nations of the earth combined, and it has exerted that influence without the use of sword or Gatling gun. Mexico and the republics of Central and South America testify to the benign influence of our institutions, while Europe and Asia give evidence of the working of the leaven of self-government. In the growth of democracy we observe the triumphant march of an idea—an idea that would be weighted down rather than aided by the armor and weapons proffered by imperialism.

Much has been said of late about Anglo-Saxon civilization. Far be it from me to detract from the service rendered to the world by the sturdy race whose language we speak. . . .

Anglo-Saxon civilization has, by force of arms, applied the art of government to other races for the benefit of Anglo-Saxons; American civilization will, by the influence of example, excite in other races a desire for self-government and a determination to secure it.

Anglo-Saxon civilization has carried its flag to every clime and defended it with forts and garrisons. American civilization will imprint its flag upon the hearts of all who long for freedom.

> To American civilization, all hail!
> Time's noblest offspring is the last!

Imperialism

Even now we are beginning to see the paralyzing influence of imperialism. Heretofore this Nation has been prompt to express its sympathy with those who were fighting for civil liberty. While our sphere of activity has been limited to the Western Hemisphere, our sympathies have not been bounded by the seas. We have felt it due to ourselves and to the world, as well as to those who were struggling for the right to govern themselves, to proclaim the interest which our people have, from the date of their own independence, felt in every contest between human rights and arbitrary power.

Three-quarters of a century ago, when our nation was small, the struggles of Greece aroused our people, and Webster and Clay gave eloquent expression to the universal desire for Grecian independence. In 1898 all parties manifested a lively interest in the success of the Cubans, but now when a war is in progress in South Africa, which must result in the extension of the monarchical idea, or in the triumph of a republic, the advocates of imperialism in this country dare not say a word in behalf of the Boers. . . .

The forcible annexation of territory to be governed by arbitrary power differs as much from the acquisition of territory to be built up into States as a monarchy differs from a democracy. The Democratic party does not oppose expansion when expansion enlarges the area of the Republic and incorporates land which can be settled by American citizens, or adds to our population people who are willing to become citizens and are capable of discharging their duties as such.

The acquisition of the Louisiana territory, Florida, Texas and other tracts which have been secured from time to time enlarged the Republic and the Constitution followed the flag into the new territory. It is now proposed to seize upon distant territory already more densely populated than our own country and to force upon the people a government for which there is no warrant in our Constitution or our laws.

Even the argument that this earth belongs to those who desire to cultivate it and who have the physical power to acquire it cannot be invoked to justify the appropriation of the Philippine Islands by the United States. If the islands were uninhabited American citizens would not be willing to go there and till the soil. The white race will not live so near the equator. Other nations have tried to colonize in the same latitude. The Netherlands have controlled Java for three hundred years and yet today there are less than sixty thousand people of European birth scattered among the twenty-five million natives. . . .

The Republican platform assumes that the Philippine Islands will be retained under American sovereignty, and we have a right to demand of the Republican leaders a discussion of the future status of the Filipino. Is he to be a citizen or a subject? Are we to bring into the body politic eight or ten million Asiatics, so different from us in race and history that amalgamation is impossible? Are they to share with us in making the laws and shaping the destiny of this nation? No Republican of prominence has been bold enough to advocate such a proposition. . . .

Let us consider briefly the reasons which have been given in support of an imperialistic policy. . . .

It is argued by some that the Filipinos are incapable of self-government and that, therefore, we owe it to the world to take control of them. Admiral Dewey, in an official report to the Navy Department, declared the Flipinos more capable of self-government than the Cubans and said that he based his opinion upon a knowledge of both races. But I will not rest the case upon the relative advancement of the Filipinos. Henry Clay, in defending the right of the people of South America to self-government, said:

> It is the doctrine of thrones that man is too ignorant to govern himself. Their partizans assert his incapacity in reference to all nations; if they cannot command universal assent to the proposition, it is then demanded to particular nations; and our pride and our presumption too often make converts of us. I contend that it is to arraign the disposition of Providence himself to suppose that he has created beings incapable of governing themselves, and to be trampled on by kings. Self-government is the natural government of man.

Clay was right. There are degrees of proficiency in the art of self-government, but it is a reflection upon the Creator to say that he denied to any people the capacity for self-government. Once admit that some people are capable of self-government and that others are not and that the capable people have a right to seize upon and govern the incapable, and you make force—brute force—the only foundation of government and invite the reign of a despot. I am not willing to believe that an all-wise and an all-loving God created the Filipinos and then left them thousands of years helpless until the islands attracted the attention of European nations. . . .

Some argue that American rule in the Philippine Islands will result in the better education of the Filipinos. Be not deceived. If we expect to maintain a colonial policy, we shall not find it to our advantage to educate the people. The educated Filipinos are now in revolt against us, and the most ignorant ones have made the least resistance to our domination. If we are to govern them without their consent and give them no voice in determining the taxes which they must pay, we dare not educate them, lest they learn to read the Declaration of Independence and Constitution of the United States and mock us for our inconsistency.

The principal arguments, however, advanced by those who enter upon a defense of imperialism are:

First—That we must improve the present opportunity to become a world power and enter into international politics.

Second—That our commercial interests in the Philippine Islands and in the Orient make it necessary for us to hold the islands permanently.

Third—That the spread of the Christian religion will be facilitated by a colonial policy.

Fourth—That there is no honorable retreat from the position which the nation has taken. . . .

It is sufficient answer to the first argument to say that for more than a century this nation has been a world power. For ten decades it has been the most potent influence in the world. Not only has it been a world power, but it has done more to shape the politics of the human race than all the other nations of the world combined. . . .

. . . the commercial argument . . . is based upon the theory that war can be rightly waged for pecuniary advantage, and that it is profitable to purchase trade by force and violence. . . .

But a war of conquest is as unwise as it is unrighteous. A harbor and coaling station in the Philippines would answer every trade and military necessity and such a concession could have been secured at any time without difficulty.

It is not necessary to own people in order to trade with them. We carry on trade today with every part of the world, and our commerce has expanded more rapidly than the commerce of any European empire. We do not own Japan or China, but we trade with their people. We have not absorbed the republics of Central and South America, but we trade with them. It has not been necessary to have any political connection with Canada or the nations of Europe in order to trade with them. Trade cannot be permanently profitable unless it is voluntary.

The music of John Philip Sousa, composer of "The Stars and Stripes Forever" and other well-known marches, might be understood as the musical equivalent of the nation's turn-of-the-century imperial ambitions. A good place to begin is an entertaining discussion about Sousa moderated by Ben Wattenberg and featuring musical scholars Jon Newsom, Jerry Rife, and Loras Schissel. A transcript of their conversation is at http://www.pbs.org/thinktank/show_903.html.

Imagining the African "Other"

Mabel E. Barnes

Touring "Darkest Africa"

America's flirtation with empire created a new and deep curiosity about "exotic" peoples and nations. The World's Fairs at Buffalo (1901) and St. Louis (1904) both had elaborate Filipino "villages," designed to show visitors what life was really like in that remote archipelago. The Filipino compound in Buffalo included houses with thatched roofs, natives making rope on a rope walk, a primitive cart drawn by water buffalo, and a reproduction of a Catholic church, where the imported Filipinos attended Sunday services.

Although not an object of the nation's imperial ambition, Africa was a compelling subject of the American imagination. In that imagination, Africa was what the United States was not: primitive, sensual, black, and (always) "dark." In the following account of a visit to the African exhibit at Buffalo's Pan-American Exposition, Mabel Barnes offers us a glimpse of how Americans understood peoples who were remote and different from themselves. According to Barnes's account, what aspects of African society and culture did the exhibit highlight? What aspects of that culture touched Barnes most deeply, and why?

VOICES

Then we went on an exploring tour into "Darkest Africa." In the ballyhoo, a real pygmy, with a sheep's skin about his head, a piece of cotton cloth about his loins and glistening flesh visible everywhere else, with a quiver full of supposedly poisoned arrows hanging from his neck, executed a few steps of a barbaric dance to attract the attention of passersby.

Within there is a presentation of real African life in a real African village. The exhibit was made possible only by the cooperation of England, France, Germany, and Italy with the Buffalo Society of National Science, which accepted the sponsorship of the expedition into Africa to gather materials under the leadership of Xavier Pené, a French geographer and explorer. The original purpose of the expedition contemplated chiefly an ethological and anthropological exhibit to specially include rare types of African natives. But it was realized that an added interest would be given if the natives could be shown in their natural surroundings—and living in the native way. To this end, these natives cut and brought with them the bamboos with which to build and the reeds with which to thatch the huts they live in. They brought, also, their primitive household utensils, implements

Mabel E. Barnes, "Peeps at the Pan-American," vol. III, August 29, 1901, Nineteenth Visit, pp. 70–72, 81–88. The Barnes diary is in the collections of the Buffalo and Erie County Historical Society.

Tickets Here for Darkest Africa. Buffalo and Erie County Historical Society.

of labor, and weapons of war and of the chase, and to make the exhibit complete, there were added to the cannibals, pygmies, and semi-barbarous natives, representative native craftsmen, cloth weavers, workers in gold, and carvers of ivory. The occasional chatter of monkeys and the constant screaming of the flock of African parrots give a final touch of local color to the scene.

There are said to be ninety-eight men, women, and children. This number includes, besides the specimens of pygmies and cannibals, representatives of eleven different tribes. The latter are, for the most part, semicivilized, as they are from the mission stations along the Congo River. This is the first time, however, that they have been outside of Africa and they are to be returned there when the exposition is over. Within their bark stockade, beyond which they are not allowed to go, they live their own lives, with some necessary concessions to the white man's ideas in the matter of clothes, etc. They may be seen at work and at play, carving ivory, weaving nets, working gold, engaging in their dances of war and peace, or indulging in the simple sports and pastimes of village life.

The headman, Chief Ogolaurie is a fine speciman [*sic*] of the semibarbarous African. He has in all fifty-six wives, fifty-three of these having been left behind. The three who are with him treat him with the deference paid by oriental women to their lords. They speak only when spoken to, but stand ready to obey his every behest. The chief's son, Ogandaga is the active head of the native life and decked out in barbarous finery conducts the fetish dances.

In one of the buildings constructed by the native workmen is a construction of musical instruments, weapons, idols, and curios. . . . Here is a queer shaped native drum, almost as high as the roof, that has sounded the call to cannibal orgies. . . . These spears have been bathed in the blood of battle, those lances have stood the lion's charge, and that quiver is filled with arrows so deadly that a prick from their poisoned tips means quick death. Here are the gods of fetishism, every one of which has a tale of human sacrifice to its credit, and in that corner is a tusk carved with a long procession of women winding round and round from base to top, a sort of family tree, the carver of which added a new figure every time he took a new wife. . . .

But the finest exhibits are the natives themselves. Their bodies are slender, strong, and clean; their eyes large, clear, and full of life; their teeth milk white, firm and well-shaped. They are great bathers, these barbarians; they demand a bath every night, and they rub themselves daily with palm oil. The result is a skin so smooth, so fine in texture that it resembles brown satin. To the unpracticed eye there is little to distinguish a native of one tribe from another, but to an expert, each tribe differs in dress, decoration, or mutilation. Some have their teeth filed in a distinctive manner; others are curiously tattooed, the tattooing being not a mere pattern printed on the skin, but markings raised by some painful process to stand out in relief against the flat surface of the body. We saw two women who were decorated in this way from the throat down with a design in arabesque. The women seem more addicted to this sort of decoration than the men. One of the latter, in whom we became especially interested, had a skin so free from blemish, so clean and smooth that it almost tempted one to lay hands upon it. Miss Hale and I were making some comment upon it, not realizing that the owner of the skin, who, moreover, was of rather an intelligent appearance, could understand English, when a knowing and amused expression on his face led me to ask hastily, "Do you understand?," and his reply was, "a little." So we had a few words of conversation as we watched him weave a net of intricate pattern which he explained was for fishing, and then he had to leave us to join in one of the native dances given in an open pavilion.

Each dance has its own significance, and this was described for the instruction of the spectators. . . . [for example], in a time of plague, a dance is begun while the obiman, or witch-doctor, moves along the line to "smell out" the witch who has laid a spell upon the people and their cattle. Imagine the terror of the natives who shrink from the man whose touch means death. Some victory must be had, and if any unfortunate has incurred the ill will of the obiman, he knows that the hour of vengeance has come. It is in such settings as these that the spectator must frame the picture on the stage and remember that the performers have gone through the same ceremonials in darkest Africa to avert threatened famine or present plague and that their hearts have throbbed to the rhythm and the drums which called for a sacrifice to the blood-thirsty deity.

The two extremes of the native religions are illustrated in the village,— Mohammedanism and Fetishism. The representative of the one—the mullah—calls the faithful to prayer with the same call that rises from the lips of the muezzin on oriental minarets. The chief priest of the other leads the barbaric fetish dance about the grotesque image of stone that he worships.

At the farther end of the enclosure are clustered the little huts in which the native craftsmen ply their arts. Here a goldworker with a few primitive tools forges and decorates a ring of yellow African gold; there a carver in ivory reproduces a Midway type with excellent fidelity, for simple as they are, these natives are also quick at observing the customs of the world outside their bark enclosure, a world of which they catch glimpses only from the watchtowers on the stockade. One ivory group shows a woman, an American, with an [*sic*] parasol in a jinrickisha, another depicts the parade of the Mexican vaqueros next door.

We spent two interesting hours in the African village, and when it began to grow dark, we left the grounds for home.

The Search for the Primitive: Tarzan of the Apes

The Cover of the September 10, 1912, Issue of *The All-Story* Magazine, in Which Edgar Rice Burroughs's *Tarzan of the Apes* First Appeared. The epic tale was very much about empire and race. The story concerns an Englishman, Lord Greystoke (Tarzan), raised from infancy entirely by apes and mothered by the ape Kala, whose death—at the hands of a black man—Tarzan avenges.

Life, as this cover suggests, should not be monotonous or overly civilized; hunting—even being hunted—offered the pleasure of danger. Tarzan's ability to act instantly and intuitively, and to kill if need be, are signs that he remains unaffected by the worst aspects of civilization. In contrast, the fear-crazed European in the background—an over-civilized product of cities and modern life—can only watch as the instinctual Tarzan, resembling an American Indian and sporting a mane not unlike the beast he is about to dispatch, saves his life.

THE BIG PICTURE

Why did the United States take on an empire—even a small one—at the turn of the century? A good question, but the question contains its own assumption: that the American empire was a truly national phenomenon, part of the "nation's" history. In their debate over empire, William Jennings Bryan and Senator Beveridge recognize the importance of that assumption, and each takes it on by offering an account of American history. Might empire be understood as the result of the desires of some groups (whites, men) rather than others (blacks, women)? Mabel Barnes's comments on the Pan-American exposition can contribute to an answer to that question, as can Frances Benjamin Johnston's photographs. Examining the racial or racist references in Lt. Connor's letter, Willard Gatewood's essay, and the statements by *both* Bryan and Beveridge, think about whether racism was a *cause* of the imperial effort, or just a kind of *rhetoric* that soldiers in any era employ in order to summon the courage (and hatred) to do their dangerous jobs. The link between the American empire and the nation's experience in the West—particularly the Indian wars of the late nineteenth century—is also worth exploring.

Chapter 6

Progressivism: The Age of Reform

*H*istorian Richard Hofstadter gave us the theme for this chapter in 1955 when he published his conclusions about populism and progressivism in a book titled *The Age of Reform*. A half century later, it is not at all clear what this phenomenon called "progressivism" was, or whether its agents, the "progressives," were really very progressive. Hofstadter in fact argued that at the heart of progressivism was a vision of the past, an attempt to restore economic individualism and political democracy, values that had been buried under giant corporations, burgeoning unions, and corrupt political bosses. With the exception of Theodore Roosevelt, who believed that most big business could not and should not be eliminated, Progressives, according to Hofstadter, generally tried to disassemble existing institutions. The progressive movement, he wrote, was "the complaint of the unorganized against the consequences of organization."

Others have argued that progressivism was not nostalgic but aggressively future-oriented. According to this view, progressivism cannot be separated from the "organizational revolution" taking place at the turn of the century. Products of that revolution include trade associations, new government agencies, the organized professions, and an increased willingness to use federal rather than state and local agencies to achieve economic and social goals. But there are real problems even in placing specific movements within this organizational context. Did new government regulations represent the past or the future? Were they designed to bring change or to preserve the status quo?

The most recent effort to understand progressivism emphasizes the prominence of women in setting the progressive agenda and in the legislative process. This view foregrounds the creation of the U.S. Children's Bureau in 1912 (the first government agency run by women), the passage of mothers' pension laws in most states, and the Sheppard-Towner Act of 1921 (money for health-care clinics and to reduce infant mortality). At bottom, this women's perspective holds that the foundations of the American welfare state were poured not by male-dominated political parties but by women—most of them still without the right to vote—organized in a variety of voluntary associations.

The title of Hofstadter's study implies the ability to recognize a reform when we see one, and much of the history of the progressive period has been written from this assumption. But here, too, there are difficulties. When Theodore Roosevelt broke with the Republican Party in 1912 and campaigned for the presidency under the banner of the Progressive Party (not to be confused with the more general term "progressivism"), his Bull Moose platform was a classic summary of social reforms long identified with progressivism—minimum wages for women, prohibition of child labor, the eight-hour workday, and workmen's compensation. For years, however, Roosevelt had been involved with birth-control advocate Margaret Sanger and with Stanford University president David Starr Jordan and other luminaries in another "reform" effort, the eugenics movement, which many Progressives found unappealing. In a letter written in 1914, Roosevelt described and explained his interest in eugenics:

> I wish very much that the wrong people could be prevented entirely from breeding; and when the evil nature of these people is sufficiently flagrant, this should be done. Criminals should be sterilized and feeble-minded persons forbidden to leave offspring behind them. But as yet there is no way possible to devise a system which could prevent all undesirable persons from breeding.

For Roosevelt, eugenics deserved the label "reform" every bit as much as the movement to abolish child labor. Others, including historians, have disagreed, and therein lies a central problem with the word *reform*.

Nor is the difficulty resolved simply by focusing on what seem to be clearly benign reforms. One of the most popular progressive-period programs was state workmen's compensation legislation, under which injured workers were compensated according to predetermined schedules, rather than by virtue of what they could recover through legal action. By what standards is workmen's compensation "reform"? Is it an example of progressivism? Feminists of the 1970s and 1980s would raise similar, and worthwhile, questions about the many progressive-era laws that regulated hours and conditions for working women. In 1910 those laws seemed to be important measures of protection; today they seem to be obstacles to equality of the sexes. Were those laws, even in 1910, a clear example of social progress?

Still, certain features of progressivism stand out. One need only mention the major regulatory measures of the period to grasp the importance of regulation (a word, it should be emphasized, with no more real content than *reform*). Out of a financial panic in 1907 came the Federal Reserve System, created in 1913 to provide a more flexible currency. Several pieces of railroad legislation, including the Elkins Act (1903) and the Hepburn Act (1906), were designed to limit rebates (unfair price cutting by the carriers) and to give the Interstate Commerce Commission, then two decades old, the authority to fix maximum rates. Congress also provided for federal inspection of meat packers that shipped in interstate commerce and created the Federal Trade Commission (1914) to supervise the competitive relations of interstate businesses. State and local governments were also active in the regulatory movement and were the major agencies of change in such social-justice areas as hours of labor, child labor, mothers' pensions, and tenement-house reform. The progressive period is also well known for a series of measures designed to change the terms of access to the political system. For example, a 1913 amendment to the Constitution provided that U.S. senators would be elected directly by the people of their states, rather than by the state legislatures. And some western states enacted reforms known as initiative (by which the electorate could make laws directly, while voting), referendum (by which voters expressed opinions on issues), and recall (allowing voters to remove public officials from office). The impact of these political reforms was mixed. They did, indeed, increase the role of ordinary citizens in public affairs. But often they were co-opted and used by big business or political machines.

Like the right-wing of the Republican Party in the late twentieth century, the Progressives were also deeply moralistic. They saw moral decay everywhere, but especially in cities, where prostitution, the unrestrained street life of boys who worked as bootblacks and messengers, and commercial recreation—pool halls, movie houses, saloons, amusement parks, excursion boats, and the dance halls described in this chapter's interpretive essay—seemed to threaten the social order.

Aside from the dramatic rise in the use of government as a social tool, the qualities that gave unity to progressivism were attitudinal and ideological. Progressives believed in data. They believed in the possibilities of "scientific" social welfare, supported by research; of market research in selling; and of measuring the abilities of employees through psychological testing. This faith in science was often accompanied by a fear of national moral collapse. It was this kind of thinking that led to the founding of the Boy Scouts of America in 1910 and to Roosevelt's enchantment with eugenics.

Finally, progressivism was not, at least on the surface, a matter of class interests, of one group seeking hegemony over another. For Progressives, the political system was not a device by which conflicting interests compromised (or failed to compromise) their essential differences; it was a means through which the essential harmony of all interests might be expressed.

Perhaps because of this emphasis on harmony, the declaration of war in April 1917 ushered in a brief period in which the progressive spirit of reform was reincarnated as a struggle against German autocracy. Led by Woodrow Wilson, Americans came to understand the war as a holy crusade, a great struggle, as Wilson put it, to "make the world safe for democracy."

INTERPRETIVE ESSAY

Cleaning Up the Dance Halls

Elisabeth Perry

In June of 2004, the New York Times *featured the new trend in "dirty dancing" at proms in the city and around the country. The dancing position, called "backing it up," placed the girl in front and the boy in back, both facing the same direction, pushing against each other, "grinding" away. Almost 100 years before, Belle Israels and the New York Council of Jewish Women, having made their own observations about the dirty dancing of their day, and concerned about the impact of dancing and alcohol on the working-class girls who frequented New York City's numerous dance halls, initiated a campaign for municipal regulation of these venues. The campaign had parallels in Progressive Era efforts to censor movies, eliminate prostitution, and turn unregulated "play" into regulated and supervised "recreation." The Progressive Era was also witness to the first efforts to understand, theorize, and control adolescence.*

The campaign to clean up the dance halls, described and interpreted by historian Elisabeth Perry (the granddaughter of Belle Israels) offers a variety of windows onto Progressive Era reform. By asking the right questions of the essay, one can begin to define and understand the perspective of Progressive Era reformers. Who were the reformers? What social class or age group did they represent? And who were the objects of the reform efforts? What basic changes in industrial and urban conditions had produced the dance halls? How did the reformers know there was a problem? Were the reformers a reasonable and flexible bunch, or were they likely to be carried away by incorrect assumptions or silly fears? How did the reformers counter the argument of critics, who said that government should stay out of "free enterprise"? Was the dance hall reform movement a success?

In 1903, a sixteen-year-old girl named Frieda left a small Eastern European village to emigrate to America. An uncle, who lived in New York City with his three daughters, took her in. Frieda knew little of the language, nothing of American customs. Her cousins, who grew up in America but who had a busy

From Elisabeth Perry, "Cleaning Up the Dance Halls," *History Today*, vol. 39, October 1989, pp. 20–26. Reprinted with permission of the publisher.

Belle Israels [Moskowitz] also worked with the New York State Factory Investigating Commission, set up to study the 1911 Triangle Shirtwaist Factory fire, which killed 146 people, and she became a trusted political advisor to Democrat Al Smith, governor of New York and candidate for president in 1928. For more on her career, see www.library.csi.cuny.edu/dept/history/lavender/386/bmoskowi. html. *The Triangle Fire, an iconic event of the Progressive Era, can be studied on any number of Web sites. A good place to begin is the exhibition at* www.ilr.cornell.edu/trianglefire/.

life of their own, did not take the time to teach her. They were happy that she spent her days in the kitchen, looking after their needs. After a while Frieda discovered life outside the kitchen. Brightly lit halls and images of forms moving to the strains of upbeat music drew her in. There she discovered laughter, joy, and other young people much like herself. As girls were always in demand at such places, and she was pretty, she soon became a popular patron at this and other dance halls. But she also learned that to keep her popularity she had to drink "stylish drinks," for dancing without drinking was "slow."

According to the social welfare workers of Frieda's day, the dance halls, then proliferating in American cities, were initiating many girls into a "fast" life. Here's how one social worker, writing about the problem for a national magazine, described Frieda's dénouement:

> One night, when her head was whirling from excitement and dazed with drink, the man who had been playing with her for weeks . . . took her not home, but to a place where she offered on the altar of her "good time" the sacred gift of her girlhood—all she had to lose. She never turned again from the path. . . . She followed it through the mazes of wretched slavery to men and walked to its end five years later in a reformatory to which she had been committed and where her nameless baby was born. It was the price paid.

Several assumptions about sexual relations in the early 1900s lie behind the way this story was told. First, that men "play" with girls, almost for sport. Second, when left to their own devices, lonely girls cannot resist the offer of a man's "love," even though accepting it means losing their "girlhood." Third, that sex for young unmarried girls leads inevitably to some form of criminal activity or worse.

Whether these assumptions were based on reality need not concern us. The important thing is that early twentieth-century social workers believed they were. They also believed that modern urban society had weakened if not destroyed the traditional family and community controls that used to protect innocent girls. In their view, men should control their urges toward sexual conquest. But since most men did not, society had to control the venue—namely, the dance hall—which clearly increased a girl's vulnerability. Thus began the campaign to clean up America's dance halls, a campaign that aroused wide public support and lasted for over two decades.

Dance halls were run for profit. Their owners or managers gave patrons, most of whom were young and unattached, what they wanted—the fast, rhythmic music of Tin Pan Alley, no restrictions on dancing styles, and plenty of drinks, usually alcoholic, to quench the thirst and arouse the spirits. Dance halls also offered girls unprecedented freedom in finding amusement and making new acquaintances. Unescorted girls often got in for half-price or free. Worse, from the point of view of social workers, dance halls made no provision for social chaperonage. Complete strangers accosted girls and invited them to dance. Such easy affability was in part what excited youth most about the dance-hall environment, but it appalled social workers.

Dance-hall reform officially began in 1908. In that year, Belle Israels (later, Moskowitz), a social worker associated with the New York Council of Jewish Women, became concerned about rising numbers of Jewish girls in homes for unwed mothers and in reformatories. Interviews with the girls produced evidence that the dance halls were where the girls had first fallen into "bad" company. Mrs Israels formed a Committee on Amusements and Vacation Resources of Working Girls to find out why. Its report disclosed that nine out of every ten girls considered dance halls their favourite resort, forty-nine out of seventy-three New York City dance halls sold alcohol, and twenty-two of these were attached to hotels known to be brothels.

Having established the popularity of dance halls among city youth, and associated them in the public mind with alcohol and sex, the report then went on to distinguish several types of halls. Most were "inside" or saloon halls that merely cleared away space for dancing to piano music. "Spielers" worked for the management, bringing customers in and dancing with wall-flowers. Frequenting such places night after night, the report surmised, girls assuaged their loneliness, felt popular, and dreamt of romance. Soon they found themselves accepting "treats" (usually alcoholic drinks) from men, in return for which they sat with them in the dark alcoves and balconies that ringed the dance floors. There, of course, they "paid the price."

Another type of dance hall was the "outside" hall or casino that offered unlimited beer and dancing during the day. At night, prices dropped and "immoral persons" arrived to use adjacent parks for assignations. Yet a third type was the "dancing academy." Some had good reputations; others were fly-by-nights that kept little order, allowed close body contact in dancing styles, improper dress, and smoking, and encouraged gambling and prostitution in back rooms. The report lamented that girls, some only fourteen, paid high fees for lessons at these places, often learning more than they bargained for.

Belle Israels and her committee recognized that commercial dance halls provided essential recreation to urban youth. They knew that the halls could not be abolished. But they did believe the halls could and ought to be controlled. Their strategy was two-pronged: first, to regulate existing halls through a licensing act; then, using both private and public funds, to substitute "decent" halls for the sleazy ones, and "proper" dancing for the "tough" or "sensual" styles then popular. These complementary themes of regulation and substitution, which seemed so sensible and moderate, drew prominent adherents to the cause.

Over the next months, committee members lobbied city and state legislators for action. Success came in 1910, when the committee proposed a bill that prohibited the sale of alcohol on dance floors and in adjoining rooms, and made conformity to strict safety and sanitation codes compulsory in both dance halls and dance academies. Few critics objected to the codes, but many fought the alcohol ban. Brewers and saloon dance-hall owners pressured legislators to reject the bill. Immigrant groups, for whom a dance without wine or beer was unthinkable, joined in. For her part, Belle Israels insisted that she was not making a temperance argument, but that her experience with hundreds of girls who had learned the taste of alcohol from the dance hall or amusement park had made her realize its "stupefying effect on the moral sensibilities."

A compromise bill passed. It stipulated that saloons could not allow dancing unless they were licensed also as dance halls. Further, no alcohol could be sold in places that taught dancing and advertised as such. The bill passed, but left reformers dissatisfied. It delayed enforcement until 1911 and exempted all hotels with more than fifty bedrooms. There were other problems, such as an inadequate budget for dance-hall inspection. Members of the Committee on Amusements became volunteer inspectors themselves, a development neither they nor the city wanted.

While awaiting the result of the licensing legislation, Mrs Israels and her committee worked on the companion side of their strategy—substitution. They opened model dance halls designed to show businessmen that decent places could be run at a profit. Such halls planned to serve only non-alcoholic drinks and be free of other objectionable features of commercial resorts.

The committee opened its first model hall the following year. Hundreds of youngsters flocked to the place, advertised by a plain sign, "General Dancing, Fifteen Cents." Because of recent dance-hall shootings, a bouncer checked for weapons at the door. Soft drinks sold briskly for five cents. The dance floor was large, the ceiling high, the room well lit and ventilated. In a space reserved for beginners, a stout dancing master—a "mixture of artist and pugilist," a reporter observed—called out the "Lancers." A young man resting his head on his partner's shoulder found himself expelled. College students dancing too wildly were told to stop. In the place of spielers, male relatives of the Committee on Amusements took care of wallflowers.

Over the next two years, the Committee on Amusements sponsored model dance halls in Manhattan, Brooklyn, and Newark. Newark's Palace Ballroom was its showplace. Located in a large rectangular building with an enclosure for a fourteen-piece orchestra and a balcony for spectators, the hall featured close supervision, especially in the balconies where an "introducer" helped young people meet "properly." There was "barn dancing" once a week, complete with two or three farmers forking hay; German dancing or waltz tournaments took place on other nights. But the hall's most dazzling feature was its streamers of rainbow-coloured lights hung from a central chandelier. Operated by a switchboard, the lights blinked on and off in time to the music, changing hues to suit moods. The hall was a splendid mixture of old-fashioned dancing decorum with the novelties of the electrical age.

In addition to regulating existing dance halls and creating model ones, the Committee on Amusements also addressed dancing styles. In the late 1890s, the waltz, polka, two-step, and "set and figure" dances were standard. But by the turn of the century, ragtime and cakewalks had moved into northern cities. There they evolved into a variety of "animal" dances named after turkeys, bunnies, monkeys, and bears. The Turkey Trot required couples to move in fast one-step circles occasionally flapping their arms. The Grizzly Bear, Bunny Hug, and Kangaroo Dip encouraged close body contact. Soon, enterprising songwriters such as Irving Berlin were putting suggestive words to the new tunes, telling dancers to "hug up close to your baby," and "everybody's doin' it." Then South American dances such as the Argentine Tango appeared, its medley of dips, glides, and sways suggesting sexual conquest and submission.

Clergymen, dancing masters, and upper-class citizens denounced the new dances as ugly and indecent. But their attempts to keep them out of ballrooms were in vain. Even at society balls, couples slipped out into the corridors to learn the forbidden steps. By 1912, letters to editors dwelled incessantly on whether to "trot" or not, and the "nots" were losing.

The Committee on Amusements took a remedial approach. Belle Israels argued that repression without substitution would fail. Her substitution plan began with a conference on the "real nature" of the new dances. Meeting in a fancy ballroom early in 1912, the conference attracted 600 observers. Israels introduced a dancing master who demonstrated how the new dances start out innocently, but then become passionate, gliding embraces. The audience gasped in horror. Next, entertainers Al Jolson and Florence Cable performed. Jolson told how he had learned to dance on San Francisco's infamous Barbary Coast. Drunken tars who could barely stand up would come alive when the orchestra "ragged it up," hitting seductive minor keys. Jolson then grabbed his partner, snapped his fingers, and drew her daringly close. The audience gasped again, but when the dancers finished they broke out with thunderous applause.

Perhaps unhappy with such a positive response to "offensive" dancing, the Committee on Amusements focused subsequent demonstrations only on the "graceful" dances that illustrated the "best standards." These promised to be "just as much of a romp" as the offensive dances, Mrs Israels declared. The committee also won the co-operation of a "better class" of dance halls and ballrooms. In return for being on an approved list, their owners and managers posted signs forbidding "immoral dancing" and inserted clauses in musicians' contracts against the playing of "rags" and "shivers."

In time, the controversy over dancing styles died down. Professional dancers "sanitized" the new dances, turning them into the elegant Castle Walk, Hesitation, or Maxixe. Popular magazines and newspapers published "how-to" dance articles, complete with photographs and diagrams. The dances forced clothing styles to change to accommodate them, skirts becoming looser, or slit at the side to allow for dips. Even the infamous Turkey Trot won admirers as physicians assured young and old that its effects benefited the circulation. "Honi soit qui mal y danse," quipped one writer in *Collier's* in 1913. Even Belle Israels admitted in 1914 that the tango was beautiful, if danced well.

Between 1910 and 1913, dance-hall reform spread across the country. By 1914, many cities, including Cleveland, Detroit, Chicago, Cincinnati, Kansas City, Minneapolis, Los Angeles, and Portland, had passed dance hall ordinances or planned to. The new ordinances shared certain features: license fees, compliance with city codes, and controls or bans on alcohol. But on other issues of social chaperonage, such as ages of admission for minors, free admission for females, "moonlight" dancing, and correct dancing positions, there was almost no agreement.

By the end of this first stage of American dance-hall reform, reformers had won the passage of a number of laws, but felt disappointed on other grounds. On the substitution side of reform, several cities set up supervised summer dance pavilions in parks or on docks, but in some cities clergy campaigned against such uses of public funds, and in Denver and Milwaukee, after the defeat of progressive governments, experiments at public dancing foundered. Worse, enforcement of the laws was never properly funded. As a result, many regulatory provisions remained dead letters.

Despite such setbacks, agitation for dance-hall reform continued throughout the 1910s, reviving vigorously after the First World War. In the 1920s, with the rise of the cheap automobile and the spread of the paved road system, urban dance halls began to crop up in mid-sized provincial cities as well as in the countryside (in this instance called roadhouses). When rural communities found themselves thus "contaminated" with city ways, they pressed for county- and state-wide regulation.

In addition, new types of dancing resorts began to appear in major northern cities. One type that reformers found particularly appalling was the "closed dance hall," so called because it was closed to women customers but not women employees. This kind of dance hall arose out of a combination of circumstances. In the 1920s, many cities were experiencing an unprecedented influx of working-class immigrants, many of whom were single, male, and of new racial and ethnic types. When these men sought amusement in dance halls, either they were denied admission or native-born girls refused to dance with them. Capitalising on this situation, and on the lack of well-paid jobs for young, unskilled urban women, entrepreneurs hired such women to provide "dance instruction" to the men in return for a commission—usually five cents on a ten-cent ticket. Halls that offered this kind of amusement became known as "taxi-dance halls," since they allowed men who "paid the fare," as in a taxi, to dance with a partner. Reformers opposed the existence of these halls because they seemed exploitative of women and to promote, if not prostitution, then at least some forms of sexual "disorder." Indeed, in the so-called "tougher" halls, women engaged in what observers euphemistically called "sensual" dancing. This was, in fact, the masturbation of their partners on the dance floor.

To deal with these developments, dance-hall reform revived, reaching a peak in mid-decade. The result was legislation that, by the end of the decade, covered 70 per cent of all American cities over 15,000 in population. Reformers were interested in more than just the extension of dance hall regulation, however. They wanted to use regulation to control the conditions in dance halls that permitted young people to flout standards of social decorum. Reformers argued that unrestrained and unsupervised dancing to jazz music was dangerous, especially to girls. Sexually aroused by the dancing, sometimes lubricated with "hooch," innocent young women left the dance halls (often in men's automobiles) to go straight to seduction. Again, as in the case of the immigrant "Friedas" of an earlier decade, there may have been some basis to such fears. But it is also clear that, in the 1920s, when the pace of change in sexual morality was accelerating, dance-hall reform became a way of resisting the prevailing trends of the day.

The story of Joseph Louis Guyon, former soap salesman turned Chicago dance-hall entrepreneur, illustrates how this resistance could be effective. Guyon had first invested in a dance hall in 1909. Then the modern dance craze hit Chicago. Tangos, Bunny-Hugs, and Turkey Trots became the rage. Worried about the falling-off of their trade, the city's dancing masters got together and voted to "go with the crowd." But not Guyon. "I am going to stick to the waltz and two-step," he declared. "In my hall, I'll make everybody keep six inches from his partner." His colleagues called him a fool. His partner left him and his hall began to fail. Even when jazz came to the Chicago dance floor in the form of "walking the dog," "ballin' the Jack," and finally the "shimmy," Guyon held out.

In 1914 Guyon invested in poster and newspaper advertisements for a new Dreamland Ballroom where "No Modern Dances Would be Allowed," and partners had to keep at least six inches between them. Young people who came to the ballroom to test him found themselves warned three times and then out on the street—Guyon, six feet tall and fifteen stone, acted as his own bouncer. The ballroom did not do well, and Guyon almost went bankrupt. Desperate, he mortgaged his household furniture, sinking the money into one final clean-dancing advertisement. At last (as he told the story at least) women responded. Juvenile protection associations, women's clubs, and other similar groups endorsed him, and gradually people in ever-increasing numbers started coming to his hall. A year later he had recouped his losses and was well on his way to making a small fortune. The continued support of reformers enabled him to carry on his campaign against jazz and improper dance-floor etiquette long into the next decade.

Much of Guyon's efforts in this campaign focused on the behaviour of girls. Every night, Guyon, his wife, and twenty staff members enforced the rules, including those against hugging, a man walking his partner backward, or any of the "clutching, writing postures of the new dances." Most significantly, however, Guyon took direct action against any display of female sexuality:

> If a girl's skirts are too high, or her dress too low, we bundle her up and send her home to her mother in the automobile that always stands outside. If she is too highly rouged, we make her take it off—if she is too young—we allow no one in the ballroom under seventeen—we send a private letter to her mother, telling just why we cannot admit her daughter. I send hundreds of letters to mothers whose daughters I see keeping undesirable company, or developing dangerous mannerisms. I accept responsibility for much of the moral standard of those who dance on my floor. Parents and preachers are my strongest supporters.

The twenties were a time when young women were freeing themselves from many restraints. Yet many Americans resisted this trend, even in a large cosmopolitan community such as Chicago, but especially in mid-sized American communities where rules like Guyon's were standard fare. Perhaps only some parts of urban America were prepared to accept, or at best tolerate, the "flapper." The successful and widespread passage of dance hall regulation indicates broad popular support for the six-inch rule.

The story of dance-hall reform offers insights into the American response to changing sexual mores in the early part of the modern era. There were some repressive variations of the reform, but most reformers argued that repression would only drive youth to experiment with worse forms of amusement. They therefore pressed communities to adopt substitution programmes, and to provide young women, especially, with a wider range of recreational choices than they had before.

Many of reformers' concerns about maintaining "standards" and protecting young women from seduction seem silly and naive to us now. But as a result of their efforts they established the principle that public amusements should be regulated in the interests of youth. They also convinced many municipalities and even some church-related groups that they ought to provide safe recreational facilities for youth where none exist, that is, facilities that do not cater to a lowest common denominator in standards of human behaviour. As we struggle today to provide our youth with drug- and alcohol-free environments, we realize that some of the concerns of the dance hall reformers of the 1910s and 1920s are still with us.

Hull-House: The Softer Side of Progressive Reform?

Jane Addams

Jane Addams (1860–1935) was the most prominent of a generation of women who committed their lives to the cause of social reform. Born in 1860, Addams returned from Europe in the 1880s convinced of the need to take action against the ills of urban America. In 1889, she established the social settlement of Hull-House—a mansion in the heart of Chicago's Italian and eastern European immigrant community that would assist the area's people in liberating themselves from their Old World cultures and customs, in overcoming their ignorance, in adjusting to modern urban life, and in securing needed changes in the neighborhood. By 1900, there were over 100 social settlements in cities across the nation, nearly all of them managed by women.

In the first section of the following account, published in 1910, Addams presents some of the ideas and attitudes she observed in the Italian immigrant community, and she explains how the immigrants' adjustment to American industrial conditions might be facilitated by a labor museum. In the second section, she describes her efforts to deal with conditions in a nearby "slum." What do you think of Addams's labor museum? Of her solution to the tenement conditions? What did area residents think of her work? According to Addams, why did the problems she uncovered exist, and, speaking generally, what needed to be done to solve them? Is there anything particularly female about Addams's approach to social reform?

This tendency upon the part of the older immigrants to lose the amenities of European life without sharing those of America, has often been deplored by keen observers from the home countries. When Professor Masurek of Prague gave a course of lectures in the University of Chicago, he was much distressed over the materialism into which the Bohemians of Chicago had fallen. The early immigrants had been so stirred by the opportunity to own real estate, an appeal perhaps to the Slavic land hunger, and their energies had become so completely absorbed in money-making that all other interests had apparently dropped away. And yet I recall a very touching incident in connection with a lecture Professor Masurek gave at Hull-House, in which he had appealed to his countrymen to arouse themselves from this tendency to fall below their home civilization and to forget the great enthusiasm which had united them into the Pan-Slavic Movement. A Bohemian widow who supported herself and her two children by scrubbing, hastily sent her youngest child to purchase, with the twenty-five cents which was to have supplied them with food the next day, a bunch of red roses which she presented to the lecturer in appreciation of his testimony to the reality of the things of the spirit.

Jane Addams, *20 Years at Hull-House*, Macmillan, New York, 1910, pp. 234–45, 292–96.

An overmastering desire to reveal the humbler immigrant parents to their own children lay at the base of what has come to be called the Hull-House Labor Museum. This was first suggested to my mind one early spring day when I saw an old Italian woman, her distaff against her homesick face, patiently spinning a thread by the simple stick spindle so reminiscent of all southern Europe. I was walking down Polk Street, perturbed in spirit, because it seemed so difficult to come into genuine relations with the Italian women and because they themselves so often lost their hold upon their Americanized children. It seemed to me that Hull-House ought to be able to devise some educational enterprise, which should build a bridge between European and American experiences in such wise as to give them both more meaning and a sense of relation. I meditated that perhaps the power to see life as a whole, is more needed in the immigrant quarter of a large city than anywhere else, and that the lack of this power is the most fruitful source of misunderstanding between European immigrants and their children, as it is between them and their American neighbors; and why should that chasm between fathers and sons, yawning at the feet of each generation, be made so unnecessarily cruel and impassable to these bewildered immigrants? Suddenly I looked up and saw the old woman with her distaff, sitting in the sun on the steps of a tenement house. She might have served as a model for one of Michael Angelo's Fates, but her face brightened as I passed and, holding up her spindle for me to see, she called out that when she had spun a little more yarn, she would knit a pair of stockings for her goddaughter. The occupation of the old woman gave me the clew that was needed. Could we not interest the young people working in the neighboring factories, in these older forms of industry, so that, through their own parents and grandparents, they would find a dramatic representation of the inherited resources of their daily occupation. If these young people could actually see that the complicated machinery of the factory had been evolved from simple tools, they might at least make a beginning towards that education which Dr. Dewey defines as "a continuing reconstruction of experience." They might also lay a foundation for reverence of the past which Goethe declares to be the basis of all sound progress.

My exciting walk on Polk Street was followed by many talks with Dr. Dewey and with one of the teachers in his school who was a resident at Hull-House. Within a month a room was fitted up to which we might invite those of our neighbors who were possessed of old crafts and who were eager to use them.

We found in the immediate neighborhood, at least four varieties of these most primitive methods of spinning and three distinct variations of the same spindle in connection with wheels. It was possible to put these seven into historic sequence and order and to connect the whole with the present method of factory spinning. The same thing was done for weaving, and on every Saturday evening a little exhibit was made of these various forms of labor in the textile industry. Within one room a Syrian woman, a Greek, an Italian, a Russian, and an Irishwoman enabled even the most casual observer to see that there is no break in orderly evolution if we look at history from the industrial standpoint; that industry develops similarly and peacefully year by year among the workers of each nation, heedless of differences in language, religion, and political experiences.

And then we grew ambitious and arranged lectures upon industrial history. I remember that after an interesting lecture upon the industrial revolution in England and a portrayal of the appalling conditions throughout the weaving districts of the north, which resulted from the hasty gathering of the weavers into the new towns, a Russian tailor in the audience was moved to make a speech. He suggested that whereas time had done much to alleviate the first difficulties in the transition of weaving from hand work to steam power, that in the application of steam to sewing we are still in the first stages, illustrated by the isolated woman who tries to support herself by hand needlework at home until driven out by starvation, as many of the hand weavers had been.

The historical analogy seemed to bring a certain comfort to the tailor as did a chart upon the wall, showing the infinitesimal amount of time that steam had been applied to manufacturing processes compared to the centuries of hand labor. Human progress is slow and perhaps never more cruel than in the advance of industry, but is not the worker comforted by knowing that other historical periods have existed similar to the one in which he finds himself, and that the readjustment may be shortened and alleviated by judicious action; and is he not entitled to the solace which an artistic portrayal of the situation might give him? I remember the evening of the tailor's speech that I felt reproached because no poet or artist had endeared the sweaters' victim to us as George Eliot has made us love the belated weaver, Silas Marner. The textile museum is connected directly with the basket weaving, sewing, millinery, embroidery, and dressmaking constantly being taught at Hull-House, and so far as possible with the other educational departments; we have also been able to make a collection of products, of early implements, and of photographs which are full of suggestion. Yet far beyond its direct educational value, we prize it because it so often puts the immigrants into the position of teachers, and we imagine that it affords them a pleasant change from the tutelage in which all Americans, including their own children, are so apt to hold them. I recall a number of Russian women working in a sewing-room near Hull-House, who heard one Christmas week that the House was going to give a party to which they might come. They arrived one afternoon when, unfortunately, there was no party on hand and, although the residents did their best to entertain them with impromptu music and refreshments, it was quite evident that they were greatly disappointed. Finally it was suggested that they be shown the Labor Museum—where gradually the thirty sodden, tired women were transformed. They knew how to use the spindles and were delighted to find the Russian spinning frame. Many of them had never seen the spinning wheel, which has not penetrated to certain parts of Russia, and they regarded it as a new and wonderful invention. They turned up their dresses to show their homespun petticoats; they tried the looms; they explained the difficulty of the old patterns; in short, from having been stupidly entertained, they themselves did the entertaining.

Because of a direct appeal to former experiences, the immigrant visitors were able for the moment to instruct their American hostesses in an old and honored craft, as was indeed becoming to their age and experience.

In some such ways as these have the Labor Museum and the shops pointed out the possibilities which Hull-House has scarcely begun to develop, of demonstrating that culture is an understanding of the long-established occupations and thoughts of men, of the arts with which they have solaced their toil. A yearning to recover for the household arts something of their early sanctity and meaning, arose strongly within me one evening when I was attending a Passover Feast to which I had been invited by a Jewish family in the neighborhood, where the traditional and religious significance of woman's daily activity was still retained. The kosher food the Jewish mother spread before her family had been prepared according to traditional knowledge and with constant care in the use of utensils; upon her had fallen the responsibility to make all ready according to Mosaic instructions that the great crisis in a religious history might be fittingly set forth by her husband and son. Aside from the grave religious significance in the ceremony, my mind was filled with shifting pictures of woman's labor with which travel makes one familiar; the Indian women grinding grain outside of their huts as they sing praises to the sun and rain; a file of white-clad Moorish women whom I had once seen waiting their turn at a well in Tangiers; south Italian women kneeling in a row along the stream and beating their wet clothes against the smooth white stones; the milking, the gardening, the marketing in thousands of hamlets, which are such direct expressions of the solicitude and affection at the basis of all family life.

There has been some testimony that the Labor Museum has revealed the charm of woman's primitive activities. I recall a certain Italian girl who came every Saturday evening to a cooking class in the same building in which her mother spun in the Labor Museum exhibit; and yet Angelina always left her mother at the front door while she herself went around to a side door because she did not wish to be too closely identified in the eyes of the rest of the cooking class with an Italian woman who wore a kerchief over her head, uncouth boots, and short petticoats. One evening, however, Angelina saw her mother surrounded by a group of visitors from the School of Education, who much admired the spinning, and she concluded from their conversation that her mother was "the best stick-spindle spinner in America." When she inquired from me as to the truth of this deduction, I took occasion to describe the Italian village in which her mother had lived, something of her free life, and how, because of the opportunity she and the other women of the village had to drop their spindles over the edge of a precipice, they had developed a skill in spinning beyond that of the neighboring towns. I dilated somewhat on the freedom and beauty of that life—how hard it must be to exchange it all for a two-room tenement, and to give up a beautiful homespun kerchief for an ugly department store hat. I intimated it was most unfair to judge her by these things alone, and that while she must depend on her daughter to learn the new ways, she also had a right to expect her daughter to know something of the old ways.

That which I could not convey to the child but upon which my own mind persistently dwelt, was that her mother's whole life had been spent in a secluded spot under the rule of traditional and narrowly localized observances, until her very religion clung to local sanctities,—to the shrine before which she had always prayed, to the pavement and walls of the low vaulted church,—and then suddenly she was torn from it all and literally put out to sea, straight away from the solid habits of her religious and domestic life, and she now walked timidly but with poignant sensibility upon a new and strange shore.

It was easy to see that the thought of her mother with any other background than that of the tenement was new to Angelina and at least two things resulted; she allowed her mother to pull out of the big box under the bed the beautiful homespun garments which had been previously hidden away as uncouth; and she openly came into the Labor Museum by the same door as did her mother, proud at least of the mastery of the craft which had been so much admired.

. . . Our experience in inspecting [the ward's garbage disposal facilities] only made us more conscious of the wretched housing conditions over which we had been distressed from the first. It was during the World's Fair summer that one of the Hull-House residents in a public address upon housing reform used as an example of indifferent landlordism a large block in the neighborhood occupied by small tenements and stables unconnected with a street sewer, as was much similar property in the vicinity. In the lecture the resident spared neither a description of the property nor the name of the owner. The young man who owned the property was justly indignant at this public method of attack and promptly came to investigate the condition of the property. Together we made a careful tour of the houses and stables and in the face of the conditions that we found there, I could not but agree with him that supplying South Italian peasants with sanitary appliances seemed a difficult undertaking. Nevertheless he was unwilling that the block should remain in its deplorable state, and he finally cut through the dilemma with the rash proposition that he would give a free lease of the entire tract to Hull-House, accompanying the offer, however, with the warning remark, that if we should choose to use the income from the rents in sanitary improvements we should be throwing our money away.

Even when we decided that the houses were so bad that we could not undertake the task of improving them, he was game and stuck to his proposition that we should have a free lease. We finally submitted a plan that the houses should be torn down and the entire tract turned into a playground, although cautious advisers intimated that it would be very inconsistent to ask for subscriptions for the support of Hull-House when we were known to have thrown away an income of two thousand dollars a year. We, however, felt that a spectacle of inconsistency was better than one of bad landlordism and so the worst of the houses were demolished, the best three were sold and moved across the street under careful provision that they might never be used for junkshops or saloons, and a public playground was finally established. Hull-House became responsible for its management for ten years, at the end of which time it was turned over to the City Playground Commission although from the first the city detailed a policeman who was responsible for its general order and who became a valued adjunct of the House.

During fifteen years this public-spirited owner of the property paid all the taxes, and when the block was finally sold he made possible the playground equipment of a near-by school yard. On the other hand, the dispossessed tenants, a group of whom had to be evicted by legal process before their houses could be torn down, have never ceased to mourn their former estates. Only the other day I met upon the street an old Italian harness maker, who said that he had never succeeded so well anywhere else nor found a place that "seemed so much like Italy."

Festivities of various sorts were held on this early playground, always a May day celebration with its Maypole dance and its May queen. I remember that one year the honor of being queen was offered to the little girl who should pick up the largest number of scraps of paper which littered all the streets and alleys. The children that spring had been organized into a league and each member had been provided with a stiff piece of wire upon the sharpened point of which stray bits of paper were impaled and later soberly counted off into a large box in the Hull-House alley. The little Italian girl who thus won the scepter took it very gravely as the just reward of hard labor, and we were all so absorbed in the desire for clean and tidy streets that we were wholly oblivious to the incongruity of thus selecting "the queen of love and beauty."

It was at the end of the second year that we received a visit from the warden of Toynbee Hall and his wife, as they were returning to England from a journey around the world. They had lived in East London for many years, and had been identified with the public movements for its betterment. They were much shocked that, in a new country with conditions still plastic and hopeful, so little attention had been paid to experiments and methods of amelioration which had already been tried; and they looked in vain through our library for blue books and governmental reports which recorded painstaking study into the conditions of English cities.

They were the first of a long line of English visitors to express the conviction that many things in Chicago were untoward not through paucity of public spirit but through a lack of political machinery adapted to modern city life. This was not all of the situation but perhaps no casual visitor could be expected to see that these matters of detail seemed unimportant to a city in the first flush of youth, impatient of correction and convinced that all would be well with its future. The most obvious faults were those connected with the congested housing of the immigrant population, nine tenths of them from the country, who carried on all sorts of traditional activities in the crowded tenements. That a group of Greeks should be permitted to slaughter sheep in a basement, that Italian women should be allowed to sort over rags collected from the city dumps, not only within the city limits but in a court swarming with little children, that immigrant bakers should continue unmolested to bake bread for their neighbors in unspeakably filthy spaces under the pavement, appeared incredible to visitors accustomed to careful city regulations. I recall two visits made to the Italian quarter by John Burns,—the second, thirteen years after the first. During the latter visit it seemed to him unbelievable that a certain house owned by a rich Italian should have been permitted to survive. He remembered with the greatest minuteness the positions of the houses on the court, with the exact space between the front and rear tenements, and he asked at once whether we had been able to cut a window into a dark hall as he had recommended thirteen years before. Although we were obliged to confess that the landlord would not permit the window to be cut, we were able to report that a City Homes Association had existed for ten years; that following a careful study of tenement conditions in Chicago, the text of which had been written by a Hull-House resident, the association had obtained the enactment of a model tenement-house code, and that their secretary had carefully watched the administration of the law for years so that its operation might not be minimized by the granting of too many exceptions in the city council. Our progress still seemed slow to Mr. Burns because in Chicago the actual houses were quite unchanged, embodying features long since declared illegal in London. Only this year could we have reported to him, had he again come to challenge us, that the provisions of the law had at last been extended to existing houses and that a conscientious corps of inspectors under an efficient chief, were fast remedying the most glaring evils, while a band of nurses and doctors were following hard upon the "trail of the white hearse."

The mere consistent enforcement of existing laws and efforts for their advance often placed Hull-House, at least temporarily, into strained relations with its neighbors. I recall a continuous warfare against local landlords who would move wrecks of old houses as a nucleus for new ones in order to evade the provisions of the building code, and a certain Italian neighbor who was filled with bitterness because his new rear tenement was discovered to be illegal. It seemed impossible to make him understand that the health of the tenants was in any wise as important as his undisturbed rents.

Nevertheless many evils constantly arise in Chicago from congested housing which wiser cities forestall and prevent; the inevitable boarders crowded into a dark tenement already too small for the use of the immigrant family occupying it; the surprisingly large number of delinquent girls who have become criminally involved with their own fathers and uncles; the school children who cannot find a quiet spot in which to read or study and who perforce go into the streets each evening; the tuberculosis superinduced and fostered by the inadequate rooms and breathing spaces. One of the Hull-House residents, under the direction of a Chicago physician who stands high as an authority on tuberculosis and who devotes a large proportion of his time to our vicinity, made an investigation into housing conditions as related to tuberculosis with a result as startling as that of the "lung block" in New York.

The Progressive Vision of Lewis Hine: A Photo Essay

"I have heard their tragic stories," wrote Lewis Hine in 1914, "watched their cramped lives and saw their fruitless struggles in the industrial game where the odds are all against them." Hine spent a decade—from 1908 to 1918—taking thousands of photographs of an estimated 2 million children who worked in the nation's factories, fields, mines, and tenements. His employer was the National Child Labor Committee, a typical Progressive-Era organization in the Jane Addams mold, whose goal it was to survey and publicize the facts of child labor and get the states to pass laws against it. Hine and his fellow reformers had some success; between 1903 and 1917, most of the states outside the South regulated child labor. Most states limited workers under age sixteen to eight hours per day; a few—Rhode Island, New York, and Utah—prohibited the employment of children under sixteen in factories. By the mid-1930s, all states but Wyoming had set a minimum age limit of fourteen years for general factory work. A national child labor law, passed by Congress in 1916 to keep employers from playing one state against another, was declared unconstitutional in 1918.

The photographs that follow show how Hine's work was used in Survey *magazine, a publication that advocated mothers' pensions, an end to child labor, and other social reforms. The photographs are documents, to be sure; they constitute a record of child labor in the early twentieth century. But Hine's vision is more complex than that. What attitude did Hine have toward these young workers? What did he think about work and the workplace? What was his opinion of the larger system of capitalism that employed children?*

Child Workers in Shrimp and Oyster Canneries, Pass Christian, Mississippi, c. 1912.

1915. Original Caption: "Alfred, 13, who lost part of a finger in a spinning machine, has worked since he was 10."

1914. This Complex Tableaux Depicts City Children Pressed into Service to Pick Cotton. Hine wrote: "A group of children who go from a nearby city after school to pick cotton on a Texas farm. Ages range from 4 to 6 years. The enlarged picture is a four-year-old youngster who works regularly."

ILLITERATES IN MASSACHUSETTS

THE THREE YOUNGEST IN THIS GROUP AT A FALL RIVER MILL ARE PORTUGUESE CHILDREN WHO COULD NOT WRITE THEIR OWN NAMES. ONE COULD NOT SPELL THE NAME OF THE STREET HE LIVED ON. ALL THREE SPOKE ALMOST NO ENGLISH.

CHILDREN IN MASSACHUSETTS ARE SUPPOSED TO PASS A FOURTH GRADE TEST BEFORE RECEIVING A WORK PERMIT, BUT THE OFFICERS WHO ISSUE PERMITS OCCASIONALLY HELP A CHILD TO READ EVEN THE SIMPLEST ENGLISH SENTENCE.

AT BEST THIS STANDARD IS SO LOW THAT THE MEAGER ENGLISH LEARNED IN SCHOOL IS SOON FORGOTTEN BY CHILDREN WHOSE WORK FAILS TO STIMULATE INTELLIGENCE AND WHO HEAR LITTLE OR NO ENGLISH AT HOME AND IN THE MILL.

1914.

Cotton Pickers, and a Cotton-Picking Machine, 1914. The copy below reads: "The manufacturers of this cotton-picking machine believe that it will not only save time and money, but will eventually drive out the child pickers. . . ."

Patriotism: A Menace to Liberty

Emma Goldman

*Just as Vietnam would a half century later, and the Iraq war after that, the
Great War divided the American people, creating a climate of hostility and
downright nastiness that spilled over into every corner of American life. Few
German Americans wanted to see the United States declare war on Germany.
Irish Americans feared United States entry into the conflict would mean assistance*

U.S. Army recruiting poster, c. 1918. Library of Congress, Prints &
Photographs Division, WWI Posters.

From Emma Goldman, *Anarchism and Other Essays*, Mother Earth Publishing, New York,
1917, pp. 127–142.

For more on Emma Goldman, see the online exhibition at www.sunsite.berkeley.edu/
Goldman/Exhibition.

to Britain in her struggle against Irish revolutionaries. Socialists—an influential faction in the 1910s—strongly opposed the American declaration of war, branding it a "crime against the people of the United States." The government responded by selling the war to Americans as if it were a used car and, in the Sedition Act of 1918, by making it illegal for people to make false statements that interfered with the conduct of the war. Among those prosecuted and imprisoned under the statute was the eloquent and distinguished leader of the Socialist Party of America, Eugene Debs.

Emma Goldman was a feisty and determined anarchist, rather than a mainstream progressive reformer. To most people, then as now, anarchism connoted violence and even political assassination. While Goldman did not entirely reject such methods, she emphasized anarchism as a philosophy of personal freedom. Freedom meant freedom from the dominion of religion; freedom from property; reproductive freedom; and, perhaps most of all, freedom from a coercive government that oppressed workers and labor unions and identified with, and supported, capitalism and big business.

Goldman was imprisoned in 1916 for publicly advocating birth control and again in 1917 for obstructing the draft. She was deported to her native Russia in December 1919—one of 249 Russian-born aliens deported—at the height of the postwar Red Scare, a phenomenon triggered by fears that the Russian Revolution of 1917 would spread radical ideas across the globe.

On what grounds does Goldman criticize patriotism? Which of her arguments are the most reasonable? And which the least? In your opinion, what is the most important positive function of patriotism?

What is patriotism? Is it love of one's birthplace, the place of childhood's recollections and hopes, dreams and aspirations? Is it the place where, in childlike naivety, we would watch the fleeting clouds, and wonder why we, too, could not run so swiftly? . . . Or the place where we would sit at mother's knee, enraptured by wonderful tales of great deeds and conquests? In short, is it love for the spot, every inch representing dear and precious recollections of a happy, joyous, and playful childhood?

If that were patriotism, few American men of today could be called upon to be patriotic, since the place of play has been turned into factory, mill, and mine, while deafening sounds of machinery have replaced the music of the birds. Nor can we longer hear the tales of great deeds, for the stories our mothers tell today are but those of sorrow, tears, and grief.

What, then, is patriotism? "Patriotism, sir, is the last resort of scoundrels," said Dr. Johnson. Leo Tolstoy, the greatest anti-patriot of our times, defines patriotism as the principle that will justify the training of wholesale murderers; a trade that requires better equipment for the exercise of man-killing than the making of such necessities of life as shoes, clothing, and houses; a trade that guarantees better returns and greater glory than that of the average workingman.

Gustave Hervé, another great anti-patriot, justly calls patriotism a superstition—one far more injurious, brutal, and inhumane than religion. The superstition of religion originated in man's inability to explain natural

Emma Goldman, riding a tram, c. 1918. Note the "Uncle Sam Wants You" sign above her.
Library of Congress.

phenomena. That is, when primitive man heard thunder or saw the light-ning, he could not account for either, and therefore concluded that back of them must be a force greater than himself. Similarly he saw a supernatural force in the rain, and in the various other changes in nature. Patriotism, on the other hand, is a superstition artificially created and maintained through a network of lies and falsehoods; a superstition that robs man of his self-respect and dignity, and increases his arrogance and conceit.

Indeed, conceit, arrogance, and egotism are the essentials of patriot-ism. Let me illustrate. Patriotism assumes that our globe is divided into little spots, each one surrounded by an iron gate. Those who have had the fortune of being born on some particular spot, consider themselves better, nobler, grander, more intelligent than the living beings inhabiting any other spot. It is, therefore, the duty of everyone living on that chosen spot to fight, kill, and die in the attempt to impose his superiority upon all the others.

The inhabitants of the other spots reason in like manner, of course, with the result that, from early infancy, the mind of the child is poisoned with blood-curdling stories about the Germans, the French, the Italians, Russians, etc. When the child has reached manhood, he is thoroughly saturated with the belief that he is chosen by the Lord himself to defend *his* country against the attack or invasion of any foreigner. It is for that purpose that we are clam-oring for a greater army and navy, more battleships and ammunition. It is for that purpose that America has within a short time spent four hundred million dollars. Just think of it—four hundred million dollars taken from the produce of *the people*. For surely it is not the rich who contribute to patriotism. They are cosmopolitans, perfectly at home in every land. . . .

But, then, patriotism is not for those who represent wealth and power. It is good enough for the people. It reminds one of the historic wisdom of Frederick the Great, the bosom friend of Voltaire, who said: "Religion is a fraud, but it must be maintained for the masses." . . .

The awful waste that patriotism necessitates ought to be sufficient to cure the man of even average intelligence from this disease. Yet patriotism demands still more. The people are urged to be patriotic and for that luxury they pay, not only by supporting their "defenders," but even by sacrificing their own children. Patriotism requires allegiance to the flag, which means obedience and readiness to kill father, mother, brother, sister. . . .

Considering the evil results that patriotism is fraught with for the aver-age man, it is as nothing compared with the insult and injury that patriotism heaps upon the soldier himself,—that poor, deluded victim of superstition and ignorance. He, the savior of his country, the protector of his nation,—what has patriotism in store for him? A life of slavish submission, vice, and perversion, during peace; a life of danger, exposure, and death, during war.

While on a recent lecture tour in San Francisco, I visited the Presidio, the most beautiful spot overlooking the Bay and Golden Gate Park. Its pur-pose should have been playgrounds for children, gardens and music for the recreation of the weary. Instead it is made ugly, dull, and gray by barracks,—barracks wherein the rich would not allow their dogs to dwell. In these mis-erable shanties soldiers are herded like cattle; here they waste their young days, polishing the boots and brass buttons of their superior officers. Here, too, I saw the distinction of classes: sturdy sons of a free Republic, drawn up in line like convicts, saluting every passing shrimp of a lieutenant. American equality, degrading manhood and elevating the uniform!

Barrack life further tends to develop tendencies of sexual perversion. It is gradually producing along this line results similar to European military conditions. Havelock Ellis, the noted writer on sex psychology, has made a thorough study of the subject. I quote: "Some of the barracks are great centers of male prostitution. . . ."

Thinking men and women the world over are beginning to realize that patriotism is too narrow and limited a conception to meet the necessities of our time. The centralization of power has brought into being an international feeling of solidarity among the oppressed nations of the world; a solidarity which represents a greater harmony of interests between the workingman of America and his brothers abroad than between the American miner and his exploiting compatriot; a solidarity which fears not foreign invasion, because it is bringing all the workers to the point when they will say to their masters, "Go and do your own killing. We have done it long enough for you." . . .

THE BIG PICTURE

Progressivism constituted one of the three most important liberal reform movements of the twentieth century (the other two were Franklin D. Roosevelt's New Deal and Lyndon Johnson's Great Society). Yet every reform movement has its limitations and its peculiarities, and the materials in this chapter can help one begin the process of understanding progressivism's qualities. One can always ask whether reformers have identified the appropriate enemy or source of the problem, and that question is a good one to apply to the effort, described by Elisabeth Perry, to regulate New York City dance halls. Similarly, Lewis Hine's photographs of children working can be examined for what they might tell us about the mind of the reformer—that is, Hine. Was he trying to show us that children were being terribly exploited—and therefore, that all child labor should be abolished? Is there anything in the photographs to suggest that Hine was opposed to capitalism itself? Or to the use of technology? Similarly, how deep was Jane Addams's desire for "reform"? Did she want to change the way factories produced goods, or was she more interested in helping workers "adjust" to existing conditions?

Chapter 7

From War to "Normalcy"

The generation that came of age in the 1920s did so in the shadow of World War I. A nation led to expect that the struggle would be morally satisfying—that had boldly announced in song that "the Yanks are coming"—would be reduced to seeking meaning in an unidentifiable soldier, buried in Arlington, Virginia. That a war of such short duration—direct American involvement lasted little more than eighteen months—could have had such an impact may seem surprising. But part of an explanation may be found by examining how Americans experienced the conflict and what they were led to believe it would achieve.

Several groups experienced the war years as a time of increased opportunity. Blacks—migrating from the South into Chicago, Detroit, New York, and other industrial cities—and women—heretofore denied most jobs open to men—found themselves suddenly employable. The same circumstances allowed organized labor to double its membership in the four years after 1914. Farmers prospered because of rising European demand and, after 1917, because of government price guarantees. Soldiers, however, experienced the typical wartime "tax" on income, and many lost their positions on promotional ladders.

Continued deficit spending fueled the economy during demobilization. In 1919, activity in automobile production and building construction, two industries held back by the war, helped the nation avoid a prolonged postwar tailspin. But economic crisis could be postponed for only so long. By mid-1921, the economy was mired in a serious depression that cut industrial output by some 20 percent. It seems likely that a downturn in the postwar economy, deeply affecting a people who had no history of planning for such events, helped to dissolve the aura of economic progress and personal success that had been part of the war and to inaugurate a decade of conflict between young and old, employer and employee, country and city, religion and science, nation and locality. In the minds of many Americans, depression was inseparably linked to demobilization and the peace settlement.

Perhaps fighting a war—especially a war with which large numbers of the population disagreed—required a kind of artificially imposed unity. But when the great crusade was over, a new crusade, called the Red Scare, took the place of wartime coercion of dissidents. When this latest hysteria subsided in the spring of 1920, hundreds of radicals of every persuasion—Socialists, Communists, even ordinary union members—had been arrested, beaten, lynched, tried, or deported.

Just as wartime coercion had yielded to the Red Scare, so was the Red Scare reincarnated in the politics of Warren Harding. In May 1920, emphasizing that "too much has been said about bolshevism in America," Harding coined the word that would capture his appeal and win him the presidency, urging return to "not heroism, but healing, not nostrums, but normalcy." With "normalcy," Harding and the American people seemed to be rejecting the world that Woodrow Wilson had sought to create—the world in which words replaced concrete realities, in which dreams of world government (the League of Nations) transcended political facts. The government's advertising agency, The Committee on Public Information, had described the war as "a Crusade not merely to re-win the tomb of Christ, but to bring back to earth the rule of right, the peace, goodwill to men and gentleness he taught." When it proved much less than this, Americans beat an emotional retreat to the comfort of Harding's slogans.

By mid-decade, when prosperity had returned and "normalcy" was in full swing, it was clear that the economy was undergoing a gradual change of enormous importance: the old economy of "production" was yielding, decade by decade, to a new economy of "consumption." This change occurred partly because many of the problems of production appeared to have been solved; the moving assembly line and Frederick W. Taylor's scientific management had made possible a new level of productive efficiency. Now the roadblock to abundance seemed to be at the level of the consumer. One approach, decidedly unpopular with business and with the Republican presidents who held office in the decade, was to encourage consumption by using the tax system to distribute money to those who would spend rather than save it. Another approach was to teach (some would say condition) people to desire, and then to buy, the available products. This teaching or conditioning was the function of advertising, which grew by leaps and bounds during the 1920s. Many advertising agencies were staffed by people who had honed their skills at the Committee on Public Information. Indeed, the ad agencies of the twenties were simply applying what appeared to be the great lesson of wartime propaganda: that the "masses" could be manipulated—made to go to war, or to buy—using the techniques of modern psychology.

The 1920s had powerful currents of individualism, of course. In fact, the decade has been rightly famed for its affection for jazz, for its compulsion for mah-jongg and flagpole sitting, for the flapper, and for the iconoclast H. L. Mencken (for whom every group, even the New England town meeting, was a mob run by demagogues). Harding's "normalcy," however, seemed to center on a program of cultural conformity, and it was to infect the entire decade. The Ku Klux Klan, revived at a Georgia meeting in 1915, grew rapidly in the early 1920s through campaigns against blacks, Catholics, Jews, and immigrants. National prohibition, which required millions to give up deeply ingrained drinking habits or evade the law, was in effect throughout the decade. The first law establishing immigration quotas was passed in 1921; a second measure passed three years later was designed to reduce immigration of peoples from eastern and southern Europe—the later immigrants discussed in Chapter 4. If "normalcy" is broad enough to encompass these aspects of the 1920s, then perhaps wartime coercion, the Red Scare, the new economy of consumption, and "normalcy" were all variations on a theme—a theme perhaps placed in bold relief by the war, demobilization, and postwar economic crisis, but ultimately one set more deeply in the nation's character and its institutions than any of these events.

Political Fundamentalism

William E. Leuchtenburg

As the nation entered the decade of the 1920s, not much remained of the progressive movement's desire—limited as it was in many respects—for social justice, or even of the impulse to regulate and restrain big business. To be sure, the self-congratulatory, even arrogant business climate of the 1920s, abetted by a trio of Republican presidents, encouraged the progressive fondness for corporate and governmental efficiency. And those elements of the progressive movement that had emphasized morality and social control—those who favored prohibiting the public consumption of alcoholic beverages, regulating the dance halls (see Chapter 6), or legislating the nation's genetic makeup by regulating immigration—were as busy and as central to the 1920s as they had been a decade or two before. But the progressive enthusiasm for protecting ordinary people, especially women, children, and workers, from the ravages of industrialization and urbanization, was moved to the margins of society.

Replacing it was an attitude and perspective that was more conservative, more mean-spirited, and more selfish. In the following selection, William Leuchtenburg, a distinguished historian and masterful writer, assembles some of the elements of this new perspective, labeling it "political fundamentalism." It is a curious and unusual phrase, combining politics and religion. What was "political fundamentalism," and why did it emerge with such strength in the 1920s? Was it the product of ignorance and superstition, or an approach advocated by the educated and knowledgeable? Was it reasonable or misguided—or both? What elements of "political fundamentalism" can one observe in today's society?

Despite prosperity, the United States in the postwar years felt deeply threatened from within. The American people suddenly had thrust upon them the responsibilities of war and the making of peace, and their contact with Europe and power politics was bitterly disillusioning. In a world of Bolshevik revolutions and Bela Kuns, of general strikes and Mussolini's march on Rome, there was danger that America, too, might be infected by the social diseases of the Old World. Yet the threat of foreign contagion was not as terrifying as the menace of change from within. In part the danger seemed to come from enclaves of the foreign-born, not yet adapted to American ways, in part from the rise of the metropolis, with values different from those of nineteenth-century America, in part from the new currents of moral relativism and cosmopolitanism. Not a little of the anxiety arose from the disturbing knowledge that Americans themselves no longer had their former confidence in democracy or religion. "They have," observed André Siegfried, "a vague uneasy fear of being overwhelmed from within, and of suddenly finding one day that they are no longer themselves."

Political fundamentalism attempted to deny real divisions in the nation by coercing a sense of oneness. Celebration of the Constitution became a tribal rite; in the 1920s, Americans, as one English writer noted, were "a people who, of all the world, craved most for new things, yet were all but Chinese in their worship of their Constitution and their ancestors who devised it." Constitution-worship was a kind of magical nativism, a form of activity in which, as the anthropologist Ralph Linton writes, "the society's members feel that by behaving as the ancestors did they will, in some usually undefined way, help to recreate the total situation in which the ancestors lived." Efforts toward social change were condemned as un-American. "Individualism?" cried an American Legion commander in California. "Down with all Isms!" This resistance to change and this insistence on conformity intertwined with the desire of rural churchmen to turn back modernism in religion and compel morality by statute. In 1924, Protestant fundamentalists wove together both movements in a "Bible-Christ-and-Constitution Campaign," while the Ku Klux Klan's warcry was "Back to the Constitution."

Many felt hostile to anything foreign. Isolationism had its counterpart in a determination to curb immigration, to avoid alien contamination and to preserve the old America ethnically before it was too late. In the late nineteenth century and the early years of the twentieth century, the drive for immigration restriction had foundered on presidential vetoes. Restrictionism could not overcome the industrialists' demand for cheap labor or, more important, America's confidence in its ability to absorb large numbers of foreign-born. World War I badly shook that confidence. The war revealed that the sympathies of millions of Americans were determined by their countries of origin, and the fight over the League of Nations reflected the animosities of Irish-Americans, German-Americans, and other "hyphenated Americans." In his defense of the Versailles Treaty, Wilson charged: "Hyphens are the knives that are being stuck into this document." By the end of the war years, many agreed with Walter Hines Page: "We Americans have got to . . . hang our Irish agitators and shoot our hyphenates and bring up our children with reverence for English history and in the awe of English literature."

The drive for immigration restriction after the war was based, to a far greater degree than before, on a pseudo-scientific racism. Men with little knowledge of either science or public affairs were accepted as experts on "race," although their writings revealed neither insight nor good judgment. In *The Passing of the Great Race* (1916), Madison Grant contended that race was the determinant of civilization and that only Aryans had built great cultures. "The man of the old stock," alleged Grant, "is being crowded out of many country districts by these foreigners, just as he is today being literally driven off the streets of New York City by the swarms of Polish Jews. These immigrants adopt the language of the native American, they wear his clothes, they steal his name and they are beginning to take his women, but they seldom adopt his religion or understand his ideals." Lothrop Stoddard in *The Rising Tide of Color* (1920) and Professor Edwin East of Harvard warned that white races were being engulfed by the more fertile colored races. Most influential of all were the widely read articles by Kenneth Roberts in the *Saturday Evening Post*. Roberts urged that the immigration laws be revised to admit fewer Polish Jews, who were "human parasites"; cautioned against Social Democrats, since "social democracy gives off a distinctly sour, bolshevistic odor"; and opposed unrestricted immigration, for it would inevitably produce "a hybrid race of people as worthless and futile as the good-for-nothing mongrels of Central America and Southeastern Europe."

In the first fifteen years of the century, an average of one million immigrants a year had entered the United States. Slowed to a trickle by the war, the stream of immigration became a swollen torrent after the armistice. From June, 1920, to June, 1921, more than 800,000 persons poured into the country, 65 percent of them from southern and eastern Europe, and consuls in Europe reported that millions more were planning to leave. By February, 1921, Ellis Island was so jammed that immigration authorities had to divert ships to Boston. Alarmed almost to the point of panic, Congress rushed through an emergency act to restrict immigration; it passed the House in a few hours without a record vote and was adopted by the Senate soon after by 78–1.

Despite initial opposition, sentiment for a more lasting form of immigration restriction soon gained increasing strength. . . . With the new prosperity of 1923 and increased mechanical efficiency, which reduced the need for mass labor, however, the chief obstacle to permanent immigration restriction was removed at the same time that industrialists, agitated by the Red Scare, grew increasingly nativist. So did unions, largely confined to skilled craftsmen, who for some time had wanted to limit new entrants into the labor market, thereby enhancing the market value of their members by reducing supply.

In 1924, Congress passed, over scant opposition, the National Origins Act, which drastically cut down the total of newcomers to be admitted each year and established quotas to be calculated on the basis of the proportion of descendants of each nationality resident in the United States at an earlier time. Under that proviso, the more "Nordic" lands of northern and western Europe got 85 percent of quotas. In addition, the law forbade all Oriental immigration—a gratuitous insult which was marked in Japan with a day of national mourning. "It is a sorry business," wrote Hughes, "and I am greatly depressed. It has undone the work of the Washington Conference and implanted the seeds of an antagonism which are sure to bear fruit in the future."

The law, reflecting racist warnings about a threat to "Anglo-Saxon" stock, aimed at freezing the country ethnically by sharply restricting the "new" immigration from southern and eastern Europe. In the debate on the bill, Congressmen reviled the foreign-born of the great cities, particularly New York, to whom were attributed every evil of the day. "On the one side," asserted a Kansas congressman, "is beer, bolshevism, unassimilating settlements and perhaps many flags—on the other side is constitutional government; one flag, stars and stripes." For three hundred years, English squires and cutthroats, French Huguenots, Spanish adventurers, pious subjects of German duchies, and, above all in recent years, peasants from Calabria to the Ukraine had come to America in search of gold, or land, or freedom, or something to which they could not put a name. Now it was over. One of the great folk movements in the history of man had come to an end.

While the immigration restriction movement drew on the apprehension that America might be transformed ethnically by an invasion of alien elements from without, the Ku Klux Klan preyed on the feeling that the country was already in peril from elements within. The KKK was organized on Stone Mountain in Georgia on Thanksgiving night, 1915, in the light of a blazing cross, by William J. Simmons, a former Methodist circuit rider and organizer of fraternal associations. Modeled on the hooded order of Reconstruction days that murdered blacks, the Klan admitted "native born, white, gentile Americans" who believed in white supremacy; by implication, they could not be Catholics. Although it took the name of an old Southern society, the Klan owed more to the nativist tradition of Know-Nothingism, having its greatest appeal not to the deep South but to the Midwest, Southwest, and Far West, where people were worried less by blacks than by the encroachment of "foreigners," especially if they were papists.

The Klan attracted its chief support from the sense of desperation experienced by old stock Protestants who felt themselves being eclipsed by the rise of the city with its polyglot masses. Though the Klan had a following in some cities, especially ones undergoing rapid growth, two-thirds of its members lived in places with a population of less than 100,000, and the KKK found metropolises with large proportions of the foreign-born hostile territory. In cities such as Boston and San Francisco, the Klan got nowhere, and in New York it did not dare show its face at a public gathering.

"The reason there is a Klan in America today," said Colorado's grand dragon, "is to make America safe for Americans." Those attracted to the KKK thought themselves engaged in a battle which their falling birth rates doomed them to lose. "The dangers," Simmons explained, "were in the tremendous influx of foreign immigration, tutored in alien dogmas and alien creeds, slowly pushing the native-born white American population into the center of the country, there to be ultimately overwhelmed and smothered." In its elaborate ritual, its stark pageantry, its white-hooded sheets, its titles of "Exalted Cyclops," "Klaliff," "Klokard," "Kligrapp," and "Klabee," the KKK appealed to the lodge vogue of blue collar and middle-class America. When the Klansman sang "klodes" with his neighbor and klasped his hand in a secret grip, he felt reassured.

In the early years of the 1920s, the Klan, which had less than 5,000 members as late as 1920, experienced a phenomenal growth, and, with probably a few million adherents at one time or other during this period, made its weight felt in politics. In Youngstown, Ohio, the KKK elected the mayor and the entire city government, and in Texas, where it ousted a four-term U.S. Senator, the Klan dominated the legislature and the cities of Dallas, Fort Worth, and Wichita Falls. Candidates running with KKK backing were elected to the United States Senate in six states, and the Klan controlled municipal governments in cities such as Denver and El Paso. In Oklahoma, the governor called all the citizens of the state into military service and declared martial law in an effort to put down the organization; the Klan-controlled legislature retaliated by impeaching him and removing him from office in November, 1923. In staunchly Republican Oregon, a state settled by Eastern and Midwestern Protestants, the Klan helped elect a Democratic governor, Walter Pierce, by the largest majority in state history and supported a law that wiped out parochial schools by requiring parents to send all children between eight and sixteen to public schools. (In 1925, the Supreme Court [*Pierce v. Society of Sisters*] declared the law unconstitutional.) For the most part, though, the Klan did not know, once it had power, what to do with it, for it was more a vehicle to express resentment than a movement with coherent policy aims.

Where the Klan entered, in its wake too often came floggings, kidnappings, branding with acid, mutilations, church burnings, and even murders. In the South, the Klan sometimes used terror to preserve a social system that was swiftly changing. Yet even in the South, intimidation, although it was used against blacks (a bellhop in Texas was branded on the forehead with the initials "KKK," and black homes were burned in Florida to discourage voting), was employed more often against Catholics or political enemies or bootleggers or, most important, against individuals deemed immoral. In Birmingham, a Klansman murdered a Catholic priest in cold blood and was acquitted; in Naperville, Illinois, two hours after a monster Klan ceremony, a Roman Catholic church was torched. When the mayor of Columbus, Georgia, ignored demands of the KKK that he remove the city manager, his home was dynamited. . . .

Such episodes did not characterize the everyday routine of the KKK, but they were symptomatic. Most Klansmen never participated in violence, and not a few viewed the organization as an interest group for white Protestants or a fraternal association that sometimes carried on benevolent activities. When the Klan did resort to flogging or social ostracism, it was less likely to do so against ethnic minorities than to people thought to have broken some moral code—by trafficking in liquor, or gambling, or carrying on an extramarital affair. (One of its avowed aims was to "break up roadside parking.") Yet, as an organization exclusively of white Protestants, there was no mistaking its hostility to Catholics and Jews and to anyone it defined as "alien." The Klansmen, who thought white Protestants were being victimized, had no comprehension of the fact that it was not they but Catholics and Jews who faced blatant discrimination in employment, and blacks who, when they were not at the mercy of lynch mobs, were denied the most fundamental Constitutional rights. Furthermore, as Don Kirschner has pointed out, while there were any number of fraternal associations that promised conviviality and solace, "the one thing that the Klan offered that was uniquely its own was extra-legal or even illegal action."

Opponents of the KKK fought fire with fire. Especially in northern cities, the order encountered resistance not only from Catholics, Jews, and liberals, but also from bootleggers and other elements of organized crime. . . .

The Klan reached the heights in Indiana, and in Indiana it toppled to its death. Hundreds of thousands of white-sheeted Klansmen took over the state. Many of them sauntered brazenly through town with their hoods flung back, not even bothering to conceal their identity. On parade nights in Kokomo, the police force vanished and white-sheeted figures, bearing a striking resemblance to the absent patrolmen, directed traffic. The Grand Dragon of the Indiana KKK, David Stephenson, extended his influence in the Klan beyond the borders of the state and into the Republican party, especially through his association with the governor of Indiana, Ed Jackson. A gross, corrupt man, who was a boozer, a womanizer, and a violent brawler, Stephenson made himself a political power and a multimillionaire overnight through his Klan activities. Finally, he overreached himself: he forced a twenty-eight-year-old State House secretary onto a Chicago-bound train and brutally assaulted her. When she took poison, his henchmen spirited her to a hotel and held her for several days without medical aid; a month later she died. In November, 1925, Stephenson was convicted of second-degree murder and sentenced to life in prison. When his crony, Governor Jackson, refused to pardon him, Stephenson opened a "little black box" which sent a congressman, the mayor of Indianapolis, and other officials to jail; Jackson was indicted for bribery but escaped because of the statute of limitations.

As early as 1924, the Klan had been put on the run in Oklahoma, Louisiana, and Texas, and the conviction of Stephenson sealed its doom. It brought into bold relief both the hypocrisy of the Klan (Stephenson had denounced petting parties and had warred on vice) and the corruption that threaded the history of the order. Many of the KKK leaders had joined the organization primarily for personal profit; many who preached righteousness were corrupt. Feeding on a millennial lust for rule by a league of the pure, the Klan, once in power, sometimes licensed the very evils it said it would exterminate. Its ugly side lay in the fact that it appealed to many who were frustrated by the rigid moral code of the small town. Klansmen often felt tempted by that which they were condemning—sexual freedom, modernity—and their frustration sometimes took a sadistic turn, as when they stripped "fallen" women naked and whipped them. The Stephenson episode revealed everything that was seamy about the organization. The KKK never recovered.

To a considerably greater degree than the Klan, the prohibition movement, which was often the focus of KKK activities, centered in the rural areas of the country, especially in the villages where the preacher could speak with authority on matters of politics and morals. Prohibition was a way that rural Americans could impose their mores on city folk; that Baptists and Methodists could badger people of other faiths, especially Catholics; that old stock Americans could compel newer arrivals to conform; and that the middle class could get workingmen to give up their favorite beverages. . . .

The campaign to preserve America as it was, which characterized both the Klan and prohibition, came to a head in the movement of Protestant fundamentalism climaxed by the Scopes trial. Although the publication of Darwin's *Origin of Species* in 1859 had touched off a controversy between science and theology that rocked the Western world for the next two decades, men such as Asa Gray in the United States and Charles Kingsley in England had succeeded in reconciling evolution and Christianity; by the time of World War I, an assault on Darwin seemed as unlikely as an attack on Copernicus. When in 1922 the Kentucky legislature came within a single vote of banning the teaching of evolution in the schools, though, the nation suddenly awoke to a deep-seated hostility to Darwinian assumptions in rural America that it thought had been scotched a half-century before.

In farmlands and small towns, particularly in the mountain country of the South, many Protestant ministers had never subscribed to Darwinism; they continued to believe that the only true account of the origin of the world could be found by a literal reading of the first two chapters of Genesis. The attempts of modernists to accommodate religion to scholarly criticism of the Bible had, the fundamentalists argued, shattered the chief tenets of Christianity. One fundamentalist wrote: "The Modernist juggles the Scripture statements of His deity and denies His virgin birth, making Him a Jewish bastard, born out of wedlock, and stained forever with the shame of His Mother's immorality." To attempt to preserve religion while denying the truth of Christ's resurrection, wrote the editor of a Baptist periodical, "is like saying that the title to the house which you prepared as a habitation for your old age is a fraud. . . . If Jesus Christ did not rise from the dead, we cannot depend upon a word of what he said."

Strengthened by popular anger against Germany (the home of modernist religion) and by the Red Scare (which linked atheism with communism), fundamentalism made modest gains during and after the war, but it amounted to little until William Jennings Bryan joined the anti-evolution movement. The Peerless Leader was a man to reckon with; for three decades, he had been the folk hero of the Mississippi Valley heartland. A man of transparent sincerity, courageous in the face of repeated defeats, a man whose belief in democracy was instinctive, Bryan was the authentic representative of the tradition of Jacksonian democracy (with a leaven of nineteenth-century evangelical Christianity) in his suspicion of the expert and the university-educated as members of a privileged class. "It is better," wrote Bryan, "to trust in the Rock of Ages than to know the age of rocks; it is better for one to know that he is close to the Heavenly Father than to know how far the stars in the heavens are apart."

Always a factionalist, Bryan threw himself into the anti-evolution campaign with the same zeal he had marshaled against the "goldbugs" in 1896. Bryan, wrote Heywood Broun, "has never lived in a land of men and women. To him this country has been from the beginning peopled by believers and heretics." Under Bryan's leadership, the campaign to compel the teaching of a biology that conformed to the account of the origin of man in Genesis quickly caught the attention of the nation. It was a war of country and small town against the city, a war largely centered in the South. In the Northeast, the anti-evolutionists got nowhere, even though fundamentalists held a number of city pulpits. When a bill was introduced in the Delaware legislature to forbid teaching that man evolved from lower animals, it was referred facetiously to the Committee on Fish, Game, and Oysters. In many Southern states, too, anti-evolution efforts were turned back by counterattacks from university presidents and urban newspapers, but in Oklahoma, Florida, and North Carolina the anti-evolutionists won partial victories. When the Texas legislature turned down a bill to censor textbooks, Governor "Ma" Ferguson took matters in her own hands and blacklisted or bowdlerized books to remove any mention of Darwinsim. "I am a Christian mother," the Governor declared, "and I am not going to let that kind of rot go into Texas textbooks."

The first smashing victory for the anti-evolutionists came in Tennessee, where a farmer who was also a part-time school teacher and clerk of the Round Lick Association of Primitive Baptists was elected to the legislature on the single plank of advocating an anti-evolution law. Bryan and a powerful fundamentalist lobby moved in on Nashville to support him; in March, 1925, the legislature made it illegal "for any teacher in any of the universities, normal, and all other public schools of the state, to teach any theory that denies the story of the divine creation of man as taught in the Bible and to teach instead that man has descended from a lower order of animals."

That spring, in the mountain town of Dayton, Tennessee, John T. Scopes, a slim, bespectacled young biology teacher at Central High School, a man of engaging modesty and wit, was sipping lemon phosphates at Robinson's Drug Store with several of his friends, and in particular with George Rappelyea, manager of the local mine, and druggist Robinson, chairman of the county schoolbook committee. They talked about the law, of which they disapproved, and about the fact that the American Civil Liberties Union had offered counsel to any Tennessee teacher who challenged it. More in the spirit of fun than of social protest, the mine manager and the teacher hatched a scheme. The next day Scopes lectured from Hunter's *Civic Biology* and Rappelyea filed a complaint with local officials; the police brought Scopes before the justices of the peace, and he was bound over to a grand jury.

To Scopes's defense came Clarence Darrow, the most famous defense lawyer in the country and an avowed agnostic, Arthur Garfield Hays, a civil liberties attorney, and Dudley Field Malone, who in other years had campaigned with Bryan for the Democratic cause. Retained by the World's Christian Fundamentals Association to assist the prosecution was William Jennings Bryan, who announced that the trial would be a "duel to the death" between Christianity and evolution. "He gave the impression," observed *Le Matin*, "of one returned to the earth from the wars of religion."

The Scopes trial is usually seen simply as a struggle of champions of truth pitted against Tennessee Hottentots. Certainly, academic freedom and respect for the findings of science constituted the most important feature of the case, and nothing is to be said for the attempt to force teachers to give their students a wholly inaccurate account of the evolution of man. It should be noted, though, Tennessee had no intention of enforcing the law, which many legislators went along with not because they doubted Darwin but because they did not want to become enmeshed in a controversy that might imperil university appropriations. Nobody ever interfered with Scopes's teaching until he and his fellow conspirator contrived their scenario, in part as a way to put their town on the map, which the "monkey trial" surely did. Quite apart from its singular origin, the case was never simply a morality play between the good forces of intellectual liberty and the evil spirits of obscurantism. In the Scopes trial, the provincialism of the city was arrayed against the provincialism of the country, the shallowness of Mencken against the shallowness of Bryan, the arrogance of the scientists against the arrogance of the fundamentalists.

The very faith in science, as C. E. Ayres pointed out, had reached the point where it had become "superstition, in another guise." In the 1920s, the nation was captivated by electricity, by the new world of radioactivity, even by more mundane matters like calories and vitamins; science, many people believed, was a universal balm that would answer every human need. High priests of the science cult dismissed traditional concerns as remnants of an irrational age. "No one," declared Watson, the behaviorist psychologist, "has ever touched a soul, or has seen one in a test tube." Churchgoers were understandably concerned about a dogma that stripped away myths, presented no adequate system of ethics, offered little sustenance in times of grief, and provided a partial, limited glimpse of man and the universe.

Fundamentalism made sense to men and women in isolated rural areas still directly dependent on nature for their livelihood; they put their trust in divine intervention and depreciated human capacity because it had been their experience that people were all but helpless when disease struck or when their corn withered in a drought. They were much less likely than city folk to believe that life had the predictable rhythm of an assembly line and more willing to hope and pray that a benign Providence would spare them the caprices of nature. Their adversaries in the city found fundamentalism incomprehensible because the rational methods of production in the factory and life in the metropolis suggested that man, through science and education, could solve the major problems of living and might even be able someday to solve the ultimate questions of human existence.

At the Dayton trial, the court maintained that the only issue properly before it was whether Scopes had violated the law, which he clearly had. The defense attempted to shift the emphasis to the questioning of the law itself. Scopes's attorneys, who argued that a belief in evolution was consistent with Christian faith and that Genesis was allegorical, were frustrated in their efforts to demonstrate that the statute was either wicked or foolish, until Hays hit upon the idea of calling Bryan to the stand as an expert on the Bible.

In the suffocatingly hot courtroom, Darrow and Bryan, each in shirt-sleeves, faced off against one another in one of the most dramatic confrontations of the twentieth century. In response to Darrow's grilling, Bryan declared that the whale had swallowed Jonah (although he thought it was a fish rather than a whale), that Eve had been made from Adam's rib, that all languages derived from the collapse of the tower of Babel, and that Joshua had literally made the sun stand still. Professing himself an authority on religion and science, Bryan was revealed by Darrow's devastating probing to be a man of dense ignorance. Bryan made a fatal admission: he conceded that when the Bible said the world had been created in six days, it did not necessarily mean that a "day" was twenty-four hours long; it might be a million years. Thus Bryan, whose position was grounded on the conviction that the Bible must be read literally, had himself "interpreted" the Bible, thereby destroying the basis for opposition to modernism.

The Dayton trial ended in victory for the fundamentalists, but it was a hollow one. Scopes was found guilty, as had been anticipated from the first, and fined $100. The Tennessee supreme court later threw out the fine on a technicality, thereby blocking his attorneys from testing the constitutionality of the law. (Scopes himself received a scholarship to attend the University of Chicago, where he was trained as a geologist.) Scopes had lost, but, in another sense, he had won. In the last minutes of Darrow's cross-examination, there was raucous laughter at Bryan, derision from his own followers. A terrible pathos filled Bryan's last days; soon after the trial, he died—after having written an autobiographical statement to prove that he was neither an ignorant nor an uneducated man. The anti-evolutionists won in three more southern states, but with Bryan's death the heart went out of the movement, and it quickly subsided.

The aftermath of the Scopes trial is symbolic of the fate of political fundamentalism in the 1920s. Immigration restriction, the Klan, prohibition, and Protestant fundamentalism all had in common a hostility to modernity and a desire to arrest change through coercion by statute. The anti-evolutionists won the Scopes trial; yet, in a more important sense, they were defeated, overwhelmed by the tide of cosmopolitanism. Such was the fate of each of the other movements. By the end of 1933, the Eighteenth Amendment had been repealed and the Klan was a dim memory. Immigration restriction, which apparently scored a complete triumph and certainly did win a major one, was frustrated when (since the law did not apply to the Western Hemisphere) Mexicans, French Canadians, Cubans, and Puerto Ricans, most of them "swarthy" Catholics, streamed in. Ostensibly successful on every front, the political fundamentalists in the 1920s were making a last stand in a lost cause.

The Scopes Trial: Testimony of William Jennings Bryan

In the spring of 1925, biology teacher John T. Scopes went on trial in Dayton, Tennessee, for teaching evolution, a practice prohibited under a new state law. Scopes was defended by Clarence Darrow, a brilliant lawyer of national reputation. The prosecution was assisted by William Jennings Bryan, the Democratic candidate for president in 1896 and 1900 and a man of deep religious conviction. There was never much doubt about the verdict, and when the judge ruled that the defense could not bring on expert witnesses to probe the subject of evolution, the trial seemed over after less than a week. Some reporters left town.

But on a Monday afternoon, following a weekend recess, the defense called Bryan as an expert witness on the Bible. "All the lawyers leaped to their feet at once," Scopes recalled. A confident Bryan agreed to take the stand, though the jury was not allowed to be present. Darrow's examination took place on the speaker's platform of the courthouse lawn, where the judge had moved the proceedings only hours before, when a rumor circulated that the courthouse was cracking from the strain of the large crowd. About 3,000 people assembled in the open air to hear the exchange.

Imagine yourself a reporter. As Bryan testifies, it becomes clear that a rare moment is taking shape. When court is adjourned, you find the nearest available phone and call your editor back home. When he comes on the line, you offer him an opening paragraph for one of the great stories of the century.

Examination of William Jennings Bryan by Clarence Darrow, counsel for the defense:

Q. You have given considerable study to the Bible, haven't you, Mr. Bryan?

A. Yes, sir, I have tried to.

Q. Then you have made a general study of it?

A. Yes, I have; I have studied the Bible for about fifty years, or sometime more than that, but, of course, I have studied it more as I have become older than when I was but a boy.

Q. You claim that everything in the Bible should be literally interpreted?

A. I believe everything in the Bible should be accepted as it is given there: some of the Bible is given illustratively. For instance: "Ye are the salt of the earth." I would not insist that man was actually salt, or that he had flesh of salt, but it is used in the sense of salt as saving God's people.

Q. But when you read that Jonah swallowed the whale—or that the whale swallowed Jonah—excuse me please—how do you literally interpret that?

A. When I read that a big fish swallowed Jonah—it does not say whale. . . . That is my recollection of it. A big fish, and I believe it, and I believe in

http://www.law.umkc.edu/faculty/projects/ftrials/scopes/day7.htm.

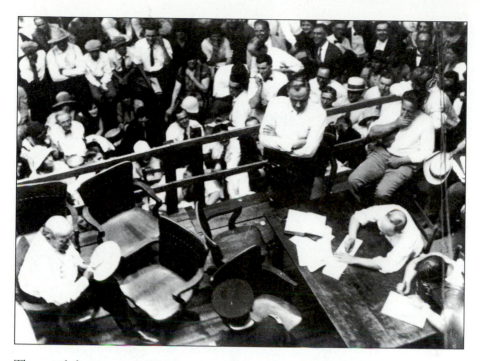

The crowded courtroom in Dayton, Tennessee, where the Scopes trial was held. William Jennings Bryan is at left, Clarence Darrow center, with his arms crossed. Library of Congress.

a God who can make a whale and can make a man and make both what He pleases.

Q. Now, you say, the big fish swallowed Jonah, and he there remained how long—three days—and then he spewed him upon the land. You believe that the big fish was made to swallow Jonah?

A. I am not prepared to say that; the Bible merely says it was done.

Q. You don't know whether it was the ordinary run of fish, or made for that purpose?

A. You may guess; you evolutionists guess. . . .

Q. You are not prepared to say whether that fish was made especially to swallow a man or not?

A. The Bible doesn't say, so I am not prepared to say.

Q. But do you believe He made them—that He made such a fish and that it was big enough to swallow Jonah?

A. Yes, sir. Let me add: One miracle is just as easy to believe as another.

Q. Just as hard?

A. It is hard to believe for you, but easy for me. A miracle is a thing performed beyond what man can perform. When you get within the realm of miracles; and it is just as easy to believe the miracle of Jonah as any other miracle in the Bible.

Q. Perfectly easy to believe that Jonah swallowed the whale?

Clifford Kennedy Berryman, "Evolution in Tennessee," 1925. Library of Congress.

A.   If the Bible said so; the Bible doesn't make as extreme statements as evolutionists do. . . .

Q.   The Bible says Joshua commanded the sun to stand still for the purpose of lengthening the day, doesn't it, and you believe it?

A.   I do.

Q.   Do you believe at that time the entire sun went around the earth?

A.   No, I believe that the earth goes around the sun.

Q.   Do you believe that the men who wrote it thought that the day could be lengthened or that the sun could be stopped?

A.   I don't know what they thought.

Q.   You don't know?

A.   I think they wrote the fact without expressing their own thoughts. . . .

MR. DARROW: Can you answer my question directly? If the day was lengthened by stopping either the earth or the sun, it must have been the earth?

A.   Well, I should say so.

Q.   Now, Mr. Bryan, have you ever pondered what would have happened to the earth if it had stood still?

A.   No.

Q.   You have not?

A. No; the God I believe in could have taken care of that, Mr. Darrow.

Q. I see. Have you ever pondered what would naturally happen to the earth if it stood still suddenly?

A. No.

Q. Don't you know it would have been converted into molten mass of matter?

A. You testify to that when you get on the stand, I will give you a chance.

Q. Don't you believe it?

A. I would want to hear expert testimony on that.

Q. You have never investigated that subject?

A. I don't think I have ever had the question asked.

Q. Or ever thought of it?

A. I have been too busy on things that I thought were of more importance than that.

Q. You believe the story of the flood to be a literal interpretation?

A. Yes, sir.

Q. When was that Flood?

A. I would not attempt to fix the date. The date is fixed, as suggested this morning.

Q. About 4004 B.C.?

A. That has been the estimate of a man that is accepted today. I would not say it is accurate.

Q. That estimate is printed in the Bible?

A. Everybody knows, at least, I think most of the people know, that was the estimate given.

Q. But what do you think that the Bible, itself says? Don't you know how it was arrived at?

A. I never made a calculation.

Q. A calculation from what?

A. I could not say.

Q. From the generations of man?

A. I would not want to say that.

Q. What do you think?

A. I do not think about things I don't think about.

Q. Do you think about things you do think about?

A. Well,sometimes.

(Laughter in the courtyard.)

POLICEMAN: Let us have order. . . .

STEWART: Your honor, he is perfectly able to take care of this, but we are attaining no evidence. This is not competent evidence.

WITNESS: These gentlemen have not had much chance. They did not come here to try this case. They came here to try revealed religion. I am here to defend it and they can ask me any question they please.

THE COURT: All right.

(Applause from the courtyard.)

Darrow: Great applause from the bleachers.

Witness: From those whom you call "Yokels."

Darrow: I have never called them yokels.

WITNESS: That is the ignorance of Tennessee, the bigotry.

DARROW: You mean who are applauding you? (Applause.)

WITNESS: Those are the people whom you insult.

DARROW: You insult every man of science and learning in the world because he does not believe in your fool religion.

THE COURT: I will not stand for that.

DARROW: For what he is doing?

THE COURT: I am talking to both of you. . . .

Q. Do you know there are thousands of books in our libraries on all these subjects I have been asking you about?

A. I couldn't say, but I will take your word for it. . . .

Q. Have you any idea how old the earth is?

A. No.

Q. The Book you have introduced in evidence tells you, doesn't it?

A. I don't think it does, Mr. Darrow.

Q. Let's see whether it does; is this the one?

A. That is the one, I think.

Q. It say B.C. 4004?

A. That is Bishop Usher's calculation.

Q. That is printed in the Bible you introduced?

A. Yes, sir. . . .

Q. Would you say that the earth was only 4,000 years old?

A. Oh, no; I think it is much older than that.

Q. How much?

A. I couldn't say.

Q. Do you say whether the Bible itself says it is older than that?

A. I don't think it is older or not.

Q. Do you think the earth was made in six days?

A. Not six days of twenty-four hours.

Q. Doesn't it say so?

A. No, sir. . . .

THE COURT: Are you about through, Mr. Darrow?

DARROW: I want to ask a few more questions about the creation. . . .

BRYAN: Your honor, they have not asked a question legally and the only reason they have asked any question is for the purpose, as the question about Jonah was asked, for a chance to give this agnostic an opportunity to criticize a believer in the world of God; and I answered the question in order to shut his mouth so that he cannot go out and tell his atheistic friends that I would not answer his questions. That is the only reason, no more reason in the world.

MALONE (for the defense): Your honor on this very subject, I would like to say that I would have asked Mr. Bryan—and I consider myself as good a Christian as he is—every question that Mr. Darrow has asked him for the purpose of bringing out whether or not there is to be taken in this court a literal interpretation of the Bible, or whether, obviously, as these questions indicate, if a general and literal construction cannot be put upon the parts of the Bible which have been covered by Mr. Darrow's questions. I hope for the last time no further attempt will be made by counsel on the other side of the case, or Mr. Bryan, to say the defense is concerned at all with Mr. Darrow's particular religious views or lack of religious views. We are here as lawyers with the same right to our views. I have the same right to mine as a Christian as Mr. Bryan has to his, and we do not intend to have this case charged by Mr. Darrow's agnosticism or Mr. Bryan's brand of Christianity. (A great applause.)

Q. . . . Does the statement, "The morning and the evening were the first day," and "The morning and the evening were the second day," mean anything to you?

A. I do not think it necessarily means a twenty-four-hour day.

Q. You do not?

A. No.

Q. What do you consider it to be?

A. I have not attempted to explain it. If you will take the second chapter. let me have the book. (Examining Bible.) The fourth verse of the second chapter says: "These are the generations of the heavens and of the earth, when they were created in the day that the Lord God made the earth and the heavens," the word "day" there in the very next chapter is used to describe a period. I do not see that there is any necessity for construing the words, "the evening and the morning," as meaning necessarily a twenty-four-hour day, "in the day when the Lord made the heaven and the earth."

Q. Then, when the Bible said, for instance, "and God called the firmament heaven. And the evening and the morning were the second day," that does not necessarily mean twenty-four hours?

A. I do not think it necessarily does.

Q. Do you think it does or does not?

A. I know a great many think so.

Q. What do you think?

A. I do not think it does.

Q. You think those were not literal days?

A. I do not think they were twenty-four-hour days.

Q. What do you think about it?

A. That is my opinion. I do not know that my opinion is better on that subject than those who think it does.

Q. You do not think that?

A. No. But I think it would be just as easy for the kind of God we believe in to make the earth in six days as in six years or in 6,000,000 years or in 600,000,000 years. I do not think it important whether we believe one or the other.

Q. Do you think those were literal days?

A. My impression is they were periods, but I would not attempt to argue as against anybody who wanted to believe in literal days. . . .

Q. Now, you refer to the cloud that was put in heaven after the flood, the rainbow. Do you believe in that?

A. Read it.

Q. All right, Mr. Bryan, I will read it for you.

BRYAN: Your Honor, I think I can shorten this testimony. The only purpose Mr. Darrow has is to slur at the Bible, but I will answer his question. I will answer it all at once, and I have no objection in the world, I want the world to know that this man, who does not believe in a God, is trying to use a court in Tennessee.

DARROW: I object to that.

BRYAN: (Continuing) to slur at it, and while it will require time, I am willing to take it.

DARROW: I object to your statement. I am examining you on your fool ideas that no intelligent Christian on earth believes.

THE COURT: Court is adjourned until 9 o'clock tomorrow morning.

 *The Scopes trial, and other trials of the 1920s, may be pursued at Douglas O. Linder's excellent Web site, "Famous Trials," at www.umkc.edu/famoustrials.*

The New Woman: A Photo Essay

Many middle-class and upper-middle-class women emerged from wartime work experiences, and from the atmosphere of democracy that permeated the conflict, invigorated and self-confident. Under these circumstances, woman suffrage was inevitable, and it came in 1920, with the Nineteenth Amendment to the Constitution. By mid-decade, black self-assurance had blossomed into the idea of a "New Negro," liberated from genteel culture, free to explore African-American identities. Similarly, many women embraced the concept of a "New Woman," freed from Victorian social and physical restraints—the corset, floor-length gowns, a full figure, and long hair. In contrast, the "flapper" look of the 1920s featured knee-length (or shorter) skirts; a thin, boyish figure; and short, bobbed hair.

The New Woman seemed poised to engage the world in a new way. But was that new way truly significant? Was the New Woman one aspect of a serious assault on the citadel of male power? Or something less meaningful, even trivial? Based on the photographs on the following pages, how would you describe the values and preoccupations of the New Woman?

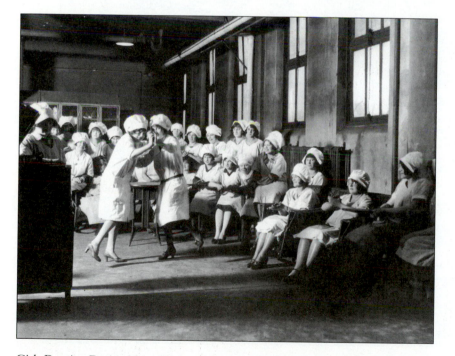

Girls Dancing During Noon Hour at Armour & Company Plant, 1927.
National Archives.

Miss Suzette Dewey, Daughter of Assistant Secretary of the Treasury and Mrs. Chas. Dewey, Beside Her Roadster, 1927. Library of Congress.

Margaret Gorman, Miss America, 1921. Library of Congress.
Contestants in this pageant were instructed not to wear makeup or bob their hair, and the outfit shown here is something less than skimpy, even for the 1920s. Why?

Tybee Beach No. 6, Savannah, Georgia. Library of Congress.

"The Gay Northeasterners" Strolling on 7th Avenue, c. 1927. Schomburg Collection, New York Public Library.

Singing the Blues

The blues had its origins in the cotton fields of Mississippi and Alabama, sometime in the late nineteenth century, and it became the musical expression of the great black migration and of the black experience in the urban North. Because Chicago was so easily accessible by rail from the Mississippi delta, that city became a center for playing and recording the blues. Between 1920, when the first blues was recorded, and 1926, when country blues played by men began to attract interest, women dominated the commercial blues scene. By far the biggest stars of the era were Gertrude "Ma" Rainey and Bessie Smith, who recorded over 250 songs, many in the mid-1920s. Their lyrics, and those of other composers whose songs they sang and recorded, are printed on the following pages.

Read the lyrics from a broad perspective. What ideas and themes can you find? What do the songs tell us about the great migration, especially as it was experienced by black women? About gender relations? Do you think Rainey and Smith should be viewed as feminists—that is, as "sisters" of the middle-class white women who had recently fought for the right to vote—or as kin to the "New Women" of the 1920s? In the hands of these composers, was the blues a music of despair, of triumph, or of survival?

 # VOICES

Gone Daddy Blues *(Gertrude Rainey)*

[Knocking]

[Spoken]

UNKNOWN MAN: Who's that knockin' on that door?
RAINEY: It's me, baby.
MAN: Me who?
RAINEY: Don't you know I'm your wife?
MAN: What?! Wife?!
RAINEY: Yeah!
MAN: Ain't that awful? I don't let no woman quit me but one time.
RAINEY: But I just quit one li'l old time, just one time!
MAN: You left here with that other man, why didn't you stay?
RAINEY: Well, I'll tell you why I didn't stay, baby. I got home and I had to come on back home to you!
MAN: Well, I'm leavin' here today, what have you got to say?
RAINEY: Well, all right, I'll tell it, baby.
MAN: Talk fast, then.

[Sung]
    I'm going away, I'm going to stay
    I'll find the man I love some day
    I've got my ticket, clothes in my hand
    Trying to find that South bound land

I'm gonna ride 'til I find that South bound land
I'm gonna ride 'til I find that South bound land
Gon' keep on ridin' 'til I shake hands with my man

I'm going away, I'm going to stay
I'll come back for my daddy someday
But, dad, you'll never know how much I've missed you 'til I'm gone

I'm going away, I'm going to stay
I'll long for my daddy some day
But, dad, you'll never know how much I've missed you 'til I'm gone.

Yes, Indeed He Do *(Porter Grainger)*

I don't know what makes it rain, can't tell what makes it snow
Well, I don't claim to know it all, but there's some things I do know

There's one thing in particular that I never have to guess
I ask myself this question, and I have to tell me yes

Oh, do my sweet, sweet daddy love me? Yes, indeed he do
Is he true as stars above me? What kind of fool is you?

He don't stay from home all night more than six times a week
No, I know that I'm his Sheba, and I know that he's my sheik

And when I ask him where he's been, he grabs a rocking chair
Then he knocks me down and says, "It's just a little love lick, dear."

But if some woman looks at him, I'll tear her half in two
Oh, do my sweet, sweet daddy love me? Yes, indeed he do

Of course my sweet daddy loves me, yes, indeed he do
If he beats me or mistreats me, what is that to you?

I don't have to do no work except to wash his clothes
And darn his socks and press his pants and scrub the kitchen floor

I wouldn't take a million for my sweet, sweet daddy Jim
And I wouldn't give a quarter for another man like him

Gee, ain't it great to have a man that's crazy over you?
Oh, do my sweet, sweet daddy love me? Yes, indeed he do.

Lost Wandering Blues *(Gertrude Rainey)*

I'm leavin' this mornin' with my clothes in my hand
Lord, I'm leavin' this mornin' with my clothes in my hand
I won't stop movin' 'til I find my man

I'm standin' here wonderin' will a matchbox hold my clothes
Lord, I'm standin' here wonderin' will a matchbox hold my clothes
I got a trunk too big to be botherin' with on the road

I went up on the mountain, turned my face to the sky
Lord, I went up on the mountain, turned my face to the sky
I heard a whisper, said, "Mama, please don't die."

I turned around to give him my right han'
Lord, I turned around to give him my right han'
When I looked in his face, I was talkin' to my man

Lord, look-a yonder, people, my love has been refused
I said, look-a yonder, people, my love has been refused
That's the reason why mama's got the lost wandering blues.

Poor Man's Blues *(Bessie Smith)*

Mister rich man, rich man, open up your heart and mind
Mister rich man, rich man, open up your heart and mind
Give the poor man a chance, help stop these hard, hard times

While you're livin' in your mansion, you don't know what hard times means
While you're livin' in your mansion, you don't know what hard times means
Poor working man's wife is starvin', your wife's livin' like a queen

Get a workin' man when you marry, and let all these sweet men be
Child, it takes money to run a business, and with me I know you girls will agree

There's one thing about this married life that these young girls have got to know
If a sweet man enter your front gate, turn out your lights and lock your door

Yes, get a working man when you marry, let all these pinchbacks be
Child, it takes money to run a business, and with me I know you girls will agree

And if this panic stay on much longer, I'll hear all these young girls say
That it's a long way to Oklahoma, but these little pinchbacks, take 'em away.

Blame It on the Blues *(Thomas Dorsey)*

I'm so sad and worried, got no time to spread the news
I'm so sad and worried, got no time to spread the news
Won't blame it on my trouble, can't blame it on the blues

Lord, Lord, Lord, Lordy Lord
Lord, Lord, Lordy Lordy Lord
Lord, Lord, Lord, Lord, Lord, Lord

[Spoken] Lord, who'm I gonna blame it on, then?

I can't blame my daddy, he treats me nice and kind
I can't blame my daddy, he treats me nice and kind
Shall I blame it on my nephew, blame it on that trouble of mine?

This house is like a graveyard, when I'm left here by myself
This house is like a graveyard, when I'm left here by myself
Shall I blame it on my lover, blame it on somebody else?

Can't blame my mother, can't blame my dad
Can't blame my brother for the trouble I've had
Can't blame my lover that held my hand
Can't blame my husband, can't blame my man
Can't blame nobody, guess I'll have to blame it on the blues.

Portrait of Bessie Smith, by Carl Van Vechten, 1936. Library of Congress.

THE BIG PICTURE

A good way to get at the big picture of the 1920s, and to appreciate the central contradictions and tensions of the decade, is to take another look at William Jennings Bryan. Bryan was sixty-five years old in 1925, when he took center stage in the Scopes trial. Despite his age—or because of it—his Dayton, Tennessee, performance remains one of the dominant images of the 1920s, along with Fords and flappers, silent movies, and two remarkable moments from 1927: Charles Lindbergh's solo flight across the Atlantic, and sixty home runs by "The Sultan of Swat," Babe Ruth. Although Bryan's views did not represent those of all Americans, or even those of a majority, he did raise issues and suggest concerns that were troubling for many people. To get at some of those issues, try to imagine what Bryan would have thought of some of the pictures of young women that appear in this chapter, of the enormous migration of African Americans from the South to northern cities, and of the blues they brought with them. How would he have come to grips with the sophisticated technology that made Lindbergh's solo flight possible, with the efficiency experts that were flooding America's factories and assembly lines, or with the new consumer ethos of the age? It would be comforting to think he was just old-fashioned, just a fuddy-duddy whose time had come and gone. But perhaps he stood for something more important—not just religion, but another way of being in the world than the one the nation would choose.

Chapter 8

The Great Depression and the New Deal

The economic decline that followed the stock market crash of October 1929 was unparalleled in the nation's history. Over 4 million people were unemployed in 1930, 8 million in 1931, and almost 13 million, or close to one-quarter of the total civilian labor force, in 1933. Detroit, a city symbolic of the high-flying consumer economy of the 1920s, suffered in proportion to its earlier prosperity. Of the city's 690,000 gainful workers in October 1930, 223,000 were without jobs in March 1931. Because millions of small farmers reacted to falling prices by continuing to produce full crops, agricultural production fell little; farm income, however, was halved in the four years after 1929.

Work for wages was the heart of the economy of the early 1930s, and when it faltered, the effects rippled through every area of American life. In one sixty-day period in Detroit, for example, some 50,000 homeowners lost the equity in their property—the banks foreclosed on their mortgages and took their homes. Children went to school without food. Throughout that city, people of all races rummaged through garbage cans in the city's alleys, stole dog biscuits from the pound, and even tried to dig homes in the ground.

Herbert Hoover was not a do-nothing president. His attempts to persuade business to maintain wage rates were moderately successful for more than two years. Through the Agricultural Marketing Act, passed four months prior to the crash, the national government sought to maintain agricultural prices. National expenditures on public works increased. The Reconstruction Finance Corporation lent funds to banks, railroads, building and loan associations, and insurance companies. It saved a number from bankruptcy.

Perhaps Hoover's greatest failure was his firm opposition to national expenditures for relief. Private charity and city government, the primary agencies of relief, soon proved inadequate. Even in Philadelphia, where philanthropic traditions ran deep, the city's Community Council described its situation in July 1932 as one of "slow starvation and progressive deterioration of family life." Detroit, with its highly developed *public* welfare system, in 1931 debated whether to cut its welfare rolls in half or reduce payments by 50 percent—whether to "feed half the people or half-feed the people."

As people gradually became aware just how deep the crisis went, and as the government under Hoover failed to deal with it, it became obvious that fundamental change of one kind or another might be the only solution. One possible direction of change was dictatorship. The Great Depression was not a domestic crisis only. European nations were hit just as severely as the United States. And there, turning to an authoritarian figure—a Hitler in Germany or a Mussolini in Italy—at least promised to restore order and a sense of purpose. Europe's dictators frightened many Americans. But they also led many to think of strong leadership as a necessary phenomenon of the age, a prerequisite to the restoration of international order and domestic prosperity.

Another possible direction—a threat or a promise, depending on where one stood politically—was revolution. To many, some sort of socialist or communist transformation of the economic and political order seemed the only answer. Early in the decade, the Communist Party did make some gains. The party tried to organize unemployed urban workers into "councils," built around neighborhoods, blocks, or even apartment houses. In 1930, these Unemployed Councils managed a series of demonstrations in major cities, drawing crowds ranging from 5,000 to 35,000. Later, after they deemphasized their talk of immediate revolution, the Communists had some substantial successes within the Congress of Industrial Organizations (CIO), a new and powerful labor union. Large numbers of intellectuals—writers, scientists, teachers, and bureaucrats—also joined the party. The Socialist Party, too, began a vigorous program of recruitment and political campaigning, with the very popular Norman Thomas as its presidential candidate.

Into this atmosphere of uncertainty came Franklin Delano Roosevelt. A master at capturing the national mood in his speeches, Roosevelt talked of action, of advance, of what he called a New Deal for the American people.

It was not all talk, of course. Within three months of his inauguration in March 1933—the so-called Hundred Days—Roosevelt had signed into law a bewildering variety of legislation, much of it designed either to restructure the economy or to bring recovery. In the Emergency Banking Act, Congress gave the president broad discretionary powers over financial transactions. The Government Economy Act cut government employees' salaries and veterans' pensions in an attempt to balance the federal budget. The Agricultural

Adjustment Act (AAA) granted subsidies to farmers who voluntarily reduced acreage or crops. In an act of boldness not to be repeated, development of the Tennessee River Valley was turned over to a public corporation.

Akin to the policy toward agriculture but more comprehensive, the National Industrial Recovery Act (NIRA) attempted to promote recovery by granting businesses the right to cooperate. Each industry wrote its own code of fair competition—setting minimum wages and maximum workweeks, limiting construction of new capacity, even fixing prices by prohibiting sales below cost. In addition, section 7(a) of the NIRA appeared to give workers the right to bargain collectively with employers. (The NIRA is perhaps the best evidence that the New Deal sought to strengthen capitalism rather than replace it with socialism.)

Relief efforts went well beyond those of the Hoover administration. To absorb the unemployed, Congress created the Civilian Conservation Corps (CCC) and set up the Public Works Administration to promote construction in the public interest. In 1935, the Works Progress Administration (WPA) was established to coordinate public works. The Emergency Relief Act directed Hoover's Reconstruction Finance Corporation to make relief funds available to the states and signaled the shift away from Hoover's opposition to using federal money for relief. The Social Security Act of 1935 brought the national government into old-age assistance and insurance and unemployment compensation.

For all its accomplishments, the New Deal made no commitment to remedying even the worst aspects of race relations: racial segregation, racial discrimination, denial of suffrage in the South, the lynching of black Americans. Fearful that a strong stand on racial issues would alienate the southern wing of his Democratic Party and bring an end to the New Deal, Roosevelt refused to use the Fourteenth Amendment to help blacks, and although sympathetic to the cause, he failed to support the growing movement for a federal antilynching statute. Because they were poor (rather than because they were black), many black Americans benefited from New Deal relief programs. For example, although blacks made up 10 percent of the population, they filled 18 percent of the WPA rolls. Yet some New Deal programs actually made life worse for blacks. When, for example, southern farmers took land out of production under the AAA, some 200,000 rural black farmworkers were left jobless. Moreover, numerous New Deal programs gave blacks less than they should have received. Many NIRA wage codes allowed businesses to pay lower wages to black than to white workers. Federal public housing programs often amounted to "Negro clearance." And the showy New Deal model communities, like Greenbelt, Maryland, had no black residents.

Historians have long debated whether the New Deal had any significant effect on the depression, and there is no more agreement on the New Deal's legacy for black Americans. But of one thing there can be little doubt. Roosevelt did manage to steal the rhetorical thunder from *both* the advocates of dictatorship and the proponents of revolution and to convince most blacks that the New Deal was worthy of their support. When he presented his legislative program to Congress, he could sound as though he meant to do everything that any European leader could, asking for "broad executive power to wage a war against the emergency, as great as the power that would be given to me if we were in fact invaded by a foreign foe." And he could now and then sound like a bit of a socialist, lambasting the "economic royalists" who controlled the nation's wealth. Most of the Rooseveltian rhetoric designed to appeal to blacks came from the lips of Eleanor rather than Franklin, but significantly, in 1936, to his famous phrase "forgotten man" he added "forgotten races."

Historians have also argued about whether Roosevelt's New Deal "saved" American capitalism or fundamentally altered it. What he was probably most anxious to save, however, was not the economic system, or even the political structure, but the faith of his constituents in the system. The nation did not respond to calls for revolution. The actual power of the Communist Party probably declined after Roosevelt's election. Blacks affirmed their commitment to a political party—the Democratic Party—with an influential southern, racist component. The "deal" Roosevelt offered the people may not have been as "new" as he made it sound, but he did convince most Americans—and most black Americans—that he was in charge of the only game in town.

Mean Streets: Black Harlem in the Great Depression

Cheryl Greenberg

On the eve of the Great Depression, the area of upper Manhattan known as Harlem was two very different places. For white, middle- and upper-class Americans, who did not live there, it was a symbol of the "jazz age," the antithesis of Main Street, a place where "expressive," "primitive," and "exotic" Negroes sang and danced and laughed and otherwise rebelled against the materialism and monotony of American life. For many of its black residents, Harlem was a slum, albeit a newly created one. As late as 1910, Harlem was a racially and ethnically diverse and reasonably prosperous community. During the 1910s and 1920s, massive in-migration of blacks from the rural South and from the West Indies, along with the out-migration of Italians, Jews, and other whites, created a community that was mostly black and very poor—in some respects, today's Harlem. Thus even before the stock market crash of October 1929 triggered economic decline, life in Harlem was difficult. Blacks paid high rents, did the menial and unskilled tasks regarded as "Negro jobs," and suffered from the highest rates of infant mortality and tuberculosis of any New York City neighborhood.

Cheryl Greenberg's essay can help us understand some of the ways in which the black people of Harlem understood and dealt with their basic poverty and with the additional burdens imposed by the Great Depression. It is a complex story, involving federal, state, and local governments, private agencies, and community organizations, as well as some creative family management. Having read Greenberg's account, do you think Harlem blacks survived the Great Depression with dignity, or were they demeaned by the crisis? What evidence is there that black economic problems were significantly exacerbated by race? And how might Greenberg's essay lead one to be more critical of the inactivity of the New Deal on racial issues (chronicled in the introduction to this chapter)?

Whether on relief or employed in private industry (and most black families experienced both at some point in the depression), few managed to make ends meet without some sort of extra income. People with little helped those with less; ties of family and community proved strong and durable. Men and women picked up temporary work whenever possible. Families took in lodgers or boarders or moved into the homes of relatives. Many borrowed money from friends or kin or bought groceries on credit from local merchants. Some engaged in illegal activities. A large proportion of Harlem arrests during the depression were for possession of policy slips, prostitution, and illegal distilling, all income-producing rather than violent crimes. These activities were certainly not new to the 1930s; blacks had been poor before this. But more families resorted to them in the years of the depression.

One woman's experiences illustrate the available choices—and their limitations. Thirza Johnson was twenty-one years old with three young children. Her husband had worked for the WPA for eighteen months. Despite that income the family could not pay its bills, and Mr. Johnson "tampered with the gas meter." For this he received sixty days in jail. The family had been receiving $5.40 every two weeks to supplement Mr. Johnson's paycheck, but without the WPA income that amount was completely inadequate. The utility companies cut off the gas and the electricity and Mrs. Johnson fell a month behind in paying the rent. When all three children fell ill, she asked her mother to come in from New Jersey to help. Her mother told her employer she needed a few days off to tend to her grandchildren. He fired her. This brought the number in the house to five, but the relief agency refused to increase the family's relief allotment because Mrs. Johnson's mother was not a New York resident. The grocery store gave her no more credit. Completely desperate, Mrs. Johnson turned to the Universal Negro Improvement Association (UNIA) for aid, and the Home Relief Bureau at last agreed to help.

Families like the Johnsons were so poor they were often forced to choose among necessities. Consumption patterns of Harlem families reveal both their real poverty and the constraints of living in a segregated community. Because of low incomes, African-Americans lived in poor, overcrowded housing, with high disease and death rates and high crime. Yet, . . . the New Deal programs had brought some progress to Harlem as well: health care, for example, improved in the depression decade, and for a few, new public housing became available.

Certainly black Harlem was not one homogeneous neighborhood. Within it lived population clusters divided by income and nativity. On some blocks only a few families received relief; on others, a majority did. Particular streets hosted the grocery stores, benefit societies, or restaurants of different national groups. As Vernal Williams, lawyer for the Consolidated Tenants League, explained:

> Why, every one of us have our own standards of living. We don't all live together. Just as you have Riverside, West End and Park Avenues, we have the same standard among our people, and you won't find that doctors [are] willing to go to the cheaper quarters along where the longshoremen live. . . . [To live in the Dunbar apartments, for example] you had to be a doctor or a wealthy business man or work in the Post Office.

Nevertheless, virtually no family was immune from the depression's ravages, and all shared both the burdens of life in a discriminatory society and the strengths found in networks of support within the black community.

Making Ends Meet

The most important first step for impoverished Harlem families was to supplement their earnings. Many families in the New Deal era turned to the long-standing practice in black communities of taking in lodgers. Perhaps because everyone was poor, the number of lodgers in black families in this period did not appear to bear a relation to any economic consideration. In the Harlem sample of the 1935 Bureau of Labor Statistics study, neither the family's earnings nor its expenditures provided a reliable predictor of whether or not that family would take in lodgers. The decision did depend on family size to some extent; families with many children seldom had lodgers. . . .

Black families in Harlem as elsewhere also turned to nonfinancial solutions, such as swapping and borrowing, and relied on the generosity of those temporarily better off. Evidence of these sorts of alternative economic strategies comes from many sources. Relief agencies, for example, demanded from applicants an accounting of expenses and income for the previous twelve months. Other agencies, such as the Bureau of Labor Statistics, investigated current earnings of nonrelief families. Private organizations conducted their own studies. Of the eighty-one Harlem families in the BLS sample, sixteen reported receiving gifts, and one a loan, from friends or relatives. Three others had picked up odd jobs and thirteen received "other income" from interest, "pool game," or sickness benefits from a lodge. If the number of families receiving money from gifts, loans, insurance, winnings, odd jobs, and lodgers were added together, over half the BLS survey families supplemented their earnings over the year, with an average of $153 per family with such added income. Families turning to the Unemployed Unit of the UNIA for help in obtaining relief also reported a heavy reliance on such means of supplementing their incomes.

Several families told of moving in with friends or relatives or receiving economic help from them. Both Nathan Campbell and Sarah Johnson told the UNIA that their family received money from friends. Minnie Jones complained she had to borrow money from her employer for food. In every income category, almost twice as many blacks as whites in New York City reported contributing to the support of relatives in 1935. Many men and women worked in exchange for free rent. Madeline Bright served as superintendent of an apartment building in return for lodgings. This, too, was common practice; one-fifth of single black women not living with families surveyed in Philadelphia, and two-fifths of such women in Chicago, engaged in this sort of exchange as well.

The proportion of all black families relying on these practices cannot be precisely documented. But impressionistic evidence suggests such interactions were commonplace. Francie, the protagonist of Louise Meriwether's Harlem-based novel, *Daddy Was a Number Runner,* borrows from her neighbor:

[Mother] gave me a weak cup of tea.
    "We got any sugar?"
    "Borrow some from Mrs. Caldwell."
    I got a chipped cup from the cupboard and going to the dining-room window, I knocked at our neighbor's window-pane. The Caldwells lived in the apartment next door and our dining rooms faced each other. . . . Maude came to the window.
    "Can I borrow a half cup of sugar?" I asked.

> She took the cup and disappeared, returning in a few minutes with it almost full. "Y'all got any bread?" she asked. "I need one more piece to make a sandwich."
>
> "Maude wants to borrow a piece of bread," I told Mother.
>
> "Give her two slices," Mother said.

Loften Mitchell remembered: "In this climate [Harlem] the cooking of chitterlings brought a curious neighbor to the door. Mrs. Mitchell, you cooking chitterlings? I thought you might need a little cornbread to go with em'. A moment later a West Indian neighbor appeared with rice and beans. Another neighbor followed with some beer to wash down the meal. What started as a family supper developed into a building party." As another contemporary wrote, "The people [of Harlem] are the kindest and most sympathetic people that can be found. They will take one into the home and share everything there except the mate or sweetheart."

Some turned to illegal activities such as bootlegging and numbers running. Between 1931 and 1935, over half of all black arrests in Harlem were for "possession of policy slips," and police charged three-quarters of all black females arrested with vagrancy and prostitution. One woman included in a Welfare Council study explained that she earned money from "rent parties and home brew sales" and rented out rooms in her apartment for "immoral" purposes. The investigator suspected another family of earning money in this fashion as well, but that family did not admit it. Several people reported altering gas pipes and electrical wiring to avoid paying utilities; arrests for "tampering with gas meter" or similar offenses dotted the Harlem precinct records.

> Our electricity had been cut off for months for nonpayment . . . [explained Francie] so Daddy had made the jumper. . . . I took the metal wire from behind the box where we hid it, and opening the box, I inserted the two prongs behind the fuse the way Daddy had showed me. . . . Daddy said almost everybody in Harlem used a jumper.

Lillian Holmes, to document her need for relief, told the UNIA how she earned money in the past. For several years, she reported, she had been "engaged in the illegitimate business of *manufacturing liquor*" (UNIA's emphasis): six gallons of 100-proof alcohol a week. Her living costs, including manufacturing, came to $199.90 a month, while she earned approximately $208. In April 1937, however, there was a "*RAID*" (UNIA emphasis), at which time she applied for relief but was rejected. Paroled, the UNIA record concludes, she "return[ed] to making 'hot stuff.'" The record does not reveal whether the UNIA persuaded the relief agency in question to accept Ms. Holmes or whether she continued her life of crime.

Income-producing strategies did not add enough income for most families to live comfortably. They had to budget carefully and often deprive themselves of one necessity to afford another. The widespread poverty of Harlem and its character as a segregated community were reflected in consumption decisions made by black families. High rents required large portions of family earnings, and family size determined the amount spent on food and other household goods. The amount families set aside for such items as recreation and personal care, by contrast, varied according to personal decision. Consumption decisions therefore depended on many factors, some beyond the control of the family. How Harlemites chose to spend their money reflected all these considerations and demonstrates the extreme poverty of the area.

The average family in the Harlem sample of the Bureau of Labor Statistics study spent $548 per person for the year. Both income and the size of the family, of course, affected this figure. Not unexpectedly, the poorer the family, the more per-person expenditures depended on the number of members; as more people sit down to eat a small pie, each slice becomes smaller. At higher income levels, families spent with fewer constraints; a larger family could spend as much per person as a smaller family and simply save less.

The typical blue-collar and clerical nonrelief black family earned $1446 and spent $1459, compared with white earnings of $1745 and expenditures of $1839. On average, black families spent just under a third of their total expenditures, $450, on food and almost as much, $417, on rent. White families, by contrast, spent approximately 40 percent of their budget on food and 20 percent on rent. Controlling for income yields similar results. Black families at each economic and occupational level spent a lower proportion of their total income on food, and a higher proportion on rent, than did comparable whites. Blacks at each level spent more than whites on other housing costs, personal care, and clothing, but less on medical care. . . .

Blacks spent less of their total income on food than whites at the same economic level, in part because their families were smaller and in part because so much of their income was used for rent. But food was costly; food prices did rise during the depression, and they were higher in Harlem. Between 1934 and 1935, for example, food prices rose 11 percent. In the later year, a dozen eggs cost approximately 40 cents in most city neighborhoods, and 42 cents in Harlem. Flour cost 6 cents a pound; cornmeal 7 cents; again slightly higher in Harlem. Milk cost 13 cents a quart, potatoes 2 cents a pound, and carrots 6 cents a bunch. Meat was more expensive. Bacon cost 37 cents a pound; ham 29 cents citywide, and more in Harlem. *Amsterdam News* columnist Roi Ottley noted that food prices in Harlem were "considerably higher" than elsewhere in the city during the depression. "For every dollar spent on food the Negro housewife has to spend at least six cents in excess of what the housewife in any other comparable section is required to pay." Adam Clayton Powell, Jr., claimed "foodstuffs were 17 percent above the general level." The Reverend Mr. Garner of Grace Church complained: "Our food in Harlem is higher than the food we can get elsewhere. Food on the east side is much cheaper than food in the immediate neighborhood." The Department of Markets received more complaints from Harlem than from anywhere else about unfair costs and "shortweight practices."

Black families spent slightly more on clothing, household furnishings, and personal care than comparably impoverished whites possibly because, poor for a longer time, they could not continue to defer those needs. For medical care, white spending exceeded black in both amount and percentage of income. For both races, families with lower incomes were less likely to have annual medical exams or to go to a private doctor rather than a free clinic. Many poor families deferred dental visits.

The poorest spent less on every item in the budget than the general pool of blacks did. In fact, in the Harlem sample the poorest blacks had so little disposable income that the amount allotted for food did not change, regardless of family size. With more members a family might vary the quality of food it bought (less meat, for example, and more vegetables), but it could not afford to increase its overall food budget. . . .

This family was by no means unique. Most of the Harlem families in the [BLS] survey did not break even; fully three-quarters of them ended the year with some small deficit. Interestingly, the percentage of families with deficits did not decline as income rose. Rather, most families appeared to live at a level slightly above their actual income. Presumably, these families had all suffered a decline in their usual earnings and had not yet adjusted completely.

Still, for each income level, the average deficit of white families far exceeded that of black. Ninety-five percent of all Harlem black families in the survey either overspent by less than 5 percent of their total income or actually saved money. Only two families exceeded their income by more than 10 percent. The average debt for whites who had debts was $265, or 15 percent of their total expenditures, according to the BLS citywide study of wage earners; while for blacks it was $115, or 8 percent. . . .

Poverty alone could not account for indebtedness, since, according to the Harlem sample, black families at all income levels were equally likely to fall into debt. Nor could family size: among nonrelief families, those with deficits were no larger than those without. In other words, families of all types used debt as one way to stretch tight budgets. This did not imply extravagance, however, since those families with surpluses and those with debts spent approximately the same amount for food, rent, and all other items. In practical terms, then, any wage-earning family could find itself in the red. An emergency need would probably force a family into debt since virtually all lived close to the edge of their income level. As Myrtle Pollard explained, impoverished Harlemites got along by buying one thing at a time. If someone needed a new coat, the rent would have to go unpaid that month. When this strategy failed, a family could find itself forced to turn to relief.

The Bennett family illustrates the preceding discussion: the all-too-common pattern of economic decline, a cut in consumption, debt, and finally application for relief. David Bennett, a thirty-three-year-old laborer, and his wife and two children lived on his WPA wages until January 1937, when he received his last $14.46 check. He had found work as a longshoreman and earned $88 that month. He also supplemented this with $32 in tips he received as a "helper" at the Washington Market. That month, despite $15 in medical bills, the family met all its obligations, paying $24 in rent, $37 on food, and an $8 insurance premium. After these costs, plus clothing, utilities, and carfare, there was still something left over for cigarettes and "entertainment." The following month David earned only $66 at the docks and $14 at the market, but the family still managed by cutting food pur-chases down to $30, paying only half the insurance, and foregoing clothing and "entertainment." The family struggled on this way for a while; David earning between $80 and $110 a month, and everyone spending less.

The third week in August, however, David lost his longshoreman's job, and his wife hired herself out as a domestic worker to two families. One paid her $7 a week, the other $4. By skimping on food they managed again, but September was much worse. With only Mrs. Bennett's wages of $44 and the $12 David earned shining shoes, they eliminated all spending but rent and food (which they had cut again). In October they decided to take in a lodger who paid $3.50 a week. They broke even only by pawning a watch and eight pairs of shoes.

In November, David's wife lost her previous jobs and hired on with two new families. She now earned $4 from one, and $3 from the other. That month the Bennetts went into debt. Food, rent, and utilities cost $65, while David's $12 from shoeshining, his wife's $28, and the lodger's $14 came to only $54. They withdrew money from their Christmas fund in December, but still could pay only half their rent that month. By the new year, they had to accept a loan of $10 and a gift of $3.50 from friends because Mrs. Bennett had again lost her jobs. Now able to afford only $22 for food, and paying no rent or utilities, they applied for public relief. Rejected with no explanation, they took another loan of $15, and turned to the UNIA for help. The file ended with the notation "no food."

Consequences

The constant choosing between necessities or going without, the struggle to maintain a livable income, and the weight of discrimination and segregation resulted in poor housing and health, high crime, and inadequate public fa-cilities in Harlem.

Neither the depression nor the New Deal lessened the segregation that trapped black families in substandard housing. Rental costs for Harlem res-idents remained high in the depression, although absolute costs fell slightly. In 1933, the City Affairs Committee reported Harlem to have "the worst housing conditions in the city. . . . Negro tenants pay from one percent to twenty percent more of their income for rent than any other group, despite the fact that the income of the Negro family is about 17 percent lower than that of the typical family in any other section of the city." This committee in fact understated the problem. The Neighborhood Health Committee sur-veyed rental costs in Manhattan in the depression's early years. It found that while the average Manhattan apartment rented for $44 a month, most in poor areas paid significantly less. In East Harlem, for example, where poor Italians and Puerto Ricans lived, rents averaged $30. In Central Harlem, however, rents never fell below $31 a month, and often ran as high as $70. The average resident of Central Harlem paid $52. The League of Mothers' Clubs found tenement-house blacks paid almost $1 more per room, per month, than comparably poor whites. Thus, for most Harlem residents, rents had not declined much; they were in some cases even higher than pre-depression rates. Even the Brotherhood of Sleeping Car Porters was forced to resort to rent parties to pay for its offices.

The policies of relief agencies aggravated housing problems. The enormous demand on their limited funds led several to provide no rent payments until eviction was threatened. Landlords learned that the sooner they made such threats the sooner they received overdue rent. Families who did not qualify for aid therefore faced eviction earlier than they otherwise might have. The Communist party, which fought eviction notices in the courts and carried the furniture of evicted families back into their apartments in an effort to stop the process, reported that hundreds of successful evictions occurred each week. . . .

Some black families economized by moving to smaller apartments of lesser quality or by moving in with relatives. The biggest problem in Harlem, the Welfare Council reported, was "the changes . . . in living conditions. . . . 'Doubling up' of families was common." Previously independent children returned to their parents' homes. The Charity Organization Society reported that, of families receiving care, twice as many families lived with relatives in 1931 as two years earlier; three times as many took in lodgers. A study of city slums found the average number of persons per room had risen in Harlem since the beginning of the depression because of such changes in household composition.

All was due not only to poverty but also to segregation. As the New York State Temporary Commission on the Condition of the Urban Colored Population pointed out, blacks gained access to apartments only when conditions there deteriorated and white tenants could not be found. In other words, blacks inherited bad conditions that simply got worse. . . .

The cost of the housing did not reflect its quality. Of the thirty-one inhabited buildings on two blocks studied by the Housing Commission, nine had been officially condemned. The Housing Authority concluded after a survey of Harlem that "due to circumstances over which they have no control, many families are compelled to accept the old law tenement accommodations [buildings erected before 1901 and therefore not subject to the health and safety codes passed that year]. These houses are usually without heat, hot water and bathrooms together with improper plumbing, inadequate light and air, and have hall party lavatories." The Citywide Citizens' Committee on Harlem found that of 2191 occupied Class B buildings they examined in West Harlem in 1941, 1979 had major violations. Over 29,000 people lived in them. (Housing was classified by the type and number of facilities—heat, hot water, toilet, bath—provided, with A as the best and F as the worst.) The Mayor's Commission estimated that 10,000 blacks lived in cellars and basements with no toilets or running water. A former manager of Harlem apartments, an "agent for one of Harlem's largest real estate concerns," the New York Life Insurance Company, informed the Mayor's Commission:

> Do you know that apartments in my houses reeked with filth through no fault of the tenant? Bad plumbing—rats—mice—bugs—no dumbwaiters—no paint—heat—water and would you believe it I have been in apartments

Palmer Hayden, "Midsummer Night in Harlem." Harmon Foundation Collection, US National Archives. What was Palmer Hayden trying to convey in this painting of Harlem street life?

where young children lived and the toilet of the floor above flushed upon them. In fact things were so bad that I even appropriated money from the rents to help make the dumps livable much to the chagrin of my superiors.

Because Harlem had been built more recently than many areas in Manhattan, some of the housing there did provide modern conveniences. A higher proportion of Harlem apartments had private bathrooms, hot water, and heat than did apartments elsewhere in Manhattan, one study found, although these amenities did not always work. It listed approximately the same proportion of Harlem as non-Harlem Manhattan apartments in "good," "fair," and "poor" condition. That these newer apartments did not receive a "good" rating more often than the rest of the borough supports the conclusion that landlords in Harlem did less to maintain properties than they did elsewhere. . . .

The Harlem River houses on Seventh Avenue between 151st and 155th streets, built by the Public Works Administration (PWA) in 1937, offered modern, clean, spacious apartments at rents of $19 to $31 a month. The Houses also provided playgrounds, a nursery school, a health clinic, and laundry facilities. The United Tenants' League of Greater New York chose it as "the cleanest and most beautifully kept project in the city." But 20,000 families applied for the 574 spots.

As a result, more people lived in a smaller area in Harlem than anywhere else in the city. As Langdon Post, commissioner of housing, testified:

> A recent survey of . . . Harlem . . . [revealed] the average family income is
> $17.14. Forty percent of that went for rent. . . . In other parts of the city it is
> 20 to 25 percent for rent. . . . There are of course violations . . . but the
> problem of Harlem is not so much the bad housing, although there are plenty
> of them, it is the congestion to which they are forced through high rents.

On the block of 133d and 134th streets between Seventh and Lenox avenues, 671 people per acre crowded together, the highest density in the city.
The block of 138th and 139th streets between the same avenues held 620
per acre. The Mayor's Commission on City Planning found 3871 people living between Lenox and Seventh avenues on 142d and 143d streets in 1935:
"the city's most crowded tenement block." As the *Herald Tribune* reported,
this block

> is tenanted exclusively by Negroes. On its four sides the area presents a front
> of gray and red brick fire escapes broken only by dingy areaway entrances to
> the littered backyard about which the rectangle of tenements had been built.
> . . . Half of all the tenants are on relief and pass their days and nights lolling
> in the dreary entrances of the 40 apartments which house them or sitting in
> the ten by fifteen foot rooms which many of them share with a luckless
> friend or two. Unless they are fortunate their single windows face on narrow
> courts or into a neighbor's kitchen and the smell of cooking and the jangle of
> a dozen radios is always in the air. . . .

Black nationalists and the Communist and Socialist parties all tried to
mobilize tenants to protest these inexcusable conditions, and occasionally
took landlords to court. While they won some victories, segregation proved
stronger than activism in Harlem. At the Harlem River Houses, for example, the long waiting list proved too great an intimidation to those lucky
enough to have an apartment there. There was nowhere else to move. In any
building, tenants who made trouble could be evicted, but in Harlem there
were low vacancy rates, and outside Harlem, few would rent to blacks. Thus,
blacks expelled from their apartments faced homelessness as their most
likely fate. Segregation, then, inhibited the emergence of black activism on
housing, despite efforts of the Consolidated Tenants League and others.

Every housing report of the period linked Harlem's poor housing to other
social ills, especially poor health. The existing situation, argued the Housing
Authority, "spells many evils the most salient of which are disease, immorality, crime and high mortality. But the vast amount of unemployment is the
greatest of all evils for that and that alone is the propelling force which
drives the populace to seek cheaper rentals and into dilapidated homes."
Harlem housing conditions constituted a "serious menace . . . not only to the
health of the residents but to the welfare of the whole city," argued the
Mayor's Committee on City Planning. It concluded that "large areas are so
deteriorated and so unsuited to present needs that there is no adequate solution but demolition."

Certainly health statistics in Harlem did not compare favorably with those in the rest of the city, because of both substandard housing and inadequate incomes. In 1934 in Central Harlem, fourteen people died per thousand, compared with ten per thousand in the city as a whole. The area's tuberculosis rate was over four times higher. Of every one thousand live births, ninety-four Central Harlem babies died, almost double the city's rate. Black women died in childbirth twice as often as whites; in part because over one-third of the black deaths compared with one-seventh of the white came as a result of an illegal abortion. For every cause of death, and virtually all health problems, Central Harlem had the highest rate of all Manhattan Health Districts. Of 1921 students registered in P.S. 157 at 327 St. Nicholas Avenue, only 248 had no "observable" health defects in 1934. With the exception of bad teeth (942 with dental problems), the largest problem was "nutrition," with 641 students suffering from inadequate diets. While citywide rates of malnutrition among school children ranged between 17 and 20 percent in the years after 1929, a 1936 study claimed that fully 63 percent of Harlem school children "suffer[ed] from malnutrition."

On the other hand, these mortality and morbidity rates, though worse than those for the rest of the city, had declined since the 1920s and the pre-New Deal years. A comparison of health statistics for these earlier periods suggests that both races had seen dramatic improvement in the quality of health care. While medical advances contributed to the mortality decline, of course, the improvement also resulted from the increased availability of free health clinics. . . . At all income levels but one, black reliance on free clinics exceeded white. (For both races these rates were comparable to those of other cities.) In many cases this meant a lessening of the gap between black and white because of a substantial improvement in black access to health care and a slowing of improvements in white health as depression conditions worsened.

Mortality statistics continued to drop during the rest of the decade. In 1940, the general death rate in Central Harlem had dropped to 12.4 per thousand, the Manhattan rate to 11.5, and, for the first time, the mortality rate in another health district surpassed Harlem's. Harlem's tuberculosis deaths and infant mortality rates declined. Because the black community had been so destitute before the depression, in some ways conditions for them had improved with the advent of New Deal programs.

Relief programs correlated with some health improvements as well. While those on relief—the poorest—had a higher overall death rate, according to E. Franklin Frazier, they had lower rates of infant mortality. Probably relief babies were healthier because caseworkers advised their parents about prenatal and child care, and because of the medical care available to them. Pregnant women also received higher home relief food allotments. Thus, in terms of public services, the depression worsened conditions in Harlem while the New Deal improved them.

Poverty, poor housing, and poor health intensified other problems in Harlem. The Citywide Citizens' Committee on Harlem argued that "the poverty, the difficulties of home life and overcrowding, and the suffering of the adult population as a result of the unemployment in [Harlem] have . . . made educational needs greater than that of the average neighborhood of the city." Yet old buildings, scarce playgrounds, and overcrowded schools worsened the educational situation, demoralizing both teachers and students. The Mayor's Commission heard testimony from the executive secretary of the Central Committee of the Harlem Parents' Associations expressing her "great distress" about overcrowding and the poor facilities in Harlem. She politely "beg[ged] and petition[ed]" the commission to "do something about this because we, the parents of the children, are suffering because our children are involved." Mrs. William Burroughs of the Harlem Teachers' and Students' Association echoed these remarks, demanding that the city

> remedy overcrowding . . . safeguard life and health of pupils—immediate abandonment of old unsanitary firetraps, four in . . . Harlem . . . clinics in schools. . . . Retardation . . . is a vital problem in Harlem. . . . Many pupils come from an area with small educational facilities. In addition to this, the scandalous conditions here, inadequate staff, crowded classes, outmoded buildings, skimpy supplies, frequent lack of sympathy, lifeless curriculum, do not help; but hinder a slow pupil.

Ira Kemp forthrightly tied these conditions to racial discrimination and advocated the nationalist position he had articulated in the "Don't Buy" campaign.

> . . . We believe that the various school institutions in Harlem are overpopulated with teachers who aren't our people. . . . We feel a considerable percentage of teachers [in Harlem] should be colored.
> Q. Do you mean to insinuate that there is discrimination?
> A. I do. . . .
> Q. The specific question is whether you know of any instances where there is a violation of the law. Do you know of any girl [teacher] that has been discriminated against?
> A. My answer is that the system of keeping colored girls off the rolls who are on the eligible lists is so systematic that you can't get at it.
> Q. We are asking for proof. . . .
> A. I explained before that it is impossible to get facts from the authorities. We have had many complaints.

Ultimately, the Mayor's Commission on Conditions in Harlem concluded:

> The school plant as a whole is old, shabby . . . in many instances not even sanitary or well-kept and the fire hazards . . . are great. The lack of playgrounds and recreational centers . . . is all the more serious when it is considered that some of the schools are surrounded by . . . corrupt and immoral resorts of which the police seem blissfully unaware. Four of the schools lack auditoriums; one endeavors to serve luncheons to 1,000 children when there are seats for only 175. Most of all, no elementary school has been constructed in Harlem in 10 years. . . .

Prejudicial discrimination appears from the fact that the Board of Education, asking funds from the federal government for 168 school buildings, asked for but one annex for Harlem. . . .

The Teachers Union, Local 5 of the American Federation of Teachers, endorsed the Mayor's Commission's findings of poor school facilities in Harlem and cited "overcrowded classes, dangerous lack of adequate recreational facilities, antiquated and unsanitary school plant, 'horrifying' moral conditions, inadequate handling of the over-age child, and shortage of teaching staff." It concluded: "The conditions described . . . make proper teaching and proper receptivity to the teaching process impossible." The union's proposals—reducing class size, funding new school buildings, modernizing the old, hiring unemployed teachers to take children to nearby parks for recreation, staffing school playgrounds until six o'clock, and providing free lunches and winter clothing to the children of the unemployed— were endorsed by, among others, the Mayor's Committee on Harlem Schools, Father Divine's Peace Mission, the Joint Conference Against Discriminatory Practices, the Adam Clayton Powells, William Lloyd Imes and other ministers, YWCA and YMCA representatives, and Countee Cullen. To spur government action, the union reminded the mayor of the link between these problems and the 1935 riot: "The unhealthful and inadequate school buildings in Harlem had much to do with the unrest which led to the disorders of March 19."

Harlem residents added their voices, circulating petitions to the Board of Education:

Public education in Harlem has been . . . long and grossly neglected. The facts are notorious.

Dirt and filth and slovenliness have no more educational value for our children than for yours. . . . New school-houses with ample grounds and appropriate modern facilities are urgently needed to supplement or replace overcrowded and outmoded structures, to provide for the large increase in our population during the past decade or more. . . .

Teachers, principals and superintendents are needed who have abiding faith in our children and genuine respect for the loins and traditions from which they have sprung. . . .

So far as public education is concerned, we beg you to dispel by concrete action the widespread conviction that this region is neglected because its people are comparatively poor in this world's goods and in social and political influence, because many of them are of African descent.

In March 1936, Harlem organizations, including the Communist party and several black churches, created a Permanent Committee for Better Schools in Harlem, meeting in the New York Urban League building "with 400 delegates representing every phase of social, political, religious, cultural and civic activity in Harlem." These efforts, the commission report, and the memory of the Harlem riot brought some improvements within the year: the city budget included appropriations for four new school buildings, some repairs were made at most Harlem schools, and "many individual cases of discriminatory zoning have been satisfactorily settled." That year for the first time students could take a course in black history.

Of course Harlem's educational problems were by no means solved. In 1941, the Citizens' Committee reported that overcrowding forced many Harlem schools to run on a three-shift school day. From West 114th Street to West 191st, there was not a single public vocational or secondary school. One junior high school served the entire area from 125th Street to 155th, between the Harlem River and St. Nicholas Avenue. In one elementary school, ten classes lacked classrooms; in another, six did.

Still, educational levels among blacks did rise in the 1930s. Whether because Harlem's schools provided a better education than those of the south, because jobs were scarce in the depression, or because relief eased families' desperation, black children from both relief and nonrelief families attended school for longer during the depression than they had before. The proportion of black children aged fourteen to twenty-four remaining in school rose through the 1930s until it approached the figures for whites. . . .

Unlike delinquency, adult crimes rose. While most death rates declined in Harlem during the depression, homicides rose from nineteen per 100,000 in 1925 to twenty-four in 1937, while city rates fell. A 1931 investigation of the relationship between housing and crime found, not unexpectedly, that Manhattan's slum areas had higher rates of arrests of all types and a higher rate of convictions than the borough's average. The top two areas were both in Central Harlem. The same held for later years. Still, like delinquency, by and large, Harlem crimes by adults were more often income-producing than violent. As already noted, arrests for prostitution, operating illegal stills, and playing the numbers rose. Of a random sample of Harlem arrests in the first six months of 1935, all types of theft, from shoplifting to grand larceny, constituted only an eighth of the total, despite the fact that the period surveyed included the riot, with its many burglary arrests. Possession of policy slips, by contrast, accounted for about a third of all Harlem arrests. Except for the rise of arrests for policy slips and the decline for other gambling offenses since the early years of the depression, the rates for the different sorts of crimes remained fairly constant.

Of those arrested statewide, a smaller proportion of blacks than whites were charged with homicide or with theft of any sort, which suggests that whites were less often arrested for minor crimes than blacks were. The black rate for these more serious crimes proportional to their population, however, was greater than the white. Statewide, the ratio of whites arrested to their total population was 140 to 100,000, compared with 853 for blacks.

As we have seen, crime statistics are not foolproof indicators of community behavior. As with delinquency, discrimination or racism may have led to selective arrest, prosecution, and conviction. Perhaps police cared less about black crime and therefore acted less vigorously on Harlem cases. This would mean that arrest rates were lower than actual criminal behavior. Similarly, the rise in Harlem homicide deaths may have been due to a new vigilance by police rather than a real rise in the number of murders. An alternative possibility is that racism provoked officers to arrest blacks more readily than whites. The greater poverty of blacks might further skew their arrest rates, since the rich are generally more able to avoid arrest for minor crimes such as disturbing the peace than the poor are. Racist juries and judges might be similarly disposed to distrust blacks. Thus high black arrest and conviction rates may reflect factors other than strictly higher rates of criminality. Nevertheless, whatever the actual rates, criminal behavior in Harlem offers hints of the problems faced by a poor black community. Criminality reflected not only black behavior, but white as well.

Police corruption led to selective and discriminatory enforcement of the laws in Harlem. An NAACP memorandum argued that Harlem's high rate of arrests for prostitution and illegal sale of alcohol was attributable to police corruption: "We are made to look more immoral, less decent than anyone else and the environment of prostitution is being fostered [sic] on our women and young girls by the Harlem police officials in their scheme and business of tribute." A second memorandum estimated "perhaps forty to fifty percent of [prostitutes] . . . (colored) are forced or semi-forced and the rest act voluntarily." This memorandum cited the Cotton Club and several Italian-owned saloons as central "clearing house[s]" for these women. While the memo noted that the NAACP did not advocate illegal activity, it pointed out that it hardly seemed fair that black women were arrested for prostitution more often than white. The NAACP was convinced police arrested black women more often because they feared public outcry if they arrested too many whites. . . .

Community

Yet while blacks in Harlem recognized the harsh conditions they lived under and the pernicious effects of their poverty, few believed the solution was wholesale abandonment of the area. Living together offered resources and strengths unavailable to dispersed individuals. Rather, African-Americans demanded better services where they lived, recognizing the positive power of community. The Reverend Mr. Garner, minister of the Grace Congregational Church, testified before the Mayor's Commission: "We find that our rents are higher than anywhere else in the city in proportion to what we get. Our food in Harlem is higher." But he refused to consider the suggestion that blacks move elsewhere to find less expensive housing:

> Our industrial life and social and economic and religious lives are centered in Harlem at the present time. We object to the beating up of our community on those grounds. . . . To break up the community in small segregated groups gives no opportunity for the friends to develop themselves on and among themselves [sic].

Street surveys of the Mayor's Commission and the "Negroes in New York" study of the Federal Writers' Project documented the large numbers of storefront churches, billiard halls, social clubs, dance halls, and mutual welfare lodges that provided social space throughout the depression decade.

Black children playing leapfrog in a Harlem street, c. 1930. National Archives.

Over two thousand social, political, and mutual aid societies flourished in Harlem, including the United Aid for Peoples of African Descent, the Tuskeegee Alumni Association, Iota Phi Lambda (a sorority for business women), the King of Clubs (half of whose members were black police officers), the Hampton Alumni Club, the Bermuda Benevolent Organization, the Southern Aristocrats, the Trinidad Benevolent Association, the Anguilla Benevolent Society, the St. Lucia United Association, California #1, the New Englanders, the Hyacinths Social Club, the Montserrat Progressive Society, St. Helena's League and Benefit Club, and hundreds of others.

Both poverty and community, then, shaped Harlem family and social life. As Loften Mitchell recalled,

[T]he child of Harlem had the will to survive, to "make it." . . . This Harlem child learned to laugh in the face of adversity, to cry in the midst of plentifulness, to fight quickly and reconcile easily. He became a "backcapping" signifying slicker and a suave, sentimental gentleman. From his African, Southern Negro and West Indian heritage, he knew the value of gregariousness and he held group consultations on street corners to review problems of race economics, of politics.

He was poor but proud. He hid his impoverishment with clothes, pseudo-good living, or sheer laughter.

. . . In the nineteen thirties we had our own language, sung openly, defiantly. . . .

We celebrated, too—our biggest celebrations were on nights when Joe Louis fought. . . . When he won a fight I went into the streets with other Negroes and I hollered until I was hoarse. . . . We had culture too. The

Schomburg collection, a mighty fortress . . . three theaters, Louis Armstrong, Cab Calloway . . . Bill "Bojangles" Robinson . . . Bessie Smith . . . Langston Hughes . . . Romare Bearden . . . Augusta Savage. . . .

Richard Wright explained the energy and joy in black culture as rooted in poverty and anger:

Our music makes the whole world dance. . . . But only a few of those who dance and sing with us suspect the rawness of life out of which our laughing-crying tunes and quick dance steps come; they do not know that our songs and dances are our banner of hope flung desperately up in the face of a world that has pushed us to the wall.

Others offered even less sanguine pictures. Alfred Smith of the FERA [Federal Emergency Relief Administration], a black man, discussed the African-American family in terms that today might be viewed as racist, but that nonetheless raised important questions about the impact of dire poverty on family life:

The comparatively unstable family life of the Negro in urban areas may be ascribed to poor living conditions. Illegitimacy, illiteracy and a lack of a sense of responsibility or obligation all have their roots in the Negroes' unfortunate past, but are nurtured and fostered in city slums. Negroes are required to pay a larger proportion of their income for rent than any other group and they get less for their expenditure. The landlord who rents to the Negro mass in urban areas has no sense of responsibility to his renters. Negroes are forced to live in proscribed areas of the city, and in quarters where their health and morals suffer. They get little attention, little notice (other than being occasionally photographed in his slums as examples of need for "better housing") and much sympathy.

One part of his equation, "unstable family life," deserves some attention. Black and white leaders lamented the frequency of female-headed households. Clayton Cook of the Children's Aid Society reported 20 percent of Harlem black children "come from 'broken homes'—that is—families that have only a woman at the head. At one school in 699 families out of 1,600 . . . the father was either dead or had deserted." Certainly the high number of widows attests to the evil effects of poverty on adult (particularly male) longevity. Some social problems such as juvenile delinquency occurred more often in families without fathers according to contemporary studies (although, interestingly, the effects were more pronounced for girls than for boys). Yet other measures of "social disorganization," such as reliance on relief, seemed to bear no relationship to whether or not a man was present at home.

Many feared an absent male would ensure that these families would live in poverty, since black women had even lower earning potential than black men did. In fact, ironically, these economic liabilities were mitigated by the depression. While black working women did earn less, on average, than working men, female-headed families more often had additional earners. Thus, in the BLS sample, for example, families without a husband present earned no less per person than those with both husband and wife. Nor were black families with women at the head more likely than others to be on relief: the figure for black female-headed families on relief, 20 percent in New York City, was no higher than the proportion of female-headed families in the black population. A study of 675 Harlem families done by the Mayor's Commission found families on different blocks had very different average incomes. But in both high-income and low-income blocks, the proportion of female-headed families was identical.

Thus, while the likelihood of some social problems (such as juvenile delinquency) seemed correlated with the presence or absence of a father, other measures of "social disorganization" (such as reliance on relief) seemed to bear no relationship to that question. It may be that the depression threw so many men out of work that their absence made little economic difference to the family. When employment opportunities improved in the next decade, two-headed families would fare better than single-parent households, on the whole. But in an era of high unemployment and highly fluid household structures in which a family's income came from a variety of contributors, the presence of a male mattered less economically than one might expect.

Making ends meet was a difficult business in depression Harlem, and families used a variety of financial and nonfinancial, legal and illegal methods to do so. No one starved, but few in Harlem prospered, and the consequences of such grinding poverty reached into all areas of life. Housing and health were poor, mortality and crime rates high. Strong kin and community networks prevented much of the worst from occurring, and New Deal programs provided some help. Harlem itself, though, remained a ghetto and a slum and its people trapped in the conditions brought on by poverty and discrimination. As the New York State Temporary Commission on the Condition of the Urban Colored Population concluded in 1939:

> While the Commission has no desire to indulge in dramatic over-statement it does earnestly wish to impress upon your honorable bodies the extreme seriousness of the conditions which it has studied. The conditions often seem almost incredible in so advanced a commonwealth as the State of New York, and they cannot remain uncorrected without general danger to the public welfare of the State as a whole.

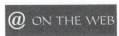

One of the most deeply felt ideas of the 1930s was that the Great Depression was somehow linked to the disintegration of city life. In response, Roosevelt's New Deal moved to reinvent the urban experience by creating a number of futuristic, model communities. One of the most famous, Greenbelt, Maryland, can be studied on the Virtual Greenbelt Web site, at www.otal.umd.edu/~vg/. Jersey Homesteads, a cooperative community that opened in 1936 with government help, is described on the Electronic New Jersey Web site, at www.scc.rutgers.edu/njh/Homesteads/jersey.htm.

Letters from the "Forgotten Man"

New York Governor Franklin Delano Roosevelt coined the term "forgotten man" during the presidential campaign of 1932. "These unhappy times," he said, "call for the building of plans . . . that build from the bottom up and not the top down, that put their faith once more in the forgotten man at the bottom of the economic pyramid."

Forgotten, perhaps. But this was no "silent majority" of the sort imagined by Richard Nixon in the late 1960s. The forgotten men (and women) were an opinionated bunch. They wrote letters by the thousands to the president, the first lady, Harry Hopkins (Federal Relief Administrator), and other public officials. A few of those letters—illustrative of the broad spectrum of voices captured by the term "forgotten man," are printed below. What is the theme of each letter? If you were handling correspondence for Hopkins or the Roosevelts, how, in each case, would you have responded?

VOICES

[New York, N. Y., May 1936]

Mr Hopkins

Dear Sir: When you opened that "Sewing Project" at 18 St N.Y.C. did you forget that there are still a few "white Americans left. Its the worst thing as far as placing is concerned. Nothing but colored, Spanish, West Indies, Italians + a hand ful of white Every colored that comes in is placed as "clerk, head or boss over tables + Knocking other people around. Well, if you dont see a race riot there its a surprise. If its colored + foreign your so interested in place them to themselves + not amongst "Humane" people—You just making the whites take a back seat. Its a very good useful project + hospitals + poor need the things that are made But the system is rotten Just like a lot of cattle Being driven around when its time to go home they all rush no matter who they bump into. Too many bosses + no one seems to Know whats to be done—Maybe a few of us whites would like to be placed in something else but a "Sweat shop" work 6 days a week its a wonder they let you have Sunday off. If you dont give American people more of a Show we will take up with President Roosevelt who did this good act so Americans dont starve.

A disgusted
American

[New York, N.Y., March 1936]

Dear President,

why is it that it is the work-man that is always kicked when things go wrong with the officials my Husband has worke on W.P.A. for some time a carpenter @ 85 dols per month + this morning he was reduced to timber-man @ 60 per month I know there was a mistake as he is a good carpenter. I am sorry to trouble you but please Dear President I need that 25 dols he is cut Do you know what it is to have money then find yourself broke, next children, + finally live in a cold water Dump get up to two children at night and find them nearly frozen from lack of clothing well I do, + struggled along although I very often thought of suicide as the best way out. I am not a coward but good Lord it is awful to stand helpless when you need things.

When that letter came from Project Labor officer Frank C. Hunt W.P.A. N.Y.C. this morning informing him that he was reduced to 60 per month. well I hate to think of what will happen. Please, get him replaced as carpenter again his tag number is "123986" + he works at 125 St. N.Y.C. I am sorry I cannot give you my name as I do not want publicity though I see no way of avoiding it if things do not pick up. Thanking you for favours + forgive scribbling as am all nerves.

[Anonymous]

[Detroit, Mich., Oct 2—1935]

Mr. Franklin D. Roosevelt.

Dear Mr. President.

In this letter I'm asking you if you are kind enough to help me out. I'm a girl of 18 years old. And I need a coat. I have no money to buy a coat I need about $25.00 Dear President are you kind to help me and send me the money so I can buy my self the coat.

My father isnt working for 5 yrs. He has a sore leg they wont take him to work any place because of that sore leg. He cant buy me a coat. Were on welfare

Dear Mr. President my father voted for you he also told lot of his friends to vote for you. He help you so please help us now.

I know that you have a kind heart and wont refuse a girl that needs help Others are dressed but me with out a coat If I wont get any help from you Dear Mr. President than I will take my life away. I can't stand it no longer. We were thrown out on the street few times I hate to live the way I'm living now.

Again please be kind and help me. I'll be waiting for your answer.

Yours Truly

M. L. [female]

Detroit, Mich.

My father reads the Bible and he has a picture of you in the bible.

[Sept. 21, 1935]

Mr. Hopkins,
Relief Administrator,
Washington, D. C.
Dear Sir:—

Why are the Relief Projects being help up in St. Louis? The Projects that have already been started and are being help up for no one knows why, but you and I do not think you know. They could be continued and at least put some of our men to work right away and not wait until all the rest are ready, for if that is done and you fool around and pass the buck like you have none will be started at all.

We are not getting the allowances we did and our children are suffering for lack of food. And some have no clothes where with to attend school. Now is that right? And we will soon need coal and will not receive the funds for it, then what about that?

Of course, you are getting yours, and never have suffered like our people have, therefore you do not care. You have never been hungry and without all the luxuries of life, let alone the bare necessities. It is not the fault of our people that this condition exzists here, for they have tried and worked at anything at all to make a few pennies, but there is not the work to be had here.

Now there is work waiting here for some of our men and you are responsible for them not getting it. How can you answer to these people for that. They demand some consideration. And I am afraid they will soon tire of this delay and take some action themselves. They have been held down long enough through your petty Political Playing. That is all it is. The red tape could have been cut long ago. But what is your excuse. We know it is not true. Petty Politics is the answer. You will never get yours later by such actions.

Your plate at the table is full. Your family can enjoy life from the peoples money, and not have a care where this and that is coming from.

You were put in that position to do a real job and now you find you cannot fulfill it, and are playing around to the interests of the most moneyed men and starve the real working people of the country. God rights everything. And I hope to live to see the day that you and yours will have a little taste of what you are giving us daily for your food. NOTHING.

The Press all over the Country is razzing you and you think you are doing a swell job. Well people are something like elephants, they never forget. And the year 1936 is not far off.

You may not take this seriously but I have heard so many comments from people who have waited and waited for you to do something and the time is not far off when they will take action themselves. No one will be to blame but you. And now you want to pass the Buck to the State Administrators and in the next word you say they cannot pass finally on these unless they are O.K'd by Washington, which is BIG YOU. Well get busy and learn how to do something for some one besides your self.

Roosevelt is a coward like you are, he was afraid to come to St. Louis to the Legion Convention and you would be afraid to come too at an invitation.

You are so yellow, but it is your type that holds such positions and should be put out. If you are afraid to fulfill your duties, why resign. there are many better and nobler men who are not afraid to do the right thing by the working people.

The women are the real ones that have to suffer when they see their children underfeed. And then they advocate to eat more food. Yes we would gladly eat more feed and give more to our children if we had work where we could earn them money to purchase more food.

Please take this situation seriously and grant these men work right away. Start them on the work that is laying waiting for them to take up. The Winter is going to be hard enough, when we are all needing so much and nothing to get it with and we are being cut here and there on our allowances. The children have to suffer.

Put a small amount of men to work and by doing that it will take that much burden off of the Relief Rolls and give more for those that have to remain on.

In the name of GOD, Start our men to work NOW. There is plenty for them to do.

A distracted Mother.

I have tried to get work and there is nothing for a woman of my age to do. There are too many young married women allowed to keep their positions after they marry and in that way throw men out of work and our young single girls who have just finished college and should be allowed to hold a position are prevented from getting one on this account. That is something else that should be taken up all over the country. Preventing young married women from continuing in their positions after marrying in order to lay up a large sum of money and there-fore keeping men out of work. When you have nothing more to do than you are doing now you might try a hand at trying to remedy this situation.

[Apr. 10, 1936, N.Y.C.]

Harry Hopkins
W.P.A. Administrator
Wash. D.C.
Dear Sir,

I am a W.P.A. worker—I have heard of your plans to lay off the W.P.A. workers and I am very much opposed to it. I come from an old American family who pioneered this country—They did not build this country so that their posterity should starve in it. I believe that this country owes a living to every man woman and child and if it cant give us this living thru private industry it must provide for us thru government means—I am ready to fight for what I believe to be an inalianable right of every person living under this govt.

A. B. [female]

[Toledo, Ohio, Feb 11, 1936]

Dear Mother

Of the Greatest country on god earth allso the father of the greatest I am one of the least and hope I am Doing Right and truely mean no Wrong by Writeing these few line I am just a voter But I Dont mean any thing all that much But Just the same I am saying this I think the President is Doing alright But what a Pull Back we have got. so many vote for him and do Difference when it com to suporting him I would call you som other Big Name But there is No other Name More Better than Mother and I Do think you and the President is the Mother and father of this Great USA Well this is What I Want to say Would it hurt to Do a little investigating lot of the People is Kicking about any and every thing the father of the house hold is Done Well far as I can see the Middle class is trying to Poison the Mind of the lower class Making it as tough as they can without you noing it althou this May be so small that you may Not Pay it No Mind But little thing som time like that help a lot. . . .

[Anonymous]

Images from the 1930s: A Visual Essay

The works of art reproduced on the following pages were among hundreds of paintings and frescoes produced under the Federal Art Project of the Works Progress Administration and other, similar programs. The New Deal found itself in the art business partly because subsidies to artists did not bring the government into competition with private enterprise; and partly because government officials understood that post office murals might have a certain public relations value.

The artists who produced these works had to pay attention to the needs of their patron, the national government; to the desires of the local community in which the finished work would reside; and to the voices of the "people" in an era of depression. While these multiple demands on the artists make it impossible to isolate any single source for a work of art, the same multiplicity ensures that the artworks have some broad, social meaning.

What do you see in the following works of art? What do they tell us about how Americans understood and coped with the Great Depression? What ideas of gender do they present? Do they suggest that Americans feared technology or welcomed it? What balance is struck between urban and rural values? What would Harlem blacks think of any one of these murals if they encountered it at their local post office?

Allan Thomas, *"Extending the Frontier in Northwest Territory,"* Crystal Falls, Michigan.
National Archives.

Xavier Gonzalez, *"Pioneer Saga,"* Kilgore, Texas. National Archives.

Paul Meltsner, *"Ohio,"* Bellevue, Ohio. National Archives.

These illustrations appear in Barbara Melosh, *Engendering Culture: Manhood and Womanhood in New Deal Public Art and Theater,* Smithsonian Institution Press, Washington, D.C., 1991. We are grateful to Professor Melosh for making the prints available for use in *The American Record.*

Caroline S. Rohland, *"Spring"* (Sketch), Sylvania, Georgia. National Archives.

Howard Cook, *"Steel Industry,"* Pittsburgh, Pennsylvania. National Archives.

Migrant Mother

*Between 1935 and 1942, photographers for the New Deal's Farm Security
Administration Photographic Project took some 80,000 photographs of depression-
era America. Together, they constitute a remarkable record of rural and small-
town life—truly one of the great achievements of "documentary" photography.
Dorothea Lange's "Migrant Mother" is the best known of all the FSA
photographs and one of the most famous photographs of the twentieth century.*

*But what does it "document"? According to historian James Curtis's account
of the evolution of this photograph, "Migrant Mother" was the sixth and last of a
series. The early photos in the series were taken from a distance and encompassed
migrant mother's tent and four children, including a teenage daughter. No. 2 is
reproduced below. The third photo was of the mother alone, breastfeeding her
baby. Photos four and five brought one young child back into the frame, looking
over the mother's shoulder toward the camera. To achieve the undeniable power of
"Migrant Mother," Lange asked the two young children to turn away from the
camera, and she told the mother to bring her hand to her face. The whole process
took only minutes.*

*Does Lange's manipulation of the mother, her children, and the scene change
your mind about "Migrant Mother" (no. 6)? Does it mean that the photograph is
somehow less truthful, less "a document"?*

Dorothea Lange, *Migrant Mother* (no. 2), Nipomo, California, March 1936 (FSA).
Library of Congress.

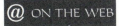 ON THE WEB   *The sequence of six photographs that compose the "Migrant Mother" set can be seen at*
xroads.virginia.edu/~UG97/fsa/lang.html.

Dorothea Lange, *Migrant Mother* (no. 6), Nipomo, California, March 1936 (FSA).
Library of Congress.

THE BIG PICTURE

It is common to think of the Great Depression as a national tragedy that cut across lines of geography, class, race, and gender. It certainly was that, but the Depression was also experienced, and survived, in a variety of different ways, depending on one's circumstances. Cheryl Greenberg's essay on Harlem tells an urban story, deeply influenced by race; the murals in the photo essay emphasize a rural (and even frontier) experience in which whites were central. Gender was important, too. Among the murals, Gonzalez's "Pioneer Saga" and Thomas's "Extending the Frontier" present images of dominant males and subordinate females, while Greenberg's Harlem featured many female-centered households. "Letters from the 'Forgotten Man'" includes a wide range of political responses to the crisis, although even the most critical reactions appear to have been within the "system." As the photograph "Migrant Mother" (no. 6) suggests, the government wanted Americans to believe that most people were getting through the Great Depression with dignity intact, and Greenberg's discussion of family and community in Harlem contributes to that assessment, as does Hayden's "Midsummer Night in Harlem"—and children playing leapfrog in the streets. Nonetheless, Greenberg's discussion of the economic decline of the Bennett family offers hints of how potentially demoralizing simple survival could be in a depression that knew no bounds.

Chapter 9

World War II: Optimism and Anxiety

When older Americans reflect on the 1940s, they recall the decade in halves: the first half, dominated by World War II, a difficult time when men and women fought for democracy against the forces of tyranny; and the second half, remembered as the beginning of a long period of prosperity and opportunity that would reach into the 1960s. There is much to be said for this view of the decade. Although Americans had been reluctant to go to war (the United States remained formally neutral when France was invaded by Germany in 1940), the Japanese attack on Pearl Harbor in December 1941 brought a flush of patriotism that temporarily buried most remaining doubts. A Virginia politician announced that "we needed a Pearl Harbor—a Golgotha—to arouse us from our self-sufficient complacency, to make us rise above greed and hate." Vice President Henry Wallace was one of many who revived Wilsonian idealism. "This is a fight," he wrote in 1943, "between a slave world and a free world. Just as the United States in 1862 could not remain half slave and half free, so in 1942 the world must make its decision for a complete victory one way or another." When the United States ended the war in the Pacific by exploding atomic bombs over Hiroshima and

Nagasaki, many Americans considered the act appropriate retribution for the attack at Pearl Harbor by a devious and immoral enemy.

In many ways, the war justified idealism, for it accomplished what the New Deal had not. Organized labor prospered. The name "Rosie the Riveter" described the new American woman who found war-related opportunities in the factories and shipyards. Black people—segregated by New Deal housing programs, injured as tenant farmers by New Deal farm policies, and never singled out as a group worthy of special aid—found skilled jobs in the wartime economy. They also received presidential assistance—in the form of the Fair Employment Practices Commission—in their struggle to end racially discriminatory hiring practices. A growing military budget in 1941 produced the nation's first genuinely progressive income tax legislation. Despite a serious and disruptive wave of postwar strikes that was triggered by high unemployment, for the most part the prosperity and economic growth generated by the war carried over into the late 1940s and 1950s.

Yet this *good war/good peace* view of the 1940s leaves too much unexplained and unaccounted for. It does not explain that the very patriotism that made Americans revel in wartime unity also had negative consequences. For example, on the Pacific coast, more than 100,000 Japanese Americans, including many American citizens, were taken from their homes and removed to distant relocation centers, where they remained for the "duration." *Good war/good peace* does not explain the popularity between 1942 and 1958 of *film noir*, a gloomy black-and-white film style that pictured a world in which ordinary, decent people were regularly victimized by bad luck. And *good war/good peace* does not reveal how thoroughly the war disrupted existing gender and race relations, setting the stage for the silly and absurd things postwar Americans did to try to restore the prewar status quo.

Beneath the surface of 1940s America was a pervasive anxiety. Some of this anxiety was economic; those who had experienced the Great Depression could never quite believe that another one wasn't around the corner. But far more important were anxieties linked to the use of the atomic bomb on the Japanese, the killing of 6 million Jews by the Nazis, the war-related deaths of 60 million people worldwide, and the increasing seriousness of the Cold War. These extraordinary facts and events created the most elemental form of insecurity: the knowledge that any human life could end senselessly and without warning. And many thoughtful Americans began to question—in a way they had not before, even during the Great Depression—whether history was still the story of civilization and progress, or a sad tale of moral decline. The concepts *good war* and *good peace* remained vital to Americans' understanding of their world, but they could not encompass the haunting feeling, so much a part of the late 1940s, that something very important had gone wrong.

Strangers from a Different Shore: The Relocation of Japanese Americans

Ronald Takaki

The beginning of the war in the Pacific on December 7, 1941, was a nightmare come true for many Japanese Americans. Americans were angry, even hysterical, and the press gave voice to their anger and fears, referring to the Japanese as "yellow men," "Nips," "vermin," and even "Mad dogs." Concerns were particularly acute on the Pacific coast, where the presence of substantial Japanese communities raised the possibility (it was never more than that) of subversive activity that could, conceivably, disrupt the war effort and endanger American lives. Within three days, the U.S. Army had proposed a mass evacuation of Japanese Americans, and by August of the following year, all West Coast Japanese Americans—some 120,000 men, women, and children—had been rounded up and put in camps of one sort or another, for the "duration." With scant regard for the Constitution, this policy was applied uniformly to those born in Japan (the Issei) and to the American-born generation (the Nisei).

Ronald Takaki's account of this experience can help us understand why and how the president of the United States made a decision that in retrospect seems shameful. The selection also describes the experience of relocation, including that of a group called the "no, no boys," who found a way to protest their treatment while living behind barbed wire.

Was the decision to relocate the Japanese on the West Coast wrong but reasonable, a product of wartime hysteria? Was the decision-making process flawed? Does Roosevelt deserve blame? Consider, too, the dilemma faced by Frank Emi and other Nisei who were asked to sign a loyalty oath and join the army. What actions were appropriate under such circumstances, and why?

The Myth of "Military Necessity" for Japanese-American Internment

"One morning—I think it was a Sunday—while I was working at Palama Shoe Factory I heard, *'Pon! pon! Pon! pon!'*" recalled Seichin Nagayama. He was only a few miles away from the navy base at Pearl Harbor. "I was drinking coffee and I thought, 'Strange. Are they having military practice?' At the corner of Liliha and Kuakini streets, a bomb fell in the back of a cement plant. We felt like going to see what happened, the noise was so loud. We found out that the war had started." The reverberations of the bombs falling near the Palama Shoe Factory and on Pearl Harbor were heard across the ocean; in a small Japanese farming community in California, Mary Tsukamoto was in church when she also suddenly felt the shocks of the explosions. "I do remember Pearl Harbor," she said years later as if it had happened that morning. "It was a December Sunday, so we were getting ready for our Christmas program. We were rehearsing and having Sunday school class, and I always played the piano for the adult Issei service. . . . After the service started, my husband ran in. He had been home that day and heard [the announcement] on the radio. We just couldn't believe it, but he told us that Japan attacked Pearl Harbor. I remember how stunned we were. And suddenly the whole world turned dark."

As it turned out, Nagayama and Tsukamoto faced very different futures during World War II. Nagayama quit his job at the Palama Shoe Factory because the pay was too low and started work at Primo Beer. His life, like the lives of most of the 158,000 Japanese in the islands representing 37 percent of Hawaii's population, was not dramatically interrupted by the war. But Tsukamoto and 94,000 fellow Japanese in California, representing only one percent of the state's population, had their lives severely disrupted: along with some 25,000 Japanese from Washington and Oregon, they were forcefully placed in internment camps by the U.S. government. Everyone was given short notice for removal. "Signs had been nailed to the telephone poles saying that we had to report to various spots," Tsukamoto recalled. "They told us to register as families. We had to report to the Elk Grove Masonic Building where we were given our family number, No. 2076." While the Japanese in the islands had become "locals," members of the community in Hawaii, their brethren on the mainland had been forced to remain "strangers." Different histories were coming home to roost in Hawaii and in California.

Shortly after inspecting the still-smoking ruins at Pearl Harbor, Navy Secretary Frank Knox issued a statement to the press: "I think the most effective fifth column work of the entire war was done in Hawaii, with the possible exception of Norway." Knox's assessment turned out to be inaccurate, for investigations by naval intelligence and the Federal Bureau of Investigation agreed that in fact no sabotage had occurred. But Knox's alarming announcement fueled rumors of sabotage committed by Japanese Americans in the islands—Japanese plantation laborers on Oahu had cut swaths in the sugar cane and pineapple fields to guide the Japanese bombers to the military installations, Japanese had parked cars across highways to block the traffic, and Japanese had given signals to enemy planes. At a cabinet meeting on December 19, Knox recommended the internment of all Japanese aliens on an outer island.

But in a radio address aired two days later, General Delos Emmons, as military governor of Hawaii declared: "There is no intention or desire on the part of the federal authorities to operate mass concentration camps. No person, be he citizen or alien, need worry, provided he is not connected with subversive elements. . . . While we have been subjected to a serious attack by a ruthless and treacherous enemy, we must remember that this is America and we must do things the American Way. We must distinguish between loyalty and disloyalty among our people."

A schism in policy was developing between Washington and Honolulu. Pursuant to Secretary Knox's recommendation, the War Department sent General Emmons a letter on January 10, 1942, asking for his view on the question of evacuating the Japanese from Oahu. Emmons replied that the proposed program would be dangerous and impractical. Such evacuation would require badly needed construction materials and shipping space, and would also tie up troop resources needed to guard the islands. Moreover, the mass evacuation of Japanese would severely disrupt both the economy and defense operations of Oahu, for the Japanese represented over 90 percent of the carpenters, nearly all of the transportation workers, and a significant proportion of the agricultural laborers. Japanese labor was "absolutely essential" for the rebuilding of the defenses destroyed at Pearl Harbor. A shrewd bureaucrat, General Emmons probably realized his analysis would fall on deaf ears in Washington and concluded his report by offering an alternative policy: if the War Department should decide to evacuate the Japanese from Oahu, it should remove them to the mainland.

In early February, Emmons informed Washington that he did not want to evacuate more than a few hundred Japanese until some 20,000 white-civilian women and children had first been transported to the mainland. He also estimated that 100,000 Japanese would have to be evacuated in order to remove all potentially disloyal Japanese, implying such a program would be impractical. On February 9, the War Department ordered General Emmons to suspend all Japanese workers employed by the army. But the order was rescinded after Emmons argued that the Japanese workers were indispensable and that the "Japanese question" should be handled "by those in direct contact with the situation."

General Emmons was hoping his bureaucratic foot-dragging and his resistance against orders from Washington would wear down the War Department. His strategy seemed to be paying off: Washington agreed to scale down the number to be evacuated. On March 13, President Franklin Roosevelt, acting on the advice of his Joint Chiefs of Staff, approved a recommendation for the evacuation of 20,000 "dangerous" Japanese from Hawaii to the mainland. Two weeks later, General Emmons reduced the number drastically to only 1,550 Japanese who constituted a potential threat. But, on April 20, Secretary Knox again insisted that "all of the Japs" should be taken out of Oahu. The War Department then circulated a report received from the Justice Department warning of dangerous conditions in Hawaii. In a letter to Assistant Secretary of War John J. McCloy, Emmons angrily dismissed the report as "so fantastic it hardly needs refuting" and then directly attacked the credibility of the War Department and the Justice Department: "The feeling that an invasion is imminent is not the belief of most of the responsible people. . . . There have been no known acts of sabotage committed in Hawaii."

The bureaucratic pushing and shoving between the War Department in Washington and the Hawaiian Department under the command of General

Emmons continued. On October 29, Secretary of War Henry L. Stimson informed President Roosevelt that General Emmons intended to remove approximately 5,000 Japanese from Hawaii during the next six months as shipping facilities became available. "This, General Emmons believes, will greatly simplify his problem, and considering the labor needs in the islands, is about all that he has indicated any desire to move although he has been given authority to move up to fifteen thousand." Irritated by Emmons, President Roosevelt wrote to Stimson four days later: "I think that General Emmons should be told that the only consideration is that of the safety of the Islands and that the labor situation is not only a secondary matter but should not be given any consideration whatsoever."

In the end, General Emmons had his way. He had seen no military necessity for mass evacuation and ordered the internment of only 1,444 Japanese (979 aliens and 525 citizens). Emmons saw that martial law had given the military government the authority to control Hawaii's Japanese population. But Emmons's success in resisting pressures from Washington depended not only on his administrative savvy and his ability to wage a waiting war of bureaucracy but also on widespread local opposition to mass internment.

In an article on "Hawaii's 150,000 Japanese" published in *The Nation* in July 1942, journalist Albert Horlings questioned whether the military authorities in Hawaii made their decision against mass internment based on their trust for the Japanese. He suspected "pressure" had been brought on the military, warning that the economic life of the islands would collapse without the Japanese. Horlings argued that businessmen appeared to favor "a liberal policy" toward the Japanese simply because they favored "business as usual."

Indeed, economic pressure groups in Hawaii were advising General Emmons to resist relocation. A few isolated local businessmen favored mass internment. "At least 100,000 Japanese should be moved to inland mainland farming states," John A. Balch of the Hawaiian Telephone Company wrote to Admiral Chester Nimitz in August 1942. "If such a step as this was taken . . . not only the danger of internal trouble could be avoided, but the future of Hawaii would be secured against the sure political and economic domination by the Japanese within the next decade." But most of Hawaii's leading businessmen and *kamaaina haoles* (old-timer whites) opposed the proposal for mass internment. The president of the Honolulu Chamber of Commerce called for just treatment of the Japanese in Hawaii: "There are 160,000 of these people who want to live here because they like the country and like the American way of life. . . . The citizens of Japanese blood would fight as loyally for America as any other citizen. I have read or heard nothing in statements given out by the military, local police or F.B.I. since December 7 to change my opinion. And I have gone out of my way to ask for the facts." The kamaaina elite, possessing a sense of genteel paternalism and a long history of interaction with the Japanese in the islands, were unwilling to permit their mass uprooting. They also knew the evacuation of over one third of Hawaii's population would decimate their labor force and destroy the economy of the islands.

Politicians and public officials also urged restraint and reason. Hawaii's congressional delegate, Sam King, advised the military that nothing should be done beyond apprehending known spies. Honolulu Police Captain John A. Burns refuted rumors of Japanese snipers firing on American soldiers during the attack on Pearl Harbor. "In spite of what . . . anyone . . . may have said about the fifth column activity in Hawaii," stated Robert L. Shivers, head of the FBI in Hawaii, "I want to emphasize that there was no such activity in Hawaii before, during or after the attack on Pearl Harbor. . . . I was in a position to know this fact. . . . Nowhere under the sun could there have been a more intelligent response to the needs of the hour than was given by the entire population of these islands." When schools were reopened in January 1942, the Superintendent of Public Instruction sent a directive to all teachers:

> Let us be perfectly frank in recognizing the fact that the most helpless victims, emotionally and psychologically, of the present situation in Hawaii will be children of Japanese ancestry and their parents. The position of loyal American citizens of Japanese ancestry and of aliens who are unable to become naturalized, but who are nonetheless loyal to the land of their adoption, is certainly not enviable. Teachers must do everything to help the morale of these people. Let us keep constantly in mind that America is not making war on citizens of the United States or on law-abiding aliens within America.

The press in Hawaii behaved responsibly. Newspaper editors like Riley Allen of the Honolulu *Star Bulletin* and Mrs. Clarence Taylor of the Kauai *Garden Island* expressed confidence in the loyalty of the local Japanese and criticized the federal government's treatment of the Japanese on the mainland. "It was an invasion of the rights of the Japanese citizens on the Pacific coast to be picked up and shipped to the interior," editorialized the *Garden Island*. Newspapers also cautioned their readers not to spread or be influenced by rumors generated by the war situation. Within days after the attack on Pearl Harbor, the Honolulu *Star Bulletin* dismissed reports of Japanese subversion in the islands as "weird, amazing, and damaging untruths." "Beware of rumors always," urged the *Paradise of the Pacific* magazine in February 1942, "avoid them like a plague and, when possible, kill them as you would a reptile. Don't repeat for a fact anything you do not know is a fact."

The reasons behind Hawaii's refusal to intern the Japanese were complex and did include the self-serving economic concern of the business community for the uninterrupted maintenance of its labor force. Still, in this moment of crisis an image of what Hawaii represented began to take a more definite form and content, drawing from the particular history of the islands and defining more sharply Hawaii's identity as a multiethnic community. Political and economic circumstances had provided an occasion for cultural development. In his radio message broadcast two weeks after the attack on Pearl Harbor, General Emmons declared: "Hawaii has always been an American outpost of friendliness and good will and now has calmly accepted its responsibility as an American outpost of war. In accepting these responsibilities, it is important that Hawaii prove that her traditional confidence in her cosmopolitan population has not been misplaced." While what Emmons described was a myth, it nonetheless also contained within it the possibility of an ideological counterpoint to the reality of racial hierarchy in the islands.

The actions of the Japanese gave concreteness to the idea of Hawaii as a cosmopolitan community. During the morning of the attack, two thousand Nisei serving in the U.S. Army stationed in Hawaii fought to defend Pearl Harbor against enemy planes. Everywhere Japanese civilians participated in the island's defense. They rushed to their posts as volunteer truck drivers for Oahu's Citizens' Defense Committee. They stood in long lines in front of Queen's Hospital, waiting to give their blood to the wounded. Many of these civilians were Issei. "Most of us have lived longer in Hawaii than in Japan. We have an obligation to this country," they declared. "We are *yoshi* [adopted sons] of America. We want to do our part for America." . . .

If the Japanese in Hawaii were not interned, why were their brethren on the mainland evacuated and imprisoned in internment camps? Why did the mainland do "things the American Way" differently?

On the day after the attack on Pearl Harbor, Representative John M. Coffee declared in Congress: "It is my fervent hope and prayer that residents of the United States of Japanese extraction will not be made the victim of pogroms directed by self-proclaimed patriots and by hysterical self-anointed heroes. . . . Let us not make a mockery of our Bill of Rights by mistreating these folks. Let us rather regard them with understanding, remembering they are the victims of a Japanese war machine, with the making of the international policies of which they had nothing to do."

Perhaps Coffee was overly hopeful and naive, but there were reasons to think Japanese Americans would not become victims of hysteria unleashed by the war. A confidential report on the question of Japanese-American loyalty had already been submitted to President Franklin Roosevelt. The president had secretly arranged to have Chicago businessman Curtis Munson gather intelligence on the Japanese in the United States and assess whether they constituted an internal military threat. After Roosevelt received the Munson report on November 7, 1941, he asked the War Department to review it. In his discussion on sabotage and espionage, Munson informed the President that there was no need to fear or worry about America's Japanese population: "There will be no armed uprising of Japanese [in this country]. . . . Japan will commit some sabotage largely depending on imported Japanese as they are afraid of and do not trust the Nisei. There will be no wholehearted response from Japanese in the United States. . . . For the most part the local Japanese are loyal to the United States or, at worst, hope that by remaining quiet they can avoid concentration camps or irresponsible mobs. We do not believe that they would be at least any more disloyal than any other racial group in the United States with whom we went to war."

A month later the assessment of the Munson report was tested at Pearl Harbor. In his investigation of the Japanese in Hawaii and on the mainland, Lieutenant Commander K. D. Ringle of the Office of Naval Intelligence found that the large majority of them were at least passively loyal to the United States. In late January 1942, Ringle estimated that only about 3,500 Japanese could potentially be military threats and stated there was no need for mass action against the Japanese. Meanwhile, the FBI had also conducted its own investigation of the Japanese. On December 10, Director J. Edgar Hoover informed Washington that "practically all" suspected individuals whom he had initially planned to arrest were in custody: 1,291 Japanese (367 in Hawaii, 924 on the mainland), 857 Germans, and 147 Italians. In a report to the Attorney General submitted in early February, Hoover concluded that the proposed mass evacuation of the Japanese could not be justified for security reasons.

Despite these intelligence findings, Lieutenant General John L. DeWitt, head of the Western Defense Command, behaved very differently from his counterpart General Emmons in Hawaii. Within two weeks after the attack on Pearl Harbor, General DeWitt requested approval to conduct search-and-seizure operations in order to prevent alien Japanese from making radio transmissions to Japanese ships. The Justice Department refused to issue search warrants without probable cause, and the FBI determined the problem was only a perceived one. In January, the Federal Communications Commission, which had been monitoring all broadcasts, reported that the army's fears were groundless. But the army continued pursuing plans based on the assumption of Japanese disloyalty. General DeWitt also wanted to be granted the power to exclude Japanese aliens as well as Americans of Japanese ancestry from restricted areas. On January 4, 1942, at a meeting of federal and state officials in his San Francisco headquarters, DeWitt argued that military necessity justified exclusion: "We are at war and this area—eight states—has been designated as a theater of operations. . . . [There are] approximately 288,000 enemy aliens . . . which we have to watch. . . . I have little confidence that the enemy aliens are law-abiding or loyal in any sense of the word. Some of them yes; many, no. Particularly the Japanese. I have no confidence in their loyalty whatsoever. I am speaking now of the native born Japanese—117,000—and 42,000 in California alone."

The Western Defense Command ignored the Munson report as well as the information from the FCC and shunned Lieutenant Commander Ringle. Serving under DeWitt, Major General Joseph W. Stilwell had an insider's view of the situation at the Command's headquarters in San Francisco. In his diary, Stilwell described how DeWitt was responding irrationally to rumors: "Common sense is thrown to the winds and any absurdity is believed." But Stilwell did not understand the reasons for DeWitt's conduct. FBI director Hoover was more perceptive: while he also saw that the WDC's intelligence information reflected "hysteria and lack of judgment," he noticed that the claim of military necessity for mass evacuation was based "primarily upon public and political pressure rather than on factual data."

Immediately after the press had been told by Navy Secretary Knox about Japanese subversive activity at Pearl Harbor, West Coast newspapers gave his claim headline attention: "Fifth Column Treachery Tool" and "Secretary of Navy Blames 5th Column for Raid." Nonetheless, newspapers were initially restrained, advising readers to remain calm and considerate toward the Japanese. But in early January, press sentiments began shifting suddenly. On January 5, John B. Hughes of the Mutual Broadcasting Company began firing a month-long salvo against the Japanese in California. The Japanese were engaged in espionage, he charged, and their dominance in produce production and control of the food supply were part of a master war plan. On January 19, *Time* reported Japanese fifth-column activities in Hawaii in an article entitled: "The Stranger within Our Gates." The next day, the *San Diego Union* stirred anti-Japanese hysteria: "In Hawaii . . . treachery by residents, who although of Japanese ancestry had been regarded as loyal, has played an important part in the success of Japanese attacks. . . . Every Japanese . . . should be moved out of the coastal area and to a point of safety far enough inland to nullify any inclination they may have to tamper with our safety here." Meanwhile the *Los Angeles Times* editorialized: "A viper is nonetheless a viper wherever the egg is hatched—so a Japanese American, born of Japanese parents—grows up to be a Japanese, not an American." On January 29, Henry McLemore blasted the Japanese in his syndicated column for the Hearst newspapers: "I am for immediate removal of every Japanese on the West Coast to a point deep in the interior. I don't mean a nice part of the interior either. Herd 'em up, pack 'em off and give 'em the inside room in the badlands." Two weeks later, in a *Washington Post* article entitled "The Fifth Column on the Coast," prominent columnist Walter Lippmann called for the mass removal of Japanese Americans: "The Pacific Coast is in imminent danger of a combined attack from within and without. . . . The Pacific Coast is officially a combat zone. . . . And nobody ought to be on a battlefield who has no good reason for being there. There is plenty of room elsewhere for him to exercise his rights."

As the press mounted its campaign for Japanese removal, it was joined by patriotic organizations. In January the California Department of the American Legion began to demand that all Japanese known to possess dual citizenship be placed in "concentration camps." Shortly afterward American Legion posts in Washington and Oregon passed resolutions urging the evacuation of all Japanese. In the January issue of their publication, *The Grizzly Bear*, the Native Sons and Daughters of the Golden West told their fellow Californians: "We told you so. Had the warnings been heeded—had the federal and state authorities been 'on the alert,' and rigidly enforced the Exclusion Law and the Alien Land Law . . . had the legislation been enacted denying citizenship to offspring of all aliens ineligible to citzenship . . . had Japan been denied the privilege of using California as a breeding ground for dual-citizens (Nisei);—the treacherous Japs probably would not have attacked Pearl Harbor on December 7, 1941, and this country would not today be at war with Japan."

Beginning in January and early February, the anti-Japanese chorus included voices from farming interests such as the Grower-Shipper Vegetable Association, the Western Growers Protective Association, and the California Farm Bureau Federation. "We've been charged with wanting to get rid of the Japs for selfish reasons," the Grower-Shipper Vegetable

Racist Hostility to the Japanese Was Not Limited to the West Coast. This billboard was in Louisville, Kentucky. Royal Photo Company Collection, Special Collections: Photographic Archives, University of Louisville.

Association stated in the *Saturday Evening Post* in May. "We might as well be honest. We do. It's a question of whether the white man lives on the Pacific Coast or the brown man. They came into this valley to work, and they stayed to take over. . . . If all the Japs were removed tomorrow, we'd never miss them in two weeks, because the white farmers can take over and produce everything the Jap grows."

Meanwhile, local and state politicians were already leading the movement for Japanese removal. The boards of supervisors of sixteen California counties, including Los Angeles County, passed resolutions urging removal. California Attorney General Earl Warren pressed federal authorities to remove Japanese from sensitive areas on the West Coast. The Japanese in California, he warned, "may well be the Achilles heel of the entire civilian defense effort. Unless something is done it may bring about a repetition of Pearl Harbor." On January 16, Congressman Leland Ford of Los Angeles wrote to the secretaries of the departments of War and the Navy and the FBI Director, insisting that "all Japanese, whether citizens or not, be placed in concentration camps." Two weeks later, several House members from the Pacific Coast states asked President Roosevelt to grant the War Department "immediate and complete control over all alien enemies, as well as United States citizens holding dual citizenship in any enemy country, with full power and authority" to evacuate and intern them.

The Western Defense Command operated within the context of this clamor for Japanese removal. The situation was very different from Hawaii's. Economic interests in California did not need Japanese labor, and many white farmers viewed Japanese farmers as competitors. Representing a small, rather than numerically significant racial minority, the Japanese were more vulnerable to xenophobic attacks. Furthermore a mythology of California as a "cosmopolitan" society did not exist to protect its Japanese residents. In fact, the state's image as projected by politicians in the 1920 vote on the alien land law was "Keep California White." On February 1, in a telephone conversation with Provost Marshal General Allen Gullion, General DeWitt said he had "travelled up and down the West Coast," talked to "all the Governors and other local civil authorities," and decided to press for mass evacuation. Protection against sabotage, he said, "only can be made positive by removing those people who are aliens and who are Japs of American citizenship." On February 5, after he had received DeWitt's views in writing, Gullion drafted a War Department proposal for the exclusion of "all persons, whether aliens or citizens . . . deemed dangerous as potential saboteurs" from designated "military areas."

But a decision on evacuation still had not been made in Washington. During lunch with President Roosevelt on February 7, Attorney General Francis Biddle said "there were no reasons for mass evacuation." In his diary on February 10, Secretary of War Henry L. Stimson wrote: "The second generation Japanese can only be evacuated either as part of a total evacuation . . . or by frankly trying to put them out on the ground that their racial characteristics are such that we cannot understand or trust even the citizen Japanese. This latter is the fact but I am afraid it will make a tremendous hole in our constitutional system to apply it."

President Roosevelt was willing to make such a tremendous hole in the Constitution. In fact, he had been considering the internment of Japanese Americans for a long time. On August 10, 1936, President Roosevelt had written a memorandum to the Chief of Naval Operations: "One obvious thought occurs to me—that every Japanese citizen or non-citizen on the island of Oahu who meets these Japanese ships or has any connection with their officers or men should be secretly but definitely identified and his or her name placed on a special list of those who would be the first to be placed in a concentration camp in the event of trouble." Thus, five years before the attack on Pearl Harbor, Roosevelt was already devising a plan for the imprisonment of Japanese aliens and citizens in a "concentration camp" without due process of law.

On February 11, 1942, Roosevelt met with Stimson, and shortly after the meeting, Assistant Secretary of War John J. McCloy telephoned the Provost Marshal General's office in San Francisco. "We talked to the President," McCloy said to Karl Bendetsen, chief of the Aliens Division, "and the President, in substance, says go ahead and do anything you think necessary. He says there will probably be some repercussions, but it has got to be dictated by military necessity. . . ." Three days after he had received his signal from Washington, General DeWitt sent Stimson his formal recommendation for removal, buttressing it with a racial justification: "In the war in which we are now engaged racial affinities are not severed by migration. The Japanese race is an enemy race and while many second and third generation Japanese born on United States soil, possessed of United States citizenship, have become 'Americanized,' the racial strains are undiluted. . . . It, therefore, follows that along the vital Pacific Coast over 112,000 potential enemies, of Japanese extraction, are at large today."

Three days later, Attorney General Biddle wrote a memorandum to President Roosevelt, opposing DeWitt's recommendation for evacuation: "My last advice from the War Department is that there is no evidence of imminent attack and from the F.B.I. that there is no evidence of planned sabotage." Biddle tried to exercise reason and restraint, and his efforts to derail DeWitt's recommendation angered Congressman John Ford. "I phoned the Attorney General's office," said Ford, "and told them to stop fucking around. I gave them twenty-four hours notice that unless they would issue a mass evacuation notice I would drag the whole matter on the floor of the House and of the Senate and give the bastards everything we could with both barrels."

The next day, February 18, Secretary of War Stimson met with Attorney General Biddle and several others from the Department of Justice and the War Department. In his autobiography, Biddle described the meeting: "The decision [for evacuation] had been made by the President. It was, he said, a matter of military judgment. I did not think I should oppose it any further." The following morning, President Roosevelt signed Executive Order 9066, which directed the Secretary of War to prescribe military areas "with respect to which, the right of any person to enter, remain in, or leave shall be subject to whatever restrictions the Secretary of War or the appropriate Military Commander may impose in his discretion." The order did not specify the Japanese as the group to be excluded. But they were the target: a few months later, when President Roosevelt learned about discussions in the War Department to apply the order to Germans and Italians on the East Coast, he wrote to inform Stimson that he considered enemy alien control to be "primarily a civilian matter except in the case of the Japanese mass evacuation on the Pacific Coast." Unlike the Germans and Italians, the Japanese were "strangers from a different shore."

President Roosevelt had signed a blank check, giving full authority to General DeWitt to evacuate the Japanese and place them in assembly centers and eventually in internment camps. And so it happened, tragically for the Japanese and for the U.S. Constitution, for there was actually no "military necessity."

Under General DeWitt's command, the military ordered a curfew for all enemy aliens and all persons of Japanese ancestry and posted orders for evacuation: "Pursuant to the provisions of Civilian Exclusion Order No. 27, this Headquarters, dated April 30, 1942, all persons of Japanese ancestry, both alien and non-alien, will be evacuated from the above area by 12 o'clock noon, P. W. T., Thursday May 7, 1942." The evacuees were instructed to bring their bedding, toilet articles, extra clothing, and utensils. "No pets of any kind will be permitted." Japanese stood in silent numbness before the notices. Years later, Congressman Robert Matsui, who was a baby in 1942, asked: "How could I as a 6-month-old child born in this country be declared by my own Government to be an enemy alien?" But the order applied to everyone, including children. An American birthright made absolutely no difference. "Doesn't my citizenship mean a single blessed thing to anyone?" asked Monica Sone's brother in distress. "Several weeks before May, soldiers came around and posted notices on telephone poles," said Takae Washizu. "It was sad for me to leave the place where I had been living for such a long time. Staring at the ceiling in bed at night, I wondered who would take care of my cherry tree and my house after we moved out." . . .

Believing the military orders were unconstitutional, Minoru Yasui of Portland refused to obey the curfew order: "It was my belief that no military authority has the right to subject any United States citizen to any requirement that does not equally apply to all other U.S. citizens. If we believe in America, if we believe in equality and democracy, if we believe in law and justice, then each of us, when we see or believe errors are being made, has an obligation to make every effort to correct them." Meanwhile Fred Korematsu in California and Gordon Hirabayashi in Washington refused to report to the evacuation center. "As an American citizen," Hirabayashi explained, "I wanted to uphold the principles of the Constitution, and the curfew and evacuation orders which singled out a group on the basis of ethnicity violated them. It was not acceptable to me to be less than a full citizen in a white man's country." The three men were arrested and convicted; sent to prison, they took their cases to the Supreme Court, which upheld their convictions, saying the government's policies were based on military necessity. Most Japanese, however, felt they had no choice but to comply with the evacuation orders. . . .

After a brief stay in the assembly centers, the evacuees were herded into 171 special trains, five hundred in each train. . . . They had no idea where they were going. In their pockets, some carried photographs of themselves and the homes they had left behind, and they occasionally turned their gaze away from the landscape whizzing by them and pulled out their pictures. . . . The trains took them to ten internment camps—Topaz in Utah, Poston and Gila River in Arizona, Amache in Colorado, Jerome and Rohwer in Arkansas, Minidoka in Idaho, Manzanar and Tule Lake in California, and Heart Mountain in Wyoming. . . .

In the camps, the internees were assigned to barracks, each barrack about twenty by 120 feet, divided into four or six rooms. Usually a family was housed in one room, twenty by twenty feet. The room had "a pot bellied stove, a single electric light hanging from the ceiling, an Army cot for each person and a blanket for the bed." . . .

Most adults went to work. Shopkeepers and farmers suddenly found themselves working as wage earners for the government, forced to abandon the virtues of self-reliance and independence that had enabled them to survive in society. Government employees in camps earned twelve dollars a month as unskilled laborers, sixteen dollars as skilled, and nineteen dollars as professionals. Busy and active people before the evacuation, many internees became bored and listless. . . . Proud people before evacuation, they felt diminished, their dignity destroyed. Some were overwhelmed by their despair. . . .

But the war had also begun to open a future for the Nisei. In September 1942, the Selective Service had classified all young Japanese men as IV-C, or enemy aliens. A month later, however, the Director of the Office of War Information urged President Roosevelt to authorize the enlistment of Nisei: "Loyal American citizens of Japanese descent should be permitted, after an individual test, to enlist in the Army and Navy. . . . This matter is of great interest to OWI. Japanese propaganda to the Philippines, Burma, and elsewhere insists that this is a racial war. We can combat this effectively with counter propaganda only if our deeds permit us to tell the truth." President Roosevelt understood the need to neutralize "Japanese propaganda": in December the army developed a plan for forming an all-Nisei combat team. On February 1, 1943, hypocritically ignoring the evacuation order he had signed a year earlier, Roosevelt wrote to Secretary of War Stimson: "No loyal citizen of the United States should be denied the democratic right to exercise the responsibilities of his citizenship, regardless of his ancestry. . . . Americanism is not, and never was, a matter of race or ancestry. Every loyal American citizen should be given the opportunity to serve this country . . . in the ranks of our armed forces. . . ."

Five days later the government required all internees to answer loyalty questionnaires. The questionnaires had two purposes: (1) to enable camp authorities to process individual internees for work furloughs as well as for resettlement outside of the restricted zones, and (2) to register Nisei for the draft. Question 27 asked draft-age males: "Are you willing to serve in the armed forces of the United States on combat duty, wherever ordered?" Question 28 asked all internees: "Will you swear unqualified allegiance to the United States of America and faithfully defend the United States from any or all attack by foreign or domestic forces, and forswear any form of allegiance or obedience to the Japanese emperor, or any other foreign government, power or organization?"

Forced to fill out and sign the loyalty questionnaire in the internment camps, Nisei stared at the form. . . . Some 4,600 or 22 percent of the 21,000 Nisei males eligible to register for the draft answered with a "no," a qualified answer, or no response. Many of them said they were not expressing disloyalty but were protesting against the internment. "Well, I am one of those that said 'no, no' on the questions, one of the 'no, no' boys," explained Albert Nakai, "and it is not that I was proud about it, it was just that our legal rights were violated and I wanted to fight back." When he was told the army wanted Nisei to volunteer for a special combat unit, Monica Sone's friend, Dunks Oshima retorted: "What do they take us for? Saps? First, they change my army status to 4-C because of my ancestry, run me out of town, and now they want me to volunteer for a suicide squad so I could get killed for this damn democracy. That's going some, for sheer brass!"

At Heart Mountain internment camp, Frank Emi studied the questionnaire. "The more I looked at it the more disgusted I became," recalled Emi, who at the time was a twenty-seven-year-old Nisei with a wife and two children. "We were treated more like enemy aliens than American citizens. And now this [the loyalty questionnaire]." Emi decided to hand print his answer and post it on the mess hall doors: "Under the present conditions and circumstances, I am unable to answer these questions." Shortly afterward, he attended a mass meeting where he heard a stirring speech by Kiyoshi Okamoto. An educated soil-test engineer from Hawaii who had moved to the mainland and become a high-school teacher, Okamoto told his fellow Nisei that as American citizens they should stand up for the rights guaranteed to them under the Constitution. He referred to himself as the "Fair Play Committee of One." The fifty-year-old Okamoto moved the younger Nisei. "At first we were naive and just felt the questionnaire was unfair," said Emi. "But Okamoto taught us about the Constitution and it came to have great meaning as we began to resist."

Though most Nisei answered Questions 27 and 28 affirmatively, they did not rush to join the army. The army was able to recruit only 1,208 volunteers—a small fraction of the 10,000 eligible Nisei. In January 1944, the Selective Service began reclassifying to I-A Nisei who had answered yes to the two questions and serving draft registration notices. At Heart Mountain, Emi and several fellow Nisei organized the Fair Play Committee and declared they would not cooperate with the draft unless their citizenship rights were restored first. Their movement spontaneously gathered widespread support. Four hundred Nisei attended their meetings and the Committee had two hundred dues-paying members. Draft resistance broke out in the other camps. Some three hundred Nisei refused to be inducted, protesting the violation of their Constitutional rights.

Worried, government authorities acted quickly to repress the protest. Emi and six other leaders of the Heart Mountain Fair Play Committee were arrested and indicted for conspiracy to violate the Selective Service Act and for counseling others to resist the draft. . . .

Emi and the others were found guilty and sentenced to four years at Leavenworth Federal Penitentiary. "What you guys are doing is all right," a Nisei told Emi. "But I don't want to go to jail so I have to register for the draft." At Leavenworth they found themselves in a prison for hardened criminals. "They asked us, 'Why are you here?'" said Emi. "And we told them, and they replied, 'It don't make sense to put you in jail.'" Altogether some three hundred Nisei refused to be inducted and many of them were sent to prison. "Look, the government took my father away, and interned him someplace," explained a Nisei draft resister. "My mother is alone at the Grenada camp with my younger sister who is only fourteen. If the government would take care of them here in America, I'd feel like going out to fight for my country, but this country is treating us worse than shit!"

The Kikuchi Diary

Charles Kikuchi

Charles Kikuchi was twenty-six years old when the Japanese attacked Pearl Harbor on December 7, 1941. He was an American citizen—born in Vallejo, California, the son of Japanese immigrants—and a resident of Berkeley, a university community. By early May 1942, he and his family had been relocated to the Assembly Center of Tanforan, where Kikuchi spent four months before being relocated again, this time to a facility in Arizona. He left that camp in April 1943 for Chicago, as part of an extended work leave for Nisei. He entered the Army in mid-1945.

The portion of Kikuchi's diary reprinted here covers the days at Tanforan. How did Charles and his parents handle the experience of relocation? What were the most important features of life in the camp? How did the camp experience affect Kikuchi's understanding of American democracy?

VOICES

December 7, 1941, Berkeley, California

Pearl Harbor. We are at war! Jesus Christ, the Japs bombed Hawaii and the entire fleet has been sunk. I just can't believe it. I don't know what in the hell is going to happen to us, but we will all be called into the Army right away. Wang* says he has to do a report, but he is so stunned that he does not know what he is doing. He is worried about his relatives as the radio says there are riots in Los Angeles, and they think it is sabotage. I can't believe that any Nisei would do anything like that, but it could be some of the Kibei† spies. I don't know what is going to happen to us, but I just can't think of it.

I think of the Japs coming to bomb us, but I will go and fight even if I think I am a coward and I don't believe in wars but this time it has to be. I am selfish about it. I think not of California and America, but I wonder what is going to happen to the Nisei and to our parents. They may lock up the

---

*Wang: Warren Tsuneishi, a friend of Kikuchi's.

†Nisei is the Japanese term, commonly used by Japanese Americans, for the children of the immigrants, the latter being known as Issei. The Kibei, also referred to, are Nisei who received much of their education in Japan.

aliens. How can one think of the future? We are behind the eightball, and that question for the California Nisei "Whither Nisei?" [is] so true. The next five years will determine the future of the Nisei. They are now at the crossroads. Will they be able to take it or will they go under? If we are ever going to prove our Americanism, this is the time. The Anti-Jap feeling is bound to rise to hysterical heights, and it is most likely that the Nisei will be included as Japs. I wanted to go to San Francisco tonight, but Pierre says I am crazy. He says it's best we stick on campus. In any event, we can't remain on the fence, and a positive approach must be taken if we are to have a place in fulfilling the Promise of America. I think the U.S. is in danger of going Fascist too, or maybe Socialist. Those Nisei progressives think it will be Socialists, but the Sacramento crowd sure sound like Fascists. "These are the days which try men's souls." I don't know what to think or do. Everybody is in a daze. Maybe I should do my report on the Nisei daze. Everybody on campus is in the same boat, and they will clear us all off to the Army and no more time for college for anyone. . . .

April 30, 1942, Berkeley

Today is the day that we are going to get kicked out of Berkeley. It certainly is degrading. I am down here in the control station and I have nothing to do so I am jotting down these notes! The Army Lieutenant over there doesn't want any of the photographers to take pictures of these miserable people waiting for the Greyhound bus because he thinks that the American public might get a sympathetic attitude towards them.

I'm supposed to see my family at Tanforan as Jack told me to give the same family number. I wonder how it is going to be living with them as I haven't done this for years and years? I should have gone over to San Francisco and evacuated with them, but I had a last final to take. I understand that we are going to live in the horse stalls. I hope that the Army has the courtesy to remove the manure first.

This morning I went over to the bank to close my account and the bank teller whom I have never seen before solemnly shook my hand and he said, "Goodbye, have a nice time." I wonder if that isn't the attitude of the American people? They don't seem to be bitter against us, and I certainly don't think I am any different from them. That General De Witt certainly gripes my ass because he has been listening to the Associated Farmers* too much.

Oh, oh, there goes a "thing" in slacks and she is taking pictures of that old Issei lady with a baby. She says she is the official photographer, but I think she ought to leave these people alone. The Nisei around here don't seem to be so sad. They look like they are going on a vacation. They are all gathered around the bulletin board to find out the exact date of their departure. "When are you leaving?" they are saying to one another. Some of those old Issei men must have gone on a binge last night because they smell like *sake*. . . .

---

*The Associated Farmers was a trade association of generally well-off California farmers; it had actively urged the relocation of the Japanese (who were in many instances competitors of theirs).

May 3, 1942 Sunday

The whole family pitched in to build our new home at Tanforan. We raided the Clubhouse and tore off the linoleum from the bar table and put it on our floor so that it now looks rather homelike. Takeshi [Tom] works pretty hard for a little guy and makes himself useful, but the gals are not so useful. They'd rather wander around looking for the boys. However, they pitched in and helped clean up the new messhall so that we could have our meals there instead of walking all the way over to the clubhouse. It's about 11:00 now and everyone has gone to bed. You can hear the voices all the way down the barracks—everything sounds so clear. Tom just stepped out to water his "victory garden." The community spirit is picking up rapidly and everyone seems willing to pitch in. They had a meeting tonight to get volunteers for cooks and waiters at the new messhall and this was done without difficulty. Rules were also made for each barracks such as radio off at 10:00 and not too many lights so that the fuse would not get overloaded.

    We have only been here three days, but it already seems like weeks. Everyone here has fallen into the regular routine, without any difficult adjustments except Pop who was a problem child this morning. He got mad because he was not getting the proper food* so he went off by himself and got lost. . . .

May 6, 1942 Wednesday

I feel like trying to join the Army also, but that's being heroic. I still can't decide whether I would be more useful doing service work among the Japanese here. I think I will be able to adjust myself easily enough although not knowing the language may be a handicap but not necessarily too big to overcome. At least I no longer feel apologetic about it. I guess it has been my emotional reactions against political Japan that have blocked my learning the language in the past few years.

    Today they have started to put Nisei police to patrol the barracks and the messhall.† There have been several cases of theft reported and the kitchen has been raided a number of times. One woman reported a fur coat stolen, but she may have just lost it as I don't see why anyone would want a fur coat in a place like this. A more serious problem is the reported solicitations by Japanese prostitutes up in the single men's dormitory. The Army M.P. are on their trails and Nisei police have been stationed to intercept them if they show up at night. (And Mr. Greene thinks we don't need social workers!) This is not so bad; but if this sort of thing starts among the young Nisei, it will be very difficult to control. This camp has a sort of pioneer atmosphere about it and if the kids are left in idleness, trouble could easily develop.

---

*The elder Kikuchi required a special diet because of his diabetic condition.

†The administration hoped to reduce their problems in patrolling their charges by employing selected evacuees as part of the "internal police." White police were less frequently seen, although present—in addition, of course, to the military guards.

Already some of the so called "rowdy Nisei"* are shooting craps so that they can get money to spend in the canteen. The development of a well balanced recreational program will be a good influence. I sound like a moralist, but I am thinking more in terms of future social adjustments of the Japanese here, which will be difficult, and morale will have to be kept at a high level if we expect progress to be made.

May 7, 1942 Thursday

A new menace has entered our lives to make the pioneer conditions more uncomfortable. We are infested with tiny fleas that bite like hell. They must be horse fleas or something that come from the old stables. Gods, they certainly make life miserable. . . .

There are all different types of Japanese in camp. Many of the young Nisei are quite Americanized and have nice personalities. They smile easily and are not inhibited in their actions. They have taken things in stride and their sole concern is to meet the other sex, have dances so that they can jitterbug, get a job to make money for "cokes," and have fun in general. Many are using the evacuation to break away from the strict control of parental rule.

Other Nisei think more in terms of the future. They want to continue their education in some sort of "career" study and be successes. The background which they come from is very noticeable: their parents were better educated and had businesses. One Nisei girl was telling me today about how Grant Avenue [San Francisco] art goods stores were sold out. They used a lot of Nisei girls and those stores that were in control of Caucasian hands paid twice as much in salary as those owned by Japanese. Many of the shrewd Jewish businessmen bought the whole store out and they got a lot of old stock out of warehouses and sold them in the evacuation sale. They used the Japanese stores as a front to unload this junk on the public. The art goods stores, even Chinese, are having a difficult time because they cannot get any more stock in from the Orient. I asked the girl what her father expected to do after the war and she said that he and his wife would probably be forced to leave this country, but the girl expects to get married and stay here.

Made me feel sort of sorry for Pop tonight. He has his three electric clippers hung up on the wall and Tom has built him a barrel chair for the barber seat. It's a bit pathetic when he so tenderly cleans off the clippers after using them; oiling, brushing, and wrapping them up so carefully. He probably realizes that he no longer controls the family group and rarely exerts himself so that there is little family conflict as far as he is concerned. What a difference from about 15 years ago when I was a kid. He used to be a perfect terror and dictator. I think most of us have inherited this tendency to be dominant, except perhaps Alice. She is not too aggressive and she would perhaps make some fellow a nice wife. She has worked hard for the past four years and helped

---

Although on the whole an extremely law-abiding community, the Japanese Americans had by 1942 discovered the problems of juvenile and postjuvenile delinquency.

support the family so that now she is more or less inclined to be a little queenish. Alice has never gone beyond her high school level of friends and this is the type that she goes around with now—nothing wrong in that, I suppose, but I do think that she should be more advanced than to confine herself with Emiko's and Bette's "jitterbug" friends.

Emiko is very boy-conscious also and her idea of life right now is good clothes, plenty of boy friends, and jitterbug music. She will probably get over the stage soon. She gets along well with the fellows and is capable of adjustments to any circumstances.

Bette is also getting at that age and sometimes she feels that Jack and I don't approve of it so she hesitates a bit at times in approving all of these light activities. She seems to be more responsible than the other two and she certainly has a clever sense of humor. She, too, is getting boystruck. Right now, she worries about her weight so that she makes Miyako or Tom walk around the track with her for the "exercise."

Mom is taking things in stride. I have a suspicion that she rather enjoys the whole thing. It certainly is a change from her former humdrum life. She dyed her hair today, and Pop made some comment that she shouldn't try to act so young. One thing about these stables is that it does cut down the amount of "nagging" because people can overhear everything that is said.

May 8, 1942 Friday

. . . The question came up as to what were we fighting for. All of us were agreed that Fascism was not the answer, but there was a difference of opinions on whether an Allied victory would be any solution to the whole mess. Jimmy thinks that it offered the most potentialities and hope for the world. Would the solution include only the white races, or will we be in a position to tackle the problem of India, China, and the other millions of "exploited" peoples? If not, our efforts will not have accomplished their purposes. The problem is so immense that it staggers the imagination.

May 17, 1942 Sunday

The importance of this Assembly Center is that some sort of organizational basis will be developed for self government, and it is not too important for us to perfect anything here, since our stay will be relatively limited in the camp. Some of the younger Nisei think that the Work Corps is a fine idea— if they get prevailing wages—and are anxious to do something as they are getting restless doing nothing here! Work opportunities will continue to be at the minimum here in this camp. . . .

Mom and Pop seem to enjoy people coming here to have fun because then they don't have to worry about what is going on. Pop even tried to jitterbug tonight and he was the hit of the evening. I was thinking tonight that the evacuation by itself has already in the past two weeks broken down some of the Japanese culture. Already some of the former causes for cultural conflict have become less intensified—with the Nisei holding the upper hand. We hold the advantage of numbers and the fact that we are citizens.

Many of the parents who would never let their daughters go to dances before do not object so strenuously now. They are slowly accepting the fact that their children cannot stay home night after night doing nothing without some sort of recreational release. Books are still a rarity. Consequently, the Thursday night talent show and the Saturday dances are jammed to capacity. There can no longer be conflict over the types of food served as everybody eats the same thing—with forks. We haven't had any Japanese food yet, thank God. The recreational program thus far has been pointed towards the Nisei and there is little for the older folks to do except go visiting.

The Nisei as a whole rejoice that they no longer have to attend Japanese language school.* This means that Japanese will be used less and less as the younger children grow up. A very few will be able to read and write it. . . .

Although we are a drop in the bucket as far as numbers are concerned, the social implications and significance are of fundamental importance to this country as well as to the rest of the democratic world. How can we fight Fascism if we allow its doctrines to become a part of government policies? The contradiction would be too obvious to ignore. Many of the American Chinese, Negroes, and Jews can see that a dangerous precedent can be set, which could easily include them later if this thing is not handled democratically. Already my Chinese, Negro, and Jewish friends have made remarks about the possibility. Perhaps we don't get enough of the other side of the picture, seeing that we are out here in California, in the hotbed of the greatest agitation. I can't blame the Nisei for being resentful when they read about "Jap soldier in U.S. uniform arrested!" I do so myself. One of the dangers of this is that many of the Nisei are getting more race conscious than even before because of this very thing—we are all lumped together as disloyal Japs. And I wonder how the Nisei soldier feels? This is one hell of a way to create national unity. . . .

July 14, 1942

Marie, Ann, Mitch, Jimmy, Jack, and myself got into a long discussion about how much democracy meant to us as individuals. Mitch says that he would even go in the army and die for it, in spite of the fact that he knew he would be kept down. Marie said that although democracy was not perfect, it was the only system that offered any hope for a future, if we could fulfill its destinies. Jack was a little more skeptical. He even suggested that we [could] be in such grave danger that we would then realize that we were losing something. Where this point was he could not say. I said that this was what happened in France and they lost all. Jimmy suggested that the colored races of the world had reason to feel despair and mistrust the white man because of

---

*The Japanese language schools, which young Nisei had more or less unwillingly attended after school at the insistence of their parents, were a prime subject for criticism by the enemies of the Japanese Americans. The complaint that emperor worship and Japanese nationalism were taught was nonsense. Most Nisei did attend at some time or other, but they learned only a little Japanese and a smattering of selected bits of old-country culture.

the past experiences. The treatment of minority groups even in this country is contradictory to democracy. Jack thought this was the reason why so many minority groups did not feel for democracy, because they have never had it. He said that before we could do anything, race prejudice had to be eliminated, and he did not see how this was possible. Marie said this feeling of hopelessness was one of the reasons why many Nisei were rejecting patriotism. But this was a negative approach. A lot of things would be cleared up if the Caucasian Americans showed their good faith by letting the bars of immigration down and by giving the Negro a democratic chance. Asia would never trust the U.S. unless we showed good faith at home first. Ann thought that it was worth the fight to make democracy right and eliminate the patronizing attitude of the white man. Whether America could shake off the stupid mistakes of prejudices was something that none of us could make a definite answer upon. We did not know whether economic greed would still be the dominant end of these nations at war. We hoped and believed that the world would be changed for the better, under a democratic system. Jack thought that this was not being practical enough, but the rest of us could not agree to that. Jack ate almost a whole box of crackers during the conversation.

August 31, 1942

In reviewing the four months here, the chief value I got out of this forced evacuation was the strengthening of the family bonds. I never knew my family before this and this was the first chance that I have had to really get acquainted. There is something wholesome about it and with the unity which it presents, one does not feel alone, knowing that there are some who will back one up in moments of crisis. It sort of binds strength to an individual thrown into a completely strange group. We have had our arguments and bickerings, but this has been a normal process which only lasts for a little while. This family is composed of very strong individualists, but the right of the individual in the family is respected by the others if it does not conflict with the whole group and is [not] harmful to it. . . .

Pop and Mom have come through a difficult adjustment period. Now I believe that they actually like it here since they don't have any economic worries. Mom still has not realized that the children have grown up, but she is strongly aware of it. Most of the family decisions are now made by the older children. They [Mom and Pop] are naturally consulted and an effort is made to believe that it came from them.

Of course, we have only had four months of this life and things may be different after we have been in a camp for a much longer period. But we always manage to get along in a fair way. I wonder what will happen if we all suddenly rebelled against this kind of living? The postwar period is going to be trying no matter which way we look at it. I may do further graduate work or else try to get into Civil Service. The latter is the only future for me that I can see at this time.

Well, the new chapter starts tomorrow. I don't feel up to the effort to attempt a review of the camp now. I'm sleepy and I have to get up at 3 o'clock!

Tanforan: A Photo Essay

The photographs on these pages were taken at the Tanforan, California, Assembly Center. Each has its original 1942 caption. Examined as a group, what is the message of the photos? Are they a form of propaganda? Do they yield the same view of the relocation effort as Charles Kikuchi's diary?

A family enjoys the sunshine on the porch of their quarters. Library of Congress.

In a watchtower a guard outside the Tanforan Assembly Center scrutinizes the landscape for fires and other hazards. Library of Congress.

An evacuee artist sketches a model. Library of Congress.

Evacuees who were citizens retained the right to vote. Photo shows city clerk Ralph E. Woodman of the San Bruno, California, municipality nearest to the Tanforan Assembly Center, accepting absentee ballots for a state election from evacuees. Library of Congress.

 ON THE WEB   *Photographs of the Manzanar, California, Relocation Center by distinguished photographer Ansel Adams can be viewed at* memory.loc.gov/ammem/aamhtml/aamhome.html. *The National Park Service Web site has solid information on all the relocation centers. Go to* www.cr.nps.gov/history/.

Bataan

On April 9, 1942, an American and Filipino force of about 70,000 soldiers, defending the Bataan peninsula in the Philippines, surrendered to the Japanese. They were among some 76,000 men, many of them ill, marched in brutal fashion to San Fernando, 55 miles away. Thousands died on what became known as the Bataan "Death March."

    The film Bataan *(1943) starred Robert Taylor as the head of a rag-tag bunch of men who had agreed to stay behind to slow the Japanese advance. The Office of War Information approved the shooting script for* Bataan, *as it did for all other films made during the war.*

    Although the American military was racially segregated until 1950, the fictional unit assembled in Bataan *included a Latino, a black, and two Filipinos, not to mention whites of different classes and ethnicities. What was the purpose of presenting the American military in this light? Was the image entirely false, or did it convey some truth?*

A still from *Bataan* (1943). The platoon leader, played by Robert Taylor, is in the back, second from left.

Truman on Hiroshima
(August 6, 1945)

Harry S Truman

One can only imagine the emotions of Japanese Americans as they heard that the Enola Gay had released an atomic bomb over the city of Hiroshima, or read the following statement by President Harry Truman, released by the White House. It is an extraordinary document, full of the twists and turns that were perhaps inevitable at this moment when the public was first introduced to the atomic bomb, told about its use at Hiroshima, and informed of its atomic future. How did Truman justify the use of this weapon? What aspects of the atomic bomb did Truman emphasize? What should or might he have said that he did not?

Sixteen hours ago an American airplane dropped one bomb on Hiroshima, an important Japanese Army base. That bomb had more power than 20,000 tons of T.N.T. It had more than two thousand times the blast power of the British "Grand Slam" which is the largest bomb ever yet used in the history of warfare.

The Japanese began the war from the air at Pearl Harbor. They have been repaid many fold. And the end is not yet. With this bomb we have now added a new and revolutionary increase in destruction to supplement the growing power of our armed forces. In their present form these bombs are now in production and even more powerful forms are in development.

It is an atomic bomb. It is a harnessing of the basic power of the universe. The force from which the sun draws its power has been loosed against those who brought war to the Far East.

Before 1939, it was the accepted belief of scientists that it was theoretically possible to release atomic energy. But no one knew any practical method of doing it. By 1942, however, we knew that the Germans were working feverishly to find a way to add atomic energy to the other engines of war with which they hoped to enslave the world. But they failed. We may be grateful to Providence that the Germans got the V-1s and the V-2s late and in limited quantities and even more grateful that they did not get the atomic bomb at all.

The battle of the laboratories held fateful risks for us as well as the battles of the air, land and sea, and we have now won the battle of the laboratories as we have won the other battles.

Beginning in 1940, before Pearl Harbor, scientific knowledge useful in war was pooled between the United States and Great Britain, and many priceless helps to our victories have come from that arrangement. Under that general policy the research on the atomic bomb was begun. With American and British scientists working together we entered the race of discovery against the Germans.

Foreign Relations of the United States, *Potsdam*, vol. 2, Washington, D.C., 1960, pp. 1380–1381.

The United States had available the large number of scientists of distinction in the many needed areas of knowledge. It had the tremendous industrial and financial resources necessary for the project and they could be devoted to it without undue impairment of other vital war work. In the United States the laboratory work and the production plants, on which a substantial start had already been made, would be out of reach of enemy bombing, while at that time Britain was exposed to constant air attack and was still threatened with the possibility of invasion. For these reasons Prime Minister Churchill and President Roosevelt agreed that it was wise to carry on the project here. We now have two great plants and many lesser works devoted to the production of atomic power. Employment during peak construction numbered 125,000 and over 65,000 individuals are even now engaged in operating the plants. Many have worked there for two and a half years. Few knew what they have been producing. They see great quantities of material going in and they see nothing coming out of these plants, for the physical size of the explosive charge is exceedingly small. We have spent two billion dollars on the greatest scientific gamble in history—we won.

But the greatest marvel is not the size of the enterprise, its secrecy, nor its cost, but the achievement of scientific brains in putting together infinitely complex pieces of knowledge held by many men in different fields of science into a workable plan. And hardly less marvelous has been the capacity of industry to design, and of labor to operate, the machines and methods to do things never done before so that the brain child of many minds came forth in physical shape and performed as it was supposed to do. Both science and industry worked under the direction of the United States Army, which achieved a unique success in managing so diverse a problem in the advancement of knowledge in an amazingly short time. It is doubtful if such another combination could be got together in the world. What has been done is the greatest achievement of organized science in history. It was done under high pressure and without failure.

We are now prepared to obliterate more rapidly and completely every productive enterprise the Japanese have above ground in any city. We shall destroy their docks, their factories, and their communications. Let there be no mistake; we shall completely destroy Japan's power to make war.

It was to spare the Japanese people from utter destruction that the ultimatum of July 26 was issued at Potsdam. Their leaders promptly rejected that ultimatum. If they do not now accept our terms they may expect a rain of ruin from the air, the like of which has never been seen on this earth. Behind this air attack will follow sea and land forces in such numbers and power as they have not yet seen and with the fighting skill of which they are already well aware.

The secretary of war, who has kept in personal touch with all phases of this project, will immediately make public a statement giving further details.

His statement will give facts concerning the sites of Oak Ridge near Knoxville, Tennessee, and at Richland near Pasco, Washington, and an installation near Santa Fe, New Mexico. Although the workers at the sites have been making materials to be used in producing the greatest of destructive force in history they have not themselves been in danger beyond that of many other occupations, for the utmost care has been taken of their safety.

The fact that we can release atomic energy ushers in a new era in man's understanding of nature's forces. Atomic energy may in the future supplement the power that now comes from coal, oil, and falling water, but at present it cannot be produced on a basis to compete with them commercially. Before that comes there must be a long period of intensive research.

It has never been the habit of the scientists of this country or the policy of this government to withhold from the world scientific knowledge. Normally, therefore, everything about the work with atomic energy would be made public.

But under present circumstances it is not intended to divulge the technical processes of production or all the military applications, pending further examination of possible methods of protecting us and the rest of the world from the danger of sudden destruction.

I shall recommend that the Congress of the United States consider promptly the establishment of an appropriate commission to control the production and use of atomic power within the United States. I shall give further consideration and make further recommendations to the Congress as to how atomic power can become a powerful and forceful influence towards the maintenance of world peace.

Dark Victory: A Visual Essay

Three of the illustrations in this grouping feature Americans dealing in ordinary ways with the fact of World War II. The other two are from 1946, a year of transition: the war was over, the Cold War not yet recognizable. Of the postwar pictures, one is an illustration from a high school yearbook, the other a film still from The Best Years of Our Lives *(1946), the winner of seven Oscars, including Best Picture. In the scene depicted, Dana Andrews plays Fred Derry, a returning veteran interviewing for work at a small department store. What does each illustration reveal about the era? About the war? About relations between men and women? In the scene from* The Best Years of Our Lives, *what emotions might be running through the head of the job-seeking young man in uniform? What do all those signs on the floor below represent? What does the setting of the scene reveal about what Derry might be feeling?*

Soldier Home on Furlough, Brown Summit, North Carolina, May 1944. Standard Oil Collection, Special Collections: Photographic Archives, University of Louisville.

For secondary and primary sources, including digital collections, on the experience of women during World War II, contact American Women's History: A Research Guide: World War II, *at www.mtsu.edu/~kmiddlet/history/women/wh-wwii.html.*

The Tanner Family—Velma, Jimmie, and Their Son—at Home in the Humble Oil Company "Poor Boy" Camp, Tomball, Texas, 1945. Standard Oil Collection, Special Collections: Photographic Archives, University of Louisville.

A Barmaid in Great Falls, Montana, 1944. Standard Oil Collection, Special Collections: Photographic Archives, University of Louisville.

Riverside High School *Skipper*, Buffalo, New York, 1946.

Returning veteran Fred Derry (Dana Andrews, right) applies for a job in a
department store in *The Best Years of Our Lives* (1946).

THE BIG PICTURE

War is a complex and transforming experience. That is especially true when the conflict is as big and important as World War II, and when the combatant is a nation with a significant commitment to democratic institutions and ideals. This chapter features two presidents, each deeply committed to preserving and enlarging the nation's democratic heritage, yet each, operating in the climate of war, taking actions that to some, even at the time, seemed indecent, seemed to violate the nation's core values. Roosevelt incarcerated American citizens who had committed no crime; Truman used the atomic bomb against civilians at Hiroshima.

But war also transforms in ways that can be revitalizing, and there are suggestions of that kind of transformation in the preceding pages, too. One can see it in Charles Kikuchi's interrogation of democracy; in Frank Emi's decision to answer "no" and "no" to questions on a loyalty questionnaire; in the film *Bataan*'s insistence that the conflict in the Pacific was between a Japanese autocracy and a vigorous, color-blind American democracy; and in returning veteran Fred Derry's discomfort with the trivial consumerism of a 1946 economy rapidly making the transition from production to consumption, and from war to peace.

Chapter 10

Cold War, Cold War at Home

The end of World War II marked a clear American military and economic success. But it also created a power vacuum in Europe and a sense of insecurity about the immediate future in Washington. Some prominent Americans, like Henry Luce, the publisher of *Life* magazine, welcomed the opportunity to inaugurate an "American Century," an era where the United States was challenged to embrace world leadership and create an environment conducive to American commercial growth and development. Should the nation fail to grasp this opportunity, Luce argued, it might find itself, as it had after World War I, hostage to the fortunes of fascist, totalitarian, or communist nations that were less keen on peace, commercial development, and democracy.

Throughout World War II, Washington's major policies were consistent with Luce's vision of an American Century. At the Bretton Woods Conference in April 1944, the World Bank, the International Monetary Fund, and a system of currency exchange were created, all aimed at facilitating and stabilizing the free flow of trade. A further American diplomatic priority was world stability, addressed through the renewed commitment to collective security as defined by the United Nations, another agency given new life by the Allies' military success.

America held one other high card in its hand, in addition to its immense military and economic and financial establishments. In August 1945, American technology and science were proved superior when the first atomic bomb was exploded over Hiroshima. In sole possession of a startling new weapon that redefined warfare, Americans felt they had a sure winner. It was, however, frustratingly difficult to find combat situations where the bomb could be profitably employed, especially since it took months to build each one. The preponderance of the American contribution in funding the war, in ending the conflict in the Pacific, and in creating the monetary environment of the future seemed to indicate that the American Century had commenced.

Yet August 1945 did not immediately usher in a secure, stable world for American workers. The problems inherent in converting the American economy to peacetime production, the demobilization of millions of servicemen, and the shift in the labor force as returning servicemen displaced recently hired women and minorities meant a period of inflation and insecurity for a nation only too familiar with the economic hardships of the recent depression. Americans became aware, once again, that they could win the war and lose the peace. The clear military victory of 1945 was followed by inconclusive diplomacy, as the Allies were unable to agree on the structure of postwar Germany; American factories were in danger of cutting production for lack of clients; and the shared goals and ideals of wartime were giving way to socialism and state economies among the Allies.

As these concerns grew and multiplied, President Truman took action. In March 1947, he boldly asked Congress for $400 million in aid to Greece and Turkey. The general anxiety and sense of crisis among the American public regarding recent world events coalesced into active fear of the Soviet Union and communist regimes. The Cold War had officially begun.

Within two months, the Truman administration would call for the largest foreign aid program in the history of the United States: the Marshall Plan. The intent was to save the economies of Europe and indirectly to provide markets to sustain America's production. In 1948, the first arguments for American defense of Europe were heard; in 1949, the North Atlantic Treaty Organization was formed, and military containment was born. The American decision to reconstruct Western Europe led the Soviet Union to retaliate by forming its own east European bloc. Truman's response to the crisis of 1947 institutionalized a military, economic, and diplomatic contest between the United States and the Soviet Union.

The 1952 election of Dwight D. Eisenhower redefined the problem. Republicans accused Truman of misunderstanding the nature of the fight; what Democrats called a relatively short-term crisis was, the Republicans argued, a long-term, ideological struggle between the forces of communism and capitalism—a struggle that threatened, if not dealt with correctly, to destroy the very foundations of American society. In this contest to the death, America's future lay in maintaining budgetary balance, military superiority, and a clear moral definition of its goals. If a "clear and present danger" existed in America's future, then all of America's promises of freedom, democracy, and individualism had to be placed on hold until security was won.

The acute insecurity expressed in the elections of 1950 and 1952 blurred the lines between foreign policy and domestic policy. Once the concept of America under siege became political consensus, dissension in actions or thoughts could easily be seen as treason, offering aid and comfort to the enemy, deeds worthy of prosecution and punishment. This was the climate that spawned the second Red Scare.

☙ INTERPRETIVE ESSAY

The Postwar Sex Crime Panic

George Chauncey, Jr.

From time to time Americans have found themselves caught up in moments of collective fear and anxiety—what is labeled a "panic" in the story that follows. In 1919, in the wake of the first world war and the Russian Revolution of 1917, the object of that fear and anxiety was the ideology of Communism. In the 1970s, the obsessive concern with cults had some of the earmarks of a panic. And so did the child-kidnapping scare of the early 1980s.

The late 1940s proved to be a particularly fertile ground for such events. The UFO scare of mid-1947 began in late June, when the pilot of a private plane claimed to have seen nine "saucerlike" objects; by mid-July, "flying saucers" had been reported in 35 states. The "sex crime panic" began that same year and held the nation's attention through the early 1950s. For more than 5 years, newspapers and magazines were full of stories and articles on brutal sex murders and assaults; state commissions studied the problem of the sexual "deviant"; and parents agonized over whether it was safe to send their children outdoors to play.

While some panics are just what they appear to be—that is, real expressions of concern over genuine social problems—others need to be read and interpreted like any other "text." When this is done, the flying saucer scare can be understood in part as a reaction to anxiety-producing events in Europe, including the failure of the United Nations to resolve a serious crisis in the Balkans and the Soviet decision not to participate in the Marshall Plan, a program for European reconstruction. The UFO sightings were one expression of Cold War anxieties.

The sex crime panic, too, was a more complicated event than it seemed at the time. Like the UFO scare, it was partly a product of the Cold War, reaching a peak of intensity in the winter of 1949 to 1950, just as the Soviet Union exploded its first atomic bomb, China fell to the Communists, and Wisconsin Senator Joseph McCarthy began charging that Communists had infiltrated the State Department.

In the following narrative, George Chauncey, Jr. probes a very different side of the sex crime panic. For Chauncey, the panic was no mere reflection of postwar anxiety over world events, although his account gives the Cold War its due. More important, he argues, the panic reflected the deep tensions in family life and sexual culture that had resulted from the upheavals of the war. The conflict had divided families, put women into men's jobs, and brought men into intimate—and sometimes sexual—contact with other men. Many Americans wanted to put an end to these and other threatening developments, and to enforce conformity to orthodox ideas of gender, sexuality, and family.

George Chauncey, Jr., "The Postwar Sex Crime Panic," from *True Stories from the American Past*, ed. William Graebner, © The McGraw-Hill Companies, Inc.

The sex crime panic evoked genuine fears about sexual violence. But it was seized on by a variety of groups that sought to mold it and use it to advance their own social programs and organizational interests. As a result of their efforts, the panic—for all the lurid tales of ice pick murders and rape mutilations of women and children—ultimately had as much to do with keeping women in the home as with keeping sex criminals off the street.

On November 14, 1949, Linda Joyce Glucoft, aged 6 years, was sexually assaulted by an elderly relative of the friend she had gone to visit in her Los Angeles neighborhood. When she cried out, her assailant, a retired baker whom the police had already charged in another child molestation case, choked her with a necktie, stabbed her with an ice-pick, and bludgeoned her with an axe, then buried her body in a nearby rubbish heap. Only a few days later, a drunken farm laborer assaulted and murdered a 17-month-old baby girl outside a dance hall in a small town near Fresno. That same week, the Idaho police found the body of 7-year-old Glenda Brisbois, who had last been seen entering a dark blue sedan near her home; she had been murdered by a powerful assailant who had heaved her body 15 feet into an irrigation canal.

The gruesome details of these murders and of the hunt for their perpetrators were telegraphed to homes throughout the country by the nation's press. According to police statistics, such assaults were proportionately no more common than in previous years, but in late 1949 these three murders epitomized to many Americans the heightened dangers that seemed to face women and children in postwar America. Many regarded them not as isolated tragedies but as horrifying confirmation that a plague of "sex crime" threatened their families.

They had reason to fear such a plague. Ever since the war's end, a growing number of newspaper and magazine articles had focused the nation's attention on the murder of women and children; even more chillingly, they had argued that the motive for such assaults was sexual and that their perpetrators were men who had lost control of deviant sexual impulses. Stories with titles such as "Murder as a Sex Practice," "The Psychopathic Sex Menace," and "What Can We Do About Sex Crimes?" appeared with growing frequency in magazines as varied as the *Saturday Evening Post, Sir!,* and *Parade.* Between July of 1949 and March of 1951, *Collier's,* a weekly magazine with a large, middle-class family readership, ran a particularly explosive series of 13 articles by Howard Whitman which identified the growing "Terror in Our Cities," particularly the terror caused by the threat of sexual violence, as a national phenomenon. Newspapers throughout the country picked up on the issue and spotlighted local incidents involving children and women. "How Safe Is Your Daughter?" J. Edgar Hoover had asked America's parents in a famous article published by *The American Magazine* in 1947; a barrage of articles on sex crime seemed to confirm his claim that she wasn't very safe at all.

Some of the reporters and editors responsible for such stories published them because they thought they would help sell papers. Other editors, genuinely convinced that the "sex criminal" posed a major new threat to

"The nation's women and children will never be secure . . . so long as degenerates run wild"

Illustrating J. Edgar Hoover's famous article, "How Safe Is Your Daughter?" (1947), this photograph evoked every parent's greatest fear—that some harm might come to his or her child—to urge support for the policing of a wide range of sexual noncomformists. The picture's giant hand also evoked the period's sci-fi horror films, which depicted the threats posed to America by alien ways of life; it suggested that every "sex deviate" was equally alien to traditional American values.

American families, hoped the articles would alert the public to the danger such criminals posed and generate popular support for the drastic new measures they thought were needed to curtail them. "Let's get cracking before it's too late," *Collier's* challenged its readers in one editorial. "Who knows where or when the next psychopath or hoodlum will strike? In your town? In your street?"

The press campaigns worked: They did not just report on the fear of sex crimes gripping many cities, but helped create it. When Michigan's newspapers spotlighted the murders of three children in the state in 1949 and 1950, for instance, many parents became so alarmed that they wrote the governor to demand action. As one father wired the governor in September 1950: "Who is going to protect my Joey when he is out playing tomorrow[?] The death of eight year old Joey Hausey only speaks to millions of how wicked sex deviates are." After hearing a radio report about sex crimes in February,

1950, a woman wrote to remind the governor that "Every mother of a daughter—and I am one—can not rest with sex perverts at large."

In many cities, parents did more than write letters. In one community after another, they organized to demand governmental protection for their children. The pattern in most cities was the same: a single violent, sometimes murderous assault on a girl, boy, or woman galvanized a public already made deeply anxious about sex crime. Local newspapers and church, women's, and parents' organizations mobilized popular support for increased police protection and more effective legislation to control sex offenders. In Philadelphia, where a newspaper poll reported that 90 percent of the city's women and 50 percent of its men were afraid to walk the streets at night, a series of incidents in 1949 resulted in neighborhood demands for increased police surveillance. On Palm Sunday in 1950, Chicago's "Fighting Priest," Father Jerome Dehnert, asked his parishioners to attend a mass protest meeting at a parochial school where two children had been attacked—and 600 people showed up.

As a result of the press's preoccupation with the issue, the problem of sex crimes and "sex deviation" became, to an astonishing extent, a staple of public discourse in the late 1940s and early 1950s. A popular topic for young orators (one Michigan girl won her high school district's first prize in oration for a talk on sex deviates in 1950 and was later asked to repeat the speech at a Lions Club luncheon), it was also a regular subject of PTA discussions ("PTA Plans Panel on Deviate," announced one banner headline; "Experts Asked to Serve"). Some high school boys heard so much discussion of "deviates" that they even began referring to certain boys they disliked as "Dee-Vees" instead of "sissies."

The local press campaigns and panics set the stage for the eruption of a genuinely national hysteria in the winter of 1949 to 1950, when newspapers riveted the nation's attention on the November murders of the three little girls in California and Idaho. Papers throughout the nation followed the story of each murder in the grim detail normally reserved for local murders. Many also exacerbated local fears by providing additional coverage of local attacks on children, which, while less severe, took on greater significance because of their association with the national stories.

The *Detroit News*, for instance, generally the least sensationalist of Detroit's three daily newspapers, devoted extensive coverage to sex crimes during the week of the girls' murders. Every day that week, the *News* carried stories, several under front-page banner headlines, about the California and Idaho murders, the attempted abduction of a 7-year-old girl in Detroit, and FBI statistics about sex crime. Three editorials in as many days demanded stronger laws to control sex criminals; one in Saturday's paper warned of the "large, potentially murderous population [of sex deviates], floating about in the larger community, [which] constitutes the problem which in the last week has reasserted itself with appalling force." The front page of Sunday's paper carried the first installment in an 18-part series of articles on "Controlling the Sex Criminal," and another page was devoted to "Michigan's Most Revolting Sex Crimes—In Words and Photos." Monday's paper inaugurated a week-long series of articles, "Somebody Knows!," which reminded readers of the circumstances of eight recent "sex murders" in the Detroit area and offered rewards for information leading to the murderers' apprehension. Not surprisingly, 9 of the 14 letters to the editor published on Tuesday focused on sex crime. The press had created the image of a country whose streets and alleyways were overrun with murderous sex psychopaths.

The sensationalist accounts of the children's murders led church and women's groups throughout the country, as well as the local and national press, to demand state action, and state governments responded in ways that focused even more attention on the issue. The two sex murders in California in mid-November prompted 1000 people to meet in Los Angeles on November 21 to demand state action. California's legislators established a Subcommittee on Sex Crimes the following week, and in December Governor Earl Warren convened both a special session of the state legislature and a conference of law enforcement agencies on "Sex Crimes Against Children" to respond to the crisis. The New Jersey Commission on the Habitual Sex Offender, established the previous spring, kept the issue alive in its state that fall by inviting some 750 judicial, medical, police, church, and civic authorities to testify at well-publicized hearings in Atlantic City and Newark. In February, 1950, it issued its report, and in March a New York study commission reported the results of its 2-year study of sex offenders confined at Sing Sing Prison and recommended legislation that was heartily endorsed by Governor Dewey. Both states' reports received nationwide press attention.

Fifteen state governments responded to the public's concern about sex crimes by establishing such study commissions, and while press reports had generated the initial panic, the commissions played the major role in its subsequent development. In Michigan, for instance, Governor G. Mennen Williams appointed a study commission on the "Deviated Criminal Sex Offender" in November of 1949 in response to the demands of civic and parents' organizations, scores of letters and petitions, and a vociferous press campaign. But a review of subsequent developments in Michigan shows that, once the commission was established, it quickly took charge of the panic, managing it and giving it direction.

The commission was well aware that the public's outrage over sex crimes might decline when the memory of particular crimes had faded, so for 2 years it worked to sustain that outrage and to channel it into support for the long-term programs it thought would effectively prevent such crimes. The commission cultivated the press in a successful effort to have itself portrayed as the major authority on the problem and to gain extensive, favorable coverage of its work (two of Detroit's three dailies, for instance, ran long series of articles explaining its proposals). In order to keep the public's attention focused on the sex crime issue the commissioners addressed public meetings sponsored by women's, farmers', and police organizations, local health councils, and PTAs. They also established official liaisons with the state's bar and medical associations and informal ties with other important civic, professional, and women's groups in order to mobilize their support for the legislation they recommended to the state assembly. In August of 1951 they mailed copies of their 245-page final report to some 2300 individuals and organizations. During the most important stages of the legislative battles that winter the commissioners sent "Legislative Bulletins" to more than 70 organizations, keeping them posted on legislative developments and urging them to orchestrate letter-writing campaigns and meetings with legislators in support of the bills they had proposed, and arranged for supportive women's and professional associations to send speakers to the public hearings on them.

The commission that so skillfully marshalled this support from the press and the public was dominated, like those in most states, by the psychiatrists and psychologists who served on it. The several clergymen, police, and court officials who served on the commission with them were accustomed to thinking of sexual behavior in terms of its morality or legality. But the psychiatrists persuaded them that unconventional sexual behavior should be considered not just immoral or illegal, but—more significantly— as a deviation from the psychological norm and the symptom of a deeper pathology or mental illness, which could be treated more effectively by medical men than by clergymen or the police. In Michigan, the one commissioner who dissented from this consensus—an attorney who denounced his colleagues' recommendations for threatening due process and individual liberty—soon stopped attending meetings because, he said, "no one listened to [his] objections."

Psychiatrists might not have had so much influence on the commissions earlier in the century, but their prestige had grown enormously during World War II because of the crucial role they had played in screening and managing the millions of people mobilized for military service. Their role in the Michigan commission both reflected their new prestige and helped them enhance it. As psychiatrists, the men who dominated the work of the commission genuinely believed that psychiatry had the most important contribution to make to the explanation of sexual "deviation" and to the solution of sex crime. As strategists, they heeded Governor Williams' advice in his address at their first meeting that they should "take advantage of the widespread public concern about this problem for the establishment of [mental health] facilities and programs dealing constructively with this situation."

Thus in the name of protecting women and children from sex deviates, the commission's psychiatrists urged the public to support the expansion of existing psychiatric institutions and the development of new ones, even if they were only peripherally related to the problem of sex crime. Before a special session of the Michigan legislature in March, the commission argued that the governor's proposal to expand psychiatric treatment programs and programs to educate clergymen, physicians, police, and school children about mental health issues should be supported because sex deviates were likely to remain undetected, untreated, and possibly dangerous without them. Eight months later, the commission urged voters to support a state bond referendum for the construction of mental hospitals; such programs, as the *Detroit Times* put it, would provide the "means of detecting the deviate before he becomes a killer."

The most innovative recommendation made by most state commissions—and the one most specifically geared to the problem of sex crime—was that the role of psychiatrists in the disposition of criminal "sex cases" be expanded. The Michigan commission's original proposal would have required the courts and prisons to cede authority to psychiatrists at every stage in such proceedings: Psychiatrists were to examine all sex offenders; those they diagnosed as dangerously psychopathic were, at their recommendation, to be sentenced to psychiatric hospitals for indeterminate terms, which would last from 1 day to life; and they were to be released only when a psychiatrist decided that they no longer posed a threat to the community. Some state commissions recommended that such commitment procedures apply to people convicted of specified offenses; others wanted anyone even suspected of psychopathic tendencies to be subject to them. Such indeterminant sentencing to psychiatric treatment, the Michigan commission argued, promised to cure and change psychopathic sex deviates, rather than just punish them; it was not only more humane but more effective than putting offenders in jail.

Several commissioners in Michigan and other states criticized such procedures for violating defendants' constitutional rights to counsel, cross-examination of witnesses, trial by jury, and other due process safeguards. They expressed particular concern about indeterminate sentencing, which allowed people labeled sex deviates to be confined indefinitely, no matter how serious their alleged offense. But the police, many judges, and the majority of commissioners in most states argued that the gravity of the danger posed by "sex deviates" justified the abrogation of traditional constitutional safeguards. As a sociologist and Nebraska municipal court judge argued in 1949:

> Such factors as the presumption of innocence, proof beyond a reasonable doubt and all of the other valuable and ancient safeguards by which the person accused of crime has been surrounded are perfectly proper in their correct application. Still they have no more logical place in the investigation of a known or suspected corrupter of the minds and bodies of little children than in the case of the insane person before the insanity board . . . for such proceedings are based upon theories utterly different from those of the criminal law.

But who was to be subject to such laws? Commissioners and other interested parties disagreed about this as well, although they agreed in general about who should be labeled a sexual deviate. Most of them put "sex murderers" at the top of the list, but they also included sadomasochists, pedophiles (adults sexually interested in children), rapists, homosexuals, exhibitionists, and voyeurs. Some extended the list to include anyone who was too "immature" to "adjust" to the "norms" of society and accept his or her gender-defined social responsibilities as a parent, husband, or wife, including people who engaged in premarital or extramarital sex. Benjamin Karpman, chief psychotherapist at the prestigious St. Elizabeth's Hospital and one of the decade's most important medical writers on sex offenses, argued that the sexual deviate displayed "patterns of sexual behavior" that

are not desirable biologically or culturally and are therefore prohibited. . . .
[Such patterns] are not directed ultimately toward procreation, the goal of all
normal sexual life. . . . [The deviate] has not matured sexually, having failed
to integrate his sexual needs and activities in such a way as to accord with
socially accepted modes of sexual expression.

The postwar consensus thus maintained that to be sexually "normal"
was to behave in a way the dominant culture considered not only socially acceptable and moral, but also statistically average and "mature"; the term
"normality" thus embodied a moral judgment, a statistical presumption, and
a psychological goal all at once. Failure to adhere to the sexual conventions,
moral standards, and (supposed) majority practices of one's culture made one
a deviate.

What contemporary authorities thought distinguished a sex criminal
from a mere deviate—and made him both especially frightening and difficult
to control—was that he was *psychopathic*, not only unconventional (or "abnormal") in his sexual impulses but unable to *control* his impulses. He was not
technically insane, as a noted psychiatrist, Edward Strecker, pointed out in
his testimony at the 1949 Philadelphia murder trial of Seymour Levin, a
teenager who had raped and killed a neighborhood boy, as he was "able to
distinguish between right and wrong behavior." But he was "still not willing
or able to exert inhibitions against anti-social behavior as strong and effective as those which can be excited by the average person." The purpose of
special sex psychopath laws was to place people capable of making such
moral distinctions (and thus legally "sane") but unwilling or incapable of acting in accordance with them (and thus "psychopathic") under the jurisdiction of psychiatrists.

The dominant public image of the psychopath—based on press accounts
of people like the Philadelphia murderer Levin—was that of a murderer out
of control. But psychiatrists and jurists regarded murder as only the most
extreme manifestation of a mental disease that more commonly resulted in less
severe forms of nonconformist behavior. The judges who convicted Levin hastened to note that while psychopaths "commit a tremendous number of anti-
social behavior acts, the [acts] are usually not in the major category. They are
misdemeanors and slight offenses against the law." Indeed, many jurists and
psychiatrists defined almost any failure to conform to social expectations as
psychopathic. The chief medical officer of the Supreme Bench of Baltimore,
Manfred Guttmacher, defined psychopaths as people "unable to conform to
the standards of their social group, . . . tragic failures in establishing lasting and
satisfying interpersonal relationships." In effect, then, some authorities regarded almost any "deviate" as psychopathic and almost any failure to conform
to social norms as a sign of mental illness.

Although most authorities shared this broad definition of sexual deviance and psychopathy, they sharply disagreed about how wide a range of
nonconformist (or "deviant") sexual behavior should render one subject to
the new laws. One group of sociologists, psychiatrists, and civil libertarians
agreed that a wide range of unconventional sexual behavior resulted from
mental disorder, but argued that deviates should nonetheless be divided into

two groups. Most deviates, they maintained, were harmless: They violated social norms but posed no direct danger to the lives or freedom of others. The state, they argued, should focus its limited resources on the apprehension, confinement, and treatment of the relatively small number of deviates whose sexual behavior posed a genuine danger, in their estimation, because it involved force or children. It should ignore relatively harmless nonconformists, such as people who engaged in premarital sex or homosexual relations, so long as they kept their behavior hidden (although most of them did still advocate the prosecution of gay people for doing some of the same things heterosexuals regularly did, such as trying to pick up a date at a bar, because they considered *any open* expression of homosexuality to be a public nuisance). They also argued that even if some currently harmless deviates might ultimately become dangerous, there was no way to determine which ones would; in particular, psychiatrists had not proven their claim that they could make such distinctions. In any case, imposing an indeterminate sentence on a man who had not even been charged with a crime—or, at most, had been convicted of a minor sex offense—simply because a psychiatrist had judged that he *might* become dangerous, would violate his constitutional rights.

A second group of psychiatrists, who received more support from police and court officials and were generally more influential in the debates of the 1940s and 1950s, regarded it as much more likely that a "minor deviate" would "degenerate" to more dangerous forms of deviance. Any nonconformist behavior, including window-peeping and consensual adult homosexual activity, they warned, might be only a symptom of a deeper pathology that would ultimately lead them to harm others. And while such officials disagreed about how likely such degeneration was, they shared the conviction that psychiatrists could be trusted to determine which sexual nonconformists posed a long-term social danger.

Accordingly, this group argued that if the state wished to prevent sex crimes, rather than simply punish or treat their perpetrators after it was too late, it should seek to identify and examine all sexual nonconformists in order to determine which ones might become dangerous—and to confine those who might, even if they had not yet committed a crime. As a policewoman on the Michigan commission argued: "The police know that although many known sex deviates cannot be charged with a crime, . . . unless these individuals receive help they will probably continue to deteriorate and many of them will be dangerous in the community." The medical director of a state hospital in California put the case even more strongly: "Whenever a doubt arises in the judge's mind . . . that [an offender] might be a sexual deviate, maybe by his mannerisms or his dress, something to attract the attention, I think he should immediately call for a psychiatric examination." Detroit's Prosecuting Attorney demanded the authority to arrest, examine, and possibly confine indefinitely *"anyone* who exhibited abnormal sexual behavior, whether or not dangerous."

The press reports that shaped public perceptions of the problem usually blurred the lines between different forms of sexual nonconformity. They did this in part simply by using a single term, sex deviate, to refer to *anyone* whose sexual behavior was different from the norm. Like the term abnormal, the term deviate made any variation from the supposed norm sound ominous and threatening, and it served to conflate the most benign and the most dangerous forms of sexual nonconformity. People who had sex outside of marriage, murdered little boys and girls, had sex with persons of the same sex, raped women, looked in other people's windows, masturbated in public, or cast "lewd glances" were all called sex deviates by the press. The term sex deviate could refer to an adult engaging in consensual homosexual relations with another adult, an adult involved in consensual sadomasochistic relations—or a sadistic murderer of children. The very ambiguity of the term served to reinforce the press's message that any "sex deviate" might engage in any such activity. As the distraught mother of a 4-year-old boy wrote Michigan's governor after the papers were filled with such stories in late 1949, "Please get some laws in Michigan that protect even a pre-school child, and that also protect boys—not just girls. These deviates do not care."

The conflation of all forms of sexual nonconformity in press accounts of sex crime had particularly significant consequences for the public image of gay men. While the officials and reporters concerned about degeneration believed in principle that almost any sexual nonconformist might become a psychopathic sex murderer, the deep-seated anti-gay prejudices of the era led them to be particularly concerned about male homosexuals. Not only did they consider homosexual behavior reprehensible and a sign of mental illness (an opinion psychiatrists later repudiated), but they rejected the contention that gay men were harmless and should be left alone so long as they kept to themselves, because they believed gay men were *incapable* of keeping to themselves. "The sex pervert, in his more innocuous form, is too frequently regarded as merely a 'queer' individual who never hurts anyone but himself," warned the Special Assistant Attorney General of California in 1949. "All too often we lose sight of the fact that the homosexual is an inveterate seducer of the young *of both sexes*," he insisted, "and is ever seeking for younger victims."

Moreover, they asserted, men who engaged in homosexual behavior had demonstrated the refusal to accommodate to social conventions that was the hallmark of the psychopath—and they could easily degenerate further. "Once a man assumes the role of homosexual, he often throws off all moral restraints," claimed *Coronet* magazine in the fall of 1950. "Some male sex deviants do not stop with infecting their often-innocent partners: they descend through perversions to other forms of depravity, such as drug addiction, burglary, sadism, and even murder."

The stereotype of the homosexual as an "inveterate" child molester had prestigious official advocates, but its most powerful proponents were the local and national press, the reports of which transformed the dominant public image of the homosexual into that of a dangerous psychopath during the postwar decade. The vast majority of cases of child sex murders reported by the press involved men attacking girls. But the press paid special attention to the murders of little boys and used them to try to persuade the public that all gay men were dangerous (attacks on little girls, it almost goes without saying, did not lead the press to make the same argument about heterosexual men). The brutal rape and murder of 6-year-old George Counter in a Detroit basement in the spring of 1949 was graphically described in the national press. Seven months later a description of the murder and the basement furnace behind which Counter's body had been hidden began Howard Whitman's *Collier's* article on crime in Detroit, and the image of it shadowed his description of his tour with a vice squad detective of a Detroit neighborhood where gay men gathered. For half an hour, according to Whitman, they followed one man whom he described as "a hefty six-footer dressed in a flowered shirt"—at once menacingly large and distinctively gay.

> Other deviates met and paired off, but this fellow stalked and hunted without success. He grew a little panicky. [. . . He moved to another block, where] he took up the hunt again—the same sordid cycle of exhibitionism, search and enticement. We saw him disappear down the steps of the latrine. . . . "That fellow is at large on the town. Who knows what he might do?" said [the detective] resignedly. Suppose he got more panicky as the evening wore on? Suppose he finally snapped up a child? In an alley somewhere. Or a basement. And if the child screamed or threatened to tell. . . . I remembered the hissing furnace against which Georgie Counter's body was crammed.

Whitman's article appeared in *Collier's* in November 1949, just as the nation's attention was riveted on the murders of the three little girls in Idaho and California. Along with other articles, it led many people to fear that tolerating homosexuals resulted in just such crimes against boys and girls. Local press campaigns against sex criminals frequently turned into campaigns against homosexuals, and thus helped turn their readers' understandable fear about the safety of women and children into an irrational fear of gay men.

At a time when few heterosexuals knew openly gay men or women who might counter such stereotypes, the public representation of gay men in the press assumed special cultural authority. If homosexuals had been relatively invisible before the war, they had also been considered fairly harmless. But press reports in the postwar period created a new, more ominous stereotype of the homosexual as a child molester, a dangerous psychopath likely to commit the most unspeakable offenses against children. Magazine reports that homosexuals were almost impossible to detect—that even your next-door neighbor could be one—heightened public fears, provided additional evidence that psychiatrists' special diagnostic skills were needed, and helped justify police surveillance of gay bars. The growing intolerance and fear of gay people forced many of them to become even more careful to hide their sexual identities from their heterosexual associates, which only increased their invisibility and vulnerability. As one gay man lamented in 1956, "To the average parent I am a menace to warn their children against."

The study commissions and press focused on men's behavior when discussing the dangers of sexual deviation, but they had much to say about women's gender roles and responsibilities as well. For although most state commissions requested sweeping new authority for the police to apprehend and investigate sexual nonconformists and for psychiatrists to supervise their treatment, they insisted with equal vigor that such emergency programs alone could not solve the problem of sex crime. Most psychiatrists had little confidence that they could do more than train particularly receptive adult sex offenders to control their impulses. "It is seldom possible," one psychiatrist emphasized at a public forum in Michigan, "to cure completely a chronic sex offender of mature years." But if sexual deviation could not be eradicated in the present generation, it might be prevented in the next. "Abnormal sex behavior, be it in the adult or child," Benjamin Karpman asserted, "derives from the unwholesome family and social atmosphere in which the child develops. The fault lies with the parents."

Many psychiatrists therefore devoted considerable effort to advising parents about the proper way to rear their children. They had done this before, but fears about sex crime made many people more receptive to their counsel, and newspapers frequently reported on their speeches at forums on sex crime sponsored by the PTA and other civic groups.

Mothers took most of the blame. "Psychopath's Start Traced: Lack of 'Mothering' in Youth Blamed" ran one headline in the *Detroit News*; "Mother Blamed for Neurotic Child" ran another. Such warnings implied that the women who failed to follow psychiatrists' advice had only themselves to blame for the men who attacked them and their children.

Much of the advice psychiatrists gave women, however, concerned their roles as wives as much as their roles as mothers. It emphasized the importance of parents making clear to their children the differences between their gender roles as husband and wife and their genuine contentment with those roles. It warned that failure to do so could confuse the child about his or her own role, undermining his or her development as a mature, gendered human being. Thus, women were encouraged to stay at home while their husbands went to work, to invest their self-worth in their "homemaking" and childrearing, and to affirm their husband's authority in the marriage.

Postwar advice also contended that "domineering mothers" were the single most important cause of homosexuality. This effectively warned women that a family structure in which women held power or refused to be subservient to their husbands (that is, were "domineering mothers" married to "passive fathers") bred pathology. The culture's simultaneous denunciation of homosexuality and glorification of women who invested their self-worth wholly in their children made the idea that domineering mothers could turn their children into homosexuals an exceptionally powerful warning to women.

Many psychiatrists and government officials were unwilling to depend on parents following their advice, however; they also recommended new government programs that would supervise the rearing of children to ensure their socialization into acceptable gender roles and sexual identities. They called for the establishment of programs to train school personnel, clergymen, and police to recognize children who displayed nonconformist sexual tendencies and to refer them to psychiatric programs for treatment. "Obviously the teaching population should be alerted to the urgency of 'typing' emotionally maladjusted children as incipient sex deviates," one Michigan consultant pointed out to a gubernatorial assistant; "all teachers should be given training to recognize the symptoms of sexual deviation," concluded the Utah study commission.

Once identified as sissies, bullies, tomboys, or some other problem type, the children were to be referred to an expanded program of child guidance clinics for treatment by psychiatrists. Many teachers took such advice seriously, although inadequate state funding meant that few clinics were established to which they could refer "deviant" children. In a Philadelphia suburb in 1950, for instance, a teacher sent the parents of a 9-year-old fourth grader a note warning them that because their son was uninterested in sports the other boys considered him a sissy and there was a danger he might grow up to be a homosexual; she recommended that they get him counseling and force him to play sports. (His parents ignored the advice about counseling, but did set up a basketball hoop in the backyard.) The panic over sex deviates gave new urgency to adults' efforts to ensure that boys turned into rugged young men and girls into proper young women; the engendering of children (their socialization into conventional gender roles), which was supposed to be so natural, had never seemed so difficult.

Police and school officials also instituted security programs to prevent children from having any contact with sexual nonconformists: They began investigating teachers and other school personnel to ensure that none were homosexual and requiring that men convicted of sex crimes register with the local police department whenever they moved. They also taught children to avoid strangers: At the height of the sex crime panic in the winter of 1949 to 1950, schools and police departments across the country began to distribute pamphlets on a massive scale to parents and children warning about the dangers of unknown adults. One photo-illustrated booklet issued to thousands of school-children in Detroit warned girls to "NEVER go with strangers when they ask for directions" and boys to "NEVER wait around toilets."

Strangers certainly could be dangerous to unsuspecting children, but according to studies conducted in the 1950s, whose methodology tended to underrepresent intrafamilial sexual activity, the majority of children who had sexual experiences with adults knew the adult involved. More recent studies have argued even more strongly that incest is more common than attacks by strangers. The postwar pamphlets nonetheless focused exclusively on "strangers" as the source of sexual danger to children, and identified the family as a sanctuary for children from the violence of the external world. Thus they misrepresented some of the real dangers facing children, but in a manner consistent with the ideology of the Cold War nuclear family. The pamphlets intended for children, like the lectures intended for their parents, embodied and defined the dominant postwar vision of the proper family.

The postwar outcry over "sex crimes" and "sex deviates" exhibited many of the characteristics of what social theorists have termed a moral panic. Moral panics usually occur in periods of social stress when large numbers of people, already apprehensive about the stability of the social order, focus those anxieties on a social phenomenon, incident, person, or social group, which comes to symbolize (even as it obscures) the forces that seem to

NEVER play alone in alleys, or in deserted buildings. Keep together.

NEVER wait around toilets. Always leave immediately.

The sex crime panic both reflected and heightened many people's fears that suburban and urban life had become more transient, anonymous, and dangerous in the wake of World War II, and prompted local police departments to distribute thousands of brochures like this one to school children, warning them of the dangers posed by strangers in the postwar urban landscape.

threaten their way of life. The mass media often exacerbate or even create such panics, by focusing public attention on the phenomenon and portraying it in stereotypical and threatening ways; public officials and professional "experts" of various sorts usually also play important roles in defining (or even creating) the "problem." The explosion of concern in the 1980s about the problem of child abuse in day care centers, for instance, could be considered such a panic. In retrospect, the problem seems to have existed not so much in the centers as in the minds of the media and the police, but the media "exposés" of abuse both evoked and focused widespread anxieties about the family, working mothers, and the problems of sexual violence and incest.

Why did a moral panic about sex crimes engulf postwar America? Although a number of horrifying murders of children did occur in the late 1940s, they alone cannot account for the panic for the simple reason that such murders were not new. Police statistics showed no disproportionate increase in the number of crimes of sexual violence; statistically speaking, there was no crime wave.

What distinguished the murders of those years was neither their number nor their intrinsic horror but the magnitude of the coverage they received and the manner in which they were interpreted. Press crusades frightened the public (and not incidentally sold papers) by using the murders to create the image of a country whose streets and alleyways were overrun with murderous sex psychopaths. The deliberations of the state study commissions then perpetuated those fears by keeping the public's attention focused on the issue even when the memory of particular crimes had faded; they expanded the panic's ideological significance by becoming an important vehicle for postwar discussions about the boundaries of acceptable sexual and gender behavior and about the extent to which the state ought to enforce such boundaries. State governments acted as forcefully as they did because of the interest several constituencies had in using the panic, once it developed, to advance their own (sometimes conflicting) interests: elected officials keen to demonstrate their ability to manage a problem that had aroused their constituents; police forces anxious to secure new mechanisms for controlling homosexuals and other people they considered "sex criminals"; psychiatrists hoping to enhance their cultural authority and institutional power.

Yet the panic could not have become so widespread and powerful had it not tapped into deep anxieties already existing within the culture about the disruptive effects of World War II on family life, sexual mores, and gender norms. The war had removed millions of men from their families, forced hundreds of thousands of those families to migrate to overcrowded military and industrial centers, and allowed unprecedented numbers of married women to enter the paid labor force and take over industrial jobs previously considered suitable only for men. Although women's industrial employment was always described as a temporary expedient, it nonetheless had demonstrated that women could do so-called "men's work" and allowed many women to live independently and earn unprecedentedly high wages, gains that many were loath to give up when the war ended.

At the war's end discriminatory management and union policies ensured that most women workers lost their new industrial jobs to returning veterans, and government policies (especially the GI Bill of Rights) allowed many of those veterans to buy suburban homes and establish families. Such efforts to reconstruct the gender order were accompanied by a postwar media campaign that championed the virtues of suburban domesticity, glorified women's roles as homemakers, and warned of the dangers posed by married women's employment. After the hardships of the depression and war, many women welcomed the postwar social order; others discovered there were risks involved in questioning it. The sex crime panic served to increase the pressure on women reluctant to leave their jobs by stigmatizing those who did not devote themselves full-time to mothering. Repeated accounts of rape and child molestation reminded women of the very real dangers they and their children faced outside the home (even as the accounts ignored the dangers they faced inside it), and the commissions provided a platform to experts (rather than to women themselves) who blamed sexual deviation and violence on women's bad mothering.

The panic also reflected and contributed to a more general effort to reimpose the social controls on sexual behavior that had been weakened by the war. The war's disruption of family life led to an increase in nonmarital sexual activity of all sorts, but its most striking effect was to facilitate the growth of urban gay and lesbian communities. By removing men from the supervision of their families and small town neighborhoods and placing them in a single-sex military environment, military mobilization increased the chances that they would meet gay men and be able to explore their homosexual interests. Many recruits met other gay people for the first time, saw the sort of gay life they could lead in large cities, and chose to stay in those cities after the war, rather than return home where they would almost surely have had to hide their sexual preferences. Some of the women who joined the military, as well as those on the homefront who shared housing and worked in defense industries with other women, had similar experiences. The number of bars and restaurants serving gay and lesbian customers grew enormously during and after the war, and in larger cities gay enclaves became noticeable in certain neighborhoods. The Kinsey Report on male sexual behavior, published in 1948, highlighted these changes—and shocked the nation—by showing how widespread homosexual behavior was.

The sudden growth in the visibility of gay people led to an upsurge in anti-gay prejudice, as many Americans sought a return to prewar "normality." Even before the war most homosexual behavior—from actual sex to one man trying to pick up another man for a date or two women dancing together at a bar—was illegal, and in many states the law prohibited bars, restaurants, and other public establishments from serving lesbians and gay men or even letting them gather on their premises. After the war the police in many cities intensified their enforcement of such laws. By 1950 Philadelphia's six-member "morals squad" was arresting more gay men than the courts knew how to handle, some 200 each month.

Local panics over sex crimes, even when they originally had nothing to do with homosexuality, often resulted in even harsher anti-gay crackdowns, as such crackdowns were often the only concrete steps (or at least the most visible ones) the police could take in response to public demands for action. One man who moved to Detroit shortly after George Counter's murder recalled how worried the gay people he met there were about the "campaign against gays" being waged by the city's newspapers and police. He met several men who had been arrested by the police while socializing in gay bars, and he knew others who would not even visit a gay bar for fear of being caught in a police raid. After only 2 months in the city he was himself arrested in such a raid and forced to spend a night in jail. The native Detroiters arrested with him, he later recalled, were terrified they would be sent to a psychiatric prison. "They hold you there," one cellmate warned, in an apparent reference to the state's new indeterminate sentencing law, "until the unlikely event that you turn straight."

Gay people were particularly hard hit by the new climate of intolerance, but the widely publicized deliberations of the state study commissions increased the cultural sanctions against unconventional sexual behavior of any sort. Even when the press reported that authorities disagreed about how dangerous gay men and other "deviates" were, the very terms in which it described those disagreements reinforced the public's anxiety that *any* form of gender or sexual nonconformity was pathologically abnormal and merited analysis and treatment, whether on a voluntary or forced basis. The wide publicity given such ideas served to establish boundaries for the gender and sexual behavior of all. The spectre of the sex psychopath led to the unfair stigmatization of all homosexuals as potential child molesters or murderers, and the spectre of the hidden homosexual contributed to the stigmatization of anyone who violated certain gender norms as "immature" and potentially (or "latently") homosexual. Boys who didn't play sports—and girls who did—were sometimes stigmatized this way, and the public's increased awareness of (and anxiety about) the extent of homosexuality in postwar society quietly contributed to the pressure put on men and women who were reluctant to marry to do so and to assume other culturally defined gender roles, lest they be considered abnormal. The spectre of the hidden homosexual haunted the cult of suburban domesticity.

That spectre haunted the Cold War as well. In February, 1950, when Senator Joseph McCarthy seized the nation's attention by charging that hundreds of Communists had infiltrated the State Department, the sex crime panic was at its height. McCarthy shrewdly played on and exacerbated Americans' apprehensions about communist subversion, and he played on their fears about sex criminals as well. From the beginning he charged that sex deviates had infiltrated the government along with communists, and the State Department fired hundreds of employees whom it discovered to be gay.

The sex crime panic was also linked to—and reinforced—the postwar hysteria about communism in other ways. Both the anti-communist and anti-sex deviate campaigns claimed that minimal deviations signaled greater dangers: Just as homosexuals were branded as child molesters or murderers, so were liberal dissenters, civil rights activists, and union organizers attacked as communists or communist dupes. Both campaigns sought to develop programs that would identify, investigate, and limit social or political nonconformity. Both argued that the dangers posed by such nonconformity justified the abrogation of traditional constitutional safeguards. And both encouraged the conformity that became a hallmark of postwar American society—and against which the social movements organized by African-Americans, students, women, and lesbians and gay men would rebel in the 1960s.

In a moral panic, diffuse public apprehensions and concerns are symbolically embodied in a single object on which public attention is focused. The national panic over sex crimes constituted such a panic, for it became one means of expressing the deep postwar apprehensions about the sexual and gender order and of weighing religious, medical, judicial, and police claims to the authority to arbitrate them. A series of murders came to symbolize, for many people, the dangers of gender and sexual nonconformity. Denounced by the press, explained by the state commissions, and burned into public consciousness by both, the "sex deviate" became a means of defining, by his transgressions, the boundaries of acceptable behavior for anyone who would be "normal."

 SOURCES

The Search for Communists: HUAC Investigates Hollywood

In the fall of 1947, only months after the Truman Doctrine and the Marshall Plan had announced a deepening Cold War, the House Un-American Activities Committee (HUAC) opened hearings designed to probe communist infiltration of the Hollywood film industry. The inquiry was only one of several attacks on communism taking place at the time. The United States Attorney General had distributed a list of "subversive" organizations with presumed communist ties; and in March, 1947, President Truman had issued an order requiring investigations of all federal employees.

HUAC called dozens of witnesses, many of them famous actors, directors, screenwriters, and studio heads. Ronald Reagan, then a movie actor and a member of the Screen Actors Guild, offered rather vague testimony about a "small clique" that had made an effort to be a "disruptive influence" in the guild, while admitting that he had no knowledge that the group included communists. Novelist and screenwriter Ayn Rand described at length the contents of the film Song of Russia, *a wartime production that Rand, and many members of the committee, considered deceitful and propagandistic. Other witnesses echoed and amplified Rand's concerns, but the HUAC hearings did not uncover much solid evidence of communist influence in Hollywood.*

Even so, the inquiry had an impact. In November, studio executives announced a "blacklist" of people who would no longer be allowed to work in the industry, and the House of Representatives held ten "unfriendly" witnesses in contempt and sent them to jail. More important, the pressure on producers, directors and screenwriters to avoid anything that smacked of radicalism shaped the content of Hollywood films for about fifteen years.

In reading the following testimony, consider the possibility that the purpose of the inquiry may have been something other than the discovery of communism or Communists. How did the witness define activities or values he deemed un-American? What people, events, or organizations were understood to be dangerous?

Besides Menjou, those speaking include Robert E. Stripling, Chief Investigator of the Committee on Un-American Activities, and Richard M. Nixon, Republican congressman from California.

U.S. Congress, House, Committee on Un-American Activities, *Hearings Regarding the Communist Infiltration of the Motion Picture Industry*, 80th Cong., 1st Sess., October 20–30, 1947, Government Printing Office, Washington, 1947.

Adolph Menjou at the Un-American Activities
Hearing, October 1, 1947 © Leonard McCombe//Time
Life Pictures/Getty Images.

✑ *Testimony of Adolph Menjou, Actor*

MR. STRIPLING. Mr. Menjou, will you please state your name and address?

MR. MENJOU. My name is Adolph Menjou, and my address is 722 North Bedford Drive, Beverly Hills, Calif. . . .

MR. STRIPLING. Mr. Menjou, what is your occupation?

MR. MENJOU. I am a motion-picture actor, I hope.

MR. STRIPLING. When and where were you born, Mr. Menjou?

MR. MENJOU. I was born in Pittsburgh, Pa., February 18, 1890.

MR. STRIPLING. How long have you been in the motion-picture industry?

MR. MENJOU. Thirty-four years.

MR. STRIPLING. And how long have you been in Hollywood?

MR. MENJOU. Twenty-seven years.

MR. STRIPLING. Mr. Menjou, were you in the First World War?

MR. MENJOU. Yes, sir.

MR. STRIPLING. In the armed services?

MR. MENJOU. Yes, sir. I served abroad for 2 years. I was in the Army 3 years, 1 year in America. I served in Italy, with the Italian Army, being attached to the Italian Army; attached to the French Army; and with the Fifth Division until the surrender on November 11, 1918.

MR. STRIPLING. Were you in World War II?

MR. MENJOU. I served 6 months with the U.S. Camp Shows, Inc., entertaining troops—for 4 months in England, 2 months in North Africa, Sicily, Tunisia, Algeria, Morrocco, Brazil, and the Caribbean.

MR. STRIPLING. Mr. Menjou, have you made a study of the subject of communism, the activities of the Communists, in any particular field in the United States?

MR. MENJOU. I have. I have made a more particular study of Marxism, Fabian socialism, communism, Stalinism, and its probable effects on the American people, if they ever gain power here.

MR. STRIPLING. Based upon your study, have you observed any Communist activity in the motion-picture industry or in Hollywood, as we commonly refer to it?

MR. MENJOU. I would like to get the terminologies completely straight. Communistic activities—I would rather phrase it un-American or subversive, antifree enterprise, anticapitalistic. I have seen—pardon me.

MR. STRIPLING. Have you observed any Communist propaganda in pictures, or un-American propaganda in pictures which were produced in Hollywood?

MR. MENJOU. I have seen no communistic propaganda in pictures—if you mean "vote for Stalin," or that type of communistic propaganda. I don't think that the Communists are stupid enough to try it that way. I have seen in certain pictures things I didn't think should have been in the pictures.

MR. STRIPLING. Could you tell the committee whether or not there has been an effort on the part of any particular group in the motion-picture industry to inject Communist propaganda into pictures or to leave out scenes or parts of stories which would serve the Communist Party line?

MR. MENJOU. I don't like that term "Communist propaganda," because I have seen no such thing as Communist propaganda, such as waving the hammer and sickle in motion pictures. I have seen things that I thought were against what I considered good Americanism, in my feeling. I have seen pictures I thought shouldn't have been made—shouldn't have been made, let me put it that way. . . .

MR. NIXON. In answer to a question by Mr. Stripling you indicated that although you might not know whether a certain person was a Communist, I think you said he certainly acted like a Communist.

MR. MENJOU. If you belong to a Communist-front organization and you take no action against the Communists, you do not resign from the organization when you still know the organization is dominated by Communists, I consider that a very, very dangerous thing.

MR. NIXON. Have you any other tests which you would apply which would indicate to you that people acted like Communists?

MR. MENJOU. Well, I think attending any meetings at which Mr. Paul Robeson* appeared and applauding or listening to his Communist songs in America, I would be ashamed to be seen in an audience doing a thing of that kind.

MR. NIXON. You indicated you thought a person acted like a Communist when he stated, as one person did to you, that capitalism was through.

MR. MENJOU. That is not communistic per se, but it is very dangerous leaning, it is very close. I see nothing wrong with the capitalistic system, the new dynamic capitalism in America today. Mr. Stalin was very worried when he talked to Mr. Stassen. He asked him four times when the great crash was coming in America. That is what they are banking on, a great crash, and I do not think it is coming.

MR. NIXON. You indicated that belonging to a Communist-front organization, in other words, an association with Communists, attending these planned meetings, making statements in opposition to the capitalistic system are three of the tests you would apply.

MR. MENJOU. Yes, sir.

*African American actor and singer Paul Robeson was associated with Communist causes in the 1930s. The PBS Web site has brief, cogent biographies of artists and writers accused of being Communists or Communist sympathizers, including novelist Dashiell Hammett, playwright Clifford Odets, and film director Elia Kazan (On the Waterfront). Go to www.pbs.org/wnet/americanmasters/database/mccarthyism.html.

During the Army-McCarthy hearings of 1954, McCarthy *(far right)* blocked an attempt by Army Counsel Joseph Welch *(far left)* to obtain names of McCarthy's office staff. McCarthy charged "a smear campaign" was under way against "anyone working with exposing communists." Harris & Ewing/Washington Star Collection, Courtesy Washingtoniana Division, Public Library.

Tail Gunner Joe: The Wheeling Address

Joseph McCarthy

McCarthyism is the name applied to the second Red Scare, a period of political repression in America, epitomized by the career of Senator Joseph McCarthy. "Tail gunner Joe" was elected as the junior senator from Wisconsin in 1946 and received little recognition until his speech in Wheeling, West Virginia, on February 9, 1950. For the next four years, he chaired Senate committee meetings where he accused first the Truman administration, and later the Eisenhower administration, of harboring known communists and probable spies in the government. He was censured by his colleagues in the Senate in 1954 and faded into obscurity.

*   McCarthy did not create the atmosphere of suspicion and anticommunism given his name. Indeed, years before McCarthy came on the scene, the Truman administration had instituted its own loyalty-security program (1947) and stepped up the use of the Smith Act throughout 1948 to prosecute Americans suspected of subversive thinking. Congress also contributed with the hearings of the House Un-American Activities Committee (HUAC) and the Alger Hiss investigation and*

trials (1948). Yet McCarthy was surely the most notorious opportunist of the era. His tactics of demagoguery, insinuation, and guilt by association defined the means by which thousands of Americans were denied their civil rights. Worse still, a public insecure about the postwar world accepted his vision of conspiracy and sanctioned his attacks.

The following is a sample of McCarthy's tactics against the State Department. How does Senator McCarthy define the threat to American security? What proof does he offer that the State Department is filled with known Communists?

Ladies and gentlemen, tonight as we celebrate the one hundred and forty-first birthday of one of the greatest men in American history, I would like to be able to talk about what a glorious day today is in the history of the world. As we celebrate the birth of this man who with his whole heart and soul hated war, I would like to be able to speak of peace in our time, of war being outlawed, and of worldwide disarmament. These would be truly appropriate things to be able to mention as we celebrate the birthday of Abraham Lincoln.

Five years after a world war has been won, men's hearts should anticipate a long peace, and men's minds should be free from the heavy weight that comes with war. But this is not such a period—for this is not a period of peace. This is a time of the "cold war." This is a time when all the world is split into two vast, increasingly hostile armed camps—a time of a great armaments race.

Today we can almost physically hear the mutterings and rumblings of an invigorated god of war. You can see it, feel it, and hear it all the way from the hills of Indochina, from the shores of Formosa, right over into the very heart of Europe itself.

The one encouraging thing is that the "mad moment" has not yet arrived for the firing of a gun or the exploding of the bomb which will set civilization about the final task of destroying itself. There is still a hope for peace if we finally decide that no longer can we safely blind our eyes and close our ears to those facts which are shaping up more and more clearly. And that is that we are now engaged in a showdown fight—not the usual war between nations for land areas or other material gains, but a war between two diametrically opposed ideologies.

The great difference between our western Christian world and the atheistic Communist world is not political, ladies and gentlemen, it is moral. There are other differences, of course, but those could be reconciled. For instance, the Marxian idea of confiscating the land and factories and running the entire economy as a single enterprise is momentous. Likewise, Lenin's invention of the one-party police state as a way to make Marx's idea work is hardly less momentous.

Stalin's resolute putting across of these two ideas, of course, did much to divide the world. With only those differences, however, the east and the west could most certainly still live in peace.

From U.S., Congress, Senate, *Congressional Record*, 81st Cong., 2d sess., 1950, 96, 1954, 1946, 1957.

The real, basic difference, however, lies in the religion of immoralism—invented by Marx, preached feverishly by Lenin, and carried to unimaginable extremes by Stalin. This religion of immoralism, if the Red half of the world wins—and well it may—this religion of immoralism will more deeply wound and damage mankind than any conceivable economic or political system. . . .

Today we are engaged in a final, all-out battle between communistic atheism and Christianity. The modern champions of communism have selected this as the time. And, ladies and gentlemen, the chips are down—they are truly down. . . .

Ladies and gentlemen, can there be anyone here tonight who is so blind as to say that the war is not on? Can there be anyone who fails to realize that the Communist world has said, "The time is now"—that this is the time for the showdown between the democratic Christian world and the Communist atheistic world?

Unless we face this fact, we shall pay the price that must be paid by those who wait too long.

Six years ago, at the time of the first conference to map out the peace—Dumbarton Oaks—there was within the Soviet orbit 180 million people. Lined up on the antitotalitarian side there were in the world at that time roughly 1,625,000,000 people. Today, only six years later, there are 800 million people under the absolute domination of Soviet Russia—an increase of over 400 percent. On our side, the figure has shrunk to around 500 million. In other words, in less than six years the odds have changed from 9 to 1 in our favor to 8 to 5 against us. This indicates the swiftness of the tempo of Communist victories and American defeats in the cold war. As one of our outstanding historical figures once said, "When a great democracy is destroyed, it will not be because of enemies from without, but rather because of enemies from within."

The truth of this statement is becoming terrifyingly clear as we see this country each day losing on every front.

At war's end we were physically the strongest nation on earth and, at least potentially, the most powerful intellectually and morally. Ours could have been the honor of being a beacon in the desert of destruction, a shining living proof that civilization was not yet ready to destroy itself. Unfortunately, we have failed miserably and tragically to arise to the opportunity.

The reason why we find ourselves in a position of impotency is not because our only powerful potential enemy has sent men to invade our shores, but rather because of the traitorous actions of those who have been treated so well by this nation. It has not been the less fortunate or members of minority groups who have been selling this nation out, but rather those who have had all the benefits that the wealthiest nation on earth has had to offer—the finest homes, the finest college education, and the finest jobs in government we can give.

This is glaringly true in the State Department. There the bright young men who are born with silver spoons in their mouths are the ones who have been worst.

Now I know it is very easy for anyone to condemn a particular bureau or department in general terms. Therefore, I would like to cite one rather unusual case—the case of a man who has done much to shape our foreign policy.

When Chiang Kai-shek was fighting our war, the State Department had in China a young man named John S. Service. His task, obviously, was not to work for the communization of China. Strangely, however, he sent official reports back to the State Department urging that we torpedo our ally Chiang Kai-shek and stating, in effect, that communism was the best hope of China.

Later, this man—John Service—was picked up by the Federal Bureau of Investigation for turning over to the Communists secret State Department information. Strangely, however, he was never prosecuted. However, Joseph Grew, the under secretary of state, who insisted on his prosecution, was forced to resign. Two days after Grew's successor, Dean Acheson, took over as under secretary of state, this man—John Service—who had been picked up by the FBI and who had previously urged that communism was the best hope of China, was not only reinstated in the State Department but promoted. And finally, under Acheson, placed in charge of all placements and promotions.

Today, ladies and gentlemen, this man Service is on his way to represent the State Department and Acheson in Calcutta—by far and away the most important listening post in the far east. . . .

This, ladies and gentlemen, gives you somewhat of a picture of the type of individuals who have been helping to shape our foreign policy. In my opinion the State Department, which is one of the most important government departments, is thoroughly infested with Communists.

I have in my hand fifty-seven cases of individuals who would appear to be either card-carrying members or certainly loyal to the Communist party, but who nevertheless are still helping to shape our foreign policy. . . .

This brings us down to the case of one Alger Hiss who is important not as an individual any more, but rather because he is so representative of a group in the State Department. It is unnecessary to go over the sordid events showing how he sold out the nation which had given him so much. Those are rather fresh in all of our minds.

However, it should be remembered that the facts in regard to his connection with this international Communist spy ring were made known to the then Under Secretary of State Berle three days after Hitler and Stalin signed the Russo-German alliance pact. At that time one Whittaker Chambers—who was also part of the spy ring—apparently decided that with Russia on Hitler's side, he could no longer betray our nation to Russia. He gave Under Secretary of State Berle—and this is all a matter of record—practically all, if not more, of the facts upon which Hiss's conviction was based.

Under Secretary Berle promptly contacted Dean Acheson and received word in return that Acheson (and I quote) "could vouch for Hiss absolutely"—at which time the matter was dropped. And this, you understand, was at a time when Russia was an ally of Germany. This condition existed while Russia and Germany were invading and dismembering Poland, and while the Communist groups here were screaming "warmonger" at the United States for their support of the allied nations.

Again in 1943, the FBI had occasion to investigate the facts surrounding Hiss's contacts with the Russia spy ring. But even after that FBI report was submitted, nothing was done.

Then late in 1948—on August 5—when the Un-American Activities Committee called Alger Hiss to give an accounting, President Truman at once issued a presidential directive ordering all government agencies to refuse to turn over any information whatsoever in regard to the Communist activities of any government employee to a congressional committee.

Incidentally, even after Hiss was convicted—it is interesting to note that the president still labeled the exposé of Hiss as a "red herring."

If time permitted, it might be well to go into detail about the fact that Hiss was Roosevelt's chief advisor at Yalta when Roosevelt was admittedly in ill health and tired physically and mentally. . . .

Of the results of this conference, Arthur Bliss Lane of the State Department had this to say: "As I glanced over the document, I could not believe my eyes. To me, almost every line spoke of a surrender to Stalin."

As you hear this story of high treason, I know that you are saying to yourself, "Well, why doesn't the Congress do something about it?" Actually, ladies and gentlemen, one of the important reasons for the graft, the corruption, the dishonesty, the treason in high government positions—one of the most important reasons why this continues—is a lack of moral uprising on the part of the 140 million American people. In the light of history, however, this is not hard to explain.

It is the result of an emotional hangover and a temporary moral lapse which follows every war. It is the apathy to evil which people who have been subjected to the tremendous evils of war feel. As the people of the world see mass murder, the destruction of defenseless and innocent people, and all of the crime and lack of morals which go with war, they become numb and apathetic. It has always been thus after war.

However, the morals of our people have not been destroyed. They still exist. This cloak of numbness and apathy has only needed a spark to rekindle them. Happily, this spark has finally been supplied.

As you know, very recently the secretary of state proclaimed his loyalty to a man guilty of what has always been considered as the most abominable of all crimes—of being a traitor to the people who gave him a position of great trust. The secretary of state in attempting to justify his continued devotion to the man who sold out the Christian world to the atheistic world, referred to Christ's Sermon on the Mount as a justification and reason therefor, and the reaction of the American people to this would have made the heart of Abraham Lincoln happy.

When this pompous diplomat in striped pants, with a phony British accent, proclaimed to the American people that Christ on the Mount endorsed communism, high treason, and betrayal of a sacred trust, the blasphemy was so great that it awakened the dormant indignation of the American people.

He has lighted the spark which is resulting in a moral uprising and will end only when the whole sorry mess of twisted, warped thinkers are swept from the national scene so that we may have a new birth of national honesty and decency in government.

The Cold War had a major effect on the climate of inquiry in American universities. The University of Washington fired three pro-Communist professors in 1949, and some 200 professors were dismissed nationally in the 1950s. Historian Michael Reese has narrated events at the University of Washington and assembled a variety of documents relevant to the Red Scare in Washington State, at www.washington.edu/uwired/outreach/cspn/curcan/main.html.

Selling America

The two photographs that follow are idealizations of American life, created by the United States Information Agency, the international propaganda arm of the American government. In a sense, they were weapons in the Cold War. According to the first photograph, what apparent relationship exists between technology and domestic bliss and harmony? What idealized notions of youth culture are present in the second photograph? What does it mean to identify someone or some group as "typical"?

Original Caption: "Takoma Park, Maryland—In the living room of their home, the A. Jackson Cory family and some friends watch a television program. Some sociologists claim the growing popularity of television will tend to make family life stronger and make the home the center of the family's recreation. 1950." United States Information Agency photo, National Archives.

Original Caption: "Washington, D.C.—Brennan Jacques, a typical American teenager, has his own orchestra, the 'Fabulous Esquires,' composed of youngsters aware of what their schoolmates like and do not like in current music. Here, young Jacques plays the piano for a group of young people, who have gathered around him. 1957." United States Information Agency photo, National Archives.

THE BIG PICTURE

This chapter introduces the idea of the "panic," which could be defined as a moment of extreme social anxiety, focused on a particular, plausible (though not necessarily real) "problem"—in this case, sex crime. Panics are frequent in democratic societies with an unfettered press—the tabloids try to sell a panic a week—and they can occur at any time. But they are most likely to take place at moments of great social tension and fear, such as that produced by the Cold War, which was a very real threat to national security, or by the events of 9/11. The panic at once feeds off and increases the tension, defines a set of problems (domineering mothers, changing gender roles), and suggests solutions (attacking deviates, enforcing traditional, "normal" gender roles) that seem to promise to make things better.

There was a lot of power in defining what was normal and typical (the good) and what was abnormal and atypical (the bad, the dangerous). The "typical teenager" in the photograph on p. 304 is white, and the music he plays (which must also be typical, or normal) is nonthreatening; it is not rock 'n' roll or rhythm and blues. In his testimony before HUAC, Adolph Menjou defined the abnormal as belonging to an organization dominated by Communists, criticizing capitalism, or showing things in motion pictures that were not "good Americanism."

There is much truth in the argument that the climate of conformity described in this chapter was a product of the Cold War, an extreme, flawed effort to confront the Soviet threat. But one must also acknowledge that anti-Communism was often less an end in itself than a useful device, one that was used to discourage criticism of the existing economic system; to criticize the New Deal heritage of the Democratic Party; or to assist anxious men in reconstituting the "normal" and "typical" gender roles and the traditional, male-dominated families that the war had left in a shambles.

Chapter 11

The Fifties

*R*eason, objectivity, dispassion—these were the qualities and values that twice elected Dwight Eisenhower to the presidency. His appeal was bipartisan. In 1948 and 1952, politicians of both major parties sought to nominate this man with the "leaping and effortless smile" who promised the electorate a "constitutional presidency"—immune from the ideological harangues of European dictators, American demagogues, and New Deal presidents—and a secure economy—immune from major dislocations.

To replace the disjointed and unpredictable insecurity of depression, war, and ideological struggle, Eisenhower offered Americans a society based on consensus. In the consensual society, major disagreements over important issues such as race, class, and gender were presumed not to exist. Conflict—serious conflict, about who had power and who did not—was considered almost un-American.

By 1960, it was clear that Eisenhower, and the nation at large, had not sought to create or maintain the consensual society through any radical departures from the past. The Cold War, anticommunism, the welfare state—all inherited from his Democratic predecessor, Harry Truman—were not so much thrown aside as modulated or refined.

Anticommunism was central to the consensus, for the existence of a powerful enemy helped define the consensus and to deflect attention from the economic and social issues on which there could be no easy agreement.

Joseph McCarthy would cease to be a factor after 1954, but otherwise, anti-communism was almost as much a part of the Eisenhower years as it had been of the Truman years. The purges that cleansed most labor unions of communist influence were completed when Ike took office, but Cold War attitudes permeated the labor movement throughout the decade. The House Un-American Activities Committee (HUAC) would never know the acclaim it had mustered in the late 1940s, but each year it received more money from Congress and continued to function. In 1959, the Supreme Court refused to declare HUAC in violation of the First Amendment. New Organizations—Robert Welch's John Birch Society and the Christian Anti-Communist Crusade, for example—emerged to carry on the struggle against internal subversion. Welch labeled Eisenhower a "dedicated, conscious agent of the Communist conspiracy."

Those who feared that the first Republican president since Herbert Hoover would grasp the opportunity to dismantle the welfare state had misunderstood both Eisenhower and the function of government at midcentury. If only intuitively, Eisenhower knew that what was left of the New Deal could not be eliminated without risking serious social and economic disruption. Countercyclical programs like old-age insurance and unemployment insurance were maintained or expanded; the Council of Economic Advisers, created in the Employment Act of 1946 to provide the president with his own planning staff, remained; spending for military hardware and interstate highways was expected to create jobs. Republicans did manage a rollback of New Deal policies in the areas of taxation and agriculture.

There was in much of this a pervasive element of acceptance—acceptance of American institutions as they were or as Americans wished they were. The power of the large corporation was accepted, its influence invited. Many agreed with General Motors president Charles E. Wilson, who during Senate hearings to confirm his nomination as secretary of defense said, "I thought what was good for our country was good for General Motors, and vice versa." Effective government was often conceptualized as the product of big business, big labor, and big government, each checking and balancing the others. The antitrust emphasis of the later New Deal was all but forgotten.

Instead, Americans took comfort in economist John Kenneth Galbraith's theory of countervailing power. While Galbraith acknowledged that many sectors of the American marketplace were dominated by just a few firms and therefore were no longer competitive by the usual standard, he argued that power on one side of the market (among sellers of a product, such as steel) usually produced a "countervailing" power on the other side of the market (among buyers of the product, such as automobile makers). Similarly, the market power of a very big seller of consumer durable goods, such as General Electric, was limited by the existence of equally powerful buyers of those goods, including Sears, Roebuck and Montgomery Ward. Because countervailing power was usually "self-generating," the role of government was limited to fine-tuning an economic system whose basic structure was understood to be reasonably competitive.

It followed that a wide variety of social problems—racism, unemployment, poverty, urban life, and the cult of domesticity, which suffocated women—were ignored, denied, accepted, or left in abeyance to be handled by some future generation. Throughout the 1950s, social commentators affirmed that America's central problems were ones of boredom, affluence, and classlessness. *The Midas Plague*, a science-fiction novel, described a world in which goods were so easily produced and so widely available that consuming had become a personal duty, a social responsibility, and an enormous and endless burden. David Riesman's *Lonely Crowd*, an influential study published in 1950, argued that the age of scarcity had ended; Americans would henceforth be concerned with leisure, play, and the "art of living."

According to Riesman, these new conditions had created a new American character type that he labeled "other-directed": gregarious, superficially intimate, deeply conformist. For many analysts of American society, the new conditions of life had eliminated old conflicts between capital and labor and ushered in what sociologist Daniel Bell referred to as "the end of ideology." In a 1960 book by that title, Bell described how most postwar intellectuals had given up on the class-based, ideological radicalism of the 1930s and adopted a new, more accommodating stance toward social and economic conditions. Economic growth—so some pundits believed—would increase the size of the total product to be distributed and soon result in a society consisting mainly of white-collar workers, who were unlikely to be critical of their circumstances or to demand profound social or economic change.

Beneath the surface of the consensual society, there were some currents that disturbed many Americans. Despite a landmark Supreme Court decision in 1954 ordering the racial integration of public schools with "all deliberate speed," black Americans remained outside the American system, gathering energies for a spectacular assault on the traditions of prejudice and exploitation. Women did not resist so overtly, but a growing body of scholarly literature suggests that many women were at best ambivalent about the June Cleaver (*Leave It to Beaver*) and Margaret Anderson (*Father Knows Best*) images that were television's contribution to the consensual society. Everyone was concerned about an apparent alienation among many young people, an alienation that expressed itself sometimes frighteningly as juvenile delinquency, sometimes just as a mystifying lack of energetic affirmation, most often in an affinity for a new music called rock 'n' roll. Following the launch of the Soviet satellite *Sputnik* in 1957, Americans began to ask whether this technological defeat reflected a general withering of national purpose (a theme taken up by Eisenhower's successor, John Kennedy). As the decade wore on, it became obvious, too, that millions of Americans were not participating in the prosperity the administration proclaimed. Eisenhower's farewell address would be silent on most of these issues; but its discussion of the military-industrial complex was perhaps Eisenhower's way of acknowledging that the consensus he had tried so hard to preserve—indeed, to create—was fundamentally unstable. If so, the next decade would prove him right.

Rebels Without a Cause? Teenagers in the 1950s

Beth Bailey

Against images of Elvis Presley's contorted torso, of Little Richard's screaming black sexuality, of Cleveland disc jockey Alan Freed introducing a generation of eager young people to the erotic pleasures of rhythm and blues, Beth Bailey offers a very different perspective on American youth in the 1950s. Using dating behavior to understand the emerging postwar youth culture, Bailey suggests that young people were responding to a climate of insecurity that had deep historical roots. Furthermore, she identifies the quest for security with a revised, "'50s" version of the American dream that also encompassed family and suburbia. In short, Bailey seems to suggest that the youth of the 1950s were as attuned to consensual values as any other group.

While reading the essay, consider some of these questions: Does Bailey's argument apply to most American youths, or only to those who were white and middle class? What did parents find objectionable in this youth behavior, and why? Might "going steady" be understood as both a form of acquiescence in dominant values and a kind of resistance? And how can one square Bailey's perspective with the Presley, Little Richard, and Freed images mentioned above?

The United States emerged from the Second World War the most powerful and affluent nation in the world. This statement, bald but essentially accurate, is the given foundation for understanding matters foreign and domestic, the cold war and the age of abundance in America. Yet the sense of confidence and triumph suggested by that firm phrasing and by our images of soldiers embracing women as confetti swirled through downtown streets obscures another postwar reality. Underlying and sometimes overwhelming both bravado and complacency were voices of uncertainty. America at war's end was not naively optimistic.

The Great War had planted the seeds of the great depression. Americans wondered if hard times would return as the war boom ended. (They wouldn't.) The First World War had not ended all wars. Would war come again? (It would, both cold and hot.) And the fundamental question that plagued postwar America was, would American citizens have the strength and the character to meet the demands of this new world?

Postwar America appears in stereotype as the age of conformity—smug, materialistic, complacent, a soulless era peopled by organization men and their (house)wives. But this portrait of conformity exists only because

Beth Bailey, "Rebels Without a Cause? Teenagers in the 1950s," *History Today*, vol. 40, February 1990, pp. 25–31. Reprinted with the permission of the publisher.

Americans created it. Throughout the postwar era Americans indulged in feverish self-examination. Experts proclaimed crises, limned the American character, poked and prodded into the recesses of the American psyche. Writing in scholarly journals and for an attentive general public, theorists and social critics suggested that America's very success was destroying the values that had made success possible. Success, they claimed, was eroding the ethic that had propelled America to military and industrial supremacy and had lifted American society (with significant exceptions seen clearly in hindsight) to undreamed-of heights of prosperity.

At issue was the meaning of the American dream. Did the American dream mean success through individual competition in a wide-open free marketplace? Or was the dream only of the abundance the American marketplace had made possible—the suburban American dream of two cars in every garage and a refrigerator-freezer in every kitchen? One dream was of competition and the resulting rewards. The *making* of the self-made man— the process of entrepreneurial struggle—was the stuff of that dream. Fulfillment, in this vision, was not only through material comforts, but through the prominence, social standing, and influence in the public sphere one achieved in the struggle for success.

The new-style postwar American dream seemed to look to the private as the sphere of fulfillment, of self-definition and self-realization. Struggle was not desired, but stasis. The dream was of a private life—a family, secure, stable, and comfortable—that compensated for one's public (work) life. One vision highlighted risk; the other security. Many contemporary observers feared that the desire for security was overwhelming the "traditional" American ethic. In the dangerous postwar world, they asserted, the rejection of the public, of work and of risk would soon destroy America's prosperity and security.

The focus for much of the fear over what America was becoming was, not surprisingly, youth. Adult obsession with the new postwar generation took diverse forms—from the overheated rhetoric about the new epidemic of juvenile delinquency (too many rebels without causes) to astringent attacks on the conformity of contemporary youth. These critiques, though seemingly diametrically opposed, were based on the shared assumption that young people lacked the discipline and get-up-and-go that had made America great.

Perhaps nowhere in American culture do we find a richer statement of concern about American youth and the new American dream than in the debates that raged over "going steady," an old name for a new practice that was reportedly more popular among postwar teenagers than "bop, progressive jazz, hot rods and curiosity (slight) about atomic energy." The crisis over the "national problem" of going steady is not merely emblematic—an amusing way into a serious question. "Going steady" seemed to many adults the very essence of the problem, a kind of leading indicator of the privatization of the American dream. Social scientists and social critics saw in the new security-first courtship patterns a paradigm for an emerging American character that, while prizing affluence, did not relish the risks and hard work that made it possible.

Certainly the change in courtship patterns was dramatic. And it was not hard to make a connection between the primary characteristics of teenagers' love lives and what they hoped to get out of American life in general. Before the Second World War, American youth had prized a promiscuous popularity, demonstrating competitive success through the number and variety of dates they commanded. Sociologist Willard Waller, in his 1937 study of American dating, gave this competitive system a name: "the campus rating complex." His study of Pennsylvania State University detailed a "dating and rating" system based on a model of public competition in which popularity was the currency. To be popular, men needed outward, material signs: an automobile, proper clothing, the right fraternity membership, money. Women's popularity depended on building and maintaining a reputation for popularity. They had to *be seen* with popular men in the "right" places, indignantly turn down requests for dates made at the "last minute," and cultivate the impression they were greatly in demand.

In *Mademoiselle*'s 1938 college issue, for example, a Smith college senior advised incoming freshmen to "cultivate an image of popularity" if they wanted dates. "During your first term," she wrote, "get 'home talent' to ply you with letters, invitations, telegrams. College men will think, 'She must be attractive if she can rate all that attention.'" And at Northwestern University in the 1920s, competitive pressure was so intense that co-eds made a pact not to date on certain nights of the week. That way they could preserve some time to study, secure in the knowledge they were not losing ground in the competitive race for success by staying home.

In 1935, the Massachusetts *Collegian* (the Massachusetts State College student newspaper) ran an editorial against using the library for "datemaking." The editors proclaimed: "The library is the place for the improvement of the mind and not the social standing of the student." Social standing, not social life: on one word turns the meaning of the dating system. That "standing" probably wasn't even a conscious choice shows how completely these college students took for granted that dating was primarily concerned with competition and popularity. As one North Carolina teenager summed it up:

> Going steady with one date
> Is okay, if that's all you rate.

Rating, dating, popularity, competition: catchwords hammered home, reinforced from all sides until they seemed a natural vocabulary. You had to rate in order to date, to date in order to rate. By successfully maintaining this cycle, you became popular. To stay popular, you competed. There was no end; the competitive process defined dating. Competition was the key term in the formula—remove it and there was no rating, dating, or popularity.

In the 1930s and 1940s, this competition was enacted most visibly on the dance floor. There, success was a dizzying popularity that kept girls whirling from escort to escort, "cut in" on by a host of popular men. Advice columns, etiquette books, even student handbooks told girls to strive to be "once-arounders," never be left with the same partner for more than one turn around the dance floor. On the dance floor, success and failure were easily measured. Wallflowers were dismissed out of hand. But getting stuck—not being "cut in" on—was taken quite seriously as a sign of social failure. Everyone noticed, and everyone judged.

This form of competitive courtship would change dramatically. By the early 1950s, "cutting in" had almost completely disappeared outside the deep south. In 1955, a student at Texas Christian University reported, "To cut in is almost an insult." A girl in Green Bay, Wisconsin, said that her parents were "astonished" when they discovered that she hadn't danced with anyone but her escort at a "formal." "The truth was," she admitted, "that I wasn't aware that we were supposed to."

This 180-degree reversal took place quickly—during the years of the Second World War—and was so complete by the early 1950s that people under eighteen could be totally unaware of the formerly powerful convention. It signaled not simply a change in dancing etiquette but a complete transformation of the dating system as well. Definitions of social success as promiscuous popularity based on strenuous competition had given way to new definitions, which located success in the security of a dependable escort.

By the 1950s, early marriage had become the goal for young adults. In 1959, 47 percent of all brides married before they turned nineteen, and up to 25 percent of students at many large state universities were married. The average age at marriage had risen to 26.7 for men and 23.3 for women during the lingering depression, but by 1951 the average age at marriage had fallen to 22.6 for men, 20.4 for women. And younger teens had developed their own version of early marriage.

As early as 1950, going steady had completely supplanted the dating-rating complex as the criterion for popularity among youth. A best-selling study of American teenagers, *Profile of Youth* (1949), reported that in most high schools the "mere fact" of going steady was a sign of popularity "as long as you don't get tied up with an impossible gook." *The Ladies' Home Journal* reported in 1949 that "every high school student . . . must be prepared to fit into a high-school pattern in which popularity, social acceptance and emotional security are often determined by the single question: does he or she go steady?" A 1959 poll found that 57 percent of American teens had gone or were going steady. And, according to *Cosmopolitan* in 1960, if you didn't go steady, you were "square."

The new protocol of going steady was every bit as strict as the old protocol of rating and dating. To go steady, the boy gave the girl some visible token, such as a class ring or letter sweater. In Portland, Oregon, steadies favored rings (costing from $17 to $20). In Birmingham, Michigan, the girl wore the boy's identity bracelet, but never his letter sweater. In rural Iowa, the couple wore matching corduroy "steady jackets," although any couple wearing matching clothing in California would be laughed at.

As long as they went steady, the boy had to call the girl a certain number of times a week or take her on a certain number of dates a week (both numbers were subject to local convention). Neither boy nor girl could date anyone else or pay too much attention to anyone of the opposite sex. While either could go out with friends of the same sex, each must always know where the other was and what he or she was doing. Going steady meant a guaranteed date for special events, and it implied greater sexual intimacy—either more "necking" or "going further."

In spite of the intense monogamy of these steady relationships, teenagers viewed them as temporary. A 1950 study of 565 seniors in an eastern suburban high school found that 80 percent had gone or were going steady. Out of that number, only eleven said they planned to marry their steady. In New Haven, Connecticut, high school girls wore "obit bracelets." Each time they broke up with a boy, they added a disc engraved with his name or initials on the chain. In Louisiana, a girl would embroider her sneakers with the name of her current steady. When they broke up, she would clip off his name and sew an X over the spot. An advice book from the mid-1950s advised girls to get a "Puppy Love Anklet." Wearing it on the right ankle meant that you were available, on the left that you were going steady. The author advised having "Going Steady" engraved on one side, "Ready, Willing 'n Waiting" on the other—just in case the boys could not remember the code. All these conventions, cheerfully reported in teenager columns in national magazines, show how much teenagers took it for granted that going steady was a temporary, if intense, arrangement.

Harmless as this system sounds today, especially compared to the rigors of rating and dating, the rush to go steady precipitated an intense generational battle. Clearly some adult opposition was over sex: going steady was widely accepted as a justification for greater physical intimacy. But more fundamentally, the battle over going steady came down to a confrontation between two generations over the meaning of the American dream. Security versus competition. Teenagers in the 1950s were trying to do the unthinkable—to eliminate competition from the popularity equation. Adults were appalled. To them, going steady, with its extreme rejection of competition in favor of temporary security, represented all the faults of the new generation.

Adults, uncomfortable with the "cult of happiness" that rejected competition for security, attacked the teenage desire for security with no holds barred. As one writer advised boys, "To be sure of anything is to cripple one's powers of growth." She continued, "To have your girl always assured at the end of a telephone line without having to work for her, to beat the other fellows to her is bound to lessen your powers of personal achievement." A male adviser, campaigning against going steady, argued: "Competition will be good for you. It sharpens your wits, teaches you how to get along well in spite of difficulties." And another, writing in *Esquire*, explained the going steady phenomenon this way: "She wants a mate; he being a modern youth doesn't relish competition."

As for girls, the argument went: "She's afraid of competition. She isn't sure she can compete for male attention in the open market: 'going steady' frees her from fear of further failures." The author of *Jackson's Guide to Dating* tells the story of "Judith Thompson," a not-especially-attractive girl with family problems, who has been going steady with "Jim" since she was fourteen. Lest we think that poor Judith deserves someone to care for her or sees Jim as a small success in her life, the author stresses that going steady is one more failure for Judith. "Now that Judith is sixteen and old enough to earn money and help herself in other ways to recover from her unfortunate childhood, she has taken on the additionally crippling circumstance of a steady boyfriend. How pathetic. The love and attention of her steady boyfriend are a substitute for other more normal kinds of success." What should Judith be doing? "A good deal of the time she spends going steady with Jim could be used to make herself more attractive so that other boys would ask her for dates."

There is nothing subtle in these critiques of going steady. The value of competition is presumed as a clear standard against which to judge modern youth. But there is more here. There is a tinge of anger in these judgments, an anger that may well stem from the differing experiences of two generations of Americans. The competitive system that had emerged in the flush years of the 1920s was strained by events of the 1930s and 1940s. The elders had come of age during decades of depression and world war, times when the competitive struggle was, for many, inescapable. Much was at stake, the cost of failure all too clear. While youth in the period between the wars embraced a competitive dating system, even gloried in it, as adults they sought the security they had lacked in their youth.

Young people and their advocates made much of the lack of security of the postwar world, self-consciously pointing to the "general anxiety of the times" as a justification for both early marriage and going steady. But the lives of these young people were clearly more secure than those of their parents. That was the gift their parents tried to give them. Though the cold war raged it had little immediate impact on the emerging teenage culture (for those too young to fight in Korea, of course). Cushioned by unprecedented affluence, allowed more years of freedom within the protected youth culture of high school and ever-more-frequently college, young people did not have to struggle so hard, compete so ferociously as their parents had.

And by and large, both young people and their parents knew it and were genuinely not sure what that meant for America's future. What did it mean— that a general affluence, at least for a broad spectrum of America's burgeoning middle class, was possible without a dog-eat-dog ferocity? What did *that* mean for the American Dream of success? One answer was given in the runaway best seller of the decade, *The Man in the Gray Flannel Suit*, which despite the title was not so much about the deadening impact of conformity but about what Americans should and could dream in the postwar world.

The protagonist of the novel, Tom Rath (the not-so-subtle naming made more explicit by the appearance of the word "vengeful" in the sentence following Tom's introduction), has been through the Second World War, and the shadow of war hangs over his life. Tom wants to provide well for his family, and feels a nagging need to succeed. But when he is offered the chance at an old-style American dream—to be taken on as the protégé of his business-wise, driven boss, he says no. In a passage that cuts to the heart of postwar American culture, Tom tells his boss:

I don't think I'm the kind of guy who should try to be a big executive. I'll say it frankly: I don't think I have the willingness to make the sacrifices. . . . I'm trying to be honest about this. I want the money. Nobody likes money better than I do. But I'm not the kind of guy who can work evenings and weekends and all the rest of it forever. . . . I've been through one war. Maybe another one's coming. If one is, I want to be able to look back and figure I spent the time between wars with my family, the way it should have been spent. Regardless of war, I want to get the most out of the years I've got left. Maybe that sounds silly. It's just that if I have to bury myself in a job every minute of my life, I don't see any point to it.

Tom's privatized dream—of comfort without sacrifice, of family and personal fulfillment—might seem the author's attempt to resolve the tensions of the novel (and of postwar American society). But the vision is more complex than simply affirmative. Tom's boss responds with sympathy and understanding, then suddenly loses control. "Somebody has to do the big jobs!" he says passionately. "This world was built by men like me! To really do a job, you have to live it, body and soul! You people who just give half your mind to your work are riding on our backs!" And Tom responds: "I know it."

The new American Dream had not yet triumphed. The ambivalence and even guilt implicit in Tom Rath's answer to his boss pervaded American culture in the 1950s—in the flood of social criticism and also in parents' critiques of teenage courtship rituals. The attacks on youth's desire for security are revealing, for it was in many ways the parents who embraced security—moving to the suburbs, focusing on the family. The strong ambivalence many felt about their lives appears in the critiques of youth. This same generation would find even more to criticize in the 1960s, as the "steadies" of the 1950s became the sexual revolutionaries of the 1960s. Many of the children of these parents came to recognize the tensions within the dream. The baby-boom generation accepted wholeheartedly the doctrine of self-fulfillment, but rejected the guilt and fear that had linked fulfillment and security. In the turbulence of the 1960s, young people were not rejecting the new American Dream of easy affluence and personal fulfillment, but only jettisoning the fears that had hung over a generation raised with depression and war. It turns out the 1950s family was not the new American Dream, but only its nurturing home.

The Suburbs

Aerial photographs of Levittown, a postwar housing development on Long Island, appear in most history textbooks, usually as evidence of the inherent sterility of life in the new American suburbs. Yet there are those who argue that this is only a superficial impression and that up-close investigation of particular houses would reveal the effort most homeowners made to customize their homes and distinguish their properties from those of their neighbors. What do you think?

A Levittown house, 1958. Library of Congress.

Levittown, New York. UPI. Corbis Images.

Rock 'n' Roll

The musical style called "rock 'n' roll" dates from the early 1950s. It is usually considered a sign of revolt, musical evidence that the generational rebellion that would sweep the 1960s was already under way even as Dwight Eisenhower was serving his first term. It was this. But rock 'n' roll was also essentially a white music, and a white music that was developed almost entirely from black musical styles.

The verses below—from the rock 'n' roll classic "Shake, Rattle and Roll" (1954)—allow us to inquire into the historical meaning of this new music. The verses on the left are from the original version, written by Charles Calhoun and recorded by Joe Turner for the black market. The verses on the right are from the more popular "cover" version by Bill Haley and the Comets. Both versions were hits in 1954.

Why did Haley change the words?

"Shake, Rattle and Roll" (1954)

**The Charles Calhoun/
Joe Turner Version**

The Bill Haley Version

Get out of that bed,
And wash your face and hands. (twice)

Get out in that kitchen,
And rattle those pots and pans. (twice)

Get into the kitchen
Make some noise with the pots and pans

Roll my breakfast
'Cause I'm a hungry man.

Well you wear those dresses,
The sun comes shinin' through. (twice)

You wear those dresses,
Your hair done up so nice. (twice)

I can't believe my eyes,
That all of this belongs to you.

You look so warm,
But your heart is cold as ice.

I said over the hill,
And way down underneath. (twice)

(the third verse of the Calhoun/Turner version is not part of the Haley version)

You make me roll my eyes,
And then you make me grit my teeth.

 *A variety of Web sites explore aspects of the popular culture of the 1950s, including rock 'n' roll and dating customs. One of the best is maintained by historian Jessamyn Neuhaus:* http://home.earthlink.net/~neuhausj/1950s/index.html.

Challenging the Consensus: Integrating the Public Schools

Melba Pattillo Beals

In a 1954 decision in Brown v. Board of Education of Topeka, Kansas, *the Supreme Court ruled that segregated public schools were unconstitutional. The decision is usually understood to mark the beginning of the modern civil rights movement, and with good reason. But* Brown v. Board *was also the culmination of a series of legal and political struggles that began during World War II, when A. Philip Randolph, head of the Brotherhood of Sleeping Car Porters, threatened to lead a march on Washington, D.C., in protest against segregation in the armed forces and race discrimination in the issuing of government contracts. Although the march did not take place, Randolph's aggressive stance put the nation's leaders on notice. Pushed and prodded by legal actions facilitated by the NAACP and its chief counsel, Thurgood Marshall, the courts were especially active on behalf of civil rights. A 1944 decision in* Smith v. Allwright *required the southern wing of the Democratic Party to open its all-white primary elections to African American voters; in* Shelley v. Kraemer *(1948), the Supreme Court struck down an important form of housing segregation—the restrictive covenants that limited sales to Caucasians; and in 1950, the decision in* Sweatt v. Painter *held that Texas's system of segregated and separate law schools did not produce equal facilities. The stage was set for* Brown.

In the early 1950s, when the several cases that would together constitute Brown v. Board of Education *were making their way through the courts, most public schools in the United States were racially segregated. In the South, the segregation was by law, underpinned by the 1896 decision in* Plessy v. Ferguson, *which held that separate railroad facilities (and hence schools) were lawful, as long as they were also equal. In the North, the segregation was* de facto—*simply a "fact"—caused, in this case, by the "fact" that blacks and whites lived in different neighborhoods and, therefore, attended different schools. The color line in the North was not absolute; many public schools in northern big cities were minimally integrated. Thus the change promised by* Brown v. Board *was enormous: the racial integration of all the nation's public schools.*

The Supreme Court set no firm deadline for implementing its decision, announcing only that schools should be integrated "with all deliberate speed." When school districts refused to present a reasonable plan for integration, they sometimes had to be forced to act. That was the situation in Little Rock, Arkansas, where, in September, 1957, Governor Orval Faubus, sustained by angry white mobs, tried to block integration on the grounds that it would lead to violence. Under Faubus's direction, the National Guard took up positions outside Little Rock's Central High School. On September 4, the guardsmen turned away nine African American teenagers, presumably to forestall conflict. In late September, under Court order, the guardsmen were withdrawn and the black youths admitted, only to be forced from the school by antagonistic students. To prevent violence, President Dwight Eisenhower sent in troops of the 101st Airborne— which is where Melba Pattillo Beals's story begins. Later, Eisenhower withdrew the 101st and left the school in the hands of the Arkansas National Guard, now under federal control.

If you were Melba Pattillo, how would you have responded to these events? How would you characterize Eisenhower's response to the situation? Should the federal government have been stronger in demanding compliance with the Court's decision?

VOICES

I arrived at school Tuesday morning, fully expecting that I would be greeted by the 101st soldiers and escorted to the top of the stairs. Instead, we were left at the curb to fend for ourselves. As we approached the stairs, we were greeted by taunting catcalls and the kind of behavior students had not dared to exhibit in the face of the 101st.

Where were the disciplined ranks we had come to count on? I looked all round, but sure enough, there were no 101st guards in sight. Just then a boy blocked our way. What were we to do? My first thought was to retreat, to turn and go back down the stairs and detour around to the side door. But that escape route was blocked by those stalking us. A large crowd of jeering, pencil-throwing students hovered around us menacingly. We had no choice but to go forward.

"Where are your pretty little soldier boys today?" someone cried out.

"You niggers ready to die just to be in this school?" asked another.

Squeezing our way through the hostile group gathered at the front door, we were blasted by shouts of "Nigger, go home. Go back to where you belong." At every turn, we were faced with more taunts and blows. There were no 101st soldiers at their usual posts along the corridors.

And then I saw them. Slouching against the wall were members of the Arkansas National Guard, looking on like spectators at a sports event—certainly not like men sent to guard our safety.

I wanted to turn and run away, but I thought about what Danny had said: "Warriors survive." I tried to remember his stance, his attitude, and the courage of the 101st on the battlefield. Comparing my tiny challenge with what he must have faced made me feel more confident. I told myself I could handle whatever the segregationists had in store for me. But I underestimated them.

Early that morning, a boy began to taunt me as though he had been assigned that task. First he greeted me in the hall outside my shorthand class and began pelting me with bottle-cap openers, the kind with the sharp claw at the end. He was also a master at walking on my heels. He hurt me until I wanted to scream for help.

Troops pf 101st Airborne Division move crowd away from in front of Central High School.
Library of Congress.

By lunchtime, I was nearly hysterical and ready to call it quits, until I thought of having to face Grandma when I arrived home. During the afternoon, when I went into the principal's office several times to report being sprayed with ink, kicked in the shin, and heel-walked until the backs of my feet bled, as well as to report the name of my constant tormenter, the clerks asked why I was reporting petty stuff. With unsympathetic scowls and hostile attitudes, they accused me of making mountains out of molehills.

Not long before the end of the school day, I entered a dimly lit rest room. The three girls standing near the door seemed to ignore me. Their passive, silent, almost pleasant greeting made me uncomfortable, and the more I thought about their attitude, the more it concerned me. At least when students were treating me harshly, I knew what to expect.

Once inside the stall, I was even more alarmed at all the movement, the feet shuffling, the voices whispering. It sounded as though more people were entering the room.

"Bombs away!" someone shouted above me. I looked up to see a flaming paper wad coming right down on me. Girls were leaning over the top of the stalls on either side of me. Flaming paper floated down and landed on my hair and shoulders. I jumped up, trying to pull myself together and at the same time duck the flames and stamp them out. I brushed the singeing ashes away from my face as I frantically grabbed for the door to open it.

"Help!" I shouted. "Help!" The door wouldn't open. Someone was holding it—someone strong, perhaps more than one person. I was trapped.

"Did you think we were gonna let niggers use our toilets? We'll burn you alive, girl," a voice shouted through the door. "There won't be enough of you left to worry about."

I felt the kind of panic that stopped me from thinking clearly. My right arm was singed. The flaming wads of paper were coming at me faster and faster. I could feel my chest muscles tightening. I felt as though I would die any moment. The more I yelled for help, the more I inhaled smoke and the more I coughed.

I told myself I had to stop screaming so I wouldn't take in so much smoke. My throat hurt—I was choking. I remembered Grandmother telling me all I had to do was say the name of God and ask for help. Once more I looked up to see those grinning, jeering faces as flaming paper rained down on me. Please, God, help me, I silently implored. I had to hurry. I might not be able to swat the next one and put it out with my hands. Then what? Would my hair catch fire? I had to stop them. I picked up my books and tossed one upward as hard as I could, in a blind aim to hit my attackers.

I heard a big thud, then a voice cry out in pain and several people scuffle about. I tossed another and then another book as fast and as hard as I could. One more of their number cursed at me. I had hit my target.

"Let's get out of here," someone shouted as the group hurried out the door. In a flash, I leaped out of the stall, trying to find my things. I decided I wouldn't even bother reporting my problem. I just wanted to go home. I didn't care that I smelled of smoke or that my blouse was singed. Later when my friends asked what happened, I didn't even bother to explain.

Much worse than the fear and any physical pain I had endured, was the hurt deep down inside my heart, because no part of me understood why people would do those kinds of things to one another. I was so stunned by my experience that during the ride home I sat silent and listened to reports from the others. They, too, seemed to have had a bigger problem that day with hecklers and hooligans.

The experiment of doing without the 101st had apparently been a fiasco. By the end of the day more than one of us had heard talk that the 101st had been brought back.

Still, despite all our complaints, there were a few students who tried to reach out to us with smiles or offers to sit at our cafeteria tables; some even accompanied us along the halls. Each of us noticed, however, that those instances of friendship were shrinking rather than growing. There was no doubt that the hard-core troublemakers were increasing their activities, and without the men of the 101st, they increased a hundredfold.

> President Eisenhower says he will remove the 101st soldiers if Governor Faubus agrees to protect the nine Negro children with federalized Arkansas National Guardsmen.

Those words from the radio announcer sent a chill down my spine as I sat doing my homework on Tuesday evening. I had hoped the rumors of the return of the 101st were true. But according to the report, the same Arkansas soldiers who had been dispatched by Governor Faubus to keep us

African American students arriving at Central High School in U.S. Army car.
Library of Congress.

out of Central High would become totally responsible for keeping us *in* school and protecting our lives.

"Sounds like the wolf guarding the henhouse to me," grandma said. "Thank God you know who your real protector is, 'cause you certainly won't be able to count on those boys for help." She was peeking at me over the pages of the newspaper.

I didn't know how to tell her how right she was. But then I couldn't tell her I had had the kind of day that was making me think about running away where nobody could find me.

"Did you see where Judge Ronald Davies will be going back to North Dakota?" Grandma continued. "He will still retain jurisdiction over your case, though."

"That really frightens me," I said. "I feel safer with Davies being here."

"He is being replaced by Judge Harper from St. Louis, it says."

"Bad news," I replied. I didn't know bad things about Harper, but I had come to trust Davies as an honest and fair man with the courage of his convictions. St. Louis bordered the South; that Judge Harper might not be as open-minded.

"Of course, there is good news here," Grandma said, rattling the newspaper. "Seems as if some moderate white businessmen are getting together to oppose that special session of the legislature Faubus wants to call."

"The one to enact laws that would make integration illegal?" I asked.

"Yes, I hope they can do something to slow him down."

Ike rejects Faubus's statement and agreement falls through
—*Arkansas Gazette*, Wednesday, October 2, 1957

The Wednesday morning *Gazette* reported that Governor Faubus and the President had come to the brink of an agreement to remove the federal troops from Little Rock the day before, but at the last minute the President called it off because he didn't believe the governor would act in good faith.

As we walked toward Central that day, I was looking forward to having the 101st come back to make my life inside school at least tolerable. But right away my hopes for a more peaceful day were dashed. Showers of loud insults greeted us. Straight ahead, in front of the school, I could see a group of about fifty boys waiting at the top of the stairs as they had the day before. This time, however, they descended on us like locusts.

"Get the coons! Get the coons!" The boys were brash and bold, behaving as though they feared no consequences. There were no parading 101st soldiers to stop them. Frantically, we looked around for someone in authority, but none was in sight.

Minnijean, Ernie, and I decided to retreat, but just then, vice-principal Huckaby made her presence known at the bottom of the stairs. Tiny, erect, and determined, she stood there all alone between us and our attackers, demanding they leave us alone. One by one she challenged the leaders, calling them by name, telling them to get to class or there would be hell to pay. I had to respect her for what she did. Whether or not she favored integration, she had a heck of a lot of guts.

We circled around to the Sixteenth and Park Street entrance. As I climbed the stairs, there was no sign of Danny—or the other 101st guards I knew. In fact, I didn't see any uniformed soldiers. Just inside of the front entrance, where Danny usually stood, I saw some of the same hooligans who had tried to block our entrance only moments before. They moved toward me, and I circled away from them and walked quickly down the hall. I was desperately trying to figure out why there weren't any teachers or school officials guarding the halls the way there usually were.

I panicked; I couldn't decide where to go or what to do next. I was being pounded on my arms, my back, and my legs by angry students. Their blows hurt so much that my desire to stop the pain and survive overpowered the fear that paralyzed me. I got hold of myself. No matter what, I knew I had to stand up to them even if I got kicked out of school for doing it.

"Dead niggers don't go to school," someone said, hitting me hard in the stomach. My first instinct was to double over. The pain burned my insides. But I stood still and stared at my attacker without flinching. He taunted me: "You ain't thinking of hitting me back?"

"I'm gonna cut your guts out," I said, standing my ground. There was a long pause while we stared each other down. It was a bluff, but it worked. Looking almost frightened and mumbling under his breath, he backed off.

Just then, I noticed the members of the Arkansas National Guard lounging against the walls like cats in sunlight. Gathered in small clusters with smug, grinning expressions on their faces, they had been watching my confrontation all along. I couldn't get used to the fact that our safety now depended on nonchalant, tobacco-chewing adolescents who were most likely wearing white sheets and burning crosses on the lawns of our neighbors after sundown.

African American student Elizabeth Eckford endures epithets of white girl outside Central High School. National Guardsman in upper left. Library of Congress.

I had walked only a few steps before I was knocked to the floor. I called out for help. Three men from the Guard gave further substance to my suspicions by taking their time to respond, moving toward me in slow motion. I scrambled to my feet.

How I longed to see Danny, standing on guard in his starched uniform, and hear the swift steps of the 101st. As I felt hot tears stinging my eyes, I heard Grandmother India's voice say, "You're on the battlefield for your Lord."

I was as frightened by the ineptness of the Arkansas soldiers as by the viciousness of the increased attacks on me. If the soldiers had been armed, I was certain they would either have shot me in the back or themselves in the foot. I watched as they stood in giggling clusters while a crowd of thugs attacked Jeff and Terry and kicked them to the floor in the hallway just outside the principal's office. A female teacher finally rescued the two.

Once I was seated in class, I felt I could take a deep breath. For the moment at least I was off the front line of battle in the hallway. But just as I was feeling a snippet of peace, a boy pulled a switchblade knife and pressed the point of the blade against my forearm. In a heartbeat, without even thinking about it, I leaped up and picked up my books as a shield to fend him off.

He responded to a half-hearted reprimand from the teacher but whispered that he would get me later. At the very first sound of the bell ending class, I ran for my life, only to encounter a group of students who knocked me down and hit me with their books. As I felt rage overtake me I recalled what Danny had told me: "When you're angry, you can't think. You gotta keep alert to keep alive."

It was still early in the day, and things were so bad that I decided I had no choice: I had to find somebody in authority who would listen to me. Outside the principal's office I found Minnijean looking as abused and angry as I was.

"We gotta get out of here!" she said breathlessly.

"You're right. They're gonna kill us today," I replied.

"Let's call our folks."

"Let's call Mrs. Bates. Maybe she can talk to the army or reporters or the President." I assumed calling the head of the NAACP would at least get some response. Merely reporting this kind of trouble to school officials might not get anything except more of the same denial that there was trouble, or perhaps reprimands for being "tattletales."

Since neither of us had change for a call, we reluctantly decided to go to Mrs. Huckaby, although we were afraid she would try and convince us to stick it out. Mrs. Huckaby greeted us in a matter-of-fact way until it dawned on her that we might be using the change we asked for to call for outside help.

"Wait a minute. What's going on?" she asked, trailing behind us.

"We're calling Mrs. Bates. We need help. Maybe she can talk to the reporters and get us some protection."

Just as we suspected, Mrs. Huckaby insisted we go to the principal's office to give him a chance to solve the problem. She assured us that he would be fair.

Principal Matthews began to speak in his slow plodding way, wearing his usual nervous smile. It was apparent he only wanted to stop us from making the call. I was in no mood to have him tell me I was imagining things, not with my leg aching and the steel flash of that switchblade knife fresh in my mind.

"Either you give us some protection so we can function without getting killed, or we go home." I heard the words come out of my mouth, but I could hardly believe it was me speaking. My knees were shaking. It was the first time in my life I had ever stood up to any adult—certainly to any white adult. But I was on the edge, ready to take the risk, because how could anything the adults might do to me be worse than the abuse I was already enduring?

"Wait here," the principal said, his tone of voice leaving no doubt he was annoyed with us. Shortly afterward, we saw the brass approaching: General Clinger and Colonel McDavid of the Arkansas National Guard, and a third military man I did not recognize.

Clinger pointed to the two of us, most especially to me, and said, "You'll sit over there where I can look you in the face." Right away, I didn't like him, but I was ready to deal with him.

The rest of our group was summoned to the office. Everyone was vocal about the severity of the attacks during the morning. Each one had a story about how the physical abuse had increased significantly. We told

Clinger that his men were not protecting us, that they stood by, socializing and flirting while we were being beaten within an inch of our lives. "Those guards are turning their backs to attacks on us, and we demand you do something about it," I insisted.

Clinger didn't deny the charges. He explained that his men had to live in the community.

"We just wanna keep living . . . period," I said.

"Don't talk directly to the guards. Go to the office and report incidents," we were told.

I said, "With all due respect, sir, how can we run to the office every time we want help. Somebody could be beating one of us at the far end of the hall, and we'd have to wait until they finished and let us up so we could come here to report it."

I felt something inside me change that day. I felt a new will to live rise up in me. I knew I wasn't just going to roll over and die. I could take care of myself and speak up to white folks, even if my mother and father sometimes feared doing so. I discovered I had infinitely more guts than I had started the school year with. I had no choice. It was my life I was dickering for. I knew that Clinger didn't care about our welfare—not even a tiny bit.

"Young lady," Clinger said, eyeballing me, "you are turning our words. I didn't say—"

But I cut him off. "My friends and I will leave school if we don't get adequate protection. It's as simple as that," I told him. The others were obviously as angry as I was as they chimed in with their complaints. They voiced their agreement that something had to be done immediately.

"You'll have bodyguards." Clinger spoke with a definite edge to his voice. He summoned another soldier and told him to select eighteen men while we waited there. Those Arkansas guardsmen were the biggest, dumbest, most disheveled hayseeds I'd ever seen. They looked as if they had slept in their rumpled uniforms. We stood there not believing our eyes, dumbfounded by the sight of them.

"These clods will trip over their own shoelaces," I whispered to Minnijean.

"Or worse yet, get us in some dark corner and beat the living daylights out of us," she replied.

After about fifteen minutes we "moved out," or in their case, shuffled out. It was a sight to behold. There we were, followed by an absurd wall of not so mighty military green trailing us like a ridiculous wagging tail.

We found ourselves laughing aloud, and the white students were laughing with us. For just one moment we all realized the ridiculous situation we were caught up in.

Four of us went to our usual table in the cafeteria; the guards took up their posts, leaning against a nearby wall. When I got up to get in line for a sandwich, they fell over each other trying to see where I was going and which of them would follow me. Two stood in line with me, arms folded, tummies out, and shoulders rounded. Each time one of us rose to get anything, two of those clowns stumbled up to follow. It was a comedy of errors.

As we moved through the halls in our oddball group, I saw, just a few feet away, the boy who had pulled the knife on me earlier. The momentary terror I felt reminded me our situation wasn't funny after all.

I missed Danny. That was another feeling taking me over. Rumor had it that the 101st waited at Camp Robinson, just outside Little Rock. But I knew that even if he came back again and again, there would come the day when he would be gone for good.

Still, I was overjoyed when on Thursday we once again had our 101st bodyguards. Maybe they were forced to come back because the morning *Gazette* had reported the story of Terry and Jeff being kicked while Arkansas National Guardsmen looked on.

As we arrived at school that morning, I noticed right away that there was a different kind of tension, as though everyone was waiting for something awful to happen, only we didn't know what. We had heard rumors of a planned student protest. I could see groups of students standing in the halls instead of in class where they would normally have been.

Just before first period, more students began walking out of classes. Rumors about a big event reverberated throughout the school. I could see and feel a new level of restlessness and a deepening sense of hostility. I was on edge, waiting for disaster any moment, like dynamite or a group attack or I didn't know what. "They're hangin' a nigger, just like we're gonna hang you," someone muttered. That's when I learned that some of those who walked out had assembled at the vacant lot at Sixteenth and Park across from the school, where they hanged and burned a straw figure.

That demonstration set the tone of the day. Belligerent student protests were firing up the already hostile attitude inside the school. Danny broke the rules by coming closer and talking to me—warning that we had to stay alert, no matter what.

Near the end of the day I was walking down a dimly lit hallway, with Danny following, when I spotted a boy coming directly toward me on a collision course. I tried to move aside, but he moved with me. I didn't even have time to call for help.

The boy flashed a shiny black object in my face. The sudden pain in my eyes was so intense, so sharp, I thought I'd die. It was like nothing I'd ever felt before. I couldn't hear or see or feel anything except that throbbing, searing fire centered in my eyes. I heard myself cry out as I let go of everything to clutch at my face.

Someone grabbed me by my ponytail and pulled me along very fast, so fast I didn't have time to resist. The pain of being dragged along by my hair was almost as intense as that in my eyes. Hands grabbed my wrists and pried my hands from my face, compelling me to bend over. Then cold, cold liquid was splashed in my eyes. The water felt so good. My God, thank you! The pain was subsiding.

"Easy, girl, easy. You're gonna be fine." It was Danny's voice, his hands holding my head and dousing my eyes with water.

"I can't see," I whispered. "I can't see."

"Hold on. You will."

Over and over again, the cold water flooded my face. Some of it went into my nose and down the front of my blouse. Bit by bit I could see the sleeve of Danny's uniform, see the water, see the floor beneath us. The awful pain in my eyes had turned into a bearable sting. My eyes felt dry, as though there were a film drawn tight over them.

"What was that?"

"I don't know," Danny said, "maybe some kind of alkaline or acid. The few drops that got on your blouse faded the color immediately. Hey, let's get you to the office so we can report this. You gotta get to a doctor."

"No. No," I protested.

"Why not?"

"School's almost over, I wanna go home, right now. Please, please don't make me. . . ." I felt tears. I knew he hated me to cry, but the thought of going to the office made me crazy. I couldn't handle having some hostile clerk telling me I was making mountains out of molehills.

"Calm down. You can do what you want but—"

"No, home right now." I said, cutting Danny off.

A short time later, an optometrist examined my eyes and studied the spots on my blouse. He put some kind of soothing substance into my eyes and covered them with eye patches. As I sat there in the dark, I heard him say, "Whoever kept that water going in her eyes saved the quality of her sight, if not her sight itself. She'll have to wear the patch overnight. She'll have to be medicated for a while. She'll need to wear glasses for all close work. I'd really like to see her wear them all the time. I'll need to see her once a week until we're certain she's all right."

Glasses, all the time, I thought. No boy wants to date a girl with glasses.

Despite the doctor's instructions to wear an eye patch for twenty-four hours, I had to take it off. I couldn't let the reporters see me with the patch because they would ask questions and make a big deal of it.

By the time we got home it was seven o'clock, and I wasn't very talkative for the waiting reporters. Once inside I fell into bed, too exhausted to eat dinner. "Thank you, God," I whispered, "thank you for saving my eyes. God bless Danny, always."

The hanging, stabbing, and burning of a Negro effigy near Central High
—*Arkansas Gazette*, Friday, October 4, 1957

The newspaper story contained several vivid pictures of Central High students gathered the day before, hanging the effigy, then burning it. They were smiling gleefully as though they were attending a festive party.

"You made it. It's Friday," Danny said, greeting me at the front of Central once more. "Your peepers okay?"

My eyes still felt very dry and tight. There were floating spots before them, but I could see. They only stung when I went too long without putting the drops in.

Later that afternoon there was a movie star—someone I'd never heard of—speaking before a pep rally: Julie Adams, a former student. She was there to boost spirits because, she said, Central High School's reputation was being tainted.

Over the weekend of October 5th, a great thing happened that took the Little Rock school integration from the front pages of the national news. The Russians launched their 184-pound satellite, Sputnik.

But as the next week began, local radio, television, and newspapers claimed that 101st guards were following us females to the lavatory and harassing white girls. GI'S IN GIRLS' DRESSING ROOMS, FAUBUS SAYS ran as a banner headline in the *Gazette* for Monday, October 7. Of course it wasn't true. However, it made the military tighten up rules about where soldiers could or could not go with us and prompted them to launch a massive internal investigation.

I could see a steady erosion in the quality of security in response to charges of interference by the soldiers. It was evident as the early days of October passed that whenever the 101st troops relaxed their guard or were not clearly visible, we were in great danger.

African American students from Little Rock's Central High School display their $1,000 awards from the National Negro Elks Convention. Melba Patillo is on the far right. Library of Congress.

 ON THE WEB   *Will Counts' superb photographs of the Little Rock segregation crisis, as well as local newspaper editorials from the period, are online at* http://www.ardemgaz.com/prev/central/.

Television: A Visual Essay

New technologies may produce pleasure and positive social change, but they are often disruptive and threatening, or perceived that way. The motion picture, introduced at the turn of the last century, was widely understood as a medium that had to be regulated, even censored, to avoid moral decline. The rapid growth of television in the 1950s (1948 was the first full season) brought a chorus of concerns, many of them dealing with the device's impact on the American home and family life. The materials in this visual essay reveal how television was presented, and understood, in its early years. What concerns do they reflect? What comforts do they provide?

"Give *your* family a Crosley for Christmas." That's what the ribbon on the television says. c. 1950. Caulfield & Shook Collection, Photographic Archives, University of Louisville.

Coffee with your TV. This photograph was made for the United States Information
Agency, probably for distribution overseas as a way of marketing American values. c. 1950.
National Archives.

RCA Eye Witness Television. November, 1948.　　Crosley Full Room Vision. November, 1950.

"Get Set for New Holiday Thrills, with a 17" Truetone Console." December, 1951.

Happiness is sure headin' your way! September, 1949.

Watching the Philco. September, 1949.

Tune in on History, with a Westinghouse. The small print below the picture of a political convention reads, "This crowd that packed the 1884 Convention was tiny compared with the millions who see them today via television." July, 1952.

THE BIG PICTURE

The 1950s is often recalled as an era of conservative, consensual perfection, a "last fine time" (think of a Norman Rockwell painting) before the upheavals of the 1960s, deindustrialization, and a new wave of immigrants set the nation on the road to decline and divided its people. Historians usually paint a different picture. They acknowledge the decade's underlying conservatism, but they point to evidence of tensions, upheavals, and changes—a youth rebellion, represented by rock 'n' roll and juvenile delinquents; conflict over racial integration on Montgomery, Alabama's buses and at Little Rock, Arkansas's Central High School; the countercultural style of Jack Kerouac and the "beats"; and middle-class women festering under a burden of family and household obligation—all signs, one might say, of the epic confrontations that were just ahead.

Beth Bailey's essay offers support for both views; the new custom of "going steady" was a form of generational rebellion, but it also indicated a deep need for security in the form of a long-lasting relationship that often anticipated an early marriage, children, and a house in a suburb such as Levittown. Similarly, "Shake, Rattle, and Roll" was the sound of teen rebellion, but the more popular, Haley version was cleaned up for white, middle-class, suburban tastes—something like what Ray Kroc did to hamburgers when he opened the first McDonald's in the midwestern suburb of Des Plaines, Illinois, in 1955. And the early ads for TV confirm that Americans sought to contain the new technology and yoke it to traditional values, among them home, family, female domesticity, print culture, and political participation.

Chapter *12*

The 1960s: Resistance

For a time, the decade of the 1960s looked very much like its predecessor. John F. Kennedy, elected by a narrow margin over Richard Nixon in 1960, sought to pump up the nation with rhetoric while practicing a brand of consensus politics designed to avoid overt conflict. The problems of the 1960s, said Kennedy at Yale University's commencement in 1962, presented "subtle challenges, for which technical answers, not political answers, must be provided." Because he believed that basic problems of adequate food, clothing, and employment had been solved through economic growth and the evolution of the welfare state, Kennedy was not the reform activist that many expected him to be. Several of his policies and programs—the commitment to space exploration, the Peace Corps, the rollback of prices in the steel industry—were essentially symbolic gestures. In foreign affairs, Kennedy carried on the Cold War in grand fashion—deeper involvement in Vietnam; a CIA-sponsored invasion of Cuba in an attempt to depose Fidel Castro; a blockade to force the Soviet Union to remove its missiles from Cuba, when less bellicose but less satisfying alternatives were available.

There were signs of change and portents of turmoil in the early years of the decade—the gathering of political youth at Port Huron, Michigan, in 1962, to write and debate a manifesto; the assassination of John F. Kennedy; the assertive youth culture fostered by the English rock 'n' roll band the Beatles; the Berkeley Free Speech Movement in 1964. Yet the Eisenhower consensus was not irrevocably shattered until mid-decade. The cause was race. During the 1950s, black efforts to achieve integration had followed mainly legal channels. Gradually, though, black activists adopted the tactics of direct action. In February 1960, black and white college students conducted sit-ins at the segregated lunch counters of Woolworth dime stores in Durham and Greensboro, North Carolina; in 1961 and 1962, "freedom" rides took activists into segregated bus terminals across the Deep South. In August 1963, Martin Luther King, Jr., brought the civil rights movement north and sharpened its political content with an enormous march on the nation's capital.

Then, in 1965, a minor summer incident involving police in Watts, a black section of Los Angeles, set off five days of looting and rioting that left thirty-four people dead. Within two years, there were over a hundred major urban riots, all centered in black ghettos in cities like Newark and Detroit. It was in this setting that young black leaders began to question whether integration was an appropriate goal. They began to talk of black power. It was in this setting, too, that two of the most charismatic black leaders, Malcolm X and Martin Luther King, Jr., were shot to death. Race relations are the focus of Chapter 13.

The urban ghetto riots of the mid-1960s occurred during times of relatively low national rates of unemployment and inflation and within the context of Lyndon Johnson's Great Society—a liberal reform program that included the Voting Rights Act of 1965 and the War on Poverty. Comparable in importance to the Fifteenth Amendment to the Constitution (1870), the Voting Rights Act made illegal the literacy tests and other measures that southern states had used to keep African Americans from voting, and it gave the attorney general new powers to monitor registration and voting procedures. The law had an immediate impact. The War on Poverty was partly a response to a new wave of African American activists who were more interested in reducing black poverty than in integrating the society. Focused on the inner cities, where the riots had occurred, this complex program included public works; job training for the poor; basic-skills training for preschool children (Head Start); VISTA, a domestic version of the Peace Corps; and the Community Action Program (CAP), which encouraged local antipoverty efforts that involved community participation. Despite billions in expenditures and a booming economy, the problems of the inner cities—problems that affected whites, Hispanics, and Asians as well as blacks—seemed intractable. "We fought a war on poverty," President Ronald Reagan later declared, "and poverty won."

If poverty won, it was in some measure because the Johnson agenda was being undermined by a growing backlash against the social unrest in the inner cities and on college campuses, and starved for money by the president's own policy of escalation in Vietnam. When Kennedy was killed in 1963, there were fewer than 20,000 American personnel in Vietnam; in 1968, there were more than 500,000. For Johnson, each new American commitment was absolutely necessary. Defeat or withdrawal, he believed, would only bring more aggression, new tests of the national and presidential will. Others, however, saw the conflict in Vietnam largely as a civil war and

American involvement as an immoral and/or unlawful interference in a domestic dispute.

Protests against the war, centered on the college campuses and utilizing the tactics of the civil rights movement, began in earnest in early 1965 and grew in number and intensity through the decade. Almost every major campus in the United States was torn by rallies, teach-ins, and riots. One climax of the youth revolt was the massive demonstration—and the violent police response to it—centered on the Democratic National Convention in Chicago in 1968. The "protesters," as they had come to be called, could not prevent the nomination of the party's establishment candidate, Hubert Humphrey, but the event so clouded his candidacy that it almost ensured his defeat by Richard Nixon.

Nixon's widening of the Vietnam War in 1970, with an invasion of Cambodia, touched off the last major round of protest on the campuses. On May 4, panicky National Guardsmen, sent to quell a protest at Kent State University in Ohio, killed four students. Ten days later, two black youths were shot by police at Jackson State College in Mississippi.

By the end of the decade, the antiwar and civil rights movements had been joined and fueled by women seeking liberation from confining social roles and by a new group of environmental and consumer activists who saw that the nation had pursued economic growth at great cost to the quantity and quality of its remaining resources and the health of its citizens. Portions of this counter-culture of protest were nonpolitical (Ken Kesey's San Francisco–based Merry Pranksters, for example, painted their faces with Day-Glo and inveigled protesters to "drop acid" and simply turn their backs on the war). But protest movements of the 1960s were by and large committed to making existing political frameworks responsive. Many believed that the Great Society could reconstruct the nation's cities, force corporations to clean up the air and water, provide for genuine equality of opportunity for all races, and even eliminate poverty. Others had faith that Ralph Nader and his "raiders" could mount and sustain a meaningful consumer movement and that Common Cause, an extensive liberal lobby established by former Department of Health, Education, and Welfare Secretary John Gardner, would significantly redress the balance in Congress. Not since the 1930s had Americans believed so mightily in the possibilities of change.

INTERPRETIVE ESSAY

Confronting the War Machine

Michael S. Foley

As I write this headnote to Michael Foley's story on the October 16, 1967, draft resistance gathering in Boston, I am reminded again of a brief, simple story from my own past. It was 1966, and I was finishing my first year as a graduate student in history at the University of Illinois in Urbana. For whatever reason, I wasn't content with my situation, and one day I phoned my draft board and asked what would happen if I were to quit school and do something else. The voice on the other end of the line was firm: "You'll be in the army in six weeks." I hung up, resolved to my fate. I stayed in school, courtesy of the 2-S (student) deferment that spared me from the draft and, later, from the first draft lottery, held December 1, 1969. By the time I completed my Ph.D. in 1970, I was too old to have to worry. As remarkable as it seems to me now, I don't think I fully understood how privileged my status had been until 1975, when I read James Fallows's account of the draft scene in Boston in the Washington Monthly, *denouncing a system that had protected the wealthy and educated and connected and sent the poor, the ignorant, the working class, and minorities off to war.*

Foley describes a transitional moment in the history of draft resistance. From the end of the Korean War in 1953, until 1965, there had been little opposition to the draft, in part because so few men were called, and in part because the system in use—the granting of deferments to those engaged in "vital activities" involving "national security" (including, apparently, the study of history) protected the middle-class students most likely to protest. By the end of 1965, with troop levels in Vietnam approaching 200,000 (they would reach 500,000 in 1968), a few young men began burning draft cards and thinking about other ways to protest the draft and end the war. (Congress made the destruction of a draft card an illegal act in 1965.) The first Boston demonstrations against the war and the draft took place in March and April of 1966. Acknowledging inequities in the deferment system, in March 1967 President Lyndon Johnson called for changes, including a lottery that was to begin in 1969. But he did not call for an end to undergraduate student deferments, and in April 1967, hundreds of thousands gathered in New York City's Central Park to protest the war, including about 170 who burned their draft cards. Over the summer, as the polls revealed that a majority of the American people disapproved of the way Johnson was handling the war in Vietnam (though not, until the following year, of the war itself), the New England Resistance looked forward to the mid-October demonstration in Boston.

Boston was a city of colleges and universities, and the resistance movement that developed there was thoughtful as well as passionate. As you read about the speeches and sermons delivered that day, think about what it was that motivated resistance to the draft and what ideas and institutions were central to it. Michael Foley has argued that the draft resisters were the antiwar equivalent of the Freedom Riders, the participants in lunch counter sit-ins, the students who integrated Little Rock High School, and others who have long been understood as heroic figures in the civil rights movement. Do you agree?

Obedience to a Higher Allegiance, Fall 1967

October 16 dawned clear and bright. Organizers carried chairs and sound equipment from the basement of the Arlington Street Church to the dewy, green rise of Flagstaff Hill, the only remaining hill on the Common. Flagstaff Hill and the parade grounds on its western slope (approaching Charles Street) have played host to innumerable public events in Boston's history, and in some ways, it was the ideal choice for the location of a rally aimed at encouraging resistance to conscription. The city once stored its gunpowder supply on top of the hill, and the Marquis de Lafayette, hero of the Revolution, ceremonially fired a cannon from the hill during a visit in 1824. Most significant for the Resistance, army officers used Flagstaff Hill as their recruiting station during the Civil War—the war to preserve the Union. Although the organizers who now set up chairs and a speaker system on that hallowed ground did so in preparation for an event that those Union officers might have found puzzling, the hill's patriotic heritage dove-tailed seamlessly with their own sense of the Resistance's adherence to—and desire to preserve—the best of American traditions.

By 10:00 A.M., small groups of young people began approaching Flagstaff Hill from all directions. When speeches began at 11:00, over 5,000 people stood or sat on the now-dry grass, listening. Buses filled with students from Dartmouth, Yale, Brown, the University of Rhode Island, the University of Massachusetts, and nearly every Boston-area college circled the Common looking for parking spots. Uniformed officers stood by with police dogs to cope with any potential violence. On the hill, in the middle of a group of seated young people, a middle-aged woman, blonde, wearing sunglasses, held a sign that read "LBJ KILLED MY *SON*." Dozens of people held signs. Some of the slogans included, "Suppose They Gave a War and Nobody Came?"; "The Resistance: Don't Dodge the Draft, Oppose It"; "Wars Will End When Men Refuse to Fight"; "The Resistance Shall Not End"; "UMB {UMass-Boston] Veterans Against the War"; "They Are Our Brothers Whom We Kill"; "No Draft—Don't Enlist—Refuse to Kill." Counterdemonstrators came armed with placards, too. One said "Tough Enough to Criticize, Too Weak to Defend—USMC," another, "Draft the Draft Dodgers—Yes LBJ." Two others, held by self-described Polish Freedom Fighter Josef Mlot-Mroz, said "Let's Fight Communism, Red Dupes, Vietniks, Peaceniks, and Clergy" and "Fight Communism and

Zionist Stooges, Peaceniks, Vietniks, and Anarchists." When Mlot-Mroz tried to disrupt the speeches, Bill Dowling attempted to force him out of the area; although the struggle did not escalate, police eventually took Mlot-Mroz into "protective custody."

Homer Jack chaired the rally and introduced the speakers, each of whom took turns at the microphone in the shadow of the Soldiers' Monument. Everyone who addressed the crowd emphasized morality, conscience, and the responsibilities of citizens. Rev. Harold Fray of the Eliot Church in Newton and chair of the Committee of Religious Concern for Peace stood first before the vast crowd in his clerical robe. "What does it profit a nation," he asked, "to impose its military might upon peoples of the world, while in so doing it loses it soul?" He called it a dark period in the nation's history but added, "The light will shine again when the moral conscience of America will not submit to national policies that violate honor, decency, human compassion and those qualities of life which alone make a nation strong." Fray praised the "great courage" of the men who would resist the draft on this day but told them that, henceforth, they would have to "bear the penalty of adverse public opinion and the long arm of government suppression." Better to endure those penalties, he concluded, "than to allow your consciences to atrophy because you were afraid to give expression to them." Ray Mungo, the director of Liberation News Service, spoke next, taking up the issue of draft resistance. He told the crowd that the prospect of going to jail should not be feared; indeed, he saw prison as "an honorable alternative to serving in Vietnam."

When Nick Egleson took the microphone next, he was not as sanguine about the prospects of a protest rooted in "individual conduct." Elgeson possessed extensive Movement credentials. He had been national president of SDS,* and in the fall of 1967 he assumed a leadership position in the Boston Draft Resistance Group. The thrust of what he said to the crowd sounded much like the SDS line—only more persuasive. First, he lamented the antiwar movement's lack of a "base of power" and what he saw as the resulting shift toward "moral acts" of protest. Specifically, he warned of the temptation to "measure actions in the movement by a code of individual conduct," to establish certain moral acts as minimum standards for appropriate dissent. He argued that "such an individual code easily becomes the primary or only standard for political conduct" and pointed to the nation's "individualist ethic," the "religious frame of reference," that so many protesters had adopted and the "absence of widespread political experience" as factors that pushed the movement toward an individual code and closed off the possibility of other political standards.

Ultimately, Elgeson acknowledged that that standard of individual conduct might be useful in organizing people on campuses—those not immediately threatened by the draft—but noted that "all the while the men of Charlestown and South Boston and Riverside, of Roxbury and Dorchester

*Founded in 1961 at the University of Michigan, SDS (Students for a Democratic Society) became the largest and most prominent of the radical, New Left organizations of the 1960s.—ed.

and of the working-class parts of cities all over the country are threatened by the draft and are more gently coerced by the security of enlistment." To address this issue he urged a prescription more consistent with the missions of the BDRG and SDS: "Our solution," he said, "must be to begin to organize those most threatened by the US armed forces. How many people gave out information about the October 16 rally in Boston in poor and working-class neighborhoods? Who put up posters speaking the language of those communities? Who tried to counter, thereby, the image the press promotes of us as hippies, cowards, and peace finks?" The BDRG, of course, had already been working in this direction for several months through the Early Morning Shows and their counseling efforts, so the Resistance saw no need to duplicate BDRG's work.

Egleson's speech startled some in the assembled crowd. Suddenly, they had to come to terms with one of the day's main speakers choosing not to provide the kind of ringing endorsement of draft resistance offered by the others. In fact, Egleson implied that draft resistance might amount to the kind of "useless martyrdom" that the BDRG had warned of in its recent newsletter. Although he did not address one of the Resistance's central hopes—that widespread resistance might actually create the base of power for which he longed (through the imprisonment of thousands of resisters and the resulting outrage of their parents)—his arguments gave some potential resisters reason to pause and reassess their plans for the day. David Clennon, a third-year graduate student at the Yale School of Drama, for instance, recalled that Egleson's speech prompted him to completely rethink his reason for being there. "When I heard Nick Egleson make his speech, I really began to have some serious doubts about what I was doing. Here was a guy who . . . had a lot of political savvy, much more than I had, [and he disagreed with the draft resistance strategy]." Clennon, who "came at [the movement] mostly from a kind of politically naive point of view [and] a very strong moral point of view" found himself "easily confused and easily swayed" by Egleson's arguments.

Just in time for Clennon and others, though, Boston University government professor and World War II veteran Howard Zinn strode to the microphone. Zinn, like Noam Chomsky, was by then a well-known critic of the war. He frequently participated in antiwar teach-ins on area campuses, and his recently published book, *Vietnam: The Logic of Withdrawal*, attracted a wide readership. Zinn did not respond directly to Egleson's critique of draft resistance as creating an uncomfortable standard of individual conduct by which all antiwar activity might be judged, however. Instead, the older man raised issues of a government's responsibilities to its citizens and the citizen's loyalty to his government. "Ever since governments were first formed and tyranny, the natural companion of government, began," he observed, "people have felt the need to gather in the forest or the mountains or in underground cellars, or, as here, under an open sky, to declare the rights of conscience against the inhumanity of government." The tyranny of the present administration had already killed 13,000 Americans, he said, and he criticized those men in positions of power for appointing themselves "guardians of every spot on the earth against Communism." Zinn derided policy makers for trying to save people everywhere from Communism, "whether the people want to be saved or not, and even if they have to kill them all to save them," and assailed President Johnson for breaking his pledge to those who supported him in the 1964 election on a peace platform. A government guilty of such betrayals and abuse of power, Zinn reasoned, no longer deserved the allegiance of its citizens. "I don't believe we owe loyalty to a government that lies to us," he said. "I do believe we owe loyalty to our fellow Americans who are in danger of being killed by the incompetence of this government."

Rather than emphasize the individual principled acts of defiance decried by Nick Egleson, Zinn argued for holding the government to a reasonable moral standard. He said he felt ashamed, "deeply ashamed," to call himself an American when he read, "and in the most conservative newspapers," that the U.S. Air Force had "bombed again and again the residential areas of North Vietnamese cities, that it has bombed, again and again—too often to be an accident—villages that are devoid of military significance, that it has bombed a hospital for lepers in North Vietnam 13 times." He repeated, "I am ashamed, and I want to disassociate myself from these acts. That is not my idea of what America should stand for." In the end, although individual morality surely intertwined with responsibilities of citizenship, for Zinn the latter provided the most compelling reason for draft resistance. "We owe it to our conscience, to the people of this country, to the principles of American democracy," he concluded, "to declare our independence of this war, to resist it in every way we can, until it comes to an end, until there is peace in Vietnam."

As the last speaker at the demonstration, Zinn called on those who planned to turn in their draft cards to assemble in one area of the hill from which they would be directed to take their places in the column of marchers that would walk to the Arlington Street Church. David Clennon, his doubts assuaged, joined the line. Zinn "spoke so eloquently about the horrors of the war," he remembered, "that I was convinced all over again that turning in my draft card was the right thing to do." He felt so committed, he began to weep. "I was crying with relief I think . . . that I was about to do the right thing as dangerous and controversial as it seemed to be. . . . I was just overcome emotionally but I really felt solid then in my decision about what I was doing."

Most participants marched purposefully, quietly. Others were more expressive and playful. Marshals organized the marchers into distinct groups. The clergy led, followed by Veterans for Peace, then the resisters. This order gave the march a well-planned look of respectability. Moreover, the resisters themselves did not look like "hippies, cowards, and peace finks." The hair on some men touched their ears and collars, but most hairstyles were fairly clean cut. A few beards could be seen, but the vast majority of men had bare faces. Many wore coats and ties, perhaps because they were going to church, or because they wanted to somehow demonstrate the gravity of the act they were about to undertake. The second Resistance newsletter had instructed its readers to "smile as you march, but think defiance." They marched across the Common to Tremont Street, down Tremont to

Boylston Street, and down Boylston to the church at the southwest corner of the Public Gardens. According to one report, a woman crossing Tremont Street saw the marchers and, obviously disgusted, turned to a police officer and said: "Why don't you send them all back to Cambridge?" "Oh, they're from all over," he answered. As the marchers approached their destination, the carillon in the tower of the church played "We Shall Overcome."

The church filled quickly, leaving nearly 3,000 other participants outside waiting to hear the service over loudspeakers. The actor Peter Ustinov, in town for a performance, mingled with the crowd. (When reporters asked him if he was with the Resistance, he responded: "No, because I am British. But if I were an American I would be part of the group.") Like some of the oldest churches in New England, the pews at Arlington Street are separated into boxes that the church's earliest parishioners (or "proprietors") could purchase. About 1,000 people squeezed into these boxes and the balconies above and sat on the lumpy cushions filled with horsehair. Reporters took notes, flashbulbs flashed, and an NBC News photographer standing in the balcony with correspondent Sander van Ocur trained his camera on the sanctuary below. The atmosphere was hushed, respectful—and *electric*.

The printed programs called it "A Service of Conscience and Acceptance," and all of the speakers emphasized moral and religious justifications for civil disobedience. After Jack Mendelsohn gave the invocation, the congregation sang "Once to Every Man and Nation":

> *Once to every man and nation*
> *Comes the moment to decide*
> *In the strife of truth with falsehood,*
> *For the good or evil side;*
> *Some great cause, God's new Messiah,*
> *Off'ring each the bloom or blight,*
> *And the choice goes by forever*
> *'Twixt that darkness and that light.*

A responsive reading ("The Young Dead Soldiers") followed, and, after that, Alex Jack read a Vietnamese prayer.

The real power of the service, however, derived from the four addresses—or sermons—given. Like the speeches on the Common, the statements given in the church are worth considering in detail because of their incomplete coverage in the press. Two graduate students spoke first. Jim Harney, a Catholic studying for the priesthood at St. John's Seminary in nearby Brighton, told the congregation that he had spent the last few weeks reading about German "men of faith" who stood up to the Third Reich and paid for it with their lives. "Their witness," he said, "has affected my life enormously." He quoted Father Alfred Delp, a German priest who did not survive the concentration camps: "The most pious prayer can become a blasphemy if he who offers it tolerates or helps to further conditions which are fatal to mankind, which render him unacceptable to God, or weaken his spiritual, moral or religious senses." Harney then cited the German peasant Franz Jagerstatter, who also died "in a solitary protest": "For what purpose did God endow all men with reason, and free will, if, in spite of this, we are obliged to render blind obedience, or if, as so many also say, the individual is not qualified to judge whether this war started by Germany is just or unjust? What purpose is served by the ability to distinguish between good and evil?"

Angered by his country's actions in Vietnam and burdened by a conscience that would not allow him to study quietly for the priesthood while his ministerial deferment protected him from the draft, the twenty-seven-year-old seminarian found inspiration in the example set by these little-known German heroes. "For me, he explained, "these words from the past have great meaning: my faith is put on the line, and above all, my life is directed to the cross-roads of the living. . . . Now I must take a stand on behalf of the living. Conscience must prevail." Harney argued that "man's transcendent dignity brings him not only inalienable rights but also an awesome responsibility" and that, consequently, he could not stand by "while the very survival of the Vietnamese people is in jeopardy." Indeed, to make his stand with Franz Jagerstatter and Father Delp, "who opted for life rather than death," Harney added his voice to the 2,500 ministers, priests, and rabbis who urged Johnson to, "in the Name of God," stop the war. "And further than this," he concluded, "on this October the 16th, I resist." A year later, Harney went on to greater notoriety as a member, with Bob Cunnane, of the Milwaukee 14, a group of Catholic pacifists who, following the examples of Daniel and Philip Berrigan, raided a Milwaukee draft board and destroyed thousands of files. As a seminarian about to break the law on October 16, however, he risked being barred from the priesthood, for which he had been preparing himself for so long.

Michael Ferber followed Harney to the pulpit. He felt comfortable in such situations. He had delivered sermons at his home church in Buffalo, and as one of the main speakers for the New England Resistance (for whom he gave talks or "raps" almost daily), his "low-key Harvard style" seemed ideally suited for this moment. In what Howard Zinn later called an "extraordinary, passionate, personal statement," the twenty-three-year-old graduate student began: "We are gathered in this church today in order to do something very simple: to say No. We have come from many different places and backgrounds and we have many different ideas about ourselves and the world, but we have come here to show that we are united to do one thing: to say No. Each of our acts of returning our draft cards is our personal No; when we put them in a single container or set fire to them from a single candle we express the simple basis of our unity."

Still, Ferber warned, they would not be able to form a real community "if a negative is all we share." Albert Camus, he noted, said that "the rebel, who says No, is also one who says Yes, and that when he draws a line beyond which he will refuse to cooperate, he is affirming the values on the other side of that line. For us who come here today, what is it that we affirm, what is it to which we can say Yes?" Before they answered that question, Ferber told the congregation, they must acknowledge the differences that existed within the inchoate Resistance community. For one, many of those assembled might feel a sense of hypocrisy for participating in the religious trappings of the day's ceremonies because they themselves were not churchgoers. In response, he told of the "great tradition within the church and synagogue which has always struggled against the conservative worldly forces that have always been in control." In modern times, he said, that radical tradition "has tried to recall us to the best ways of living our lives: the way of love and compassion, the way of justice and respect, the way of facing other people as human beings and not as abstract representatives of something alien and evil." That religious tradition, he said, "is something to which we can say Yes."

Ferber then warned the assembly not to "confuse the ceremony and symbolism" of the service with the "reality" that they were only a few hundred people "with very little power." He told them that American policy would not change overnight, that, indeed, the "world will be in pretty much the same mess it is in today" and that because they, as a community, would have to "dig in for the long haul," October 16 represented not the end, but the beginning. To change the country, he said, would mean "struggles and anguish day in and day out for years . . . it will mean people dedicating their lives and possibly losing them for a cause we can only partly define and whose outcome we can only guess at."

As he moved toward his conclusion, in the most important part of the sermon, Ferber engaged the critique of "moral acts" as protest made by his old friend and former roommate at Swarthmore, Nick Egleson. To Egleson's charge that resistance grew from moralistic and personal, rather than political, motivation, Ferber again cited Camus, who, he said, "believed that politics is an extension of morality, that the truly moral man is engaged in politics as a natural outcome of his beliefs." The issue is not the difference "between the man whose moral thinking leads him to political action and the man whose moral thinking leads him no farther than to his own 'sinlessness.' It is the difference between the man who is willing to go dirty himself in the outside world and the man who wishes to stay 'clean' and 'pure.'"

Ferber, therefore, acknowledged the potential damage that moral actions could have on the antiwar movement. This kind of "sinlessness" and "purity," he said, is "arrogant pride" and "we must say No to it." "The martyr who offers himself meekly as a lamb to the altar is a fool," he warned. "We cannot honor him . . . unless he has helped the rest of us." The morally pure act of draft resistance would be useful in ending the war only if it produced a tangible political effect beyond cleansing the souls of those who carried it out. Ferber concluded:

> Let us make sure we are ready to work hard and long with each other in the months to come, working to make it difficult and politically dangerous for the government to prosecute us, working to help anyone and everyone find ways to avoid the draft, to help disrupt the workings of the draft and the armed forces until the war is over. Let us make sure we can form a community. Let us make sure we can let others depend on us. If we can say Yes to these things, and to the religious tradition that stands with us today, and to the fact that today marks not the End but a Beginning, and to the

long hard dirty job ahead of us—if we can say Yes to all this, then let us come forward together and say No to the United States Government. Then let our Yes be the loudest No our government ever heard.

Michael Ferber's emphasis on community formation as the key to supporting the moral purpose of the Resistance and moving it into the political arena highlighted an issue about which organizers truly worried. Up until the end of the ceremony, planners thought that everyone who resisted might well be rounded up and arrested on the spot. When that did not happen, they committed themselves to maintain the solidarity felt in the church among the now-scattered brethren of the Resistance. It would not be easy. They soon learned that the government would not go after them as a community, but individually. Building a community under such circumstances could be difficult. But in the church on that day, the sense of fellowship engendered by Ferber's speech and the simple feeling of being surrounded by others who were equally passionate about ending the war inflated their hopes.

For the keynote address of the service, Alex Jack had recruited Rev. Coffin, a veteran of the Second World War, a former CIA operative, and now a chaplain at Yale University and a tireless antiwar protester. He also had a playful sense of humor. When he arrived that morning and encountered Jack Mendelsohn, he told him that he wished the service were taking place in a Presbyterian church but said, "I have to hand it to you Unitarians: you really know how to combine a thin theology with a thick ethic."

For nearly two years, Coffin had been one of the leading lights of Clergy and Laymen Concerned About Vietnam (CALCAV) and gained considerable notoriety as one of its most articulate spokesmen. That quality was in evidence on October 16. He began by quoting Socrates and St. Peter, both of whom chose to follow their consciences before obeying others. Their words, Coffin said, "tell us that because there is a higher and hopefully future order of things, men at times will feel constrained to disobey the law out of a sense of obedience to a higher allegiance." To hundreds of history's most revered heroes, he said, "not to serve the state has appeared the best way to love one's neighbor," and he cited Milton, Bunyon, Gandhi, Nehru, as examples. Coffin then answered the charges of critics who argued that civil disobedience is the first step on the road to anarchy. The "heroes" he listed did not try to "destroy the legal order," Coffin said. In fact, "by accepting the legal punishment, they actually upheld it." Furthermore, like those assembled before him, these men broke the law as "a last, not as a first resort" and once they did, "they were determined to bend their every effort to the end that the law reflect and not reject their best understanding of justice and mercy."

The central force driving the incipient Resistance, Coffin argued, was the issue of conscience: "Let us be blunt. To us the war in Vietnam is a crime. And if we are correct, if the war is a crime, then is it criminal to refuse to have anything to do with it? Is it we who are demoralizing our boys in Vietnam, or the Administration which is asking them to do immoral things?" He then called on churches and synagogues to provide sanctuary for draft resisters. He quoted from the twenty-third Psalm ("Thou spread-

Dr. William Sloan Coffin, Jr., Yale University chaplain, waits for verdict on draft conspiracy charges against him in Boston, Massachusetts, June 14, 1968. Coffin and three others were found guilty of counseling young men to avoid the military draft. AP/Wide World Photos.

est a table before me in the presence of mine enemies") and explained that the passage referred to "an ancient desert law which provided that if a man hunted by his enemies sought refuge with another man who offered him hospitality, then the enemies of the man had to remain outside the rim of the campfire light for two nights and the day intervening." In the Middle Ages, Coffin explained, this practice expanded until every church in Europe was considered a sanctuary even for common criminals. Coffin acknowledged that if the American government decided that "the arm of the law was long enough to reach inside a church," the church would be unable to prevent an arrest. "What else can a church do?" he asked. "Are we to raise conscientious men and then not stand by them in their hour of conscience?" He concluded by noting that the resisters assembled that day were taking action within two weeks of the 450th anniversary of the Reformation. He urged them on in their new reformation, their reformation of conscience: "You stand now as Luther stood in his time. May you be inspired to speak, and we to hear, the words he once spoke in conscience and in all simplicity: 'Here I stand, I can do no other. God help me.'"

The Reverend George H. Williams, also recruited by Alex Jack, his nephew, spoke last and gave the call for draft cards, the "Call to Acceptance." The appearance of this very distinguished looking man, a Harvard professor and one of the nation's leading scholars in religious history, shocked many of the faculty and students at Harvard. Few of them would have expected him to align himself so publicly—and so forcefully—with the leading edge of the antiwar movement. Alex Jack remembers that "the general feeling about my uncle was that he was trapped in the twelfth century . . . people would assume he was conservative." Williams himself stated on October 16 that he was one of the more "conservative" members of the clergy to participate. On this day, though, he displayed a moral outrage that belied that image.

Williams began by explaining that during a just war he would view the exemption of clergy and conscientious objectors favorably, as an act representative of "a high degree of moral sensibility" on the part of the society in question. But he did not believe the war in Vietnam to be a just war. Therefore, he agreed to stand with the resisters in their protest. He told the congregation that, like "countless others," he had sought to register his opposition to the war in Vietnam through all the "appropriate channels of democratic, academic, and religious activity." When that failed, however, Williams concluded that the administration would "only take notice of a resolute show of moral force." He said, "I am driven to show my solidarity with fellow seminarians in an act of civil disobedience out of moral indignation at the miscarriage of American ideals of international behavior. What we are doing in Vietnam is not appropriate for a great society with a long religious heritage."

Perhaps more important, Williams made a case for draft resisters as acting within firmly established democratic and religious traditions: "We interpret the action of these seminarians as moral courage, and we trust that the democratic society of which we are a part will look upon this solemn action of moral dissociation as redemptive for our society, that the Church herself in all lands and in times to come will count these young men as true servants of the peaceable kingdom." To understand the act of resistance in this way, Williams said, did not detract from the heroism of "our fighting men in Vietnam," and he also recognized that "an orderly nation has the right to make grave demands upon its citizens in time of conflict or emergency." But citizens also have the right "to determine what constitutes licit demand" upon their lives—"in other words," he argued, "what constitutes a just war."

As he neared the end of his address, perhaps anticipating that in addition to the collection of draft cards, some men might burn their cards, he argued against such an act. "I deplore the burning of draft cards," he said. "The more solemn and responsible act is to withdraw from the social covenant on this specific issue of conscience against a barbaric, unnecessary war being waged between pitifully unmatched opponents in quite disparate stages of national and social evolution. The manner of dissociation from this unjust war should be solemn and not impetuous, anguished but not disorderly, respectful but resolute." He then asked the resisters to come forward, and he stepped down from the pulpit to the edge of the chancel, where the

Reverends Mendelsohn and Coffin, Father Cunnane, and Harvard philosopher Hilary Putnam (who had been recruited to accept cards from the nonreligious resisters) joined him. Each held an offering plate for the collection of draft cards.

All eyes (and cameras) turned toward the forward pews. Flashes popped as the first man rose, jiggled the stubborn latch on the old door at the end of the pew, and stepped out into the aisle. As he walked forward, several other men stood and began moving toward the aisle and their moment of truth. Although the promotional leaflets predicted that 500 men would turn in their draft cards and join the Resistance in Boston, organizers had commitments from only about 20 to 25 men. They were hopeful for maybe 50. It soon became apparent that many, many more would resist on this day. The first trickle of men quickly became a steady stream that continued to swell for over twenty minutes. They came not just from the pews reserved for resisters but from all corners of the church. At one point, someone pushed open the massive church doors to let resisters in from outside. At least one woman, the Reverend Nan Stone, joined the long line as it moved slowly, quietly. When she reached the altar, she burned Steve Pailet's card in the flame of a candle held by one of William Ellery Channing's own candlesticks. As they turned over or burned their cards, some of the men smiled. Others wept softly. No one spoke above a whisper. The loudest sounds came from the TV cameras whirring away in the balcony. It seemed like the procession would never end. There were brief exchanges of encouragement between the resisters and their older accomplices holding the plates. When a student he recognized from the law school at Yale handed him his card, though, Coffin tried to give it back. "Don't be a fool," he said. "With this on your record you would destroy a law career." The resister replied, calmly, "I don't care. I know I'm not going to become a lawyer." He then broke the law.

When the last man placed his card on top of the pile sprouting from one of the collection plates, elated Resistance organizers hugged one another. "The most irreligious of us," Bill Dowling later said, "perhaps, are ready now to believe in miracles." After the service ended, they counted 214 cards turned in with another 67 burned at Channing's flame. NBC News correspondent Sander van Ocur, tears in his eyes, descended from the balcony to speak to his friend Bill Coffin. "What a country this would be," he said, "if something like this were now to take place in every church."

Indeed, it had been a surprisingly moving day for many of those in attendance and a gratifying culmination to many long hours of planning by New England Resistance organizers. As the strategy of noncompliance came under attack by other antiwar and New Left groups in preceding weeks, few of them could have predicted the success of October 16. The call for draft resistance resulted in the mobilization of the largest antiwar rally the city had yet seen and a much greater number of returned draft cards than anyone anticipated. More important, the day signaled the successful transformation of the CNVA pacifists' individual defiant acts into a large-scale, mass protest that organizers believed would have lasting political effect. And, as Sander van Ocur's reaction indicated, the moral clarity of the participants came through in a serious, respectful, and thoughtful confrontation with the government. In the days and weeks that followed, the media and the public often missed that point, but leaders of this new driving force in the antiwar movement were heartened by the extensive coverage they did receive. Draft resistance, it seemed, could not now be ignored.

Resisting the Draft: A Statistical Profile

The tables in this section offer a statistical profile of the draft resisters and their parents. Who were the draft resisters? And who were they not?

Resisters' Parents' Level of Education

Highest Level of Education Achieved	Fathers		Mothers	
	No.	%	No.	%
Some grade school	6	5.1	3	2.6
Completed grade school	4	3.4	3	2.6
Some high school	6	5.1	9	7.7
Completed high school	18	15.4	26	22.2
Some post–high school training	10	8.5	9	7.7
Some college	16	13.7	19	16.2
Completed college	13	11.1	27	23.0
Some graduate school	7	6.0	4	3.4
M.A. or M.S.	7	6.0	11	9.4
Professional degree	16	13.7	5	4.3
Master's plus additional grad work	3	2.6	0	0.0
Doctorate	11	9.4	1	0.9
Total	117	100	117	100

Source: 1997 Boston Draft Resistance Survey.

Resisters' Parents' Occupations

Occupation	Fathers		Mothers	
	No.	%	No.	%
Semiskilled or unskilled	5	4.3	2	1.7
Skilled	13	11.3	1	0.9
Farmer	2	1.7	0	0.0
Clerical or sales	15	13.0	20	17.2
Proprietor	13	11.3	2	1.7
Professional	67	58.3	31	26.7
Homemaker	0	0.0	60	51.7
Total	115	99.9[a]	116	99.9[a]

Source: 1997 Boston Draft Resistance Survey.

[a]Percentages do not total 100 due to rounding.

From *Confronting the War Machine: Draft Resistance During the Vietnam War* by Michael S. Foley. Copyright © 2003 by the University of North Carolina Press. Used by permission of the publisher.

Resisters' Class Status

Class Description	No.	%
Working class	12	10.0
Lower middle class	13	10.8
Middle class	53	44.2
Upper middle class	40	33.3
Upper class	2	1.7
Total	120	100

Source: 1997 Boston Draft Resistance Survey.

Religious Affiliations of Resisters and Their Parents

Denomination	Fathers		Mothers		Resisters	
	No.	%	No.	%	No.	%
Agnostic	8	7.1	5	4.3	30	25.4
Atheist	10	8.8	6	5.2	20	16.9
Baptist	0	0.0	1	0.9	0	0.0
Congregational	6	5.3	5	4.3	3	2.5
Episcopal	16	14.2	17	14.7	7	5.9
Jehovah's Witness	0	0.0	0	0.0	0	0.0
Jewish	27	23.9	29	25.0	18	15.3
Lutheran	1	0.9	1	0.9	1	0.8
Mennonite	0	0.0	0	0.0	0	0.0
Methodist	8	7.1	10	8.6	4	3.4
Presbyterian	11	9.7	10	8.6	3	2.5
Quaker	0	0.0	0	0.0	4	3.4
Unitarian-Universalist	10	8.8	12	10.3	15	12.7
Roman Catholic	11	9.7	14	12.1	5	4.2
Other	5	4.4	6	5.2	8	6.8
Total	113	99.9[a]	116	100.1[a]	118	99.8[a]

Source: 1997 Boston Draft Resistance Survey.

[a]Percentages do not total 100 due to rounding.

Political Leanings of Resisters and Their Parents

Political Identity	Fathers		Mothers		Resisters	
	No.	%	No.	%	No.	%
Conservative Republican	15	13.0	6	5.2	1	0.9
Moderate Republican	27	23.5	28	24.1	1	0.9
Moderate Democrat	21	18.3	28	24.1	6	5.1
Liberal Democrat	41	35.7	46	39.7	48	41.0
Socialist/Communist	4	3.5	4	3.4	29	24.8
Anarchist	1	0.9	1	0.9	17	14.5
No preference	3	2.6	3	2.6	7	6.0
Other	3	2.6	0	0.0	8	6.8
Total	115	100.1[a]	116	100.0	117	100.0

Source: 1997 Boston Draft Resistance Survey.

[a]Percentage does not total 100 due to rounding.

Vietnam

For more than two decades, the United States tried, and failed, to create a Vietnam suitable to its own vision of the postwar world. This failure became most apparent in the 1960s, when the fighting of the war divided Americans into bitter factions. Apologists for John Kennedy believed that he would have avoided full-scale involvement. But Kennedy had remarked that a withdrawal from Vietnam would mean collapse in Southeast Asia; and by 1963 he had sent 15,000 advisers to the country, more than fifteen times Dwight Eisenhower's commitment. Lyndon Johnson also believed in the domino theory and defined the Vietnam problem as simple communist aggression, and in 1964, he inaugurated systematic air attacks on North Vietnam. But neither the air war nor an additional half-million American troops were sufficient to bring anything resembling victory. Even before the January 1968 Tet offensive, when Viet Cong and North Vietnamese attacks on major South Vietnamese cities made clear that the American claim to be winning the war was a sham, many Americans had come to question the war in moral terms. Over 200,000 marched against the war in Washington, D.C., in 1967. When Richard Nixon in 1970 moved ground troops into Cambodia, students closed down many colleges and universities in protest. By 1973, as Nixon withdrew the last of the nation's ground troops, the Eisenhower consensus lay in ruins.

To illustrate the polarization that the Vietnam War produced, and to offer some sense of how reasonable people could find themselves at loggerheads over this conflict, we have assembled two disparate views on the war. The first, a 1965 address by President Lyndon Johnson, reveals how a socially engaged, activist president could see the war as a high priority and, indeed, allow the war to interfere with his domestic agenda.

The second perspective is a 1971 statement delivered to a Senate committee by John Kerry, a future senator from Massachusetts. In 2004, when Kerry ran unsuccessfully for president, these remarks, and his antiwar position, were condemned by some Vietnam veterans, who argued that Kerry had demeaned American soldiers and prolonged the war.

How did Johnson defend the war in Vietnam? How would Kerry have responded to Johnson's arguments? Were twenty-first century veterans right to be upset with Kerry for a position he had taken more than three decades before?

DEBATES

Lyndon Johnson

Pattern for Peace in Southeast Asia (1965)

Last week seventeen nations sent their views to some two dozen countries having an interest in Southeast Asia. We are joining those seventeen countries and stating our American policy tonight, which we believe will contribute toward peace in this area of the world.

I have come here to review once again with my own people the views of the American government.

Tonight Americans and Asians are dying for a world where each people may choose its own path to change. This is the principle for which our ancestors fought in the valleys of Pennsylvania. It is a principle for which our sons fight tonight in the jungles of Vietnam.

Vietnam is far away from this quiet campus. We have no territory there, nor do we seek any. The war is dirty and brutal and difficult. And some 400 young men, born into an America that is bursting with opportunity and promise, have ended their lives on Vietnam's steaming soil.

Why must we take this painful road? Why must this nation hazard its ease, its interest, and its power for the sake of a people so far away?

We fight because we must fight if we are to live in a world where every country can shape its own destiny, and only in such a world will our own freedom be finally secure.

This kind of world will never be built by bombs or bullets. Yet the infirmities of man are such that force must often precede reason and the waste of war, the works of peace. We wish that this were not so. But we must deal with the world as it is, if it is ever to be as we wish.

The world as it is in Asia is not a serene or peaceful place.

The first reality is that North Vietnam has attacked the independent nation of South Vietnam. Its object is total conquest. Of course, some of the people of South Vietnam are participating in attack on their own government. But trained men and supplies, orders and arms, flow in a constant stream from north to south.

This support is the heartbeat of the war.

Speech made at Johns Hopkins University, Baltimore, Maryland, April 17, 1965, Department of State *Bulletin*, April 26, 1965, pp. 606–610.

And it is a war of unparalleled brutality. Simple farmers are the targets of assassination and kidnapping. Women and children are strangled in the night because their men are loyal to their government. And helpless villages are ravaged by sneak attacks. Large-scale raids are conducted on towns, and terror strikes in the heart of cities.

The confused nature of this conflict cannot mask the fact that it is the new face of an old enemy.

Over this war—and all Asia—is another reality: the deepening shadow of Communist China. The rulers in Hanoi are urged on by Beijing. This is a regime that has destroyed freedom in Tibet, attacked India, and has been condemned by the United Nations for aggression in Korea. It is a nation that is helping the forces of violence in almost every continent. The contest in Vietnam is part of a wider pattern of aggressive purposes.

Why Are We in South Vietnam?

Why are these realities our concern? Why are we in South Vietnam?

We are there because we have a promise to keep. Since 1954 every American president has offered support to the people of South Vietnam. We have helped to build, and we have helped to defend. Thus, over many years, we have made a national pledge to help South Vietnam defend its independence.

And I intend to keep that promise.

To dishonor that pledge, to abandon this small and brave nation to its enemies, and to the terror that must follow, would be an unforgivable wrong.

We are also there to strengthen world order. Around the globe, from Berlin to Thailand, are people whose well-being rests in part on the belief that they can count on us if they are attacked. To leave Vietnam to its fate would shake the confidence of all these people in the value of an American commitment and in the value of America's word. The result would be increased unrest and instability, and even wider war.

We are also there because there are great stakes in the balance. Let no one think for a moment that retreat from Vietnam would bring an end to conflict. The battle would be renewed in one country and then another. The central lesson of our time is that the appetite of aggression is never satisfied. To withdraw from one battlefield means only to prepare for the next. We must say in Southeast Asia—as we did in Europe—in the words of the Bible: "Hitherto shalt thou come, but no further."

There are those who say that all our effort there will be futile—that China's power is such that it is bound to dominate all Southeast Asia. But there is no end to that argument until all the nations of Asia are swallowed up.

There are those who wonder why we have a responsibility there. Well, we have it there for the same reason that we have a responsibility for the defense of Europe. World War II was fought in both Europe and Asia, and when it ended we found ourselves with continued responsibility for the defense of freedom.

Our objective is the independence of South Vietnam and its freedom from attack. We want nothing for ourselves—only that the people of South

Vietnam be allowed to guide their own country in their own way. We will do everything necessary to reach that objective, and we will do only what is absolutely necessary.

In recent months attacks on South Vietnam were stepped up. Thus it became necessary for us to increase our response and to make attacks by air. This is not a change of purpose. It is a change in what we believe that purpose requires.

We do this in order to slow down aggression.

We do this to increase the confidence of the brave people of South Vietnam who have bravely borne this brutal battle for so many years with so many casualties.

And we do this to convince the leaders of North Vietnam—and all who seek to share their conquest—of a simple fact:

We will not be defeated.

We will not grow tired.

We will not withdraw, either openly or under the cloak of a meaningless agreement.

We know that air attacks alone will not accomplish all these purposes. But it is our best and prayerful judgment that they are a necessary part of the surest road to peace.

The Path of Peaceful Settlement

We hope that peace will come swiftly. But that is in the hands of others besides ourselves. And we must be prepared for a long continued conflict. It will require patience as well as bravery—the will to endure as well as the will to resist.

I wish it were possible to convince others with words of what we now find it necessary to say with guns and planes: armed hostility is futile—our resources are equal to any challenge—because we fight for values and we fight for principle, rather than territory or colonies, our patience and our determination are unending.

Once this is clear, then it should also be clear that the only path for reasonable men is the path of peaceful settlement. Such peace demands an independent South Vietnam—securely guaranteed and able to shape its own relationships to all others—free from outside interference—tied to no alliance—a military base for no other country.

These are the essentials of any final settlement.

We will never be second in the search for such a peaceful settlement in Vietnam.

There may be many ways to this kind of peace: in discussion or negotiation with the governments concerned; in large groups or in small ones; in the reaffirmation of old agreements or their strengthening with new ones.

We have stated this position over and over again fifty times and more to friend and foe alike. And we remain ready with this purpose for unconditional discussions.

And until that bright and necessary day of peace we will try to keep conflict from spreading. We have no desire to see thousands die in battle— Asians or Americans. We have no desire to devastate that which the people of North Vietnam have built with toil and sacrifice. We will use our power with restraint and with all the wisdom that we can command.

But we will use it.

A Cooperative Effort for Development

This war, like most wars, is filled with terrible irony. For what do the people of North Vietnam want? They want what their neighbors also desire— food for their hunger, health for their bodies, a chance to learn, progress for their country, and an end to the bondage of material misery. And they would find all these things far more readily in peaceful association with others than in the endless course of battle.

These countries of Southeast Asia are homes for millions of impoverished people. Each day these people rise at dawn and struggle through until the night to wrest existence from the soil. They are often wracked by diseases, plagued by hunger, and death comes at the early age of forty.

Stability and peace do not come easily in such a land. Neither independence nor human dignity will ever be won, though, by arms alone. It also requires the works of peace. The American people have helped generously in times past in these works, and now there must be a much more massive effort to improve the life of man in that conflict-torn corner of our world.

The first step is for the countries of Southeast Asia to associate themselves in a greatly expanded cooperative effort for development. We would hope that North Vietnam would take its place in the common effort just as soon as peaceful cooperation is possible.

The United Nations is already actively engaged in development in this area, and as far back as 1961 I conferred with our authorities in Vietnam in connection with their work there. And I would hope tonight that the secretary-general of the United Nations could use the prestige of his great office and his deep knowledge of Asia to initiate, as soon as possible, with the countries of that area, a plan for cooperation in increased development.

For our part I will ask the Congress to join in a billion-dollar American investment in this effort as soon as it is under way. And I would hope that all other industrialized countries, including the Soviet Union, will join in this effort to replace despair with hope and terror with progress.

The task is nothing less than to enrich the hopes and existence of more than a hundred million people. And there is much to be done.

The vast Mekong River can provide food and water and power on a scale to dwarf even our own TVA [Tennessee Valley Authority]. The wonders of modern medicine can be spread through villages where thousands die every year from lack of care. Schools can be established to train people in the skills needed to manage the process of development. And these objectives, and more, are within the reach of a cooperative and determined effort.

I also intend to expand and speed up a program to make available our farm surpluses to assist in feeding and clothing the needy in Asia. We should not allow people to go hungry and wear rags while our own warehouses overflow with an abundance of wheat and corn and rice and cotton.

So I will very shortly name a special team of outstanding, patriotic, and distinguished Americans to inaugurate our participation in these programs. This team will be headed by Mr. Eugene Black, the very able former president of the World Bank.

The Dream of Our Generation

This will be a disorderly planet for a long time. In Asia, and elsewhere, the forces of the modern world are shaking old ways and uprooting ancient civilizations. There will be turbulence and struggle and even violence. Great social change—as we see in our own country—does not always come without conflict.

We must also expect that nations will on occasion be in dispute with us. It may be because we are rich, or powerful, or because we have made some mistakes, or because they honestly fear our intentions. However, no nation need ever fear that we desire their land, or to impose our will, or to dictate their institutions.

But we will always oppose the effort of one nation to conquer another nation.

We will do this because our own security is at stake.

But there is more to it than that. For our generation has a dream. It is a very old dream. But we have the power, and now we have the opportunity to make that dream come true.

For centuries nations have struggled among each other. But we dream of a world where disputes are settled by law and reason. And we will try to make it so.

For most of history men have hated and killed one another in battle. But we dream of an end to war. And we will try to make it so.

For all existence most men have lived in poverty, threatened by hunger. But we dream of a world where all are fed and charged with hope. And we will help to make it so.

The ordinary men and women of North Vietnam and South Vietnam, of China and India, of Russia and America, are brave people. They are filled with the same proportions of hate and fear, of love and hope. Most of them want the same things for themselves and their families. Most of them do not want their sons to ever die in battle, or to see their homes, or the homes of others, destroyed.

Well, this can be their world yet. Man now has the knowledge—always before denied—to make this planet serve the real needs of the people who live on it.

I know this will not be easy. I know how difficult it is for reason to guide passion, and love to master hate. The complexities of this world do not bow easily to pure and consistent answers.

But the simple truths are there just the same. We just all try to follow them as best we can.

Power, Witness to Human Folly

We often say how impressive power is. But I do not find it impressive at all. The guns and the bombs, the rockets and the warships, are all symbols of human failure. They are necessary symbols. They protect what we cherish. But they are witness to human folly.

A dam built across a great river is impressive.

In the countryside where I was born, and where I live, I have seen the night illuminated, and the kitchen warmed, and the home heated, where once the cheerless night and the ceaseless cold held sway. And all this happened because electricity came to our area along the humming wires of the REA [Rural Electrification Administration]. Electrification of the countryside—yes, that, too, is impressive.

A rich harvest in a hungry land is impressive.

The sight of healthy children in a classroom is impressive.

These—not mighty arms—are the achievements that the American nation believes to be impressive. And if we are steadfast, the time may come when all other nations will also find it so.

Every night before I turn out the lights to sleep I ask myself this question: Have I done everything that I can do to unite this country? Have I done everything I can to help unite the world, to try to bring peace and hope to all the peoples of the world? Have I done enough?

Ask yourselves that question in your homes—and in this hall tonight. Have we, each of us, all done all we can do? Have we done enough?

We may well be living in the time foretold many years ago when it was said: "I call heaven and earth to record this day against you, that I have set before you life and death, blessing and cursing: therefore choose life, that both thou and thy seed may live."

This generation of the world must choose: destroy or build, kill or aid, hate or understand. We can do all these things on a scale that has never been dreamed of before.

Well, we will choose life. And so doing, we will prevail over the enemies within man, and over the natural enemies of all mankind.

President Lyndon Johnson listens to a tape recording from his son-in-law, Capt. Charles Robb, who was a Marine Corp Company Commander in Vietnam. July 31, 1968. Photo by Jack Kightlinger. Lyndon Baines Johnson Library, National Archives.

John Kerry

Vietnam Veterans Against the War (1971)

Thank you very much, Senator Fulbright, Senator Javits, Senator Symington, Senator Pell. I would like to say for the record, and also for the men behind me who are also wearing the uniform and their medals, that my sitting here is really symbolic. I am not here as John Kerry. I am here as one member of the group of 1,000, which is a small representation of a very much larger group of veterans in this country, and were it possible for all of them to sit at this table they would be here and have the same kind of testimony.

I would simply like to speak in very general terms. I apologize if my statement is general because I received notification yesterday you would hear me and I am afraid that because of the court injunction I was up most of the night and haven't had a great deal of time to prepare for this hearing.

I would like to talk on behalf of all those veterans and say that several months ago in Detroit we had an investigation at which over 150 honorably discharged, and many very highly decorated, veterans testified to war crimes committed in Southeast Asia. These were not isolated incidents but crimes committed on a day to day basis with the full awareness of officers at all levels of command.

It is impossible to describe to you exactly what did happen in Detroit—the emotions in the room and the feelings of the men who were reliving their experiences in Vietnam. They relived the absolute horror of what this country, in a sense, made them do.

They told stories that at times they had personally raped, cut off ears, cut off heads, taped wires from portable telephones to human genitals and turned up the power, cut off limbs, blown up bodies, randomly shot at civilians, razed villages in a fashion reminiscent of Genghis Khan, shot cattle and dogs for fun, poisoned food stocks, and generally ravaged the countryside of South Vietnam in addition to the normal ravage of war and the normal and very particular ravaging which is done by the applied bombing power of this country.

We call this investigation the Winter Soldier Investigation. The term Winter Soldier is a play on words of Thomas Paine's in 1776 when he spoke of the Sunshine Patriot and summer time soldiers who deserted at Valley Forge because the going was rough.

We who have come here to Washington have come here because we feel we have to be winter soldiers now. We could come back to this country, we could be quiet, we could hold our silence, we could not tell what went on in Vietnam, but we feel because of what threatens this country, not the reds, but the crimes which we are committing that threaten it, that we have to speak out.

I would like to talk to you a little bit about what the result is of the feelings these men carry with them after coming back from Vietnam. The country

Statement by John Kerry, April 23, 1971, to the Senate Committee on Foreign Relations, *Congressional Record*, vol. 117, pp. 11738–11740.

doesn't know it yet but it has created a monster, a monster in the form of millions of men who have been taught to deal and to trade in violence and who are given the chance to die for the biggest nothing in history; men who have returned with a sense of anger and a sense of betrayal which no one has yet grasped.

As a veteran and one who feels this anger I would like to talk about it. We are angry because we feel we have been used in the worst fashion by the administration of this country.

In 1970 at West Point Vice President Agnew said "some glamorize the criminal misfits of society while our best men die in Asian rice paddies to preserve the freedom which most of those misfits abuse," and this was used as a rallying point for our effort in Vietnam.

But for us, as boys in Asia whom the country was supposed to support, his statement is a terrible distortion from which we can only draw a very deep sense of revulsion, and hence the anger of some of the men who are here in Washington today. It is a distortion because we in no way consider ourselves the best men of this country; because those he calls misfits were standing up for us in a way that nobody else in this country dared to; because so many who have died would have returned to this country to join the misfits in their efforts to ask for an immediate withdrawal from South Vietnam; because so many of those best men have returned as quadruplegics and amputees—and they lie forgotten in Veterans Administration Hospitals in this country which fly the flag which so many have chosen as their own personal symbol—and we cannot consider ourselves America's best men when we are ashamed of and hated for what we were called on to do in Southeast Asia.

In our opinion, and from our experience, there is nothing in South Vietnam which could happen that realistically threatens the United States of America. And to attempt to justify the loss of one American life in Vietnam, Cambodia or Laos by linking such loss to the preservation of freedom, which those misfits supposedly abuse, is to us the height of criminal hypocrisy, and it is that kind of hypocrisy which we feel has torn this country apart.

We are probably much more angry than that, but I don't want to go into the foreign policy aspects because I am outclassed here. I know that all of you talk about every possible alternative to getting out of Vietnam. We understand that. We know you have considered the seriousness of the aspects to the utmost level and I am not going to try to dwell on that. But I want to relate to you the feeling that many of the men who have returned to this country express because we are probably angriest about all that we were told about Vietnam and about the mystical war against communism.

We found that not only was it a civil war, an effort by a people who had for years been seeking their liberation from any colonial influence whatsoever, but also we found that the Vietnamese whom we had enthusiastically molded after our own image were hard put to take up the fight against the threat we were supposedly saving them from.

We found most people didn't even know the difference between communism and democracy. They only wanted to work in rice paddies without helicopters strafing them and bombs with napalm burning their villages and tearing their country apart. They wanted everything to do with the war, particularly with this foreign presence of the United States of America, to leave them alone in peace, and they practiced the art of survival by siding with whichever military force was present at a particular time, be it Viet Cong, North Vietnamese or American.

We found also that all too often American men were dying in those rice paddies for want of support from their allies. We saw first hand how monies from American taxes were used for a corrupt dictatorial regime. We saw that many people in this country had a one-sided idea of who was kept free by our flag, and blacks provided the highest percentage of casualties. We saw Vietnam ravaged equally by American bombs and search and destroy missions, as well as by Viet Cong terrorism, and yet we listened while this country tried to blame all of the havoc on the Viet Cong.

We rationalized destroying villages in order to save them. We saw America lose her sense of morality as she accepted very cooly a My Lai and refused to give up the image of American soldiers who hand out chocolate bars and chewing gum.

We learned the meaning of free fire zones, shooting anything that moves, and we watched while America placed a cheapness on the lives of orientals.

We watched the United States falsification of body counts, in fact the glorification of body counts. We listened while month after month we were told the back of the enemy was about to break. We fought using weapons against "oriental human beings." We fought using weapons against those people which I do not believe this country would dream of using were we fighting in the European theater. We watched while men charged up hills because a general said that hill has to be taken, and after losing one platoon or two platoons they marched away to leave the hill for re-occupation by the North Vietnamese. We watched pride allow the most unimportant battles to be blown into extravaganzas, because we couldn't lose, and we couldn't retreat, and because it didn't matter how many American bodies were lost to prove that point, and so there were Hamburger Hills and Khe Sahns and Hill 81s and Fire Base 6s, and so many others.

Now we are told that the men who fought there must watch quietly while American lives are lost so that we can exercise the incredible arrogance of Vietnamizing the Vietnamese.

Each day to facilitate the process by which the United States washes her hands of Vietnam someone has to give up his life so that the United States doesn't have to admit something that the entire world already knows, so that we can't say that we have made a mistake. Someone has to die so that President Nixon won't be, and these are his words, "the first President to lose a war."

We are asking Americans to think about that because how do you ask a man to be the last man to die in Vietnam? How do you ask a man to be the last man to die for a mistake? But we are trying to do that, and we are doing it with thousands of rationalizations, and if you read carefully the President's last speech to the people of this country, you can see that he says, and says clearly, "but the issue, gentlemen, the issue, is communism, and the question is whether or not we will leave that country to the communists or whether or not we will try to give it hope to be a free people." But the point is they are not a free people now under us. They are not a free people, and we cannot fight communism all over the world. I think we should have learned that lesson by now.

But the problem of veterans goes beyond this personal problem, because you think about a poster in this country with a picture of Uncle Sam and the picture says "I want you." And a young man comes out of high school and says, "that is fine, I am going to serve my country," and he goes to Vietnam and he shoots and he kills and he does his job. Or maybe he doesn't kill. Maybe he just goes and he comes back, and when he gets back to this country he finds that he isn't really wanted, because the largest corps of unemployed in the country—it varies depending on who you get it from, the Veterans Administration says 15 percent and various other sources 22 percent—but the largest corps of unemployed in this country are veterans of this war, and of those veterans 33 percent of the unemployed are black. That means one out of every ten of the nation's unemployed is a veteran of Vietnam.

The hospitals across the country won't, or can't meet their demands. It is not a question of not trying; they haven't got the appropriations. A man recently died after he had a tracheotomy in California, not because of the operation but because there weren't enough personnel to clean the mucus out of his tube and he suffocated to death.

Another young man just died in a New York VA Hospital the other day. A friend of mine was lying in a bed two beds away and tried to help him but he couldn't. He rang a bell and there was nobody there to service that man and so he died of convulsions.

I understand 57 percent of all those entering the VA hospitals talk about suicide. Some 27 percent have tried, and they try because they come back to this country and they have to face what they did in Vietnam, and then they come back and find the indifference of a country that doesn't really care.

Suddenly we are faced with a very sickening situation in this country, because there is no moral indignation and, if there is, it comes from people who are almost exhausted by their past indignations, and I know that many of them are sitting in front of me. The country seems to have lain down and shrugged off something as serious as Laos, just as we calmly shrugged off the loss of 700,000 lives in Pakistan, the so-called greatest disaster of all times.

But we are here as veterans to say we think we are in the midst of the greatest disaster of all times now because they are still dying over there—not just Americans, but Vietnamese—and we are rationalizing leaving that country so that those people can go on killing each other for years to come.

Americans seem to have accepted the idea that the war is winding down, at least for Americans, and they have also allowed the bodies which were once used by a President for statistics to prove that we were winning that war, to be used as evidence against a man who followed orders and who interpreted those orders no differently than hundreds of other men in Vietnam.

We veterans can only look with amazement on the fact that this country has been unable to see there is absolutely no difference between ground troops and a helicopter crew, and yet people have accepted a differentiation fed them by the administration.

No ground troops are in Laos so it is all right to kill Laotians by remote control. But believe me the helicopter crews fill the same body bags and they wreak the same kind of damage on the Vietnamese and Laotian countryside as anybody else, and the President is talking about allowing that to go on for many years to come. One can only ask if we will really be satisfied only when the troops march into Hanoi.

We are asking here in Washington for some action; action from the Congress of the United States of America which has the power to raise and maintain armies, and which by the Constitution also has the power to declare war.

We have come here, not to the President, because we believe that this body can be responsive to the will of the people, and we believe that the will of the people says that we should get out of Vietnam now.

We are here in Washington also to say that the problem of this war is not just a question of war and diplomacy. It is part and parcel of everything that we are trying as human beings to communicate to people in this country—the question of racism, which is rampant in the military, and so many other questions such as the use of weapons; the hypocrisy in our taking umbrage in the Geneva Conventions and using that as justification for a continuation of this war when we are more guilty than any other body of violations of those Geneva Conventions; in the use of free fire zones, harassment interdiction fire, search and destroy missions, the bombings, the torture of prisoners, the killing of prisoners, all accepted policy by many units in South Vietnam. That is what we are trying to say. It is part and parcel of everything.

An American Indian friend of mine who lives in the Indian Nation of Alcatraz put it to me very succinctly. He told me how as a boy on an Indian reservation he had watched television and he used to cheer the cowboys when they came in and shot the Indians, and then suddenly one day he stopped in Vietnam and he said "my God, I am doing to these people the very same thing that was done to my people," and he stopped. And that is what we are trying to say, that we think this thing has to end.

We are also here to ask, and we are here to ask vehemently, where are the leaders of our country? Where is the leadership? We are here to ask where are McNamara, Rostow, Bundy, Gilpatric and so many others? Where are they now that we, the men whom they sent off to war, have returned? These are commanders who have deserted their troops, and there is no more serious crime in the law of war. The Army says they never leave their wounded. The Marines say they never leave even their dead. These men have left all the casualties and retreated behind a pious shield of public rectitude. They have left the real stuff of their reputations bleaching behind them in the sun in this country.

Finally, this administration has done us the ultimate dishonor. They have attempted to disown us and the sacrifices we made for this country. In their blindness and fear they have tried to deny that we are veterans or that we served in Nam. We do not need their testimony. Our own scars and stumps of limbs are witness enough for others and for ourselves.

We wish that a merciful God could wipe away our own memories of that service as easily as this administration has wiped away their memories of us. But all that they have done and all that they can do by this denial is to make more clear than ever our own determination to undertake one last mission—to search out and destroy the last vestige of this barbaric war, to pacify our own hearts, to conquer the hate and the fear that have driven this country these last ten years and more, so when 30 years from now our brothers go down the street without a leg, without an arm, or a face, and small boys ask why, we will be able to say "Vietnam" and not mean a desert, not a filthy obscene memory, but mean instead the place where America finally turned and where soldiers like us helped it in the turning.

Thank you.

Vietnam veteran John Kerry talks at a press conference in Washington, DC, urging President Richard Nixon to accept a Viet Cong proposal to release prisoners in exchange for a total withdrawal of U.S. troops. Kerry was a member of the group Veterans Against the War, and was joined by POW family members (L-R) Richard Sigler, Francis Young, and Mrs. Sigler. July 22, 1971. © Bettmann/Corbis.

Resisting the Dominant Culture: Playing the Intersection Game

Charles Perry

While some resisted the draft, opposed the war, or took other obviously political stands, thousands of young people built a new "counterculture" that focused on music, dance, clothes, drugs, sexual freedom, and mystical religion. One element or another of the counterculture stood in opposition to nearly every value of the dominant, middle-class culture, including order, discipline, self-control, passivity, patriotic nationalism, the work ethic, profit making, consumerism, the system of capitalism, and the importance of the state. The counterculture valued spontaneity, self-discovery, the pleasures of the body, participation, egalitarianism and the sharing of income, resources, and responsibility, playfulness, and the small community.

By the summer of 1967, the San Francisco Bay area was home to Ken Kesey and his band of Merry Pranksters; to Augustus Owsley Stanley III, the chemist who supplied the LSD for Kesey's "acid tests"; to the Grateful Dead and Janis Joplin; to Emmett Grogan, the founder of an urban commune known as The Diggers; to the San Francisco Mime Troupe; and to thousands of young people who had come to the area to experience the new "hippie" counterculture.

The center of San Francisco's counterculture community was a neighborhood called Haight-Ashbury (after two intersecting streets), or simply "the Haight." It was there that Grogan's Diggers distributed free food and it was there, in the fall of 1967, that The Diggers and the Mime Troupe introduced the residents of the Haight to the Frame of Reference and to the Intersection Game. What was the point of this famous episode in street theater?

The Diggers' event, a Full Moon Public Celebration, had been publicized with 1,500 leaflets passed out in the Haight and another 500 in Berkeley, despite the Diggers' distaste for the grandstanding habits of the Berkeley left. An experiment in psychedelico-political theater and provocation, it started earlier than the other two events and lasted, for some participants, much longer.

At 5:30 everyone in the Mime Troupe who had shown interest in the plans gathered at the corner of Haight and Masonic, where the leaflets, headlined "PUBLIC NONSENSE NUISANCE PUBLIC ESSENCE NEWSENSE PUBLIC NEWS," had announced the "intersection game" was to begin. The Mime Troupers brought the thirteen-foot-square wooden frame, painted yellow, that they called the Frame of Reference and through which people were required to walk before being served at the daily free feeds. They also had the Mime Troupe's eight-foot-high satirical puppets. By six o'clock about 600 people had gathered, including school-age trick-or-treaters as well as hippies.

The Diggers passed out about 75 six-inch replicas of the Frame of Reference to be worn around the neck. They performed a playlet called "Any Fool on the Street" and then started the intersection game, which was, as it were, a lesson in the Digger theory of ownership of the streets. Leaflets gave instructions to walk across the intersection in different directions to form various polygons, relying on the pedestrian's right of way over automobiles: "Don't wait don't walk (umbrella step, stroll, cake walk, sombersault, finger-crawl, squat-jump, pilgrimmage, Phylly dog, etc.)." It was a translation of the civil rights sit-in technique directed against automobiles, and at the same time a terrific goof.

While people were walking in close order around the sidewalks and tying up traffic, an improvised puppet drama was going on around the Frame of Reference. The giant puppets, operated with one man holding the puppet up by a pole and speaking its lines while another manipulated its hands with sticks, were bobbing absurdly around the frame and urging people to walk through it. Police had responded to the traffic jam in progress with five patrol cars and a paddy wagon. While some of the policemen began directing traffic and ordering people to clear the sidewalks, one cop, looking for the perpetrators of the nuisance, somehow decided to address the eight-foot-tall puppets.

"You are creating a public nuisance," he called up to the puppet. "We warn you that if you don't remove yourselves from the area you'll be arrested for blocking a public thoroughfare."

Street theater! Heaven-sent absurdity! The Diggers answered back through the puppets. "Who is the public?" asked one puppet, bobbing its gawky arms around.

"I couldn't care less," replied the policeman. "I'll take you in. Now move on."

"I declare myself public—I am a public," insisted the puppet. "The streets are public, the streets are free." Then the puppets walked on and the four Diggers operating them, plus the sculptor who had made them, were arrested as warned. About 200 of the crowd were still present to boo the proceedings. From inside the paddy wagon, where the puppets had with difficulty been stuffed beside their human agents, the Diggers could be heard chanting, "Public, public," on their way to Park Station.

The intersection game started up again in the meanwhile, and somebody set up a phonograph for dancing. The police drifted off about twenty minutes later, the main body of the crowd having dispersed. At Park Station the Diggers were booked for creating a public nuisance. They spent part of the night in their cells singing Mime Troupe warm-up songs such as the Italian Communist anthem "Avanti Popolo," and were released the next morning without bail.

The bust endeared the Diggers to the Berkeley left even more. The following week the *Barb* not only reported on the Halloween event but began listing the daily free food in its entertainment and events column. It reported that the Diggers were renovating a garage on Page Street where they would open a "24-hour Frame of Reference exchange" to facilitate community self-help projects, all free. The Diggers were also going to develop sewing and babysitting circles, said the *Barb*, and planned to challenge the paramilitary right-wing Minutemen to a football game. The *Barb* soon reprinted "The Ideology of Failure" and "In Search of a Frame" from the Digger broadsides.

The San Francisco Mime Troupe Entertains. A routine feature of life in Haight-Ashbury is outdoor theater, admission free. July 1, 1967. UPI/Bettmann.

The San Francisco Diggers can be further explored at The Digger Archives, a rich Web site at www.diggers.org/. The Sixties Project, a Web site maintained at the University of Virginia, offers a wide range of scholarly literature, filmographies, bibliographies, personal memoirs, and fiction from the decade. It can be accessed at http://lists.village.virginia.edu/sixties/HTML_docs/resources. html. The Free Speech Movement, which in the fall of 1964 set the tone for student protest movements, is well served by The Bancroft Library's "Free Speech Movement Digital Archive," available at http://bancroft.berkeley.edu/FSM/.

THE BIG PICTURE

You're home for the holidays. Dad has a few beers and gets riled up. He rants and raves about the glorious and orderly 1950s, and he explains how the "sixties" came along and ruined everything with needless attacks on authority. You have just finished reading about both eras. How do you respond?

Chapter 13

Under Siege, Coming Apart

Whether understood as an era of destructive social upheaval or of productive social reformism, the "sixties" had a number of hard and bitter endings. Politically, the sixties began to end in 1968, when many union and working-class voters, long the mainstay of the Democratic Party, helped elect Richard Nixon. The era definitively terminated in 1972, when Nixon thrashed the liberal Democratic candidate, George McGovern, whose nomination had been made possible by internal changes in the party (motivated by the reformist energies of the sixties) that had given blacks and women larger roles in the political process. Economically, the sixties may have ended in 1971, when the United States experienced its first international trade deficit since 1893. Or they may have ended on October 16, 1973, when the Arab-dominated Organization of Petroleum Exporting Companies (OPEC) responded to American intervention in the Arab-Israeli war by cutting off oil shipments to the United States, Japan, and Western Europe. By early 1974 the stock market was in free fall and problems of inflation and economic stagnation had surfaced that would last nearly another decade. Culturally, one might mark the end of the 1960s by the breakup of the Beatles in 1970, an event that brought to an end the band's effort to produce creative music in a framework of group cooperation—and ushered in an era focusing on self and family, typified by Paul McCartney's self-conscious anthem to his wife, "Lovely Linda" (1971), in which McCartney played all the parts himself.

For those who would like to see the "fall" of the 1970s as a product of the excesses of the 1960s, consider the event known as Watergate. Watergate had its origins in 1969, when the Nixon administration embarked on a campaign to isolate and discredit the peace movement. By 1971 the people charged with this responsibility had moved to the Committee for the Reelection of the President (CREEP), where they were working with former Attorney General John Mitchell on an illegal effort to gather information on political opponents. In June 1972, five CREEP operatives were apprehended at Democratic National Committee headquarters in Washington's Watergate apartment complex. Two years later, when the president's own tape recordings revealed that he had conspired to cover up the break-in, a humiliated Nixon resigned. His legacy (although it also owed something to Lyndon Johnson's lack of candor in handling the war in Vietnam) focused on a new and troublesome attitude toward politics: credibility. He didn't have any. Simply put, many Americans no longer believed what the politicians told them.

Given the depressed economic conditions of the decade, the crisis of confidence in politics, and the working-class-led backlash against the social reform energies of the sixties, it is not surprising that there was little progress made on "reform" fronts in the seventies. To be sure, powerful lobbies of the elderly were able to bring their constituents tangible gains: a new system that indexed social security to changes in the cost of living and a 1978 law that abolished mandatory retirement in most employment. Campaigns for gay rights and women's rights also remained vital through the 1970s. And environmental issues proved able to generate an ongoing consensus for continued government action. But on the critical issues that the sixties had courageously and optimistically raised to prominence—poverty, racism, the decaying inner cities—the consensus was washing away. What was left was a new and mistaken reliance on the mandatory busing of schoolchildren as the solution to all these ills. It was a solution that relied too much on the sacrifices of the white working class and on schools that were inadequate no matter who attended them. It was a solution bound to fail.

Of all the forces remaking the nation's political agenda in the 1970s, none loomed so large as the rise of the Sunbelt, a vast region encompassing the old South, the southwest, and parts of California. One mark of the Sunbelt's burgeoning influence was its ability to send its own to the White House: Texans Lyndon Johnson, elected in 1964, and George W. Bush, in 2000 and 2004; Georgian Jimmy Carter in 1976; Californians Richard Nixon (in 1968 and 1972) and Ronald Reagan (in 1980 and 1984); Arkansas's William Jefferson Clinton in 1992 and 1996. Ironically, the political turnaround represented in that list owed much to the civil rights movement of the 1950s and 1960s, which removed from the region the taint of racism and made southern politicians acceptable nationally. The civil rights movement also had everything to do with the decline of the "solid [Democratic] South," which had been based for decades on an intersectional deal: the South would support some liberal causes, and the North would let the South deal with race in its own way. When that bargain dissolved in the 1960s, southerners were free to vote their ideological preferences. By 2004, the South was "solid" again—but Republican.

Although no region entirely escaped the downdraft of the economy in the 1970s, the Sunbelt boomed, relatively at least. The same rising oil prices that dampened growth in the Great Lakes rustbelt fueled growth in energy-rich Oklahoma, Louisiana, and Texas. Attracted by low levels of unionization, low wages, and state governments less inclined to regulate industry, corporations moved workers south or built new plants in rapidly growing cities such as Houston, Dallas, Atlanta, Charlotte, Jacksonville, and Nashville. One could track the Sunbelt's rise by charting the football teams that located in most of those places, or through the emergence of redneck rock. Responding to Neil Young's criticism of the South in a 1971 song, the band Lynyrd Skynyrd had announced the region's resurgence in "Sweet Home Alabama," recorded in 1974: "We hope Neil Young will remember," went the song, "Southern Man don't need him around anyhow."

Above all, the 1970s was an age of survival, of getting by until things got better, of coming to terms with limited opportunities. Hence the quintessential movie star of the day was John Travolta, whose characters were ordinary guys whose main task was to achieve a modicum of self-respect, and

John Travolta in His Famous Disco-Dancing Pose in *Saturday Night Fever* (1977). Travolta's characters were working-class young men operating within the economic and social constraints of the 1970s. Corbis Images.

whose triumphs were limited ones—learning to ride a mechanical bull, or winning a dance contest—won in bars and discos. As for discos, there was no more consensus over the music than over anything else in the 1970s, and its origins in the gay and black communities in the early part of the decade did not endear it to the white working class. Yet disco was enormously popular because it spoke so clearly to the question of survival, with the darkened disco a haven of refuge from a difficult world and the pulsating, irrepressible beat a pacemaker for the walking (or dancing) wounded. In the words of the Bee Gees' 1977 hit, it all came down to "stayin' alive."

Jimmy Carter spoke this language, too, and for four years he ministered to the needs of the population like Mom with a bowl of chicken soup. He worked at labeling the nation's illness—a "malaise" in one speech, a "crisis of purpose" in another. And he patiently explained to Americans how they could survive the new regime of limits by conserving energy and living simpler lives. It was not bad advice at all, and for a time Americans responded enthusiastically to a president who at least seemed honest and credible. But Carter could not solve the riddle of "stagflation"—high rates of inflation and unemployment at the same time. Nor could he do anything much about the Iranian militants who in 1979 took fifty-two American hostages and held them for 444 days—for many Americans, the last in a long series of national humiliations. By 1980, Americans wanted more than survival, and they were willing to listen to anyone who promised to give them back the nation they had lost.

The atmosphere of the late 1970s is perhaps best captured in Jimmy Carter's extraordinary July 15, 1979, address, "Energy and the National Goals—a Crisis of Confidence." It can be read (and heard) at the award-winning American Rhetoric Web site, which presents the Top 100 American speeches. Go to www.americanrhetoric.com/speeches/jimmycartercrisisofconfidence.htm.

From Integration to Diversity

Bruce J. Schulman

"Americans," wrote historian Peter N. Carroll, "approached the nation's two hundredth birthday with the ambivalence of tourists dipping their toes into shark-infested waters." There was some interest in the flotilla of tall ships that sailed into New York harbor to remind Americans of their eighteenth-century heritage, but by and large there wasn't much enthusiasm in 1976 for celebrating the nation's birthday or, for that matter, for the nation itself. Some of the reasons were obvious: a terrible defeat in Vietnam, the legacy of Watergate, and a once-invincible economy threatened by Japanese imports and Arab oil producers.

All true. But there was something else at work, pulling American society apart, chipping away at the sense of national unity that Americans had struggled to develop and maintain through a Civil War and a Great Depression—the sense that they were "one people"—one out of many, to be sure—but somehow deeply united in their shared values and experiences, ready to celebrate that shared core—ready to celebrate the birthday of the nation.

That "something else at work," as Bruce Schulman reveals in this provocative, sweeping essay on race and ethnicity, was an idea that at first blush seems as American as apple pie: diversity. What was diversity? What forces—economic, political, social—produced it? From the perspective of the present, did the diversity chickens of the 1970s come home to roost? Or did the nation manage to overcome the challenge of diversity?

In January 1975 a new situation comedy debuted on CBS. The latest in a series of spin-offs from *All in the Family*, Norman Lear's comedy about the lovable bigot Archie Bunker and his working-class family in Queens, *The Jeffersons* focused on the adventures of Archie's black neighbors, George and Louise Jefferson. Unlike the Bunkers, who remained resolutely shabby and blue collar, the Jeffersons enjoyed social mobility. They had "moved on up to a deluxe apartment in the sky."

The new series prompted viewers and reviewers to take stock of the civil rights revolution. On the one hand, *The Jeffersons* signaled real racial progress: the nation accepted a television series about a middle-class black family in a mostly white neighborhood. At a time when few black characters appeared regularly on television, and most of those lived in stereotypically dire straits, that was quite an achievement. The series even featured an interracial couple, the Willises, who kissed passionately on the screen.

The Jeffersons. © CBS Photo Archive/Getty Images.

Naming its principals "Jefferson," after the founding father most closely associated with the notion of human equality, the series touted the fundamental equality of all Americans; it envisioned a place where individuals were judged by the content of their characters, not the color of their skin. Some critics wondered whether the show was not too optimistic. The interracial Willis family encountered hostility from no one but the insufferable George Jefferson. And George's frequent troubles owed more to his own boorishness than to the trials of institutional discrimination. *Washington Post* reporter Joel Dreyfuss worried about the "dangerous political message" in a program "that never seems to show George challenged by racism."

But if *The Jeffersons* offered a world without overt racial hostility, it still depicted the clash of irreconcilably conflicting white and black cultures. It seemed to concede the ultimate futility of integration in American life. Most of the series' humor—George Jefferson's disdain for and inability to understand "honkies," the liberal white characters' amusing and patronizing efforts to talk jive—derived from the juxtaposition of utterly foreign manners and morals. *The Jeffersons* were foreigners in upper-class New York society; it was as if the series had placed a Frenchman on the Upper East Side or, as *The Jeffersons* actually did for comic effect, an Englishman.

The Jeffersons marked the crest of the civil rights movement, the summit of its material achievements, and the beginning of the end of the integrationist ideal. The public purpose of the Sixties—the shared commitment of minority activists, liberal intellectuals, and northern white voters to removing explicit racial barriers—gave way in the Seventies. "Separate but equal," the mantra of southern segregationists, had become anathema as a concept and as public policy. But the idea of distinct groups, with their own culture and politics, their own objectives and destinies, would prove more enticing and more enduring than Sixties Americans might have imagined. George Jefferson, and the new ideal of diversity, would take Americans far from Thomas Jefferson's vision of equality.

The Civil Rights Revolution: A Scorecard

The civil rights revolution breached the previously insurmountable wall of racism in American law, politics, education, and economic life. Black students flooded into the nation's colleges and universities; by the mid-1970s, black enrollments in institutions of higher learning equaled the representation of African Americans in the nation at large, and as many black high school graduates (in percentage terms) went on to college as did their white counterparts. In 1974, 600 black students matriculated at the University of Alabama. Once a symbol of the white South's massive resistance to the struggle for racial justice, the university's famous football squad fielded an integrated roster, and segregationist governor George Wallace was on hand to crown a black woman as the school's 1973 homecoming queen.

African Americans also moved into politics and public life. In the decade after the passage of the Voting Rights Act, the polls opened to millions of previously disfranchised and dispossessed voters. In the southern states, where blacks had never exercised the fundamental rights of democracy, registration rates doubled and the number of black public officials multiplied. In 1967, Cleveland voters elected Carl Stokes the first African American mayor of a major American city. Stokes and new black mayors in Detroit and Atlanta launched a wave of "firsts" during the early 1970s: the first African American admiral in the U.S. Navy, the first black southerners elected to Congress since Reconstruction, the first black secretary of the army, the first black bishop in the Episcopal church, the first black member of the New York Stock Exchange.

Desegregation opened hotels, restaurants, and other public accommodations to people of all races and helped narrow the economic gap between whites and minorities. As the federal government moved aggressively to end legal segregation, the budget of the Equal Employment Opportunity Commission exploded, from a token $3 million in 1966 to more than $111 million by the end of the Seventies. By 1972, every department of the federal government possessed its own equal opportunity office. Meanwhile, the poverty rate for black households declined. Although black families remained far more likely to suffer deprivation than whites, the racial gap closed steadily between 1959 and 1974.

Even some of the most encrusted attitudes about race seemed to be falling by the wayside. In 1963, half of white survey respondents said they would object if a member of their family "wanted to bring a black friend home for dinner"; by 1982, only 22 percent demurred. In 1958, nearly two-thirds of white voters told pollsters that they would refuse to vote for a "generally well-qualified" black candidate for president, even if nominated by their own party. A quarter-century later, 80 percent of white voters claimed they would support such a candidate.

But the rise of the black middle class offered the most dramatic evidence of racial progress. Over the past thirty years, the number of black families officially labeled as "affluent" by the Census Bureau—with household incomes exceeding $50,000—mushroomed by more than 400 percent. A "church-going, home-owning, child rearing, back-yard barbecuing, traffic jam-cursing black middle class" flourished, notable only, according to one analyst, "for the very ordinariness with which its members go about their classically American suburban affairs." . . . The civil rights revolution had won a great triumph.

But it had also been a horrible failure. Stagnation settled onto the United States in the mid-1970s, slowing the economic progress of black Americans. Economic malaise particularly injured working-class blacks, many of whom fell into poverty and despair. At the same time, a disproportionately large number of middle-class blacks drew their sustenance from government jobs. Many private employers remained unwilling to hire, and especially to promote, racial minorities. It was no accident that Prince Georges County bordered the nation's capital.

"The desegregation of public facilities cost nothing," Martin Luther King, Jr., noted just before his death, "neither did the election and appointment of a few black public officials." True racial justice could not be had at such bargain prices. The failure of true racial integration, the principal goal of early civil rights activists, highlighted this somber fact. Segregation disappeared in arenas of casual contact between Americans—restaurants, airports and train stations, hotel lobbies. But schools and neighborhoods remained rigidly separated. Even thriving middle-class blacks continued to face residential segregation. When a subdivision acquired a visible black presence, it usually "tipped," shifting from overwhelmingly white to nearly all black practically overnight.

In this respect, the experience of African Americans contrasted sharply with that of other racial minorities. Prospering Latinos and Asian Americans moved into integrated suburbs without substantial white flight. One leading study of race relations concluded that white Americans simply did not wish to live among black neighbors.

In the aftermath of the civil rights revolution and urban racial disturbances of the 1960s, whites fled the triple-decker row houses and high-rise apartments of urban America. In Boston, blacks had accounted for less than 10 percent of the Hub's population in 1960; by 1980, they made up 22 percent. Whites emptied out of Detroit, Cleveland, Baltimore, St. Louis, Milwaukee, Brooklyn, and Buffalo. It was not the allure of greener suburban pastures but discontent over school desegregation, welfare, and rising black militance that drove city dwellers to the lily-white suburbs. Cities with small black populations continued to grow. It was once "one big happy Flatbush family," a nostalgic Brooklynite explained to an inquiring sociologist, referring to the borough's main thoroughfare. "But now? Ninety-five percent of them have been mugged and moved away."

Nothing else so promoted white flight or exacerbated racial hostility as court-ordered busing. In a series of decisions during the early 1970s, the Supreme Court addressed the persistent problem of school segregation, still lingering fifteen years after the court's landmark *Brown* decision. In *Swann v. Charlotte-Mecklenburg Board of Education* (1971), a unanimous Court ruled that preservation of neighborhood schools could no longer justify racial imbalance. *Swann* authorized drastic measures, "awkward, inconvenient and even bizarre in some situations," to maximize desegregation and specifically recommended busing as a remedy. Two years later, the Court applied this doctrine outside the South for the first time. In *Keyes v. Denver School District #1* (1973), the Court found northern communities responsible for school board decisions and public policies that had isolated black students just as effectively as any Jim Crow law. Federal courts around the country began issuing desegregation plans.

A third ruling, however, *Milliken v. Bradley* (1974), established the limits for forced busing. In a contentious five-to-four decision, the Supreme Court struck down a lower court's plan to bus students between overwhelmingly black Detroit and neighboring white suburbs. Outlying communities, Chief Justice Burger asserted, must not be held responsible for the problems of the cities they surrounded. *Millikin* spared the suburbs the agonies of busing, hastened white flight beyond the city limits, and made it possible for those with means to abandon any commitment to city schools or to education for their less advantaged neighbors.

The nation's struggling city dwellers, black and white, Latino and Asian American, would bear the brunt of the struggle for integration and the agonies of busing. Boston dramatized the nation's anguish. In 1974, a federal judge ordered mandatory busing to desegregate the city's schools, sparking bitter protests and violent outbursts in classrooms and schoolyards. Armed riot police patrolled South Boston and Charlestown, white neighborhoods that greeted black children with derisive signs taunting, "We don't want any niggers in our school" and "Monkeys get out of our neighborhood." The nation's cradle of liberty, the city that begot the abolitionists and helped educate Martin Luther King, became the home of "the bean, the cod, and the bigot." In April 1976, as Boston prepared to celebrate the nation's bicentennial, antibusing protesters attacked Ted Landsmark, a Yale-educated black lawyer and architect, as he rushed across City Hall Plaza to a meeting. A stunning *Boston Herald* photograph broadcast the grisly scene to a horrified world: white boys trying to impale a black man with the American flag.

Frustration, disappointment, and feelings of betrayal increasingly gripped black America. Early in the decade, an overwhelming majority of African Americans told pollsters that they wanted to live in integrated neighborhoods and send their children to racially mixed schools. By the end of the Seventies, alienation had prevailed. By more than a two-to-one majority, surveyed African Americans declared that they felt closer to black people in Africa than to white people in America. African Americans had lost faith in the responsiveness of American institutions, in the possibility of redressing grievances through the normal channels in American society. It appeared that the civil rights movement had reached the limits of its achievements. A profound disillusionment developed, and withdrawal from frustrating, seemingly useless public discourse quickly followed.

The Collapse of the Integrationist Ideal

From World War II until the early 1970s, liberal universalism—a belief in the fundamental unity and sameness of all humanity—had undergirded social activism and political reform in the United States. Nazism in Europe and segregation in the Jim Crow South had made liberal Americans suspicious of any claims of racial and ethnic difference. Beliefs that blacks or Latinos or women possessed distinctive natures or cultures were dismissed as prejudiced. Remaining differences were but an unfortunate legacy of discrimination and oppression.

Until about 1970, Americans had largely shared a core belief that all human beings were essentially the same, that differences among people did not—or at least should not—matter. In the words of Lyndon Johnson, "They cry the same tears, they feel hungry the same, they bleed the same." This universalism reflected the public purpose of the postwar generation, especially northern liberals and intellectuals. Southern segregation—with its active, overt separation of the races, its colored and white drinking fountains and bathrooms—became the scourge of the northeastern establishment. Union leaders, big city mayors, and university professors condemned southern Jim Crow. Even blue-collar white voters, the hard hats and schoolteachers uneasy about crime in their streets and new faces in their neighborhoods, admired Dr. King and supported the southern civil rights movement.

Integration remained their principal objective in the 1950s and early 1960s. Civil rights protesters demanded acknowledgment of blacks' essential human dignity and their fundamental rights as American citizens. "There will be nobody among us who will stand up and defy the Constitution of this nation," the Rev. Martin Luther King, Jr., asserted in Montgomery. King and his fellow protesters wanted to fulfill the Constitution, to purify American democracy, to take their rightful place at the national table.

At the same time, scholarly writing stressed the essential Americanness of the black community and deemphasized cultural and racial distinctions. African Americans, according to one academic, were no more than "white men in black skins." Popular culture celebrated this same universalism. The 1950s opened what critic Gerald Early has dubbed the "age of cultural crossover for the American Negro." Poet Gwendolyn Brooks won the Pulitzer Prize and novelist Ralph Ellison the National Book Award. Sidney Poitier emerged as a major film star. Harry Belafonte broke through as a popular singer. Jackie Robinson and Bill Russell won their respective sports' Most Valuable Player Awards. In Detroit, Berry Gordy, Jr., built the most successful company in the history of popular music. Unlike earlier black recording labels, Gordy's Motown aimed for the mainstream. In the midst of the integrationist age, Gordy could imagine a black company not restricted to the black market.

The fabulous success of Sly and the Family Stone marked the apex of integrationism in American popular culture. Born Sylvester Stewart in Texas, Sly Stone came of age in Vallejo, California, a grim northern California port city beset with gang fights and youth riots during Sly's adolescence. Stone eventually attended radio school and landed a job as a disc jockey on KSOL, a San Francisco Bay Area station. He soon departed from the station's restrictive format; he played all types of music, even seasoning the station's soul specialties with Bob Dylan and the Beatles. At the same time, he formed a band—and what an unusual band it was. "The Family" included blacks and whites, women—not just as vocalists but as principal instrumentalists—and men. Sly donned outrageous clothes: one critic compared him to a "Fillmore district pimp gone stone crazy." His performances were even more outrageous and dynamic; he and the Family produced a startling fusion of white San Francisco rock, soul, British pop, jazz, and dance tunes—a music they called "a whole new thing."

Sly and the Family's music evinced an incredible freedom—freedom of form, with band members trading lead vocals and instrumental solos, and freedom of content. And this integrated family sang of "different strokes for different folks," of an America with room for everyone. "Makes no difference what group I'm in," the Family declared in "Everyday People." "We got to live together." The Family's early hits, a smash with white and black kids alike, possessed, according to rock critic Greil Marcus, "all the good feeling of the March on Washington."

In 1969, Sly and the Family Stone hit their peak at Woodstock, breaking the color line at the legendary countercultural festival. The band's essential optimism was not untempered—"there's cost for you to bear, they will try to make you crawl," as one hit put it—but the songs remained hopeful about the possibilities for individual achievement and racial concord in American life.

By 1970, however, black America betrayed a mounting suspicion about the loving, unified American family that Sly Stone envisioned, of the integrationist ideal itself. Who is being integrated into what? critics asked. Civil rights activists, frustrated with the slow pace of racial progress and anxious to develop black power, denounced integration as a sell-out, the equivalent of assimilation. Integration meant merging into white society and adopting white culture, and newly race-conscious minorities rejected such "whitening." Black activists felt that even their liberal allies had thought of them as "white men with black skins"—had not granted them a heritage worthy of preservation and respect. . . .

By 1970, millions of black Americans were arriving at similar conclusions. To be sure, the most extreme forms of separation never caught on with rank-and-file African Americans (polls showed that more whites than blacks favored the establishment of a separate black nation). But widespread approval of black cultural nationalism accompanied that suspicion of the most militant enunciations of black power. A 1970 *Time* magazine survey found the black mood more militant, more hopeful, more determined, and noted overwhelming support in the black community for Afro-American studies programs and other efforts to promote black pride. The new natural Afro hairstyles (which rejected the previously popular straightened look as assimilationist), the study of African languages, the celebration of distinctive clothing, food, and music all won mounting support.

With the abandonment of the integrationist ideal, American conceptions of race shifted, in Harold Cruse's terms, from a "politics of civil rights" to a "politics of black ethnicity." The critique of integration reverberated throughout American cultural and intellectual life in the 1970s. Academic critics scoured the American past for alternative communitarian and republican traditions, and even defended a tolerant form of "ethnocentrism" as the proper way of conceiving of the self and the world.

In this indictment of integration, ivory tower intellectuals harmonized with popular entertainers. Funk impresario George Clinton celebrated "Chocolate City," the all-black enclaves of urban America, imagining an administration with Ali as President, Richard Pryor Minister of Education, Stevie Wonder Secretary of Fine Arts, and Aretha Franklin the First Lady. Clinton neither lamented white flight nor ignored the hardscrabble realities of the black ghettoes; he simply accepted—and liked—what he found. "It's my piece of the rock and I dig you, CC," Clinton's group Parliament sang in 1975. "God bless Chocolate City and the vanilla suburbs."

Sly and the Family Stone abandoned the integrationist ideal with less humor and more pain. In 1971, Sly and the Family released *There's a Riot Goin' On*, an album that issued a grim new report on the state of the nation. The album seemed to reconsider all of the earlier, optimistic tunes, to recall them to the factory. *Riot*'s lyrics focused on betrayal, failure, oppression, on being trapped; the music, lacking the raucous, celebratory quality of Sly's earlier records, offered just as much a reversal as the lyrics. The title track, "There's a riot goin' on," was blank. An old hit, "Thank You fallentinme be mice elf Agin," reappeared transmogrified. No longer an expression of gratitude for an American freedom, it became "Thank You for talkin' to me Africa," a thanksgiving prayer for the strength to stop running from the pistol-packin' devil, stand your ground, and wrestle him to the ground.

Riot offered a black musician's anguished rejection of a nation that limited his freedom in palpable and disturbing ways. *There's a Riot Goin' On* was an album that Sly and the Family's audience, particularly its white listeners, did not want to hear. To a large extent, African Americans were rejecting the integrationist ideal, abandoning the hope of joining a single American community and actively shaping its destiny. Instead they increasingly saw themselves as a separate nation within a nation, with distinct needs and values. Nor were blacks the only Americans to reject integration as an assimilationist nightmare. Chicanos, Indians, Asian Americans, even white ethnics and the elderly would follow suit.

From "Power" to Cultural Nationalism

The critique of integration began with the emergence of the black power movement in the mid-1960s. Militant black nationalism received its most potent enunciation from Malcolm X, a former street hustler and convict who in prison converted to the Nation of Islam and became the minister of the Nation's New York City mosque. Born Malcolm Little, the militant leader scorned integration, rejected nonviolence in favor of self-defense "by any means necessary," and urged pride in blackness. His message appealed most strongly to northern urban blacks who had not participated in the early civil rights struggles. They admired Malcolm's radicalism, his background, his audacious willingness to stand up to whites. But his teachings also caught on among younger civil rights activists in the Student Non-Violent Coordinating Committee (SNCC), who became disillusioned with King's strategy of nonviolence. "The lie-down-before-your-oppressor philosophy," one young militant declared, "is now a treadmill upon which the Negro is running but getting nowhere fast."

Black power, of course, meant different things to different people, but its central message was an assertion of political power. Defining black power in 1967, James Boggs insisted that the movement must "concentrate on the issue of political power, refusing to redefine and explain away Black Power as *Black Everything except black political power.*" In October 1966, Bobby Seale and Huey P. Newton formed the Black Panther party in Oakland, California. Merging black nationalism with Marxist-Leninist doctrine, the party described black ghettoes as exploited colonies of the United States trapped within its borders. The party called itself a revolutionary vanguard that would lead the urban masses against their oppressors, first targeting "the military arm of our oppressors"—the police and the criminal justice system. It recruited heavily among ex-convicts and prison inmates and engaged in several bloody confrontations with police, including a 1967 fray that left one officer dead and a wounded Huey Newton in custody.

Even the black arts movement, a self-consciously aesthetic endeavor, stressed political power. The movement's leader, poet and dramatist Amiri Baraka, called for a socially powerful, politically functional form of black expression. "We want 'poems that kill,'" Baraka wrote in his 1968 poem "Black Art." We want "Assassin poems, poems that shoot guns. Poems that wrestle cops into alleys and take their weapons leaving them dead with tongues pulled out and sent to Ireland." What distinguished these lethal stories, poems, and plays? They exploded in the mind of the reader or audience, shocking the oppressors, but most important, shocking the oppressed so that they would acquiesce no longer in their own oppression, cease to misunderstand and even to participate in their own degradation. Art was a vehicle to concrete economic and political power.

Over the course of a decade, the cultural element of black power gradually supplanted the political as the movement's basic thrust. In the 1970s, many activists concluded that "black culture *was* Black Power"—that an assertion of power lay inherent in maintaining and expressing a distinctive culture through clothing, music, hairstyle, literature, cuisine, and the arts. For the dispossessed, denied access to wealth and political institutions, cultural nationalism enhanced group autonomy and diminished black dependence on white society. Black culture staked out a sphere of activity relatively free from white influence and domination; it also advanced a positive, black-defined black identity that rejected white stereotypes. . . .

Just as Stokely Carmichael and the Black Panther party represented a younger, angrier generation than that of Martin Luther King, Jr., and Whitney Young and other established civil rights leaders, so a new cohort arose within other minority communities. These young activists also rejected integration and despised assimilation. In *Chicago Manifesto*, Armando Rendon renounced the success he had acquired in the white man's world and denounced the older generation—the Mexican American businessmen, politicians, and civic leaders who disclaimed their heritage "and will have nothing to do with *la causa*." Unlike African Americans, who had vainly sought integration into and equality within an "Anglo dominated world" and "only recently sought anew a black identity and cultural separateness," the Chicano movement and those of American Indians and Asian Americans almost immediately advanced an anti-assimilationist, cultural nationalist agenda.

In 1972, Rodolfo Acuna, founding chairman of the pioneering Chicano Studies Program at California State University at Northridge, published *Occupied America: The Chicano's Struggle Toward Liberation*. Acuna's book, one of the earliest academic studies of Mexican Americans, also offered the manifesto of a self-described activist-academic—one who captured a wider mood by titling his final two chapters "Goodbye America." The 1960s, Acuna wrote, "represented a decade of both awareness and disillusionment. Many Chicanos participated actively in the political life of the nation, during which they took a hard look at their assigned role in the United States, evaluated it and then decided that they had had enough, and so they bid good-bye to America." "Good-bye America" meant not leaving the soil, but denying the legitimacy of the name—recognizing that *America* was a "European term of occupation and colonization." "Good-bye America" signaled resistance against integration, oppression, "captivity." The cry of "Goodbye America" also represented an assertion of political power for Chicanos, akin to the cry of black power. . . .

By the 1970s, the Mexican American experience had become mostly urban, and it was in the cities that Chicano nationalism would flourish. The founding figure was Rodolfo "Corky" Gonzales, a one-time boxer and Democratic party operative who became disillusioned with conventional reform politics. In 1966, Gonzales formed the Crusade for Justice in Denver, an organization devoted to reform of the police and courts, better housing, more economic opportunity, and, significantly, "relevant education" for Chicanos. The Crusade became strongly nationalistic; at one point Gonzales considered appealing to the United Nations for a plebiscite in the Southwest to determine whether the people—*la raza*—might desire independence from the United States. Gradually Gonzales came to stress culture. During a Denver teachers' strike, Crusade volunteers stepped in to teach basic subjects, like science and math, but also offered courses in Chicano history, Spanish, and Mexican culture. A similar program continued after the strike ended. Crusade for Justice promulgated a "Plan of the Barrio," demanding housing that would meet Chicano cultural needs, education in Spanish, and *barrio*-owned businesses. Gonzales also founded the annual Chicano Youth Liberation Conferences, energizing young activists on college campuses.

The 1970s and 1980s witnessed a broad acceptance of this cultural nationalist agenda throughout Mexican American politics—in the drive for ethnic studies programs on college campuses, for bilingual education in the public schools, for community control. Critiques of integration and assimilation became *de rigeur*; dissenting voices portraying Mexican Americans as the latest in a series of immigrant success stories met scorn and derision.

The same trend asserted itself among American Indians and Asian Americans. During the late 1960s and early 1970s, Indian activists invoked "red power" and launched militant protests against conditions on reservations, treaty violations by the U.S. government, and corrupt and abusive practices by the federal Bureau of Indian Affairs (BIA). Young activists increasingly allied with traditionalists, resisting both white society and the moderate, assimilationist leadership of many tribal governments. In 1969, three hundred Indians from fifty different tribes occupied Alcatraz Island in San Francisco Bay. They claimed a treaty right to take over surplus federal property and demanded conversion of the island into an Indian cultural center. The institution would revive "old Indian ways" and operate an Indian college, museum, and ecology center. The occupation lasted nineteen months before federal marshals peacefully removed the remaining protesters from the island. In 1973, two hundred armed Indians took over the South Dakota hamlet of Wounded Knee. In the end, two Indians lay dead and one federal marshal was severely wounded. The conflict revolved around demands for Indian sovereignty, treaty rights, and preservation of Native American cultural traditions. Throughout the country, Indians made clear that conventional methods of political participation and protest were no longer consistent with their unique history and cultural goals.

Asian Americans reached similar conclusions, only more slowly, with cultural nationalism not really emerging until the late 1970s. It manifested itself in the campaign for ethnic studies programs on campus and for cultural institutions—museum exhibitions, theater works, newspapers, literary journals. It also appeared in efforts to take seriously their status as an ethnic minority in a society that continued to view issues of race in black and white terms. Indeed, until 1980, the U.S. Census Bureau listed Asians as "Other" on the census forms. "You're not accepted in minority circles," one Asian American complained, "but you're not part of the majority either. Where do you stand?"

One violent incident—the murder of Vincent Chin in Detroit in 1982—added urgency to the Asian American quest for cultural identity. Two white autoworkers accosted the young Chinese American in a bar, denounced him as a "Jap," and blamed him for the loss of their jobs. A fistfight started; the autoworkers chased Chin with a baseball bat and beat him to death. The assailants were convicted of manslaughter, and the judge released them on probation, demanding that they pay only a small fine. The murder and lenient sentencing aroused widespread protest. Eventually the U.S. Department of Justice interceded and the principal assailant was sentenced to prison on federal civil rights charges. The Chin case aroused a determination to break silence, to speak out, to organize. At the same time, many young Asian Americans felt the need to seek out their roots—to reassert cultural identity in the arts, literature, and education and to reestablish community control of local institutions. . . .

By the mid-1970s, cultural nationalism had become the dominant force in minority activism. The old drive toward integration had been thoroughly discredited. But the emphasis on preserving and expressing distinctive racial and ethnic cultures posed an obvious problem. Could America successfully combine several different types of cultural nationalism? Could Americans acknowledge difference and still share the same city, the same university, the same polity?

Inventing "Diversity"

During the 1970s Americans hit on an answer to those thorny questions: the idea of diversity. For policymakers, the prospect of unlike, unassimilable groups appeared as a good to be valued—not a problem but a promise. This emerging ideal of "diversity" reflected a variety of social, legal, and ideological developments in the 1970s and early 1980s.

The new thinking built on a demographic foundation—a massive new wave of immigration that literally changed the face, and the faces, of the nation's population. A torrent of new arrivals, both illegal and legal, streamed in from Asia and Latin America. It included the refugees from Vietnam after the fall of Saigon and the 1979–1980 *Mariel* boatlift from Cuba, but owed mainly to the reform of the immigration laws in 1965. Eliminating the odious quota system, which since 1921 had pretty much closed the gates to all but Western Europeans, LBJ's immigration reforms ushered in a flood of new arrivals from the Third World. In 1965, only 5 percent of new arrivals had embarked from Asia; by 1980, nearly half the immigrants had journeyed across the Pacific. Latin Americans also entered in droves. Unlike earlier waves of mass immigration, most of these sojourners arrived with families intact, not as single men, and they quickly established their own businesses and communities. By the 1980s, Koreans owned and operated more than 500 businesses in Chicago, "minorities" made up a majority of the city of Los Angeles, and West Indian blacks outnumbered native-born African Americans in the outer boroughs of New York City.

But demographics alone did not reshape America's understanding of racial differences; law and public policy actively encouraged the shift from integration to diversity. Over the course of the 1970s, the rationale for affirmative action and the contours of civil rights programs slowly metamorphosed. The practical goal of such policies—increasing the representation of certain minority groups in universities, occupations, institutions—remained the same. But the justification for them shifted from integration—including disadvantaged minorities so they could become like everybody else—to diversity—welcoming racial and cultural differences into institutions so that they would reflect the multicultural nature of American society. Affirmative action was now supposed to promote and celebrate differences rather than eliminate distinctions.

While high-profile fights over busing captured the nation's attention, the federal government quietly expanded the reach of affirmative action. In 1969, the Office of Federal Contract Compliance (OFCC) promulgated the so-called Philadelphia Plan, requiring proportional representation of minorities in construction employment. . . .

The U.S. Supreme Court accelerated the drift toward diversity with its 1978 decision in *Regents of the University of California v. Bakke.* In 1973, Allan Paul Bakke, a balding, blond, blue-eyed thirty-two-year-old engineer applied for admission to the Medical School at the University of California, Davis. By all accounts, Bakke was a strong candidate; his academic record and standardized test scores placed him well above the average for students admitted to the medical school. The faculty interviewer who evaluated Bakke personally concluded that he was "a well-qualified candidate for admission whose main hardship is the unavoidable fact that he is now 33. . . . On the grounds of motivation, academic records, potential promise, endorsement by persons capable of reasonable judgments, personal appearance and decorum, maturity, and probable contribution to balance in the class, I believe Mr. Bakke must be considered as a very desirable applicant and I shall so recommend him." Nonetheless, the medical school did not admit Bakke. The school reserved 16 percent of the slots in the entering class for minority students, many of whom were recruited by a special minority admissions task force. Task force admittees presented substantially lower undergraduate grade point averages and dramatically lower test scores than did Bakke and other regular admittees to the medical school. After unsuccessfully petitioning the university and the Department of Health, Education and Welfare for redress, Bakke filed a suit in Yolo County Superior Court, maintaining that by reserving places for minority students "judged apart from and permitted to meet lower standards of admission than Bakke," the institution's affirmative action program denied him equal protection of the law.

Bakke's suit eventually reached the U.S. Supreme Court. While the case was pending, the dispute filled the pages and airwaves of the national press, sparking protest marches on college campuses, vigorous debate within the White House, and frenzied lobbying in Washington corridors. The Court heard oral arguments in the fall of 1977 but did not hand down a decision until the following June. By a five-to-four margin, a bitterly divided court upheld Allan Bakke's claim that the University of California had wrongfully denied him admission to its medical school. Four justices ruling in Bakke's favor held all race-based programs illegal, arguing that the "plain language" of the 1964 Civil Rights Act forbade excluding any individual from a public benefit on racial grounds. The four dissenters affirmed the legality of race-based affirmative action programs to relieve the debilitating effects of discrimination. Justice Lewis Powell's swing vote in favor of Bakke split the difference on the fundamental question; institutions could not exclude individuals solely on the basis of race, but race and ethnicity could be considered in a broader assessment of admission qualifications. "It was a landmark occasion," one distinguished law professor conceded, "but the court failed to produce a landmark decision."

Although the Court had struck down so-called reverse discrimination in admissions and hiring, it did not outlaw all race-conscious affirmative action. Justice Powell's decisive opinion held that "a diverse student body" remained "a constitutionally permissible goal for an institution of higher education," even where remedying past discrimination or promoting racial integration would not pass judicial muster. To comply with the law, universities, businesses, and other institutions began to stress diversity rather than eliminating discrimination or promoting integration.

Inadvertently, *Bakke* encouraged the triumph of diversity. Universities actually stepped up affirmative action in the wake of the decision, using the Court-approved need to achieve cultural diversity as their rationale. In many cases, such as at UCLA, earlier efforts to recruit students gave way to hard-target proportional representation schemes.

Meanwhile, law and public policy also reinforced the celebration of diversity in regard to bilingual education. In *Lau v. Nichols* (1974), the Supreme Court required that school districts take affirmative steps to identify and teach students with limited English proficiency (LEP). . . . The prevailing idea was not integration, but to respect and preserve the cultural integrity of non-English speakers, primarily of Hispanics, who made up 80 percent of LEP students in the late 1970s. In 1979 the newly created U.S. Department of Education moved to expand and formalize bilingual education. The proposed regulations would have forced districts to hire 50,000 new certified bilingual teachers and to establish hundreds of new programs. An uproar ensued; Chicago school officials, for instance, complained that they were expected to find native-language instructors for 90,000 students in 139 separate languages. The new regulations were never imposed.

Still, the rollback never challenged the fundamental legal and ideological rationale for bilingual, bicultural education in the nation's schools. Many school districts, especially in areas with large Latino populations, maintained booming programs in service of the now-triumphant ideal of diversity. In fact, in 1979, black parents in Michigan sued to have their children taught in black English. A federal judge ordered the school district in Ann Arbor, Michigan, to offer special language programs for African American students. These policies revised the basic notions of citizenship, challenging the very idea of a national community.

The ideological shift to diversity led to a reconception of the very nature of America—to see the nation not as a melting pot where many different peoples and cultures contributed to one common stew, but as discrete peoples and cultures sharing the same places—a tapestry, salad bowl, or rainbow. "The American flag," the Reverend Jesse Jackson declared at the 1988 Democratic National Convention, "is red, white and blue. But America is red, white, black, brown, and yellow—all the colors of a rainbow."

In this view, which became the dominant way of conceiving of race relations in the 1970s and 1980s, there was no such thing as American culture. Instead, there were many American cultures. The "discriminatory separate-but-equal doctrine of the past," Harold Cruse asserted, would give way to a democratic "plural-but-equal" future. Indeed, the emphasis on diversity, on cultural autonomy and difference, echoed throughout 1970s America. White ethnics picked it up, as did feminists and gay rights advocates and even the elderly. A new conception of the public arena emerged: Americans based their claims on the commonweal (and, increasingly, their demands for exemption from its responsibilities) less on their common rights and privileges as citizens than on their specific cultural identities.

The idea of diversity won such broad (if only shallow) acceptance that during the 1980s, diversity management became a multimillion-dollar industry. Thousands of American businesses hired diversity consultants to relieve racial tensions and train employees to "value difference." By 1990, almost half of the Fortune 500 companies employed full-time staff responsible for managing diversity. Textbooks, university curricula, and museum exhibitions reflected the new emphasis on multiculturalism, and government bureaucrats routinely received sensitivity training.

This shift from integration to diversity was neither unchallenged nor complete. But the center of gravity had drifted toward multiculturalism. If Americans remained suspicious of minority cultural nationalism, assimilation and integration had few champions. The prominent Catholic intellectual Michael Novak encapsulated the era's prevailing mood when he called the 1970s the "decade of the Ethnics." Pausing on his intellectual odyssey from Sixties radical to Eighties conservative at the waystation of cultural diversity, Novak celebrated the new ethnic politics. "It asserts that *groups* can structure the rules and goals and procedures of American life," Novak declared in *The Rise of the Unmeltable Ethnics*. "It asserts that individuals, if they do not wish to, do not have to 'melt.'" For better or worse, the nation's diverse subcultures would no longer submit to a single dominant, universalizing, WASP "Superculture."

The New Feminism

ᐁ *Visualizing Feminism*

Modern feminism emerged in the early 1960s, with John Kennedy's Commission on the Status of Women, the Equal Pay Act of 1963, and the publication that year of Betty Friedan's The Feminine Mystique. *During the 1960s, feminists emphasized their exclusion from the mainstream—from politics, from the professions, from Princeton and Yale, from ordinary good jobs. Through the National Organization for Women (NOW) and other organizations, they demanded equality in the workplace and assailed the idea, captured in the phrase "the feminine mystique," that women could live full, rich lives in purely domestic roles. By the 1970s, vocal critics of this position had emerged. Some believed that there could be no equality that did not involve significant changes in the family and domestic relations. Others rejected the assumption, implicit in the earlier view, that women should strive to be like men. This new-style feminism emphasized that feminists should understand, value, and utilize their qualities as* women.

The following photographs illustrate the enormous changes that occurred in feminism between 1945 and 1975. The first photograph, of a display celebrating the 100th anniversary of the Women's Rights Convention at Seneca Falls, New York, reflects the ambivalence of women's position at midcentury. The second, of a 1971 rally in Washington, D.C., reveals no ambivalence at all. Look at the photographs carefully. What can be learned from each of them?

The Woman Citizen, 1948. National Archives, Women's Bureau.

The Woman Citizen, 1971. Photo by Dennis Brack/stock photo.com.

❧ The Equal Rights Amendment

Section 1. Equality of rights under the law shall not be denied or abridged
  by the United States or by any state on account of sex.
Section 2. The Congress shall have the power to enforce, by appropriate
  legislation, the provisions of this article.
Section 3. This amendment shall take effect two years after the date of
  ratification.

*The ERA was approved by Congress in 1972 and by the end of that year had
been ratified by twenty-two of the required thirty-eight states. By 1977, 35 states
had ratified. The deadline for ratification was extended in 1979 to June 30,
1982, but no more states ratified the amendment, and it failed when time ran
out. Some of the arguments for and against the ERA are listed below. Which do
you find persuasive?*

❧ For the ERA

1. America has a long history of defending the equal rights of its citizens.
2. In the absence of the ERA, women are governed by hundreds of state
   statutes, rules, and regulations that include sex-based preferences.
3. The Supreme Court has been slow in applying the fourteenth
   amendment to discrimination based on sex.
4. The amendment is necessary to overcome discrimination based on
   sex that affects property and inheritance rights, among others.

5. The ERA would not result in men suddenly withdrawing support from their families, thus forcing their wives to go to work.

6. Under an all-volunteer army, the issue of women being drafted is moot. If the draft was reinstated, women would have deferment rights just as men do.

7. Under the ERA, the law would still allow reasonable classifications based on characteristics unique to men or women (e.g., child-bearing).

8. Unisex toilets would not be required under the amendment; the courts have held that the right to privacy takes precedence in that case.

9. Women and men would be more likely to share child care responsibilities; men would spend more time with their children.

10. Equality should not be subject to the whim of state legislatures.

11. All citizens have a right to equal protection under the law.

Against the ERA

1. The language of the ERA is rigid rather than flexible.

2. The ERA would destroy all state legislation designed to protect women, including laws dealing with employment, child support, alimony, rape, and the military draft.

3. The ERA would require shared, rather than separate, toilet facilities.

4. It is foolish to tinker with the Constitution just to satisfy a philosophical desire for equality.

5. The amendment would take away the important right of states to legislate on behalf of women.

6. The ERA would have results that we cannot predict; we shouldn't gamble with so general an enactment.

7. The states have been active in passing laws providing equal pay for equal work. Let them continue to do so.

8. The ERA could have a profoundly negative impact on the American family.

 ON THE WEB   *For a detailed chronology of the Equal Rights Amendment, beginning in 1923, see the National Organization for Women (NOW) Web site at www.now.org/issues/economic/cea/history.html.*

The Decline of the Hero

❧ Polling for Heroes

The "decline of the American hero" was a staple argument of the 1970s. The popular magazines of the day carried one article after another on the theme: "Why We Kill Our Heroes," "Disappearing Heroes," "The Vanishing American Hero," "The End of the American Hero." The Alamo loomed large in this discussion, because, in an age that valued mere survival, the defense of the Alamo seemed so clearly to have involved genuine personal risk. "In death," wrote journalist Peter Axthelm in a 1979 story in Newsweek, *"the heroes of the Alamo had reshaped their world. In doing so, they had taken a fierce self-respect to the level of heroism—and provided a working definition that endures and illuminates."*

Axthelm had also decided who was not *heroic: aggressive, controversial women who were vocal advocates of liberal and radical causes, including whale-saving actress Vanessa Redgrave and Margaret Trudeau, the free-spirited ex-wife of the Canadian prime minister. At the top of his list was movie star and antiwar protester Jane Fonda, whose "spotlighted harangues inspire the wish that she would shut up."*

Reprinted below are the results of a 1977 poll conducted by Senior Scholastic, *a magazine regularly used for teaching purposes by junior high and high school teachers. Thirty thousand readers had been asked to answer the question, "Is there a man or woman living today whom you consider your personal hero?" About half responded. Some of the names will be familiar; information on others can be found on the Internet.*

From the list provided,* do you agree with the claim that the American hero is in decline? Why or why not? If the claim is so obvious, why does Peter Axthelm's argument, paraphrased above, seem shrill and biased? Is it possible there is a "politics" to heroes, or even to the idea of heroes? How does the "end of the American hero" argument resonate with the strength of feminism in the 1970s?

1. Farah Fawcett Majors
2. Jerry Lewis
3. Nadia Comaneci
4. No hero at all
5. Paul Michael Glazer
6. Lee Majors
7. John Wayne
8. Dorothy Hamill
9. Bruce Jenner
10. O. J. Simpson

Lee Majors (center), star of the popular television series, *The Six Million Dollar Man*, and his wife, Farah Fawcett Majors (right), star of *Charlie's Angels.* Photos12.com-Collection Cinema.

*Reprinted by permission of Scholastic, Inc.

THE BIG PICTURE

It is the fall of 2004, and the problems presented to Americans in the 1970s remain unresolved or, in some cases, have grown in importance. More than thirty years after the Arab oil boycott revealed the nation's dependence on imports, oil hovers at $50 a barrel and the country drifts from oil crisis to oil crisis, lacking even the semblance of an energy policy that would address the basic problem. Three decades after it became clear that the United States would suffer defeat in Vietnam because it had underestimated the commitment of the Vietnamese to national sovereignty, the American nation is mired in a war caused by a similar, arrogant ignorance of how an invaded Iraq would respond to an alien armed force. The globalization of the American economy continues unabated, visible in the 1970s in rising imports of Japanese automobiles, in large, new inflows of immigrants under the Hart-Cellar Act of 1965, in the decline of the dollar and, in the early 1980s, in hostility toward Asian Americans (among other minorities) that caused the 1982 Detroit murder of Vincent Chin (described in Bruce Schulman's essay). American manufacturing remains in long-term decline, whittling away at the incomes of working Americans. One result of all this was a deadly multiethnic riot in Los Angeles in 1994.

In the midst of these challenges, Americans confronted social problems old and new, including racial integration and feminism. By the end of the 1970s they had turned away from integration, forging a new suburbia that left blacks and other minorities in the inner cities. And they were on the verge of rejecting the foremost symbol of the feminist movement, the Equal Rights Amendment. And heroes? There was something real, and poignant, in the rather thin list of personal heroes posted by *Senior Scholastic* in 1977. But the list did include several women, an African American, and a person from another country (Nadia Comaneci)—signs of the culture of "diversity," perhaps. Behind the call for new American heroes was, as Peter Axthelm's remarks suggest, a rejection of minorities and women, and a nostalgic longing for the return of the male warrior and, in the largest sense, for the American nation that was no more. In a word, Rambo.

Chapter 14

Reagan's America

When he took office as president in 1981, Ronald Reagan had many constituencies. As the oldest man ever to assume the presidency, he was the candidate of the elderly. His promises to restore American "strength" and "pride" brought him the support of millions of working-class and middle-class Americans who could not understand or accept the defeat in Vietnam, humiliation at the hands of the Arab nations, or the nation's weakness in the international marketplace. Reagan appealed to the business community and to growing numbers of other Americans who believed that welfare, the welfare state, liberalism, big government, unions, or high taxes were responsible for the nation's ills. And he had the support of fundamentalist Christians, who interpreted the nation's troubles as a fall from grace and sought a remedy in the restoration of traditional values and practices: an end to abortion, prayer in the public schools, sexual abstinence before marriage, old-fashioned gender roles, censorship of the pornographic or salacious.

For twelve years Reagan and his successor, George Bush, held this curious coalition together. They did it partly with bravado and posturing, partly with American lives. Reagan did his best to revive a foundering Cold War and to restore the Soviet Union as the "evil empire" that Americans loved to hate. He even imagined a technology, familiarly known as "Star Wars," that would miraculously protect Americans from missile attacks. Americans responded by shelling out billions for Star Wars and celebrating the October 1983 invasion of the tiny Caribbean island of Grenada, with its

Marxist government, as a sign of a reemerging America that once again had control of its destiny. Almost a decade later, when the Cold War had ended, Bush found a new, and even worthy, enemy: Iraq's Saddam Hussein, who had invaded oil-rich Kuwait. Once again, the American public responded, greeting "Operation Desert Storm" with a frenzy of patriotism and, rather pointedly, offering returning troops (136 Americans were killed) the lavish homecomings that Vietnam veterans had been denied.

On the domestic front, Reagan and Bush appeared to have made some progress, especially in reconstructing the nation's faltering economy. The catastrophic inflation rates of the Carter years had been dramatically reduced. Unemployment, which had reached a post–World War II peak of 10 percent in the second year of Reagan's first term, had been reduced as well. The Reagan administration had found a remedy for "stagflation."

Yet problems remained. In the midst of the prosperity of the mid-1980s, unemployment stayed at a level more than twice that considered reasonable a generation earlier. Major industries, including machine tools, clothing, steel, and automobiles, remained at the mercy of foreign competition. The United States was losing its heavy industry and, increasingly, its light industry, too. Most of the new jobs—and there were millions of them—were in nonunion service industries that paid low wages and did not offer their employees health insurance or pension plans. More Americans were working, but poor, too—and frightened about the future. When Bush proved ineffectual at dealing with recession in 1992, the voters replaced him with Arkansas Governor Bill Clinton.

Facing the economic uncertainties that were part of the ordinary round of life, Americans turned mean, aggressive, and deadly. Violent crimes—assaults, murders, and rapes—became commonplace events in major cities, and the ghettos of some cities, where drug traffic was heavy, became zones of terror, where people were afraid to leave their homes. Despite Bush's call for a "kinder, gentler" nation, all manner of real and fictitious Americans—talk show hosts, comedians, rock stars, cartoon characters—seemed to revel in insults, abuse, and hate-mongering. The victims were predictable: blacks, women, Asians, Arabs, welfare recipients, Jews, homosexuals, and (for rap artists like N.W.A.) the police. It was an ugly age.

As the twenty-first century approached, the search for ways of understanding the nation's difficult recent history increasingly took the form of forays into the realm of culture. One set of conservative critics attacked the emerging "multicultural" focus of the high schools and universities, calling for a return to a traditional curriculum that emphasized the nation's European roots. Book-banning made a comeback when fundamentalist, "pro-family" groups went to court to prove that some school districts were using public-school textbooks to teach the "religion" of secular humanism. Under Reagan and Bush—but not Clinton—the National Endowment for the Arts withdrew its support from projects—usually ones with some erotic content—that did not have "the widest audience."

One of the more interesting cultural battles of the 1980s was waged by Tipper Gore, the wife of Albert Gore, Jr., the Tennessee senator who would become Clinton's vice president. Working through a variety of family groups, including her own Parents' Music Resource Center, Gore focused her criticism on heavy metal rock music, a genre she claimed was characterized by harmful images of sadism, brutality, and eroticism. After congressional hearings in 1985, the record industry agreed to a voluntary system of warning labels. Later in the decade and into the 1990s, cultural censors turned their guns on the misogynist lyrics of rap group 2 Live Crew and the violent lyrics of what had become known as "gangsta" rap. And the beat goes on.

Americans have always had a prudish streak, and perhaps the culture wars of the 1980s and 1990s were just another outbreak of the nation's obsession with morality. More likely they are the other face of the American postindustrial economy. One face—whether under Reagan, Bush, or Clinton seems to make no difference—looks outward toward a new, post-American world in which the United States is just another player in the international marketplace. The other face looks inward, contemplating the damage already wrought by these changes and anticipating problems to come. It is this face—the face of a pervasive anxiety about the future—that seeks some modicum of control in the "culture wars."

INTERPRETIVE ESSAY

Reckoning with Reagan

Michael Schaller

When Ronald Reagan died on June 5, 2004, after a long struggle with Alzheimer's disease that had kept him from the public for most of the preceding fifteen years, the nation paused to pay its respects to a politician and ideologue who seemed, nonetheless, to have transcended politics and ideology. "Friend and foe acknowledge the Great Communicator," read the headline in one newspaper. Suspending his campaign for the presidency, the future nominee of the Democratic Party, John Kerry, said "even when he was breaking Democrats' hearts, he did so with a smile and in the spirit of honest and open debate. . . . He was the voice of America in good times and in grief." "He was a very charismatic president," added Democrat and former astronaut John Glenn, "and had a very friendly nature that people responded to." George Pataki, the Republican Governor of New York, announced that "the sun has set on the remarkable life of the great man who reminded us it is always morning in America," and President George W. Bush, proclaiming Reagan's death "a sad hour in the life of America," said that he "leaves behind a nation he restored and a world he helped save."

Comments such as these should be understood as part of a myth-making process, a process required by the public (or a good portion of it, anyway), and a ritual in which everyone—right and left, both sides of the aisle—was required to participate. In the selection that follows, historian Michael Schaller offers us something different: an effort to take a reasonably objective measure of the two-term Reagan presidency. What conclusions does he draw? What were Reagan's strengths and weaknesses? What is his legacy?

Ronald Reagan had an impact on American government and society that was both less than he claimed and greater than his critics admitted. The president took credit for what he called the longest post-1945 period of economic growth, a reduction in the size, cost, and scope of government, a rebirth of national spirit, and the restoration of "traditional" values in such varied spheres as judicial decision making and private moral behavior. Administration policies affected all this and more, although not always in ways Reagan understood.

Late in 1987, about the time the collapse in stock prices rocked the Reagan Recovery, director Oliver Stone released the film *Wall Street*, a cautionary tale about the rise and fall of a tycoon named Gordon Gekko. Gekko specialized in buying up shares in undervalued companies through "leveraged buyouts," a fancy term for borrowed money. To finance the deals, he sold off, or "stripped," assets of the acquired corporation, reaping large personal profits. Often, however, little remained of the original company. In a climactic scene, a group of stockholders opposed to Gekko's acquisition of an airline berates him for his greed and fixation with profits. With disdain, Gekko retorts that "greed is good, greed is healthy" because it promotes growth and success in the free market. In the end, however, Gekko is exposed as a crook who secretly broke the law to build his fortune. This parable of deceit was, in fact, a case of art imitating life.

In May 1986 financier Ivan F. Boesky—the Gekko prototype—addressed, for the second time that year, graduating business students at the University of California at Berkeley. At forty-eight years of age, Boesky was already a legend among aspiring MBAs. The child of immigrant parents, he earned over $100 million in 1985 buying underpriced shares of stock in companies about to be acquired in lucrative mergers. Boesky summarized his recent book, *Merger Mania*, by saying that his success reflected the tried and true virtues of hard work, common sense, and luck. "There are no easy ways to make money in the securities market," he observed. Boesky assured the students that "greed is healthy." Earning and flaunting great wealth was the mother's milk of capitalism, growth, and prosperity. The audience sat rapt as he recited the canon of the free market. He admonished them that as they "accumulated wealth and power," they ought to remain "God-fearing and responsible to the system that has given you this opportunity." They should "give back to the system with humility, and don't take yourself too seriously."

In November 1986 the Securities Exchange Commission and New York prosecutors announced that Ivan Boesky had pled guilty to illegally buying "inside" information from corporate officials which he used to manipulate stock prices, acquire companies, and earn a fortune. As part of the plea bargain, Boesky paid a civil fine of $100 million (half of which was tax deductible), pled guilty to a criminal charge which carried up to five years in prison, and promised to cooperate in the prosecution of corrupt business associates. In several important ways, Boesky's rise and fall mirrored the ambiguities of the Reagan era.

Economic Imbalances

Economic growth during the Reagan Recovery proved highly selective. In general, prosperity and wealth flowed to the East and West coasts, partly because of defense spending. The Northeast and California thrived even as farm and energy-producing regions stagnated. After having been given up for dead in the 1970s, Boston and Manhattan blossomed during the 1980s. Real estate values skyrocketed for both residential and commercial property.

In contrast, the so-called rust belt of the upper Midwest experienced a loss of high-paying industrial jobs. The steel industry, for example, lost over $12 billion during the 1980s. Employment fell by 58%. Even as Reagan spoke of "morning in America," the sun began to set on traditional industries such as steel, rubber, machine tools, and automobile manufacturing. Farmers also faced hard times. Following a boom in the 1970s, land value declined as did the prices farmers received for their products. By mid-decade, farm income declined to a point below where it had been in 1970. The country avoided a national recession between 1983 and 1989, but rolling, regional recessions were common phenomena. . . .

Both the government and private industry thrived on unprecedented levels of indebtedness. During Reagan's two terms the cumulative national debt tripled, from about $900 billion to almost $2.7 trillion. Interest payments alone cost taxpayers $200 billion per year. Government borrowing absorbed three-fourths of the annual net savings of families and businesses. In light of this, some cynics labeled Reagan's talk of balanced budgets a "classic case of a drunk preaching temperance."

The domestic borrowing pool had to be supplemented by large infusions of foreign capital, especially from Japan and Germany. By the late-1980s, foreign investors held as much as 20% of the national debt. In less than a decade, the United States went from being the world's biggest creditor to the world's biggest debtor. Instead of interest payments on the debt flowing into private American coffers, a growing portion of the payments flowed out of the country.

The nation's foreign trade deficit also grew dramatically during the 1980s. Near the start of the decade, the value of foreign manufactured imports surpassed by about $26 billion the value of American manufactured products sold abroad. By the end of the decade, the United States ran a deficit of more than $150 billion per year. Every week, on average during the 1980s, American consumers spent about $2 billion more abroad than foreigners spent on American products. The cumulative trade imbalance for the decade approached $1 trillion.

Foreign investors used their dollar surpluses to buy American real estate, factories, and stock shares. Some economists considered this a healthy vote of confidence. Foreign investments provided jobs for Americans. But business profits—and decision-making power—flowed abroad. Economic security depended increasingly on Japanese, British, German, Dutch, and Saudi willingness to buy the public and private debt of the United States.

The New Federalism

As a presidential candidate, Ronald Reagan pledged to shrink the scope of the federal government by returning greater authority and responsibility to the states. In practice, the Reagan administration shifted costs, not power, to local government. Under the so-called "new federalism," Washington burdened state, county, and city governments with many new, expensive to administer regulations, such as monitoring pollution, removing asbestos from schools, and supervising nursing homes—but provided less federal money than before.

During the 1980s, federal allocations to states fell by almost 13%, from $109 to $94 billion calculated in constant 1982 dollars. As Carroll A. Campbell, Jr., the Republican governor of South Carolina, complained: "instead of giving power to the states and giving us the flexibility of addressing problems," the states had new federal mandates imposed upon them. Even though state officials often agreed with the purpose of the new mandates (such as controlling pollution), they considered the Reagan administration's denial of funds a "cruel deception."

Other forms of cost cutting affected states negatively. For example, federal agencies postponed repairs of highways, bridges, and other parts of the transportation system to save money. These savings were really costs passed down to those who followed. Far from sharing in the "Reagan Recovery," by 1989 half the fifty states listed themselves as suffering from "fiscal distress." To pay for vital services, many states raised taxes. This negated a large part of the federal income tax reduction.

The Culture of Greed

Supply-siders certainly achieved their goal of reversing New Deal style income redistribution programs. Not only did resources cease to flow from wealthier to less well off Americans, but a substantial portion of national wealth was redistributed to Germany and Japan. Reagan-era policies practically doubled the share of national income going to the wealthiest 1% of Americans, from 8.1 to about 15%. In 1980, 4,400 individuals filed income tax returns reporting an adjusted gross income of over $1 million. By 1987, over 35,000 taxpayers filed such returns. The net worth of the 400 richest Americans nearly tripled. In 1980 a typical corporate chief executive officer (CEO) made about 40 times the income of an average factory worker; nine years later the CEO made 93 times as much. Lawyers handling business mergers also gained great wealth. Over 1,300 partners of major law firms averaged higher pay than the 800 top executives in industry.

Not since the Gilded Age of the late nineteenth century or the Roaring Twenties had the acquisition and flaunting of wealth been so publicly celebrated as during the 1980s. Income became the accepted measure of one's value to society. Professional athletes earned immense sums as teams scrambled to recruit basketball, football, and baseball players from colleges. Congressman Kemp, economist Laffer, and writers Jude Wanniski and George Gilder celebrated financiers and deal makers as secular saints, enriching society. In his bestselling book *Wealth and Poverty* (1981) and opinion pieces appearing in the *Wall Street Journal*, Gilder emerged as a theologian of capitalism. "Faith in man, faith in the future, faith in the rising returns of giving, faith in the mutual benefits of trade, faith in the providence of God are all essential to successful capitalism," he wrote. In the gospel according to Gilder, "Capitalism begins with giving . . . thus the contest of gifts leads to an expansion of human sympathies." Accumulating wealth represented the highest morality. Only the unsuccessful blamed the system for their problems. The poor of the 1980s, he claimed, "are refusing to work hard."

Gilder, Laffer, and Wanniski identified the true heroes of the age as Wall Street operators such as Carl Icahn, T. Boone Pickens, Ivan Boesky, and Michael Milken and real estate speculator Donald Trump—men who earned billions of dollars buying and merging companies and in construction. They were celebrated as role models and builders of a better world.

A "merger mania," fueled by changes in the 1981 tax law and a relaxed attitude toward enforcement of anti-trust statutes by the Reagan Justice Department, gripped Wall Street through 1987. Boesky and Milken exemplified the "risk arbitrager," financiers who discovered ways to make fortunes by borrowing money to merge and acquire large enterprises. Many of the nation's biggest companies bought up competitors or were themselves swallowed up in leveraged buyouts, financed by huge loans bearing high interest rates. Corporate raiders argued that these deals rewarded stockholders and got rid of incompetent management, thus increasing competitiveness.

Because many multi-billion dollar deals were too risky for banks, insurance, or pension funds to finance, Milken and others pioneered the use of "junk bonds." Corporate raiders issued these I.O.U.s that paid very high rates of interest. Repayment of the heavy debt often compelled the purchaser to sell off or "strip" portions of the newly acquired business.

Many of the nation's largest corporations, including R. J. Reynolds, Nabisco, Walt Disney, Gulf, Federated Department Stores, and R. H. Macy were the objects of leveraged buyouts, some willingly and others under protest. Between 1984 and 1987, twenty-one mergers valued at over $1 billion each occurred. Many corporations sought to avoid hostile takeovers by boosting immediate profitability to stockholders by going heavily into debt through issuing bonds or paying special dividends. This increased indebtedness made a buyout more expensive and less attractive to outsiders. It left the company less able to raise funds for investment in plants and new products. . . .

Critics of these activities charged that money spent on acquisitions contributed nothing to the productive capacity of the economy since it did not go into research or new product lines. The debt incurred by mergers became a long-term burden. Corporate profits went mainly to paying bondholders, not investing in new plants. In any period of recession, when profits dipped, it seemed likely that leveraged corporations would have difficulty paying interest on the costly junk bonds.

Following Boesky's conviction at the end of 1986, a series of probes revealed evidence of widespread insider trading among some of the most successful financiers. By the end of the decade Boesky, Milken, and many others pled guilty to a variety of illegal practices. Drexel, Burnham, Lambert, Inc., Milken's trading firm and the giant of the junk bond industry, pled guilty to legal violations and went bankrupt. The junk bond market shrank dramatically by 1988, especially as heavily indebted companies began to default on payments and go into bankruptcy.

Yuppies

In mid-decade, a new social category emerged on the American scene. *Newsweek* magazine called 1984 "The Year of the Yuppie," an acronym for young, urban, upwardly mobile professionals. For a time, this group seemed as charmed as the Wall Street wizards. *Newsweek*, in particular, applauded the group's eagerness to "go for it" as a sign of the "yuppie virtues of imagination, daring and entrepreneurship." Yuppies existed "on a new plane of consciousness, a state of Transcendental Acquisition."

Demographers and advertisers first used the term. Journalists popularized it in 1983–84, partly to explain Senator Gary Hart's unexpected popularity among young Americans as he campaigned for the Democratic presidential nomination. Unlike radical protesters or hippies of the 1960s, these young adults were hardly social rebels. They plunged joyously into the American mainstream ready to consume.

Certified yuppies—people born between 1945 and 1959, earning over $40,000 as a professional or manager, and living in a city—totaled about 1.5 million. As candidate Hart learned, they were not a reliable constituency for Democratic liberals. Yuppies tended to be "pro-choice" on the abortion issue, enjoyed "recreational drugs," and supported Reagan's economic policies. They aspired to become investment bankers, not social workers. In 1985, for example, one-third of the entire senior class at Yale sought jobs as financial analysts at First Boston Corporation.

Yuppies enjoyed creature comforts, indulging themselves, when possible, with "leisure products" like Porsches and BMWs, expensive sneakers, state-of-the-art electronic equipment, and gourmet foods. They flocked to health spas, wore designer clothes made of natural fibers, jogged, and put a high value on "looking good." . . .

The Wall Street Crash of October 19, 1987, ended the mystique surrounding young entrepreneurs. That day, as the dimension of the collapse expanded, anxious crowds gathered outside the New York Stock Exchange. A man began shouting, "The end is near! It's all over! The Reagan Revolution is over! Down with MBAs! Down with Yuppies!" Another member of the crowd tried to bolster confidence by yelling, "Whoever dies with the most toys wins!"

After only four years of grace, the term yuppie evolved into a slur. In 1988 *Newsweek* declared the group in "disgrace" and even suggested that the '80s were over, two years early. The *Wall Street Journal* reported "conspicuous consumption is passé." *New York* magazine, a purveyor to yuppie tastes, ran a cover story celebrating altruism and asked its readers: "HAD IT WITH PRIDE, COVETOUSNESS, LUST, ANGER, GLUTTONY, ENVY AND SLOTH? IT'S TIME TO START DOING GOOD."

The Other Americans

Far less glamorous than either the risk arbitrageurs of Wall Street or the yuppies of Los Angeles were the people of average income and the poor. Their experience during the 1980s differed markedly from the fables of wealth told by George Gilder. Measured in constant dollars, the average family income of the poorest fifth of the population dropped (from $5,439 to $4,107) while the income of the richest fifth swelled from $62,000 to $69,000. During the Reagan Recovery, the most affluent fifth of American households experienced a 14% increase in their wealth while the middle three-fifths experienced little or no improvement. Put simply, the rich got richer and everyone else tread water.

As a justification of his tax policy, President Reagan maintained that despite the cut in tax rates after 1981, federal revenues had grown. He neglected to mention that they never increased enough to cover the large expansion in military expenditures. But his assertion obscured the fact that the rate reductions favored the wealthy and that the total tax bite (which included Social Security, state, and sales taxes) paid by the average American family did not diminish and even increased slightly during the 1980s.

Economic growth after 1983 seemed impressive when compared to the late 1970s, but appeared less so when the base of comparison became the period from the Second World War through the Carter administration. Overall, the economy grew at a faster rate during the 1960s and 1970s than in the 1980s. Unemployment remained higher during the 1980s than in most years from 1947 to 1973. Real wages, which began to stagnate during the 1970s, continued to do so. In aggregate, individual salaries declined slightly during the Reagan years. The impact of this, however, was hidden because of a substantial increase in the number of working wives and mothers who boosted total family income. By 1989, the wealthiest two-fifths of American families received 67.8% of national income, while the bottom two-fifths earned a mere 15.4%—a larger spread than at any time since 1945.

Women and children were the most likely to be poor. The number of children living in poverty, one in five, had grown by 24% during the 1980s. The so-called feminization of poverty also grew more severe during the Reagan decade. The percentage of children living with a never married mother more than doubled during the 1980s, from 2.9 to 7%. By 1989 one of every four births in the United States was to an unwed woman. African-American and Hispanic women had the highest likelihood of becoming single mothers. Unwed mothers were less likely to receive prenatal care, finish high school, or hold a paying job.

These problems had complex causes and Reagan's policies were by no means responsible for creating them. But the refusal of his administration to address them seriously made the situation worse. In a particularly counterproductive move, the Reagan administration slashed spending for the WIC (Women-Infants-Children) program that provided pre- and post-natal care to poor women and helped reduce infant mortality rates and future medical costs.

Reagan defended reductions in social welfare spending with a typical quip. America, he remarked, had fought a war on poverty for nearly twenty years before he took office "and poverty won." At first glance, statistics he quoted seemed to confirm his dismal assessment. After an initial decline in the poverty rate to about 13% during the late Johnson and early Nixon administrations, the rate stalled at this level through the early 1980s.

But these aggregate numbers masked a major transformation in the nature of poverty. Increased spending on programs such as Social Security and Medicare dramatically improved the lot of the elderly and handicapped. They were much less likely to be poor by the 1980s than at any time since

1945. The bulk of the poor after 1980 consisted of single mothers, young children, and young minority men with little education and few job skills. These groups had either not been the beneficiaries of anti-poverty programs during the 1970s or were left in the lurch by spending cuts in such programs.

Rather than welfare spending "causing" dependency, as many conservatives argued, the surging rates of teen pregnancy, the breakdown of stable family structures in the minority community, and the loss of millions of basic manufacturing jobs in cities, where most of the poor now lived, contributed to the creation of the "new poor."

Supply-siders made much of the fact that the American economy produced 18 million jobs under Reagan. Yet, nearly as many jobs were created during the 1970s. The new jobs varied a good deal. About half paid $20,000 or more annually. Of the remainder, many paid minimum wage and were part-time only. Administration boosters blamed President Carter for the fact that between 1979 and 1984, some 11.5 million workers lost jobs because of plant closings. Deindustrialization in the so-called rust belt of the upper Midwest meant that laid-off skilled steel and auto workers often found replacement jobs paying much less than they earned previously.

Between 1981 and 1989, according to an estimate by the private Economic Policy Institute, the real hourly wage of the typical production worker had fallen by about 6% in terms of what it could buy in the marketplace. Young males with high school diplomas but no college had fared even worse, losing almost 20% of their purchasing power during the 1980s.

Both conservatives and liberals were troubled by the increasing size of a permanent homeless population and a seemingly unreachable urban "underclass." The underclass consisted largely of minorities, especially African-Americans. The homeless were divided among women and children fleeing abusive spouses, unskilled individuals with social problems, and the chronically mentally ill. Many lived on city streets, in parks, or in subway stations, begging for money and food. Reagan dismissed the problem by suggesting homeless people were either nuts or people who enjoyed their lifestyle. While true in some cases, it vastly oversimplified the problem. The President showed no interest in boosting support for community mental health programs that might aid the chronic mentally ill.

The specter of the homeless and urban underclass unsettled American sensibilities but had little effect on public policy. Conservatives saw poverty primarily as a personal failure. Government efforts to help only made matters worse and provided a disincentive for individual effort. Liberals believed government had a responsibility to help, but offered few suggestions beyond restoring funds cut from social service programs.

Conservative Justice

. . . Reagan's Justice Department took an especially dim view of enforcing civil rights legislation during the 1980s. The president had opposed most of the civil rights acts passed since the 1960s and supported a constitutional amendment to outlaw school busing. Early in his presidency he criticized

Martin Luther King, Jr., as immoral, tainted by communist affiliation, and someone who should not be honored with a federal holiday. When Congress enacted such a holiday in 1983, Reagan signed the law with great fanfare and spoke eloquently about King's contribution to American justice.

This did not change administration policy. Shortly after taking office, Reagan outraged civil rights groups by ordering the Justice Department to argue before the Supreme Court that tax benefits be restored to segregated private schools and colleges. (The IRS had stripped such schools of their preferred tax status.) In 1983 the high court rebuffed the administration and ruled that the IRS had acted properly in denying tax benefits.

The Justice Department attacked affirmative action programs—preferential hiring plans designed to offset the legacy of discrimination—as a "racial spoils system." Until 1988, a majority of Supreme Court justices voted to uphold many affirmative action plans. But following the confirmation of Justice Kennedy, a majority of the justices voted in a series of cases during 1989 (the most important of which was *City of Richmond* v. *J. A. Corson, Co.*) to forbid as reverse discrimination government or private employers from setting aside a quota of jobs or contracts for minorities. In five related decisions, the justices made it more difficult for women, the elderly, and minorities to sue employers accused of job discrimination.

Administration hostility toward civil rights was frequently expressed by the conscious maladministration of law by executive agencies. For example, Clarence Thomas, whom President George Bush appointed to the Supreme Court in 1991, served as director of civil rights in the U.S. Department of Education and as chairman of the Equal Employment Opportunity Commission under Reagan. While in the Education Department he acknowledged in a court hearing that he was violating court-ordered deadlines for processing complaints of discrimination in higher education because they ran counter to the administration's philosophy. As EEOC chair, he permitted age-discrimination claims by thousands of older workers to lapse without action and declined to press many class-action discrimination suits because he objected to the principle of class-action suits.

Further evidence of hostility toward racial minorities emerged when the Reagan administration urged Congress not to renew the landmark 1965 Voting Rights Act that assured African-Americans in the South federal protection in registering and voting. When Congress renewed the law anyway, the Justice Department declined to investigate many allegations of interference with voting rights. Instead, officials made a special effort to investigate possible fraud in voter registration projects, especially those that succeeded in electing blacks to office. . . .

Private Spheres and Public Policies

Throughout his presidency, Ronald Reagan spoke out strongly on a number of moral issues, including abortion, drug use, prayer in school, sexuality, and the importance of traditional family values. At the same time, Reagan avoided expending very much political capital in pursuit of these controversial goals. For example, he addressed the annual "pro-life," anti-abortion rally in Washington by telephone, making certain that he would not be photographed alongside the strident movement leaders. Reagan worked hard to keep social conservatives in his corner but avoided political confrontations with Congress. . . .

Religion and Public Life

The influence of politically active fundamentalists and evangelical Christians continued well into the Reagan administration. Religious broadcasters prospered as never before. By 1985, the combined take of several hundred electronic ministries totaled well over $1 billion annually. Donations from viewers supported a variety of religious, charitable, political, and business causes, often funneled through unregulated funds such as the Moral Majority, the 700 Club, and the PTL ministry.

Televangelists preached at least two sermons. One fulminated against the threat posed by immorality, communism, abortion, and "secular humanism," a belief that humans, not God, were the basis for morality. The other celebrated a "gospel of wealth." Rev. Jimmy Swaggart epitomized the former style and Rev. Jim Bakker the latter. Both promised grace and a place in heaven via generous donations while here on earth.

Hellfire-and-brimstone preachers, along with the "feel good" variety, tapped into major trends in the 1980s. President Reagan's campaign against Godless communism and the Soviet Union's evil empire (discussed below) resembled Jimmy Swaggart's talk of sin and Satan. Jim and Tammy Faye Bakker's PTL show celebrated wealth and conspicuous consumption as a form of divine grace. The Bakkers told their viewers words to the effect "you can't do good unto others unless you feel good about yourself, and you can't feel good about yourself unless you have a lot of neat stuff." Tammy Faye practiced what she preached. For husband Jim's televised birthday party, she gave him a present of two live giraffes. On another show, Tammy had Jim preside over a wedding for two pet dogs.

Assessing the influence of the electronic ministries is difficult. Not all, or even most, televangelists were flimflam artists. Nor did all viewers accept the political doctrines put forth by media preachers. Many who watched the shows simply enjoyed the hymns, entertainment, and patriotic symbolism. Even a large number of donors, pollsters reported, contributed money out of a sense of responsibility to pay for watching the spectacle, just as those watching public TV gave during "pledge week."

Several of the most powerful televangelists fell from grace during 1987, while President Reagan became deeply embroiled in the Iran-Contra scandal. Money and sex proved their undoing. Federal prosecutors indicted Jim Bakker on numerous counts of fraud and conspiracy for bilking followers who invested $158 million in a combined hotel and religious theme park called Heritage USA and for stealing some $3 million in ministry funds. In essence, PTL operated as a pyramid scheme. Around the same time, a rival TV preacher revealed that Bakker had forced a female church member,

Jessica Hahn, to have sex with him and used donations to pay her over $200,000 in hush money.

Bakker resigned from PTL, blaming his troubles on rival Jimmy Swaggart who, he charged, lusted after the PTL theme park. Hahn, interviewed for a nude *Penthouse* magazine feature, explained that Bakker forced her to have sex by saying, "When you help the shepherd, you help the sheep." A jury convicted Bakker of cheating investors and he received a stiff jail term. The *Charlotte Observer*, whose reporters won a Pulitzer Prize for their exposure of Bakker's scheme, remarked in an editorial that it was fine for a preacher to promise his flock eternal life in a celestial city, "but if he promises an annual free stay in a luxury hotel here on earth, he'd better have the rooms available."

The revelations about popular media preachers came to resemble a soap opera. Jimmy Swaggart, Bakker's nemesis, was fingered by one of his rivals for frequenting prostitutes. After one prostitute described Swaggart as "really kinky," the minister made a tearful, televised confession. Faith healer Oral Roberts became an object of derision when he locked himself in a prayer tower claiming that "God would take him away" unless his flock mailed him several million dollars in a few weeks. Roberts' salvation came when a gambler made a large contribution. Reverend Pat Robertson, who controlled the large and profitable Christian Broadcasting Network, saw his campaign for the Republican presidential nomination collapse amidst laughter after he described how his prayers had diverted a hurricane from Virginia Beach to the more Godless New York City. Jerry Falwell, though not tainted by scandal, quit the Moral Majority in 1988 and devoted himself to church activities.

President Reagan distanced himself from the media preachers in time to avoid any direct taint. The so-called Gospel-Gate scandals came as little surprise to journalists covering the electronic church. Personal and financial lapses among certain televangelists had long been rumored. The Internal Revenue Service, Federal Communications Commission, and Justice Department had sought to investigate evidence of fraud and tax evasion but were pressed not to do so by the White House, which saw the Bakkers, Swaggart, and other media preachers as important allies. As historian Frances Fitzgerald observed, the televangelist empire, like Reagan's trust in the Laffer Curve, was built largely on faith and not-quite-innocent belief in miracles.

Sex and Gender in the 1980s

Through their public pronouncements and support for new laws, Ronald and Nancy Reagan attempted to alter the sexual behavior of many Americans and their attitudes toward abortion and the rights of women. During the 1980s, fear of sexually transmitted disease, bolstered by conservative opposition to abortion and the Equal Rights Amendment, dominated discussion of sex and gender issues. President Reagan, who condemned abortion as murder, urged pre-marital chastity and championed the "traditional" family of husband as breadwinner, wife as mother and homemaker. Conservatives predicted that the decade would assure the "end of the sexual revolution."

The president's words, critics charged, rang false. Reagan was the first divorced man elected president and had married two career women. He had a distant relationship with his children, two of whom, Patti and Michael, had written books that criticized their parents as hypocrites. Reagan's personal life aside, the traditional family he celebrated was an endangered specie. The number of households composed of a married couple and one or more children under age 18 had declined steadily over recent decades. In 1970, 40% of the nation's households mirrored this ideal. By 1980, ony 31% did. Barely a fourth of households were "traditional" as of 1991.

Reagan won plaudits for appointing a few women to high-profile positions during his first term. These included Jeane Kirkpatrick as ambassador to the United Nations, Margaret Heckler to head the Health and Human Services Department, and Sandra Day O'Connor as the first female associate justice of the Supreme Court. Overall, however, Reagan appointed fewer women to influential jobs than his three predecessors.

Feminists raised other concerns about private and public policies relating to gender. They decried women's lack of access to well-paying jobs, affordable child care, and reproductive freedom. They noted the growing number of women and young children living in poverty. Under Reagan, government either ignored these problems or took actions that made them worse.

The public debate over appropriate sexuality was complicated by the appearance of AIDS (acquired immune deficiency syndrome) in the early 1980s. A disease thought to have originated in Africa, the AIDS virus destroyed victims' immune systems and left them vulnerable to opportunistic infections. After much confusion, doctors determined that the main source of infection was through bodily fluids, such as semen and blood. Male homosexuals, intravenous drug users, and hemophiliacs faced the greatest risk of infection. As of 1991, the disease had killed over 100,000 Americans. Health experts predicted that over 200,000 victims would die by the end of 1993. In Africa, AIDS struck even harder.

Before 1985, Reagan all but ignored the epidemic. Although he had homosexual friends from his days in Hollywood, the president seemed uneasy discussing the disease, its mode of transmission, or preventive measures. The president appeared to find the entire subject distasteful and felt that anything he said expressing a sympathetic attitude toward its victims might upset religious conservatives who called the illness divine punishment of sinners. Among his own staff, this attitude was forcefully expressed by Patrick Buchanan who wrote: "The poor homosexuals. They have declared war on nature and now nature is exacting an awful retribution."

Scientists, including Surgeon General Dr. C. Everett Koop, urged public officials to endorse a "safe sex" program, since use of condoms reduced transmission of the virus. Fundamentalists, as well as the president, took "safe sex" to mean "no sex." During his first term, Reagan avoided discussing the AIDS problem, opposed spending much federal money on research, and exercised no leadership.

The president's attitude began to change after October 1985 when actor and matinee idol Rock Hudson died of the disease. He was a friend of

the Reagans and his death humanized AIDS for the first family and many ordinary Americans. By early 1986, the president called AIDS research a top
priority (though he still resisted spending additional money to study it) and
asked the Surgeon General to prepare a report on the affliction.

Koop's recommendations, issued in October 1986, called on Americans
to change their personal behavior. He described his remedy as "one, abstinence; two, monogamy; three, condoms." Conservatives such as Jerry Falwell,
Phyllis Schlafly, and Education Secretary William Bennett condemned Koop
for encouraging immorality by stressing the need for sexually active people to
use condoms. The Surgeon General urged Reagan to take the lead in telling
Americans more about the disease and how to prevent it. But the President
shied away from personal involvement with this public health crisis. In his one
major speech on AIDS, in May 1987, he merely said that scientists were "still
learning about how AIDS is transmitted" and that the public should not be
afraid to donate blood. He never mentioned sex or condoms.

Reagan imposed his conservative sexual mores on other public issues.
He persuaded Congress to bar most public funding for birth control and stop
Medicare from funding abortions for poor women. An administration measure provided funding for religiously oriented "chastity clinics" where coun-
selors advised teenage girls and women to "just say no" to avoid pregnancy.

As noted earlier, Reagan endorsed the so-called Right to Life movement and supported a constitutional amendment barring abortion except to
save the life of a mother. At least one member of the president's inner circle
had a unique perspective on the subject. Shortly before the president left office, Peter Grace, who chaired the Grace Commission to recommend efficiency in government, introduced Reagan at a banquet of anti-abortion
advocates. It took a man like Reagan, Grace explained, to point out the simple truth that "all living people started life as feces." When some listeners
gasped, Grace repeated himself forcefully: "Yes, even you started out as feces. And now dinner is served."

Reagan, like many conservatives, pursued the goal of recoupling sex
and reproduction, two activities which since the 1960s had been decoupled.
Women's access to abortion and contraception, like gay sex, defied the link-
age of sex, reproduction, and marriage. Despite the president's effort to affect public opinion, at the end of his term a strong majority of Americans
continued to favor the right of a woman to choose abortion.

The generally more conservative public view toward gender issues did
permit Republican members of Congress in 1982 to block reconsideration
of the Equal Rights Amendment to the Constitution when its deadline for
approval lapsed. Reagan also succeeded in blocking congressional efforts to
develop a national child-care policy, even though a majority of women with
young children had entered the workforce.

Although Reagan failed to persuade Congress to pass a constitutional
amendment banning abortion, he selected Supreme Court justices who, he
hoped, would eventually form a majority voting to strike down constitutional protection for abortion and privacy rights. In something of an irony,

the president who advocated "judicial restraint" relied on activist judges to implement his social agenda. . . .

Reagan era policy affected events only at the margins. The President's tax and spending initiatives did not alter the economic situation of most Americans. The conservative social agenda generated controversy without changing personal behavior. The appointment of conservative judges at all levels of the federal judiciary will probably have the most lasting impact on issues of privacy, civil rights, and civil liberties.

 SOURCES

The Reagan Image: A Photo Essay

Unlike most presidents, Ronald Reagan—the "Teflon" president as he was labeled by Congresswoman Pat Schroeder—remained popular with the American people even when his administration pursued unpopular or controversial policies—even when, for example, it was discovered that he had secretly funded the right-wing contras in Nicaragua, violating a congressional ban on such aid. To be sure, his continuing appeal says something about his personality, but it was also a product of a carefully cultivated image that was, especially in Reagan's case, consistent with the man. The photos in this essay are part of that cultivated image. What do they tell us about why Reagan was so well thought of during his presidency, and so fondly remembered at his death?

Ronald Reagan reading his morning papers while eating breakfast in the Oval Office. 1982.
Ronald Reagan Library.

 ON THE WEB   *The "Final Report of the Independent Counsel for Iran/Contra Matters" (1993) is available online at www.fas.org/irp/offdocs/walsh.*

Ronald Reagan riding at the ranch. 1983. Ronald Reagan Library.

Ronald Reagan after a day's work on the ranch. 1983. Ronald Reagan Library.

Ronald and Nancy Reagan taking a boat ride at the ranch. 1983. Ronald Reagan Library.

The Homeless: a Photo Essay

Of all the issues on which Reagan was found wanting, none seemed so obvious as his failure to deal with, or even to understand, the problem of the homeless. Noting that the nation had already renamed a Washington, D.C., airport in honor of the former president, one critic suggested that a "more fitting tribute to his legacy would be for each American city to name a park bench—where at least one homeless person sleeps every night—in honor of our fortieth president." One of the founders of the Oakland (Calif.) Union of the Homeless (1986–) charged that Reagan "was a catastrophe. He was single-handedly responsible for homelessness as we know it today—and he did it to feed the wealthy and the Pentagon."

For the most part, what we know about the history of homelessness supports these claims. Indeed, homelessness increased so rapidly during the Reagan years that the word itself, and the social problem it labels, is perhaps irrevocably linked to the 1980s. Why this is so is not entirely clear. Monies spent on subsidized housing may actually have increased during most of the Reagan presidency, largely because of sums appropriated in previous years that had not been spent. However, the Reagan budgets included dramatic cuts in new spending for low-income housing. Falling real wages and the declining value of the minimum wage took money out of the pockets of workers; about 25 percent of the homeless were working poor. Even so, the Teflon president might have deflected even this criticism had he not twice made comments that suggested an insensitivity to the plight of the homeless. In 1984, on Good Morning America, he fended off critics with the claim that "people who are sleeping on the grates . . . the homeless . . . are homeless, you might say, by choice." And four years later, asked what he thought of the people sleeping in Lafayette Park, across from the White House, he said, "There are always going to be people. They make it their own choice for staying out there."

Original caption: A homeless man lies under a clear blanket in Lafayette Square across the street from the White House, during the first snow of the season. Washington, D.C., November 11, 1987. UPI/Bettmann Newsphotos.

Original caption: One of a new breed of "cart" people, George Morris pushes a battered
grocery cart loaded with recyclable aluminum cans near Baltimore's Memorial Stadium.
Although at first glance seemingly belonging to the mass of the homeless, most of the "cart"
people are "entrepreneurs," reminiscent of old-fashioned rag pickers. Baltimore, 1986.
UPI/Bettmann Newsphotos.

Original caption: Delia Torres, 33, serves food to some of the homeless in front of the tar paper and plywood shanties they call home in a vacant lot on the lower east side. Torres sued New York City for the right to stay in the makeshift homes, claiming the city's homeless shelters are too dangerous. New York City, November 23, 1986. UPI/Bettmann.

Original caption: A homeless couple, identified as Andrew and Lydia, rest in a cardboard box near Madison Square Garden, at left, in New York on July 3. City officials are attempting to sanitize the area around the Garden, the site of the Democratic Convention. 1992. Reuters/Bettmann.

Reagan and the Religious Right

Ronald Reagan was not alone among late-twentieth century presidents in paying special attention to religion. Dwight Eisenhower instituted White House prayer breakfasts and helped put "In God We Trust" on the coinage. In 1972, Richard Nixon wooed blue collar workers to the Republican party with a "Catholic strategy" that included opposition to abortion. And Jimmy Carter, a Southern Baptist who claimed to have been "born again," won the presidency in 1976 in part because he convinced the small but growing Religious Right that he would provide sound moral leadership for the nation, rather than just more government. George W. Bush, who also claimed to have been "born again," advocated using the nation's churches to achieve social goals traditionally accomplished by government—what he called "faith-based initiatives."

Although religious faith and attention to moral values is required of all serious presidential aspirants, Republicans have been especially attentive to such issues. Because the Republican Party takes positions that favor big business and the wealthy, to win majorities it must convince large numbers of middle-class and working-class voters to abandon the Democratic Party, and often their economic self-interests. To do that, the Republicans have become the party of "family values," taking what they believe or claim are moral positions on abortion, school prayer, teenage sexual activity, drugs, pornography, and, in the 2004 campaign, same-sex marriage.

Ronald Reagan's March 1983 speech to the Annual Convention of the National Association of Evangelicals in Orlando, Florida, excerpted below, was a landmark in presidential attention to religious issues. In reading his remarks, think about whether it is appropriate for the leader of a nation to interpret and understand issues—especially issues of foreign policy—in religious terms. Does it advance the cause of international understanding to mark another nation as an "evil empire"? Is the United States always "good" and our enemy always "bad"? Domestically, would a school prayer amendment be appropriate in a nation that values religious diversity and tolerance for all religious views? Who is Reagan's god?

❧ Remarks at the Annual Convention of the National Association of Evangelicals in Orlando, Florida

March 8, 1983

The other day in the East Room of the White House at a meeting there, someone asked me whether I was aware of all the people out there who were praying for the President. And I had to say, "Yes, I am. I've felt it. I believe in intercessionary prayer." But I couldn't help but say to that questioner after he'd asked the question that—or at least say to them that if sometimes when he was praying he got a busy signal, it was just me in there ahead of

From http://www.reagan.utexas.edu/resource/speeches/1983/30883b.htm.

him. [Laughter] I think I understand how Abraham Lincoln felt when he said, "I have been driven many times to my knees by the overwhelming conviction that I had nowhere else to go." . . . There are a great many God-fearing, dedicated, noble men and women in public life, present company included. And, yes, we need your help to keep us ever mindful of the ideas and the principles that brought us into the public arena in the first place. The basis of those ideals and principles is a commitment to freedom and personal liberty that, itself, is grounded in the much deeper realization that freedom prospers only where the blessings of God are avidly sought and humbly accepted. . . . That shrewdest of all observers of American democracy, Alexis de Tocqueville, put it eloquently after he had gone on a search for the secret of America's greatness and genius—and he said: "Not until I went into the churches of America and heard her pulpits aflame with righteousness did I understand the greatness and the genius of America. . . . America is good. And if America ever ceases to be good, America will cease to be great."

Well, I'm pleased to be here today with you who are keeping America great by keeping her good. Only through your work and prayers and those of millions of others can we hope to survive this perilous century and keep alive this experiment in liberty, this last, best hope of man.

I want you to know that this administration is motivated by a political philosophy that sees the greatness of America in you, her people, and in your families, churches, neighborhoods, communities—the institutions that foster and nourish values like concern for others and respect for the rule of law under God.

Now, I don't have to tell you that this puts us in opposition to, or at least out of step with, a prevailing attitude of many who have turned to a modern-day secularism, discarding the tried and time-tested values upon which our very civilization is based. No matter how well intentioned, their value system is radically different from that of most Americans. And while they proclaim that they're freeing us from superstitions of the past, they've taken upon themselves the job of superintending us by government rule and regulation. Sometimes their voices are louder than ours, but they are not yet a majority.

An example of that vocal superiority is evident in a controversy now going on in Washington. And since I'm involved, I've been waiting to hear from the parents of young America. How far are they willing to go in giving to government their prerogatives as parents?

Let me state the case as briefly and simply as I can. An organization of citizens, sincerely motivated and deeply concerned about the increase in illegitimate births and abortions involving girls well below the age of consent, sometime ago established a nationwide network of clinics to offer help to these girls and, hopefully, alleviate this situation. Now, again, let me say, I do not fault their intent. However, in their well-intentioned effort, these clinics have decided to provide advice and birth control drugs and devices to underage girls without the knowledge of their parents.

For some years now, the Federal Government has helped with funds to subsidize these clinics. In providing for this, the Congress decreed that every effort would be made to maximize parental participation. Nevertheless, the drugs and devices are prescribed without getting parental consent or giving notification after they've done so. Girls termed "sexually active"—and that has replaced the word "promiscuous"—are given this help in order to prevent illegitimate birth or abortion.

Well, we have ordered clinics receiving Federal funds to notify the parents such help has been given. One of the Nation's leading newspapers has created the term "squeal rule" in editorializing against us for doing this, and we're being criticized for violating the privacy of young people. A judge has recently granted an injunction against an enforcement of our rule. I've watched TV panel shows discuss this issue, seen columnists pontificating on our error, but no one seems to mention morality as playing a part in the subject of sex.

Is all of Judeo-Christian tradition wrong? Are we to believe that something so sacred can be looked upon as a purely physical thing with no potential for emotional and psychological harm? And isn't it the parents' right to give counsel and advice to keep their children from making mistakes that may affect their entire lives?

Many of us in government would like to know what parents think about this intrusion in their family by government. We're going to fight in the courts. The right of parents and the rights of family take precedence over those of Washington-based bureaucrats and social engineers.

But the fight against parental notification is really only one example of many attempts to water down traditional values and even abrogate the original terms of American democracy. Freedom prospers when religion is vibrant and the rule of law under God is acknowledged. When our Founding Fathers passed the first amendment, they sought to protect churches from government interference. They never intended to construct a wall of hostility between government and the concept of religious belief itself.

The evidence of this permeates our history and our government. The Declaration of Independence mentions the Supreme Being no less than four times. "In God We Trust" is engraved on our coinage. The Supreme Court opens its proceedings with a religious invocation. And the Members of Congress open their sessions with a prayer. I just happen to believe the schoolchildren of the United States are entitled to the same privileges as Supreme Court Justices and Congressmen.

Last year, I sent the Congress a constitutional amendment to restore prayer to public schools. Already this session, there's growing bipartisan support for the amendment, and I am calling on the Congress to act speedily to pass it and to let our children pray. . . .

More than a decade ago, a Supreme Court decision literally wiped off the books of 50 states statutes protecting the rights of unborn children. Abortion on demand now takes the lives of up to 1½ million unborn children a year. Human life legislation ending this tragedy will some day pass the Congress, and you and I must never rest until it does. Unless and until it can be proven that the unborn child is not a living entity, then its right to life, liberty, and the pursuit of happiness must be protected. . . .

Recent legislation introduced in the Congress by Representative Henry Hyde of Illinois . . . increases restrictions on publicly financed abortion. . . .

Now, I'm sure that you must get discouraged at times, but you've done better than you know, perhaps. There's a great spiritual awakening in America, a renewal of the traditional values that have been the bedrock of America's goodness and greatness.

One recent survey by a Washington-based research council concluded that Americans were far more religious than the people of other nations; 95 percent of those surveyed expressed a belief in God and a huge majority believed the Ten Commandments had real meaning in their lives. And another study has found that an overwhelming majority of Americans disapprove of adultery, teenage sex, pornography, abortion, and hard drugs. And this same study showed a deep reverence for the importance of family ties and religious belief.

I think the items that we've discussed here today must be a key part of the Nation's political agenda. For the first time the Congress is openly and seriously debating and dealing with the prayer and abortion issues—and that's enormous progress right there. I repeat: America is in the midst of a spiritual awakening and a moral renewal. And with your Biblical keynote, I say today, "Yes, let justice roll on like a river, righteousness like a never-failing stream."

Now, obviously, much of this new political and social consensus I've talked about is based on a positive view of American history, one that takes pride in our country's accomplishments and record. But we must never forget that no government schemes are going to perfect man. We know that living in this world means dealing with what philosophers would call the phenomenology of evil or, as theologians would put it, the doctrine of sin.

There is sin and evil in the world, and we're enjoined by Scripture and the Lord Jesus to oppose it with all our might. Our nation, too, has a legacy of evil with which it must deal. The glory of this land has been its capacity for transcending the moral evils of our past. For example, the long struggle of minority citizens for equal rights, once a source of disunity and civil war, is now a point of pride for all Americans. We must never go back. There is no room for racism, anti-Semitism, or other forms of ethnic and racial hatred in this country.

I know that you've been horrified, as have I, by the resurgence of some hate groups preaching bigotry and prejudice. Use the mighty voice of your pulpits and the powerful standing of your churches to denounce and isolate these hate groups in our midst. The commandment given us is clear and simple: "Thou shalt love thy neighbor as thyself."

But whatever sad episodes exist in our past, any objective observer must hold a positive view of American history, a history that has been the story of hopes fulfilled and dreams made into reality. Especially in this century, America has kept alight the torch of freedom, but not just for ourselves but for millions of others around the world.

And this brings me to my final point today. During my first press conference as President, in answer to a direct question, I pointed out that, as good Marxist-Leninists, the Soviet leaders have openly and publicly declared that the only morality they recognize is that which will further their cause, which is world revolution. I think I should point out I was only quoting Lenin, their guiding spirit, who said in 1920 that they repudiate all morality that proceeds from supernatural ideas—that's their name for religion—or ideas that are outside class conceptions. Morality is entirely subordinate to the interests of class war. And everything is moral that is necessary for the annihilation of the old, exploiting social order and for uniting the proletariat.

Well, I think the refusal of many influential people to accept this elementary fact of Soviet doctrine illustrates an historical reluctance to see totalitarian powers for what they are. We saw this phenomenon in the 1930's. We see it too often today.

This doesn't mean we should isolate ourselves and refuse to seek an understanding with them. I intend to do everything I can to persuade them of our peaceful intent, to remind them that it was the West that refused to use its nuclear monopoly in the forties and fifties for territorial gain and which now proposes a 50-percent cut in strategic ballistic missiles and the elimination of an entire class of land-based, intermediate-range nuclear missiles.

At the same time, however, they must be made to understand we will never compromise our principles and standards. We will never give away our freedom. We will never abandon our belief in God. And we will never stop searching for a genuine peace. But we can assure none of these things America stands for through the so-called nuclear freeze solutions proposed by some. . . .

A number of years ago, I heard a young father, a very prominent young man in the entertainment world, addressing a tremendous gathering in California. It was during the time of the cold war, and communism and our own way of life were very much on people's minds. And he was speaking to that subject. And suddenly, though, I heard him saying, "I love my little girls more than anything—" And I said to myself, "Oh, no, don't. You can't—don't say that." But I had underestimated him. He went on: "I would rather see my little girls die now, still believing in God, than have them grow up under communism and one day die no longer believing in God."

There were thousands of young people in that audience. They came to their feet with shouts of joy. They had instantly recognized the profound truth in what he had said, with regard to the physical and the soul and what was truly important.

Yes, let us pray for the salvation of all of those who live in that totalitarian darkness—pray they will discover the joy of knowing God. But until they do, let us be aware that while they preach the supremacy of the state, declare its omnipotence over individual man, and predict its eventual domination of all peoples on the Earth, they are the focus of evil in the modern world. . . .

So, I urge you to speak out against those who would place the United States in a position of military and moral inferiority. You know, I've always believed that old Screwtape reserved his best efforts for those of you in the church. So, in your discussions of the nuclear freeze proposals, I urge you to beware the temptation of pride—the temptation of blithely declaring yourselves above it all and label both sides equally at fault, to ignore the facts of history and the aggressive impulses of an evil empire, to simply call the arms race a giant misunderstanding and thereby remove yourself from the struggle between right and wrong and good and evil.

I ask you to resist the attempts of those who would have you withhold your support for our efforts, this administration's efforts, to keep America strong and free, while we negotiate real and verifiable reductions in the world's nuclear arsenals and one day, with God's help, their total elimination.

While America's military strength is important, let me add here that I've always maintained that the struggle now going on for the world will never be decided by bombs or rockets, by armies or military might. The real crisis we face today is a spiritual one; at root, it is a test of moral will and faith.

Whittaker Chambers, the man whose own religious conversion made him a witness to one of the terrible traumas of our time, the Hiss-Chambers case, wrote that the crisis of the Western World exists to the degree in which the West is indifferent to God, the degree to which it collaborates in communism's attempt to make men stand alone without God. And then he said, for Marxism-Leninism is actually the second oldest faith, first proclaimed in the Garden of Eden with the words of temptation, "Ye shall be as gods."

The Western World can answer this challenge, he wrote, "but only provided that its faith in God and the freedom He enjoins is as great as communism's faith in Man."

I believe we shall rise to the challenge. I believe that communism is another sad, bizarre chapter in human history whose last pages even now are being written. I believe this because the source of our strength in the quest for human freedom is not material, but spiritual. And because it knows no limitation, it must terrify and ultimately triumph over those who would enslave their fellow man. For in the words of Isaiah: "He giveth power to the faint; and to them that have no might He increased strength. . . . But they that wait upon the Lord shall renew their strength; they shall mount up with wings as eagles; they shall run, and not be weary. . . ."

Yes, change your world. One of our Founding Fathers, Thomas Paine, said, "We have it within our power to begin the world over again." We can do it, doing together what no one church could do by itself.

God bless you, and thank you very much.

The best Web site on the cultural history of the 1980s is that maintained by Peggy Whitley for the Kingwood College Library. Among the topics covered are Art & Architecture, Fashion & Fads, Music & Media, and Theater, Film & Television. Go to kclibrary.nhmccd.edu/decade80.html.

THE BIG PICTURE

There are a couple of aspects to the big picture. One is that the legacy of the Reagan presidency is complex. For example, Reagan is often given credit for ending the Cold War. But most scholars acknowledge that the Soviet Union was in dire economic straits very early in Reagan's first term and was incapable of carrying on an expensive arms race. "Not everything that improves international relations," writes historian James T. Patterson, "has its origins in the United States." Although Reagan's domestic policies have been described by his chief domestic and economic policy adviser as a "revolution," Michael Schaller suggests that the policy impact was much more limited.

A second element of the big picture is that Reagan and his presidency (indeed, all presidencies) should be understood and evaluated in a long-term context. For example, Reagan and his policies now appear to have been responsible for a dramatic increase in homelessness. But the falling incomes that were part of the problem preceded his presidency by a decade, and homelessness remains a serious problem. Similarly, Reagan was more outspoken than the average president on behalf of religion and moral values, but when George W. Bush courts the Pope and calls for a constitutional amendment banning same-sex marriage, it is clear that something larger is involved than the political or moral agenda of one president. Finally, although Schaller's account presents a good case for the Reagan eighties as the greedy, "Gilded Age" of the late twentieth century, one must remember that the dot-com "bubble" occurred under Bill Clinton's watch, and that Kenneth Lay (Enron), Martha Stewart (Kmart), and Halliburton are watchwords of the first George W. Bush administration.

New World Order

The phrase "New World Order" was first used by George Herbert Walker Bush, whose presidency is identified with the first [Persian] Gulf War, which ended in 1991 with a U.S.-led international force driving Saddam Hussein's Iraqi troops from Kuwait, where in retreat they had set dozens of oil wells ablaze. Despite the phrase, in many ways the last decade of the twentieth century resembled the one before it. Liberalism of the New Deal/Great Society kind remained an endangered species. The liberal panaceas of the 1970s—affirmative action and mandatory busing—were increasingly seen as wrong or harmful. Bill Clinton's two-term presidency, hamstrung politically after a strong Republican showing led by the Christian Coalition in the 1994 elections, produced remarkably few liberal gains. A major administration effort to revamp the nation's medical care delivery system to produce something close to universal coverage found little support among Americans too selfish to care about the basic needs of others or wary of anything that smacked of bureaucracy and big government.

The most important piece of domestic legislation passed in the 1990s—the Personal Responsibility and Work Opportunity Act (1996)—had been on the conservative agenda for decades. The law did what Clinton had promised to do in the 1992 campaign, "to end welfare as we know it." It ended the federal government role in AFDC (Aid to Families with Dependent Children, the heart of the welfare system since 1935) and required the states to develop their own programs under restrictive federal guidelines. The legislation assumed that the welfare system was somehow responsible for the nation's ills, and especially for conditions in the inner cities, and that welfare mothers were black, lazy, and promiscuous. Whatever the erroneous assumptions, the result of the law was that poor, single women with children were forced to work outside the home or to rely on charity.

The economy absorbed much of Clinton's attention, and here, too, the administration held the political center. Participating in his own way in the construction of the New World Order, the president was an ardent supporter of the North American Free Trade Agreement (1994), which incorporated Mexico into a free-trade zone with the United States and Canada. He also embraced the Republican ideal of a balanced budget. Driven by expanding international markets and a revolution in computer technology that dramatically increased the productivity of American workers, the economy responded with year after year of strong growth and low inflation. The stock market soared to a new record, led by Internet stocks and claims that the boom-and-bust business cycle had become a thing of the past. As unbelievable as it would seem only four years later, the central issue in the presidential election of 2000, featuring Democrat Al Gore and Republican George W. Bush, was what to do with a huge anticipated surplus in government revenues.

Though real enough in some ways, the prosperity of the 1990s, like that of the 1980s, was appallingly uneven. While a small percentage of Americans made huge profits in a raging bull market on Wall Street, millions of others just survived, holding down low-wage jobs in service industries and in a declining manufacturing sector buffeted by foreign competition and damaged by free trade. Hispanics, African Americans, women who headed households, and inner-city youth were groups that had substantial rates of poverty in a decade described by one magazine as "a golden age in American history."

The new century, which opened with the inauguration of George W. Bush, stripped away any remaining illusions. The stock market collapsed in the summer of 2001, contributing to a deepening depression that eventually made Bush the only president since Herbert Hoover to have presided over an economy that had fewer jobs than when he took office. Both major parties agreed that a tax cut was needed to stimulate spending and investment, but the administration measure passed in June, 2001 was destined to fail. Most of its benefits went to the wealthiest 10 percent of Americans, rather than to poor and middle-class people who were most likely to spend the windfall and stimulate the economy. Moreover, the tax cut was financed by borrowing—that is, by the next generation—and it contributed to an emerging budget deficit of historic proportions. Although there were signs that the economy was reviving in 2004 and early 2005, the decline of manufacturing jobs and the "outsourcing" of service jobs to India and other countries remained important issues in the fall, 2004 election, particularly in Ohio, Pennsylvania, Michigan, and other industrial "swing" states whose economies had been severely damaged by the depression and globalization.

"New World Order" took on another meaning altogether on September 11, 2001, when nineteen suicide commandos, most of them citizens of Saudi

Arabia, flew hijacked jetliners into the north and south towers of the World Trade Center in New York City and into the Pentagon near Washington, D.C., killing almost 3,000 people. A fourth airliner, probably heading for the Capitol Building or the White House, was brought down in Pennsylvania by a heroic revolt among its passengers before it could accomplish its mission.

It was understood almost immediately that the attacks had been carried out by the terrorist organization Al Qaeda, founded in 1990 by Islamic fundamentalist Osama bin Laden. Bin Laden wanted to end American influence in the Middle East and especially in his native Saudi Arabia, where American troops remained since the Gulf War, and he also wanted—in the words of one historian—to affect the "heart of Western civilization." In 1996, bin Laden had called for jihad (holy war) against American troops in Saudi Arabia; in early 1998 he had publicly called on any Muslim to kill any American, anywhere in the world; and later that year, at a press conference, he had announced his goal of "bringing the war home to America." When bin Laden's Al Qaeda was identified as the source of truck bombs that killed 224 people, including 12 Americans, at the U.S. embassies in Kenya and Tanzania in August 1998, the Clinton administration sent cruise missiles into Afghanistan in an effort to destroy Al Qaeda training camps and kill bin Laden. Some have been critical of the Clinton administration for not retaliating for the attacks on the USS *Cole*, docked in Yemen in October 2000. But the attack on the *Cole* took place in the last months of Clinton's second term, and by the time Al Qaeda had been identified as the source, the transition to the Bush administration had begun. The Bush team, with full knowledge of Al Qaeda's role, also chose not to retaliate for the *Cole* incident.

The response of the Bush administration to terrorism in the nine months between the January inauguration and 9/11 was soon to become the subject of much debate. By most accounts, the administration seems to have been less interested in the problem posed by terrorism than was its predecessor. Richard Clarke, National Coordinator for Counter-Terrorism in the Clinton and Bush administrations, had briefed Clinton on terrorism on a regular basis, but he was not given permission to do so under the Bush regime. "My view," he told the commission investigating 9/11 in 2004, "was that this administration, while it listened to me, didn't either believe me that there was an urgent problem or was unprepared to act as though there were an urgent problem." Bush had said much the same thing to reporter Bob Woodward: "I didn't feel a sense of urgency [about terrorism]." National Security Adviser Condoleezza Rice disputed this view of the Bush camp, arguing that the administration was being thorough rather than slow, that it was developing a "comprehensive strategy" to deal with Al Qaeda, a strategy that meant developing new policies toward Afghanistan and its sympathetic neighbor, Pakistan. President Bush, she later testified, "told me that he was tired of swatting flies."

Even after the 9/11 attacks, the Bush administration moved slowly. It took almost a month to launch air strikes against Afghanistan and its fundamentalist Taliban government, which was harboring bin Laden and had refused American requests to turn him over. In two months, operation

"Enduring Freedom" had driven the Taliban from power, but bin Laden had not been found. Even in the immediate aftermath of 9/11, key people in the Bush administration, including the president, seemed overly preoccupied by the issue of Iraq. Although there was (and is) no evidence that Iraq was behind the 9/11 attacks or was a sponsor or supporter of terrorism, the Bush administration seemed determined to implicate Iraq and its dictator, Saddam Hussein. On September 12, according to Clarke, Bush pressured him to "see if Saddam did this," even as Clarke insisted that there was no relationship. Secretary of Defense Donald Rumsfeld had described Iraq as a supporter of terrorism at a September 4 meeting and, a week after 9/11, Deputy Defense Secretary Paul Wolfowitz inaccurately called Saddam Hussein "one of the most active supporters of state terrorism."

By February 2003, when Secretary of State Colin Powell presented the American position for war against Iraq to a skeptical United Nations, the Bush administration's case focused on Iraq's presumed possession of weapons of mass destruction (often referred to as WMD). To be sure, American intelligence was faulty, and CIA Director George Tenet erred in characterizing the available intelligence to Bush as "a slam dunk." Even so, statements from Bush officials were misleading. Vice President Dick Cheney was most vocal on the WMD issue, telling the Veterans of Foreign Wars in August 2002 that "simply stated, there is no doubt that Saddam Hussein now has weapons of mass destruction [and] there is no doubt that he is amassing them to use against our friends, against our allies and against us." General Tommy Franks, who was preparing the Iraq war plan, wasn't so sure; in September he told the president, "We've been looking for Scud missiles and other weapons of mass destruction for ten years and haven't found any yet." While there is evidence that Bush was not fully convinced by the WMD intelligence, he kept whatever doubts he had out of the public arena. Selling the impending war to members of the House of Representatives only a couple of weeks after his conversation with General Franks, Bush claimed that Saddam Hussein and his weapons of mass destruction were a bigger threat than Al Qaeda: "He can blow up Israel and that would trigger international conflict." A week later he told another group of House members that the Iraqis had biological and chemical weapons and were building facilities to make more.

Determined to engage in a preemptive war—and perhaps even convinced that intelligence proved that Saddam had weapons of mass destruction—a coalition dominated by the United States invaded Iraq with 116,000 troops on March 19, 2003. Baghdad fell on April 9, and on the first of May, Bush was flown onto the aircraft carrier USS *Abraham Lincoln* where, attired in a flight suit, he announced that major combat was over. No weapons of mass destruction had been found, and more than twenty-two months later it seemed clear that none would be.

Hostility to the American occupation grew rather than diminished. The occupying coalition army—mostly American and British troops— proved too small to keep order or to restore essential services with the speed necessary to earn the confidence of the Iraqi people. Even as the United

States turned the country's day-to-day operations over to an Iraqi interim government in June 2004, the war raged on in Fallujah, Najaf, and other major cities, where coalition forces fought day after day against large, well-armed, informal militias. Some opponents of the American occupation and of the change in government turned to terrorist tactics, kidnapping truck drivers, journalists, and other foreigners and sometimes beheading the hostages when their demands were not met.

Meanwhile, federal agencies spent billions to provide "homeland security" against an enemy that could strike anywhere, any time. The fall 2004 presidential elections, with Bush squaring off against Senator John Kerry (D-Massachusetts), a decorated Vietnam veteran, would turn in part on voters' perceptions of the candidates' ability to prosecute the "war on terror." As of this writing, there has been no repeat of 9/11 on American soil, but terrorists remained active abroad, carrying out deadly attacks in Indonesia, Thailand, the Philippines, and Spain in the spring of 2004. Bush insisted that the conflict in Iraq had made Americans safer, but others thought the American/coalition invasion had provided terrorists with proof of American imperial ambitions in the Middle East. "By invading Iraq," Richard Clarke told the National Commission on Terrorist Attacks (the 9/11 commission), "the president of the United States has greatly undermined the war on terrorism."

So great was the shock of watching the burning and collapse of the twin towers of the World Trade Center on September 11, 2001, that the events of that day can easily seem to be entirely without precedent and beyond context. But 9/11, and the wars in Afghanistan and Iraq that followed, did not take place outside of history. The Middle East emerged as a central concern of American foreign policy in the early 1970s, when hostilities between Arabs and Israelis threatened stability in the region, and when Americans first became conscious that Arab states had control of a significant percentage of the world's oil and could use that control to raise the price. In 1979, the taking of hostages at the American embassy in Tehran brought Americans face to face with Islamic fundamentalism and virulent Iranian opposition to U.S. and western control and influence.

The moralistic tone with which the Bush administration prosecuted the war in Iraq—all the talk about "democracy" for Iraq and the region—also had its precedents. There were echoes of Woodrow Wilson's insistence that the United States was making the world "safe for democracy," and of Lyndon Johnson's claim that the war in Vietnam would do for the Vietnamese what the Tennessee Valley Authority had done for the rural South in the Great Depression. President George Herbert Walker Bush had invoked the goal of democracy in 1989, when the American military overthrew Panamanian dictator Manuel Noriega.

Perhaps most important, the wars in Afghanistan and Iraq were very much a result of the end of the Cold War, an event symbolized by the tearing down in 1989 and 1990 of the concrete block wall constructed between East and West Berlin in 1961. One consequence was immediate. When the Soviet Union withdrew from Afghanistan in 1989, Arab fighters who had come there to fight the Soviets were left wondering what to do next and confident that they could defeat any "infidel" enemy. The demise of the Soviet Union set the stage, too, for the emergence of the United States as the world's only "super-power," a status that was sure to encourage the sort of arrogant unilateralism that the Clinton administration showed when it refused to sign an international treaty on land mines (1997) and that escalated in the Bush administration, which abandoned the Kyoto Protocol on global warming in spring 2001 and, in July, rejected an international ban on biological weapons.

For many years, the Cold War had functioned to contain forces of nationalism, ethnicity, and religion in places like Afghanistan and Yugoslavia. The end of the Cold War unleashed those forces. And, with the Soviet Union out of the picture and Communism all but dead, the United States was free to intervene in places like Iraq that had once been off limits, and free, too, to stir up ethnic and religious rivalries once held in check by Saddam Hussein's brutal dictatorship. This "New World Order" was new, to be sure, and it took America on a wild ride across the globe. But it was messy and dangerous and, one is tempted to add, "disorderly."

The war in Iraq was increasingly unpopular with the American people, and for a time in the fall of 2004 it seemed that the administration's failures there, and its commitment to global economic changes that were damaging American workers, would make George W. Bush a one-term president like his father. Instead, he won a second term by a narrow margin, winning every southern state except Maryland and most states in the West. The election turned on the vote in Ohio, where evangelical Christians gave Bush a narrow plurality. They ignored huge job losses in Ohio during his presidency and the deteriorating situation in Iraq. Instead, in the latest battle in the "culture wars" that had taken shape under Ronald Reagan, they cast their vote for Republican "moral values," rejoicing in Bush's opposition to same-sex marriage, stem cell research, and abortion, and hoping for a series of Bush appointments that would reshape the Supreme Court and overturn *Roe v. Wade*. To Kerry supporters, it seemed a curious response, indeed, to a president who had made one bad decision after another.

The staff reports and full text of the report of the National Commission on Terrorist Attacks Upon the United States (2004) is available on the Commission's Web site, www.9-11commission.gov/.

The Vulcans

James Mann

As the introduction to this chapter suggests, the controversial foreign policy of the George W. Bush presidency was the product of powerful historical forces and important events, especially the end of the Cold War. But it was also made by men and women, who were free to make choices between a variety of policies and strategies. Bush's foreign policy team had a name for their group: the Vulcans. Vulcan was the Roman God of Fire and the inspiration for a 56-foot Vulcan statue in Birmingham, Alabama, where steel had been made and where Condoleezza Rice, Bush's national security adviser, had grown up. Because the president had no foreign policy experience (indeed, he had not even traveled much outside the country), Bush administration foreign policy was made by the Vulcans.

As James Mann uses the term, a "Vulcan" was anyone who served in a foreign policy role under a previous Republican administration and returned to office under George W. Bush. There were six: Vice President Dick Cheney, Secretary of State Colin Powell, Secretary of Defense Donald Rumsfeld, Deputy Defense Secretary Paul Wolfowitz (serving under Rumsfeld), Deputy Secretary of State Richard Armitage (serving under Powell), and Condoleezza Rice. They had plenty of experience, especially in the Pentagon. Cheney and Rumsfeld were former secretaries of defense; Powell had been chairman of the joint chiefs of staff under George Herbert Walker Bush, as well as national security adviser under President Ronald Reagan; Rice had worked for the joint chiefs early in her career. Only Powell and Armitage (interestingly, doves in comparison to the others) had served in combat in Vietnam, though all the Vulcans were influenced by the desire to see the nation regain the military power and reputation that the United States had enjoyed before the defeat in Vietnam. Wolfowitz, who had a Ph.D. in political science, and Rice, who had taught at Stanford University, bridged academia and government service.

In the selection below, James Mann describes and interprets an important change in American foreign policy. What were the central ingredients in the new Bush foreign policy? What were the causes? Was the new approach essential? Were the Vulcans optimists or pessimists? Should the Vulcans have paid more attention to the war on terrorism, and less to the threat posed by Iraq?

Also in the cast of characters:
    Henry Kissinger
Assistant for national security affairs and, later, secretary of state in the administration of Richard Nixon. He supported U.S. disengagement from

Vietnam in the early 1970s. In contrast to the Vulcans, Kissinger is usually described as a foreign relations "realist," who favored an approach to foreign affairs based on the idea of the balance of power.

During the early stages of the war on terrorism the Vulcans had concentrated primarily on the specific tasks they had set out for themselves: defeating the Taliban and ousting Al Qaeda from Afghanistan. By early 2002, after roughly one year in office, they were ready to move on to something larger—not merely another country or another terrorist group but a whole new way of thinking about America's relations with the world. They were preparing to wage a new campaign in the realm of ideas. "Phase two," it turned out, would be conducted not with troops and warplanes but through speeches and strategy papers. Although the Vulcans had for decades operated within the framework of the ideas developed during the cold war, by 2002, more than a decade after the collapse of the Soviet Union, many of them seemed to be eager to cut loose from these intellectual moorings.

The underlying ethos of the cold war had been a sense of caution and limits. There were some things the United States had been unwilling to do because of the risks of a full-scale war with the Soviet Union (or, for a time, China). President Truman had fought a limited war in Korea, firing General Douglas MacArthur after he sought to carry the war onto Chinese soil. The Eisenhower administration had held back from supporting freedom fighters in Hungary; the Kennedy, Johnson and Nixon administrations had waged another limited war in Vietnam. The principal strategies of the cold war had been essentially defensive in nature: containment and deterrence.

After the fall of the Berlin Wall it had taken some time for the United States to absorb the implications of the change. In 1991 President George H. W. Bush had vaguely spoken of a new world order, an idea that rested on the unprecedented, temporary cooperation between America and the Soviet Union against Iraq. Yet there had been little time to rethink the underlying principles governing American foreign policy; the members of the first Bush administration had been obliged to spend most of their time simply coping with the massive changes around the world, including the Soviet collapse and the reunification of Germany. The first signs of a new intellectual framework had emerged from the Pentagon in 1992, when Paul Wolfowitz and his aides had sketched out their vision for a world in which America was the world's only superpower. These novel ideas, however, were never officially embraced because they were too controversial to win approval at the White House and because in any event, the Bush administration was forced to leave office less than a year later.

Over the following decade the United States had continued to augment its military power to the point where by 2002 it had surpassed not merely that of any other country, but that of any imaginable combination of nations. At the same time, the nature of potential threats to American security was also changing. The dangers seemed to arise not from a rival power like Nazi Germany or the Soviet Union but from what was called asymmetric warfare. A "rogue" nation or a terrorist group could not defeat the U.S.

Army on the battlefield, but it might launch missiles or crash airplanes in ways that could kill thousands of Americans.

In the 1970s and 1980s many of the Vulcans had proposed a greater American effort to confront the Soviet Union. Rumsfeld had challenged dé-tente. Dick Cheney had led the way in accepting the "Morality in Foreign Policy" plank at the 1976 Republican National Convention. Wolfowitz had questioned Kissinger's belief in realpolitik, his preoccupation with balance of power diplomacy. Armitage had helped implement the Reagan doctrine, the efforts to challenge the Soviet Union in the third world. At the time, how-ever, none of these men had questioned the underlying doctrine of contain-ment that lay at the heart of American strategy. All had accepted the cold war framework and the limits it imposed.

But by early 2002 the Vulcans were in a hurry for new ideas. After the shock of September 11 their inclination was to reach for broad, enduring changes in the underlying principles guiding American foreign policy. They were convinced America had entered a new era and needed new concepts to guide it. While Winston Churchill provided inspiration for the Vulcans in the midst of the September 11 crisis, in its aftermath they began turning to other historical models: to Harry Truman, George Kennan and Dean Acheson, the group of men who had crafted a new foreign policy and a new set of ideas to help America cope with the Soviet Union after World War II.

The Vulcans' eagerness to jettison the past did not begin with the terrorist attacks of September 11. In one policy area, at least, the Bush administration had come into office with the specific intent of burying the legacy of the cold war. In its determination to push forward with missile defense, the new ad-ministration regularly and explicitly questioned the underlying assumptions that had governed national security for decades.

Touring Europe in the first months after he took office, Wolfowitz re-peatedly argued that the Anti-Ballistic Missile Treaty negotiated by the Nixon administration no longer made sense. "The world of 2001 is fundamentally dif-ferent from that of 1972," he said. America faced new challenges from the pro-liferation of missiles and weapons of mass destruction. In Berlin, Wolfowitz questioned why twelve years after the Berlin Wall came down, "we are still in some ways . . . wedded to old Cold War notions of deterrence." From the White House, Condoleezza Rice poked a bit of self-mocking fun at the old cold war mind-set. "For much of my career, I was a Soviet specialist. . . . I was one of the High Priestesses of Arms Control—a true believer."

Then September 11 greatly accelerated the administration's willingness to rethink cold war ideas about national security. Far from forcing the admin-istration to revert to the time-honored multilateral approaches of the past, as many analysts predicted immediately afterward, the attacks instead created a new climate in which the administration was prepared to reconsider the fun-damental tenets that had guided American security since World War II.

A half year after September 11 a veteran intelligence official said he thought the operating style of the George W. Bush administration was dif-ferent from its predecessors. The foreign policy team, he said, seemed to have a sense of impatience that was unlike anything he had observed in either the first Bush administration or the Reagan administration. "I'm surprised every day, because I've been schooled for thirty years that things go back to normal within six weeks or two months or so after a crisis. But these people aren't changing. There's a clear commitment on their part to make a difference. They refuse to go back to business-as-usual."

In December 2001 the administration took its first big step toward abandoning the rules and restrictions of the cold war when President Bush announced that the United States would withdraw from the ABM Treaty. That agreement, he said, "was written in a different era, for a different enemy."

The abandonment of the ABM Treaty represented the culmination of efforts that had begun in the Reagan administration and picked up momentum in the late 1990s. Rumsfeld had played a central role. He had not only headed the formal commission that warned in 1998 of missile attacks on American soil but had also been in charge of the more secretive campaign group that had planned for missile defense while Bush was running for president.

Powell had supported missile defense since the days when he served as Reagan's national security adviser. In 2001, however, he had sought to work out a compromise with Moscow that would enable the United States to move ahead on missile defense without withdrawing from the ABM Treaty. In the end the secretary of state's attempts to preserve the treaty fell through. Bush and Rice sided with Rumsfeld, opting for a complete break with the past.

There were soon signs that the drive for missile defense, while extraordinarily important on its own, represented only one facet of a broader change in strategy. In early 2002 the Pentagon delivered to Congress a classified document called the Nuclear Posture Review. In it, the administration proposed the development of new, smaller nuclear weapons that could be used not just against the major nuclear powers, Russia and China, but also against Iraq, North Korea, Iran, Syria, and Libya. The Clinton administration had laid the groundwork to some extent. It had drawn up a presidential directive that included some contingency plans for targeting "rogue nations" with nuclear weapons. The Bush team made this policy explicit. The thrust of the new Bush strategy was to shift the underlying purpose of America's nuclear weapons away from the notions of defense and deterrence and toward the goal of war fighting. Bunkerbusting nuclear weapons, the report envisaged, could be employed against enemy supplies of chemical or biological weapons. America's nuclear weapons might also conceivably be used in response to "an Iraqi attack on Israel or its neighbors, or a North Korean attack on the South, or a military confrontation over the status of Taiwan," the document said. Washington was no longer worrying about all-out nuclear exchanges with Moscow that could lead to Armageddon. It was, instead, thinking about the role that America's nuclear weapons might play in future conflicts in the third world.

"The terrorists who struck us on Sept. 11 were clearly not deterred from doing so by the massive U.S. nuclear arsenal," explained Rumsfeld in a speech in January 2002. Deterrence, the central element of American military strategy for decades, was a concept coming into disfavor. Increasingly the Vulcans were gravitating toward strategies that focused on offensive military action. "Defending against terrorism and other emerging 21st Century threats requires that we take the war to the enemy," said Rumsfeld. "The best and in some cases the only defense is a good offense."

The central figure in these larger conceptual changes was Condoleezza Rice. Bush's national security adviser was outweighed in the administration's inner circles by the older, more experienced figures of Cheney, Powell and Rumsfeld. Yet she was of critical importance in several ways. Of all the top-level officials, she was by far the closest to Bush. When the Defense and State departments were divided, or when Rumsfeld and Cheney advised one course of action and Powell a different one, it was Rice who helped the president reach a decision. She operated at the interface between the president and his political advisers, on the one hand, and his foreign policy team, on the other.

Of all the Vulcans, it was Rice who best personified the profound intellectual shift from the first Bush administration to the second one. Rice had not merely been a "high priestess of arms control." She had risen to prominence as the heir to the foreign policy traditions of Henry Kissinger and Brent Scowcroft. At Stanford and during the first Bush administration she had been an avowed proponent of the doctrine of realism, the belief in a tough-minded foreign policy based on national interests and balance of power diplomacy. During the 2000 presidential campaign and during Bush's initial months in office, Rice appeared to be advocating an updated, modified version of those same realist traditions. American foreign policy, she argued, should focus on the biggest, most powerful countries, particularly China and Russia, and should avoid becoming bogged down in nation-building enterprises. America should not use its military as "the world's 911," she wrote. ". . . This overly broad definition of America's national interest is bound to backfire as others arrogate the same authority to themselves."

Still, Rice had taken care to avoid alienating the conservatives, who bitterly opposed Kissinger-style realism. Like George W. Bush himself, Rice sought to avoid being swept up in the factional disputes among Republicans that had badly damaged Bush's father and, long before him, Gerald Ford. She made sure that the younger Bush, during his presidential campaign, called for "realism in the service of ideals," a slogan that sought to straddle the old Republican divide.

In mid-2001, not long after the editors of the *Weekly Standard* had excoriated the new president for his handling of the spy plane dispute with China, Rice quietly reached out to the neoconservative movement that the magazine represented. Come by my office some time, she told William Kristol, the neoconservative leader; let's talk, instead of merely reading each other's quotes in the newspapers. When Kristol went into the White House for a chat, Rice told him that during a visit to Poland she had been personally moved by the importance and power of democracy there. She had become, she suggested to Kristol, a bit less of a believer in realpolitik.

It was Rice, more than anyone else, who viewed the mission of the Vulcans after September 11 as a historic one comparable to that of the post–World War II generation. America was not merely combating terrorism but constructing a whole new order. "The international system has been in flux since the collapse of Soviet power," she told one audience. "Now, it is possible—indeed probable—that that transition is coming to an end. . . . This is, then, a period akin to 1945 to 1947, when American leadership expanded the number of free and democratic states—Japan and Germany among the great powers—to create a new balance of power that favored freedom."

When Richard Haass, a senior Powell aide and the director of policy planning at the State Department, drafted for the administration an overview of America's national security strategy, Rice ordered that the document be completely rewritten. She thought the Bush administration needed something bolder, something that would represent a more dramatic break with the ideas of the past. Rice turned the writing over to her old colleague, University of Virginia Professor Philip Zelikow, who had worked alongside Rice in the first Bush administration and had been her coauthor for a book about the unification of Germany.

In November 2001, during the last stages of the war in Afghanistan, there was a curious, subtle shift in the public rhetoric of the Bush administration. Top officials increasingly emphasized the danger that Al Qaeda might obtain weapons of mass destruction. Rumsfeld said in one television interview that it was "reasonable to assume" Osama bin Laden had some access to chemical and biological weapons. Speaking to the UN General Assembly, Bush warned that terrorists were "searching for weapons of mass destruction, the tools to turn their hatred into holocaust."

On the surface the administration was offering merely one more rationale for the war on terrorism—and seemingly an unnecessary one. Al Qaeda had just killed three thousand Americans with its attacks on the World Trade Center and Pentagon. What more justification was needed? In fact, although this was little recognized at the time, the administration's new stress on weapons of mass destruction was the earliest sign of a far broader campaign, one that would dominate the Bush administration's policy long after Afghanistan, Operation Enduring Freedom and even Al Qaeda were out of the headlines.

At the time the government of Pakistan had just arrested three scientists working on the country's nuclear weapons program for questioning about their visits to Afghanistan and their ties to the Taliban. Inside the United States, five people had died and more than twenty others were infected when letters containing anthrax spores were put into the mail. In the end neither of these incidents was tied to Al Qaeda. But the terrorist attacks had prompted the administration to examine the "what if" scenarios: What if on September 11 the terrorists had used a nuclear weapon, or a chemical or biological one? What if, instead of three thousand deaths, there had been three hundred thousand?

Initially the focus was on the terrorists who might obtain weapons of mass destruction. But of course the weapons had to be obtained somewhere. Before long the administration began to switch its attention to the potential suppliers.

On January 29, 2002, Bush took the next, momentous step in the redirection of the war on terrorism. In his State of the Union address he surprised the nation and the world by proclaiming that the administration was seeking to combat an "axis of evil," a group of nations that were seeking to develop weapons of mass destruction and could potentially provide these weapons to terrorists. He specifically named North Korea, Iran and Iraq as members of the "axis."

Thus over a period of less than five months the administration had progressively shifted the focus of the war on terrorism from (a) retaliating against the perpetrators of the September 11 attacks to (b) stopping terrorists from acquiring weapons of mass destruction to (c) preventing states from supplying terrorists with these weapons. Indeed, there were suggestions in Bush's speech that a link between the states and terrorism wasn't absolutely necessary; what mattered above all were (d) the axis-of-evil states and their weapons programs. "By seeking weapons of mass destruction, these regimes pose a grave and growing danger," the president said.

David Frum, then one of Bush's speechwriters, later claimed that the original aim of the axis-of-evil speech was specifically to target Iraq. Mark Gerson, Bush's chief speechwriter, had asked Frum first to find a justification for war against Iraq, he wrote; later Iran was added, and finally North Korea as a seemingly casual afterthought. Frum's perspective reflected both his experience as a speechwriter and also the thinking of neoconservatives within the administration, who were eager for a regime change in Iraq.

Yet Frum was not himself part of the Vulcans' foreign policy deliberations, and his analysis overlooked the other, broader dimensions of the axis-of-evil speech. Iraq, Iran, and North Korea weren't joined together entirely randomly or just for Bush's State of the Union. Rumsfeld's 1998 commission on missile threats had cited precisely these three countries as ones of special worry. The Clinton administration too had singled out Iraq, Iran, and North Korea—not as "evil" or an "axis" but as the three nations that had rapidly advancing nuclear and missile programs in seeming violation of the nuclear nonproliferation treaty and that were also considered hostile to American interests.

Thus, for the Bush administration, the axis-of-evil speech served several purposes. It underscored the Vulcans' mounting concern about terrorist groups' acquiring nuclear, chemical or biological weapons. It enabled the Bush White House to shift attention away from the murky, often frustrating task of catching terrorists with no fixed address (where was Osama bin Laden?) to the more familiar ground of dealing with conventional states, such as Iraq, North Korea and Iran. It linked up the new war on terrorism, which had been in need of new direction after Afghanistan, to long-standing U.S. policies aimed at stopping the spread of weapons of mass destruction.

Finally, for those within the Bush administration, such as Wolfowitz, who had argued long before September 11 for the overthrow of Saddam Hussein, Bush's axis-of-evil speech also provided a new, broader conceptual framework within which to pursue the goal of regime change in Iraq. Yet in this respect the axis-of-evil speech had profound implications for the eventual campaign against Iraq. Over the next fourteen months, as the Bush administration moved toward military action against Iraq, officials repeatedly emphasized the theme that Saddam Hussein was developing weapons of mass destruction; this, more than the Iraqi leader's brutality or danger to the region, became the primary justification for war. In the months after the war ended, Iraq's weapons of mass destruction could not be found, and the administration faced a torrent of questions about its previous claims.

The State of the Union address set the Bush administration on a new course. Hunting terrorists was deemphasized, at least in public; instead, stopping rogue states from developing weapons of mass destruction became the administration's top priority. Bush's speech led to abrupt changes in American foreign policy. The State Department's intermittent attempts at diplomacy with North Korea and with Iran were temporarily frozen. The American people were unlikely to support any broad accommodation with regimes branded as evil, and conversely, North Korean and Iranian leaders labeled as evil were less likely to negotiate with the United States. Thus the Vulcans were once again reverting to the approach they had taken when they opposed détente in the 1970s and when they labeled the Soviet Union an evil empire in the early 1980s: Avoid compromise or accommodation with morally objectionable regimes, and rely instead on American military power.

After Bush's State of the Union, a myth developed that the phrase *axis of evil* represented only empty rhetoric or the last-minute wording of the speechwriters. "Some senior State Department officials, for example, didn't find out that Mr. Bush would refer to the three nations as an 'axis of evil' until the rest of America did," reported the *New York Times*. That may indeed have been true of some State Department officials, yet in fact, Powell and Armitage, the two top State Department officials, had carefully reviewed and signed off on Bush's speech, including the *axis-of-evil* phraseology. "It [the speech] was cleared completely here," acknowledged Armitage in an interview later that year. "The secretary [Powell] and I had read it time and again, had made a lot of changes to it. It didn't go through the whole bureaucracy, but it went through us, in several iterations. Never did we look at [changing the phrase] 'axis of evil.' That just didn't strike us as out of the ordinary." Powell and Armitage had heard comparable words before; both were serving in government when Ronald Reagan branded the Soviet Union "the evil empire."

The Bush speech took many governments overseas by surprise. They included America's allies in Europe, many of which had ongoing relationships with Iran, and in Asia, where Japan and South Korea were trying to figure out how to deal with North Korea. The administration had not warned the allies in advance of what was, by any measure, a significant change in direction for the war on terrorism.

Wolfowitz insisted that the Bush administration was not downgrading the importance of its allies. Asked if the administration had consulted with them about the State of the Union speech, he replied that the speech itself represented the beginning of a process of consultation. "They could read it," he said. ". . . The State of the Union speech, I consider, was an invitation to a whole bunch of people to consult, to discuss, to debate, to get on board hopefully [*sic*]." He argued that America was simply demonstrating leadership and telling its allies what the United States wanted to undertake, then asking the allies for their views. By way of comparison, Wolfowitz pointed out that after Iraq invaded Kuwait in 1990, the first Bush administration had gone to Saudi Arabia not to ask what the United States should do but to state clearly that America planned and intended to drive Saddam Hussein's forces back to Iraq.

However, Wolfowitz's explanation papered over a significant change. During the cold war, "consultation" with allies hadn't usually meant giving a landmark public speech and then asking afterward what other governments thought about it; rather, it had meant talking and soliciting ideas in private before such a speech was given. The comparison to the 1990 diplomacy with Saudi Arabia underscored this crucial difference; Cheney and Wolfowitz had consulted with Saudi officials in private, not in public. The axis-of-evil speech represented a different form of "consultation" with America's allies—on television in prime time. It seemed like an unnecessary slight.

The reaction among America's allies was compounded by the further problem that other than Pakistan, the only countries singled out for praise in the State of the Union were Russia, China, and India; this was a reflection of Rice's belief in the importance of great powers. Bush's speech never referred to South Korea or Japan. Nor did the president thank (or mention) NATO, which after September 11 had passed an unprecedented resolution in support of the United States; or Germany, which ventured to send troops on an overseas combat mission for the first time since World War II; or even Britain, whose troops and warplanes fought alongside the Americans in Afghanistan. Crediting these overseas partners in Bush's speech would have cost the administration nothing more than a few words.

As it turned out, the axis-of-evil speech represented a watershed for American relations with Europe. The transatlantic tensions that had been slowly heating up throughout the late 1990s and simmering during the first year of the Bush administration now came to a boil. French Foreign Minister Hubert Védrine called the State of the Union speech "simplistic." German Foreign Minister Joschka Fischer warned that "alliance partners are not satellites." Christopher Patten, the British Conservative party leader working for the European Union, reminded Washington of the words of Winston Churchill: "In working with allies, it sometimes happens that they develop opinions of their own." That was, as Patten undoubtedly realized, a gibe at the Churchill admirers in the Bush administration.

Americans inside and outside the administration were equally caustic about the Europeans, arguing that they were blind to the dangers from weapons of mass destruction and in any event had been marginalized by their own prolonged unwillingness to spend money on defense. Neoconservative columnist Charles Krauthammer called Europe an "axis of petulance. . . . The ostensible complaint is American primitivism. The real problem is their irrelevance." Taking the lead for the Bush administration, Powell dismissed the French criticisms by saying that Védrine was "getting the vapors." The stage was being set for the drama that was to unfold one year later at the United Nations.

Debates: Nation-Building and the New World Order

George W. Bush and Al Gore

Although foreign policy was not the issue on which the 2000 election turned, Bush's first term was defined by the president's handling of the 9/11 crisis and the problem of terrorism and by his decision to go to war against Iraq. Given this history, those portions of the 2000 presidential debates dealing with foreign relations take on special meaning. The following selection is taken from the October 11 debate between the Democratic candidate, Vice President Al Gore, and the Republican candidate, Texas Governor George W. Bush. The moderator was PBS news anchor Jim Lehrer. The debate took place in Wait Chapel at Wake Forest University in Winston-Salem, North Carolina.

In the following exchange, the candidates talked in general terms about how the United States should present itself and act in the world. The discussion turned to nation-building, a term which refers to the practice or goal of generating major social, economic, and political change in a foreign country, usually after a conflict or war has taken place, and often applying some measure of military force. The United States had engaged in successful nation-building in Germany and Japan after World War II.

After a long period in which nation-building was especially risky, the end of the Cold War freed the United States and other countries to engage once again in comprehensive nation-building, often beginning with military intervention and ending in social transformation. During the 1990s, the United States engaged in some form of nation-building in Somalia, Haiti, Bosnia, and Kosovo. So it was reasonable that Bush and Gore would debate the issue during the 2000 campaign. Of course, the effort to rebuild and transform Iraq may be the largest and most expensive nation-building effort in American history; it is certainly the most controversial.

In reading through the transcript of the October 11 debate, ask yourself whether a reasonable person could have predicted the Iraq experience with nation-building from the comments made by Governor Bush. On the basis of this exchange, do you think that Al Gore—had he won the presidency—would have been the nation-builder that George Bush became?

DEBATES

MODERATOR: Should the people of the world look at the United States, Governor, and say, should they fear us, should they welcome our involvement, should they see us as a friend, everybody in the world? How would you project us around the world, as president?

From http://www.debates.org/pages/trans2000b.html.

BUSH: Well, I think they ought to look at us as a country that understands freedom where it doesn't matter who you are or how you're raised or where you're from, that you can succeed. I don't think they'll look at us with envy. It really depends upon how our nation conducts itself in foreign policy. If we're an arrogant nation, they'll resent us. If we're a humble nation, but strong, they'll welcome us. And it's—our nation stands alone right now in the world in terms of power, and that's why we have to be humble. And yet project strength in a way that promotes freedom. So I don't think they ought to look at us in any way other than what we are. We're a freedom-loving nation and if we're an arrogant nation they'll view us that way, but if we're a humble nation they'll respect us.

MODERATOR: A humble nation.

GORE: I agree with that. I agree with that. I think that one of the problems that we have faced in the world is that we are so much more powerful than any single nation has been in relationship to the rest of the world than at any time in history, that I know about, anyway. That there is some resentment of U.S. power. So I think that the idea of humility is an important one. But I think that we also have to have a sense of mission in the world. We have to protect our capacity to push forward what America's all about. That means not only military strength and our values, it also means keeping our economy strong.

MODERATOR: People watching here tonight are very interested in Middle East policy, and they are so interested they want to base their vote on differences between the two of you as president how you would handle Middle East policy. Is there any difference?

GORE: I haven't heard a big difference in the last few exchanges.

BUSH: That's hard to tell. I think that, you know, I would hope to be able to convince people I could handle the Iraqi situation better.

MODERATOR: Saddam Hussein, you mean, get him out of there?

BUSH: I would like to, of course, and I presume this administration would as well. We don't know—there are no inspectors now in Iraq, the coalition that was in place isn't as strong as it used to be. He is a danger. We don't want him fishing in troubled waters in the Middle East. And it's going to be hard, it's going to be important to rebuild that coalition to keep the pressure on him.

MODERATOR: You feel that is a failure of the Clinton administration?

BUSH: I do.

GORE: Well, when I got to be a part of the current administration, it was right after—I was one of the few members of my political party to support former President Bush in the Persian Gulf War resolution, and at the end of that war, for whatever reason, it was not finished in a way that removed Saddam Hussein from power. I know there are all kinds of circumstances and explanations. But the fact is that that's the situation that was left when I got there. And we have maintained the sanctions. Now I want to go further. I want to give robust support to the groups that are trying to overthrow Saddam Hussein, and I know there are allegations that they're too weak to do it, but that's what they said about the forces that were opposing Milosevic in Serbia, and you know, the policy of enforcing sanctions against Serbia has just resulted in a spectacular victory for democracy just in the past week, and it seems to me that having taken so long to see the sanctions work there, building upon the policy of containment that was successful over a much longer period of time against the former Soviet Union in the communist block, seems a little early to declare that we should give up on the sanctions. . . .

MODERATOR: Did he state your position correctly, you're not calling for eliminating the sanctions, are you?

BUSH: No, of course not, absolutely not, I want them to be tougher. . . .

GORE: . . . Now, I did want to pick up on one of the statements earlier, and maybe I have heard, maybe I have heard the previous statements wrong, Governor. In some of the discussions we've had about when it's appropriate for the U.S. to use force around the world, at times the standards that you've laid down have given me the impression that if it's something like a genocide taking place or what they called ethnic cleansing in Bosnia, that that alone would not be, that that wouldn't be the kind of situation that would cause you to think that the U.S. ought to get involved with troops. Now, there have to be other factors involved for me to want to be involved. But by itself, that to me can bring into play a fundamental American strategic interest because I think it's based on our values. Now, have I got that wrong?

MODERATOR: Trying to figure out who the questioner was.

BUSH: If I think it's in our nation's strategic interest I'll commit troops. I thought it was in our strategic interests to keep Milosevic in check because of our relations in NATO, and that's why I took the position I took. I think it's important for NATO to be strong and confident. I felt like unchecked Milosevic would harm NATO, and so it depends on the situation, Mr. Vice President.

MODERATOR: Well, let's stay on the subject for a moment. New question related to this. I figured this out; in the last 20 years there have been eight major actions that involved the introduction of U.S. ground, air or naval forces. Let me name them. Lebanon, Grenada, Panama, the Persian Gulf,

Somalia, Bosnia, Haiti, Kosovo. If you had been president for any of those interventions, would any of those interventions not have happened?

GORE: Can you run through the list again?

MODERATOR: Sure. Lebanon.

GORE: I thought that was a mistake.

MODERATOR: Grenada.

GORE: I supported that.

MODERATOR: Panama.

GORE: I supported that.

MODERATOR: Persian Gulf.

GORE: Yes, I voted for it, supported it.

MODERATOR: Somalia.

GORE: Of course, and that again—no, I think that that was ill-considered. I did support it at the time. It was in the previous administration, in the Bush-Quayle administration, and I think in retrospect the lessons there are ones that we should take very, very seriously. . . .

MODERATOR: . . . Want me to do it with you? Lebanon.

BUSH: Make a couple comments.

MODERATOR: Sure, absolutely, sure. Somalia.

BUSH: Started off as a humanitarian mission and it changed into a nation-building mission, and that's where the mission went wrong. The mission was changed. And as a result, our nation paid a price. And so I don't think our troops ought to be used for what's called nation-building. I think our troops ought to be used to fight and win war. I think our troops ought to be used to help overthrow the dictator when it's in our best interests. But in this case it was a nation-building exercise, and same with Haiti. I wouldn't have supported either. . . .

GORE: I'd like to come back to the question of nation-building, but let me address the question directly, first. Fine. We did, actually, send troops into Rwanda to help with the humanitarian relief measures. My wife Tipper, who is here, actually went on a military plane with General Sholicatchvieli on one

Republican presidential candidate George W. Bush (left), Democratic presidential candidate Al Gore (right), and moderator Jim Lehrer at the second presidential debate, Wake Forest University, Winston-Salem, North Carolina, October 11, 2000.

of those flights. But I think in retrospect we were too late getting in there. We could have saved more lives if we had acted earlier. But I do not think that it was an example of a conflict where we should have put our troops in to try to separate the parties for this reason, Jim. One of the criteria that I think is important in deciding when and if we should ever get involved around the world is whether or not our national security interest is involved, if we can really make the difference with military forces. We tried everything else. If we have allies in the Balkans we have allies, NATO, ready, willing and able to go and carry a big part of the burden. In Africa we did not. . . .

MODERATOR: So what would you say, Governor, that somebody would say hey wait a minute, why not Africa, I mean why the Middle East, why the Balkans, but not Africa, when 600,000 people's lives are at risk?

BUSH: Well, I understand, and Africa is important. And we've got to do a lot of work in Africa to promote democracy and trade, and there are some— the Vice President mentioned Nigeria is a fledgling democracy. We have to work with Nigeria. That's an important continent. But there's got to be priorities, and Middle East is a priority for a lot of reasons, as is Europe and the Far East, our own hemisphere. And those are my four top priorities should I be the president, not to say we won't be engaged nor work hard to get other nations to come together to prevent atrocity. I thought the best example of a way to handle the situation was East Timor when we provided logistical support to the Australians, support that only we can provide. I thought that was a good model. But we can't be all things to all people in the world, Jim. And I think that's where maybe the vice president and I begin to have some differences. I'm worried about overcommitting our military around the world. I want to be judicious in its use. You mentioned Haiti. I wouldn't have sent troops to Haiti. I didn't think it was a mission worthwhile. It was a nation-building mission, and it was not very successful. It cost us billions, a couple billions of dollars, and I'm not so sure democracy is any better off in Haiti than it was before.

MODERATOR: Vice President Gore, do you agree with the governor's views on nation-building, the use of military, our military, for nation-building as he described and defined it?

GORE: I don't think we agree on that. I would certainly also be judicious in evaluating any potential use of American troops overseas. I think we have to be very reticent about that. But look, Jim, the world is changing so rapidly. The way I see it, the world is getting much closer together. Like it or not, we are now—the United States is now the natural leader of the world. All these other countries are looking to us. Now, just because we cannot be involved everywhere, and shouldn't be, doesn't mean that we should shy away from going in anywhere. Now, both of us are kind of, I guess, stating the other's position in a maximalist extreme way, but I think there is a difference here. This idea of nation-building is kind of a pejorative phrase, but think about the great conflict of the past century, World War II. During the years between World War I and World War II, a great lesson was learned by our military leaders and the people of the United States. The lesson was that in the aftermath of World War I, we kind of turned our backs and left them to their own devices and they brewed up a lot of trouble that quickly became World War II. And acting upon that lesson in the aftermath of our great victory in World War II, we laid down the Marshall Plan, President Truman did. We got intimately involved in building NATO and other structures there. We still have lots of troops in Europe. And what did we do in the late '40's and '50's and '60's? We were nation-building. And it was economic. But it was also military. And the confidence that those countries recovering from the wounds of war had by having troops there. We had civil administrators come in to set up their ways of building their towns back.

MODERATOR: . . . Some people are now suggesting that if you don't want to use the military to maintain the peace, to do the civil thing, is it time to consider a civil force of some kind that comes in after the military that builds nations or all of that? Is that on your radar screen?

BUSH: I don't think so. I think what we need to do is convince people who live in the lands they live in to build the nations. Maybe I'm missing something here. I mean, we're going to have kind of a nation-building core from America? Absolutely not. Our military is meant to fight and win war. That's what it's meant to do. And when it gets overextended, morale drops. I strongly believe we need to have a military presence in the peninsula, not only to keep the peace in the [Balkan] peninsula, but to keep regional stability. And I strongly believe we need to keep a presence in NATO, but I'm going to be judicious as to how to use the military. It needs to be in our vital interest, the mission needs to be clear, and the exit strategy obvious.

GORE: I don't disagree with that. I certainly don't disagree that we ought to get our troops home from places like the Balkans as soon as we can, as soon as the mission is complete. That's what we did in Haiti. There are no more than a handful of American military personnel in Haiti now. And Haitians have their problems, but we gave them a chance to restore democracy. That's really about all we can do. But if you have a situation like that right in our backyard with chaos about to break out and flotillas forming to come across the water, and all kinds of violence there, right in one of our neighboring countries there, then I think that we did the right thing there. And as for this idea of nation-building, the phrase sounds grandiose. And, you know, we can't be—we can't allow ourselves to get overextended. I certainly agree with that. And that's why I've supported building up our capacity. I've devoted in the budget I've proposed, as I said last week, more than twice as much as the governor has proposed. I think that it's in better shape now than he generally does. We've had some disagreements about that. He said that two divisions would have to report not ready for duty, and that's not what the joint chiefs say. But there's no doubt that we have to continue building up readiness and military strength. And we have to also be very cautious in the way we use our military.

The Web site of the Commission on Presidential Debates has the full text of presidential debates since 1948. There were no presidential debates in 1964, 1968, and 1972. See www.debates.org/pages/history.html.

The Bush Record on Foreign Relations: A Collage

In this section, we have assembled three brief excerpts from speeches and policy documents, each representing a step in the evolution of a new Bush administration approach to foreign relations.

The first document, the "Statement of Principles" developed by the Project for the New American Century, a right-wing advocacy group, was issued more than three years before Bush took office. Significantly, its signatories include three Vulcans: Dick Cheney, Paul Wolfowitz, and Donald Rumsfeld. The entire statement is printed here.

The second document is a portion of the 2002 State of the Union Address, delivered by President George W. Bush on January 29, 2002, less than five months after 9/11.

The third document is from "The National Security Strategy of the United States of America," developed by the White House and issued in September 2002. The excerpt printed here explains how the Bush administration planned to deal with the threat of weapons of mass destruction.

Taken together, these texts trace the development of the Bush administration's vision of America's role in world affairs. What are the basic ingredients of that vision? On what assumptions does it rest? With what "tone" is it delivered or presented?

✑ *Project for the New American Century, "Statement of Principles," June 3, 1997*

American foreign and defense policy is adrift. Conservatives have criticized the incoherent policies of the Clinton Administration. They have also resisted isolationist impulses from within their own ranks. But conservatives have not confidently advanced a strategic vision of America's role in the world. They have not set forth guiding principles for American foreign policy. They have allowed differences over tactics to obscure potential agreement on strategic objectives. And they have not fought for a defense budget that would maintain American security and advance American interests in the new century.

We aim to change this. We aim to make the case and rally support for American global leadership.

As the 20th century draws to a close, the United States stands as the world's preeminent power. Having led the West to victory in the Cold War, America faces an opportunity and a challenge: Does the United States have the vision to build upon the achievements of past decades? Does the United States have the resolve to shape a new century favorable to American principles and interests?

From http://www.newamericancentury.org/statementofprinciples.htm.

We are in danger of squandering the opportunity and failing the challenge. We are living off the capital—both the military investments and the foreign policy achievements—built up by past administrations. Cuts in foreign affairs and defense spending, inattention to the tools of statecraft, and inconstant leadership are making it increasingly difficult to sustain American influence around the world. And the promise of short-term commercial benefits threatens to override strategic considerations. As a consequence, we are jeopardizing the nation's ability to meet present threats and to deal with potentially greater challenges that lie ahead.

We seem to have forgotten the essential elements of the Reagan Administration's success: a military that is strong and ready to meet both present and future challenges; a foreign policy that boldly and purposefully promotes American principles abroad; and national leadership that accepts the United States' global responsibilities.

Of course, the United States must be prudent in how it exercises its power. But we cannot safely avoid the responsibilities of global leadership or the costs that are associated with its exercise. America has a vital role in maintaining peace and security in Europe, Asia, and the Middle East. If we shirk our responsibilities, we invite challenges to our fundamental interests. The history of the 20th century should have taught us that it is important to shape circumstances before crises emerge, and to meet threats before they become dire. The history of this century should have taught us to embrace the cause of American leadership.

Our aim is to remind Americans of these lessons and to draw their consequences for today. Here are four consequences:

- we need to increase defense spending significantly if we are to carry out our global responsibilities today and modernize our armed forces for the future;
- we need to strengthen our ties to democratic allies and to challenge regimes hostile to our interests and values;
- we need to promote the cause of political and economic freedom abroad;
- we need to accept responsibility for America's unique role in preserving and extending an international order friendly to our security, our prosperity, and our principles.

Such a Reaganite policy of military strength and moral clarity may not be fashionable today. But it is necessary if the United States is to build on the successes of this past century and to ensure our security and our greatness in the next.

Elliott Abrams	Gary Bauer	William J. Bennett	Jeb Bush
Dick Cheney	Eliot A. Cohen	Midge Decter	Paula Dobriansky
Steve Forbes	Aaron Friedberg	Francis Fukuyama	Frank Gaffney
Fred C. Ikle	Donald Kagan	Zalmay Khalilzad	I. Lewis Libby
Norman Podhoretz	Dan Quayle	Peter W. Rodman	Stephen P. Rosen
Henry S. Rowen	Donald Rumsfeld	Vin Weber	George Weigel
Paul Wolfowitz			

❧ *President George W. Bush,*
State of the Union Address, January 29, 2002

What we have found in Afghanistan confirms that, far from ending there, our war against terror is only beginning. Most of the 19 men who hijacked planes on September the 11th were trained in Afghanistan's camps, and so were tens of thousands of others. Thousands of dangerous killers, schooled in the methods of murder, often supported by outlaw regimes, are now spread throughout the world like ticking time bombs, set to go off without warning.

Thanks to the work of our law enforcement officials and coalition partners, hundreds of terrorists have been arrested. Yet, tens of thousands of trained terrorists are still at large. These enemies view the entire world as a battlefield, and we must pursue them wherever they are. (Applause.) So long as training camps operate, so long as nations harbor terrorists, freedom is at risk. And America and our allies must not, and will not, allow it. (Applause.)

Our nation will continue to be steadfast and patient and persistent in the pursuit of two great objectives. First, we will shut down terrorist camps, disrupt terrorist plans, and bring terrorists to justice. And, second, we must prevent the terrorists and regimes who seek chemical, biological or nuclear weapons from threatening the United States and the world. (Applause.) . . .

Our second goal is to prevent regimes that sponsor terror from threatening America or our friends and allies with weapons of mass destruction. Some of these regimes have been pretty quiet since September the 11th. But we know their true nature. North Korea is a regime arming with missiles and weapons of mass destruction, while starving its citizens.

Iran aggressively pursues these weapons and exports terror, while an unelected few repress the Iranian people's hope for freedom.

Iraq continues to flaunt its hostility toward America and to support terror. The Iraqi regime has plotted to develop anthrax, and nerve gas, and nuclear weapons for over a decade. This is a regime that has already used poison gas to murder thousands of its own citizens—leaving the bodies of mothers huddled over their dead children. This is a regime that agreed to international inspections—then kicked out the inspectors. This is a regime that has something to hide from the civilized world.

States like these, and their terrorist allies, constitute an axis of evil, arming to threaten the peace of the world. By seeking weapons of mass destruction, these regimes pose a grave and growing danger. They could provide these arms to terrorists, giving them the means to match their hatred. They could attack our allies or attempt to blackmail the United States. In any of these cases, the price of indifference would be catastrophic.

We will work closely with our coalition to deny terrorists and their state sponsors the materials, technology, and expertise to make and deliver weapons of mass destruction. We will develop and deploy effective missile

From http://www.law.ou.edu/hist/state2002.shtml.

defenses to protect America and our allies from sudden attack. (Applause.) And all nations should know: America will do what is necessary to ensure our nation's security.

We'll be deliberate, yet time is not on our side. I will not wait on events, while dangers gather. I will not stand by, as peril draws closer and closer. The United States of America will not permit the world's most dangerous regimes to threaten us with the world's most destructive weapons. (Applause.)

Our war on terror is well begun, but it is only begun. This campaign may not be finished on our watch—yet it must be and it will be waged on our watch.

We can't stop short. If we stop now—leaving terror camps intact and terror states unchecked—our sense of security would be false and temporary. History has called America and our allies to action, and it is both our responsibility and our privilege to fight freedom's fight. (Applause.) . . .

On May 1, 2003, President Bush landed on the flight deck of the USS *Abraham Lincoln*, aboard a US Navy S-3B Viking Jet. His announcement, that major combat operations in Iraq were over, proved to be in error. © Stephen Jaffe/AFP/Getty Images.

❧ The White House, "The National Security Strategy of the United States of America," September 2002.

At the time of the Gulf War, we acquired irrefutable proof that Iraq's designs were not limited to the chemical weapons it had used against Iran and its own people, but also extended to the acquisition of nuclear weapons and biological agents. In the past decade North Korea has become the world's principal purveyor of ballistic missiles, and has tested increasingly capable missiles while developing its own WMD arsenal. Other rogue regimes seek nuclear, biological, and chemical weapons as well. These states' pursuit of, and global trade in, such weapons has become a looming threat to all nations.

We must be prepared to stop rogue states and their terrorist clients before they are able to threaten or use weapons of mass destruction against the United States and our allies and friends. Our response must take full advantage of strengthened alliances, the establishment of new partnerships with former adversaries, innovation in the use of military forces, modern technologies, including the development of an effective missile defense system, and increased emphasis on intelligence collection and analysis. . . .

In the Cold War, especially following the Cuban missile crisis, we faced a generally status quo, risk-averse adversary. Deterrence was an effective defense. But deterrence based only upon the threat of retaliation is less likely to work against leaders of rogue states more willing to take risks, gambling with the lives of their people, and the wealth of their nations.

- In the Cold War, weapons of mass destruction were considered weapons of last resort whose use risked the destruction of those who used them. Today, our enemies see weapons of mass destruction as weapons of choice. For rogue states these weapons are tools of intimidation and military aggression against their neighbors. These weapons may also allow these states to attempt to blackmail the United States and our allies to prevent us from deterring or repelling the aggressive behavior of rogue states. Such states also see these weapons as their best means of overcoming the conventional superiority of the United States.
- Traditional concepts of deterrence will not work against a terrorist enemy whose avowed tactics are wanton destruction and the targeting of innocents; whose so-called soldiers seek martyrdom in death and whose most potent protection is statelessness. The overlap between states that sponsor terror and those that pursue WMD compels us to action.

For centuries, international law recognized that nations need not suffer an attack before they can lawfully take action to defend themselves

From http://www.informationclearinghouse.info/article2320.htm.

against forces that present an imminent danger of attack. Legal scholars and international jurists often conditioned the legitimacy of preemption on the existence of an imminent threat—most often a visible mobilization of armies, navies, and air forces preparing to attack.

We must adapt the concept of imminent threat to the capabilities and objectives of today's adversaries. Rogue states and terrorists do not seek to attack us using conventional means. They know such attacks would fail. Instead, they rely on acts of terror and, potentially, the use of weapons of mass destruction—weapons that can be easily concealed, delivered covertly, and used without warning.

The targets of these attacks are our military forces and our civilian population, in direct violation of one of the principal norms of the law of warfare. As was demonstrated by the losses on September 11, 2001, mass civilian casualties is the specific objective of terrorists and these losses would be exponentially more severe if terrorists acquired and used weapons of mass destruction.

The United States has long maintained the option of preemptive actions to counter a sufficient threat to our national security. The greater the threat, the greater is the risk of inaction—and the more compelling the case for taking anticipatory action to defend ourselves, even if uncertainty remains as to the time and place of the enemy's attack. To forestall or prevent such hostile acts by our adversaries, the United States will, if necessary, act preemptively.

The United States will not use force in all cases to preempt emerging threats, nor should nations use preemption as a pretext for aggression. Yet in an age where the enemies of civilization openly and actively seek the world's most destructive technologies, the United States cannot remain idle while dangers gather. We will always proceed deliberately, weighing the consequences of our actions. To support preemptive options, we will:

- build better, more integrated intelligence capabilities to provide timely, accurate information on threats, wherever they may emerge;
- coordinate closely with allies to form a common assessment of the most dangerous threats; and
- continue to transform our military forces to ensure our ability to conduct rapid and precise operations to achieve decisive results.

The purpose of our actions will always be to eliminate a specific threat to the United States or our allies and friends. The reasons for our actions will be clear, the force measured, and the cause just.

Politics is a serious business, but it can be serious and entertaining, too. One of the funniest and most widely circulated products of the 2004 presidential race was a 2-minute film, "This Land," by Gregg and Evan Spiridellis, featuring puppetlike figures of Bush and Kerry insulting each other to the tune of Woody Guthrie's 1940 folk song classic, "This Land Is Your Land." It was a hot item in the summer of 2004 and might still be seen on the JibJab Media Web site, at www.jibjab.com.

THE BIG PICTURE

The Iraq war, and the new, more aggressive foreign policy of which it was a part, were not the result of 9/11, though the events of that day presented the Bush administration with an unparalleled window of opportunity. Despite George W. Bush's disavowal of nation-building in his 2000 debate with Al Gore, the people he selected to serve him—the Vulcans—came to his administration already committed to what the Project for the New American Century described as a "Reaganite policy of military strength and moral clarity." Before and after 9/11, the Bush administration foreign policy team was less concerned with terrorism than with its goal of using American military and economic might to reshape the globe in the American image. (It is significant that the project's "Statement of Principles" does not mention terrorism.) As a result, the administration failed to adequately assess the threat from terrorism in the spring and summer of 2001 and, after 9/11, it moved immediately to broaden the enemy from Al Qaeda to "rogue states" and the "axis of evil." On September 12, when Bush asked Richard Clarke to "see if Saddam did this," he was expressing the Vulcan goal of asserting American power worldwide, in this case in the Middle East. War with Iraq—war to remove Saddam, but also to build a new Iraqi nation based on free enterprise and democratic institutions (and, in the largest sense, with Iraq as a test case for future interventions)—was already on the table.

Bush would have been wise to have heeded the warning of Secretary of State Colin Powell, who in August 2002 met privately with the president in the oval office. "You are going to be the proud owner of 25 million people," Powell told the president, anticipating the difficulties of nation-building in Iraq. "You will own all their hopes, aspirations and problems. You'll own it all." It was an idea known in foreign policy circles as the "Pottery Barn" rule: You break it, you own it. Two years later, when voters cast their ballots in the fall elections, Iraq was barely a nation, and it was more "broken" than "built." Bush kept his presidency, but perhaps only because Christian evangelicals, panicked at the thought of same-sex marriage, chose to ignore the "mess" in Iraq.